Aristotle:
the desire to understand

Jonathan Lear

Professor of Philosophy
Yale University

CAMBRIDGE
UNIVERSITY PRESS

CAMBRIDGE UNIVERSITY PRESS
Cambridge, New York, Melbourne, Madrid, Cape Town,
Singapore, São Paulo, Delhi, Tokyo, Mexico City

Cambridge University Press
32 Avenue of the Americas, New York NY 10013-2473, USA

www.cambridge.org
Information on this title: www.cambridge.org/9780521347624

First published 1988
23rd printing 2010

A catalogue record for this publication is available from the British Library

ISBN 978-0-521-34762-4 Paperback

Aristotle:
the desire to understand

This is a philosophical introduction to Aristotle, and
Professor Lear starts where Aristotle himself starts. The
first sentence of the *Metaphysics* states that all human
beings by their nature desire to know. But what is it for
us to be animated by this desire in this world? What is it
for a creature to have a nature? What is our, human,
nature? What must the world be like to be intelligible,
and what must we be like to understand it systematically? Through a consideration of these questions Professor Lear introduces us to the essence of Aristotle's
philosophy and guides us through the central Aristotelian texts – selected from the *Physics, Metaphysics,
Ethics,* and *Politics* and from the biological and logical
works.

The book is written in a direct, lucid style which engages
the reader with the themes in an active, participatory
manner. It will prove a stimulating introduction for all
students of Greek philosophy and for a wide range of
others interested in Aristotle as a giant figure in Western
intellectual history.

For Cynthia Farrar

τί οὖν κωλύει λέγειν εὐδαίμονα τὸν κατ’ ἀρετὴν
τελείαν ἐνεργοῦντα καὶ τοῖς ἐκτὸς ἀγαθοῖς
ἱκανῶς κεχορηγημένον μὴ τὸν τυχόντα χρόνον
ἀλλὰ τέλειον βίον;

Contents

Contents

Preface

I wrote this book as a way of saying goodbye. I first went to Cambridge on a Mellon Fellowship when I graduated from Yale in 1970, and with occasional excursions back to the United States I ended up staying there for almost twelve of the next fifteen years. Cambridge is in many ways my intellectual and emotional home: I had never seen before such a warm, supportive, yet challenging intellectual environment. Perhaps that is why I stayed so long. When I decided to return to the U.S. in 1985, I wanted somehow to mark, intellectually if not emotionally, the time I had spent in Cambridge. Most of my research on Aristotle was done while I was first a student and later a Fellow at Clare College, so I decided to write an introduction to his philosophy. I liked the idea of an introduction, first, because I thought it would force me to work on a broad canvas: to elucidate the thoughts of years rather than detail a single argument. Second, I wanted to write a book that was accessible to my friends who are not Aristotelian scholars – friends who would ask me in countless casual conversations, 'What do you think Aristotle would have thought about *this*?' I am not going to mention my many Cambridge friends by name: if you are one of them and are reading this, suffice it to say that you are very much in my heart and mind. I would, however, like to mention those who helped me in my study of Aristotle. First, I would like to thank that part of my Cambridge life which accompanied me back to America: my wife, Cynthia Farrar. I won't indulge in the usual cliché, '...without whose support...', in part because it is a cliché, in part because I am not sure it is true: even if Cynthia had not been supportive I think I still would have written this book. I mention her here solely because she helped me to understand what is involved in Aristotle's claim that man is by nature a political animal. It was in attending her lectures on Thucydides in Cambridge and watching her live her life that I learned how theorizing about politics and actively living the life of a citizen in a *polis* might form a coherent whole. Let me also thank the ancient philosophy mafia of which I was once part. It is from countless seminars, classes, individual discussions with Myles Burnyeat, Geoffrey Lloyd, M. M. Mackenzie, David Sedley, Malcolm Schofield and (for two years) Gregory Vlastos, that I learned how to read ancient philosophical texts. Indeed, virtually every week I spent in Cambridge had a day in it which was spent with one or the other of them translating and interpreting an Aristotelian text. Finally, I would like to mention Timothy Smiley and Bernard Williams, two friends from whom I have learned most about how to do philosophy. However, I have no interest in bidding them a fond farewell. In saying goodbye to a way of life, I do not intend to be saying goodbye to the people who helped to constitute it.

There is one person I do want to say goodbye to, but I can't. Charles Parkin, the soul of Clare College, died suddenly of a heart attack in the fall of 1986. He was one of those modest men who knew everything and published nothing. He loved the people he knew and remained a bachelor living in College rooms. The world did not know him, and the students and Fellows of Clare loved him. He was an historian of political thought, but his interests spanned the world. When I first arrived in Cambridge, we would spend evenings looking at bacteria under his microscope, photographing craters on the moon through his telescope, sitting quietly and listening to recordings of trains pulling out of various European stations. And we would discuss Aristotle. Just after World War II, Charles contracted tuberculosis and spent two years in a sanatorium outside of Cambridge. It was in this period that he had an epiphany in which he felt he really understood the identity of subject and object. He once told me that he thought that the rest of his life was an attempt to recapture that moment. I think he would have liked this book.

I should like to thank: the National Endowment for the Humanities (U.S.) for a Fellowship for Independent Research in which some of the research and writing of this book were accomplished; the Andrew W. Mellon Foundation for administering the Fellowship which first sent me to Cambridge; the Masters and Fellows of Clare College, Cambridge, for providing the ideal atmosphere in which to carry out my studies; the Whitney Humanities Center at Yale for providing a second hide-away office in which I could write this book undisturbed by the usual demands of the semester.

An earlier draft of this book was read by Alan Code, Geoffrey Lloyd, Jeremy Mynott, Malcolm Schofield, Timothy Smiley, Bernard Williams and Michael Woods. They all offered extensive and valuable comments. Although Code and I talked about Aristotle so often and so long on the transatlantic telephone that I suspect we supported the launching of a communications satellite, I would especially like to thank him for his suggestion of Kermit as a candidate for the non-human individual I needed to make the point I was trying to make about levels of potentiality and actuality. Christopher Dustin, who was a teaching assistant in a lecture course I gave at Yale, wrote copious comments on my lectures which greatly helped me to unify the material I have presented in this book.

Above all, I would like to thank the undergraduate students at Cambridge and Yale to whom I have lectured about Aristotle. They persuaded me that material at this level of difficulty is interesting to them and that a book of this sort would be a help to them.

I

The desire to understand

Aristotle's *Metaphysics* begins:

> All men by nature desire to know. An indication of this is
> the delight we take in our senses; for even apart from
> their usefulness they are loved for themselves; and above
> all others the sense of sight. For not only with a view to
> action, but even when we are not going to do anything,
> we prefer sight to almost everything else. The reason is
> that this, most of all the senses, makes us know and
> brings to light many differences between things.[1]

Aristotle is attributing to us a desire, a force, which urges us on
toward knowledge. Of course, for some this desire does not exercise great influence; but for some of us it plays an important role in
our lives. Aristotle no doubt believed it was this desire that motivated him to do the research and thinking that led to his writing the
Metaphysics, and he trusted in this desire to lead others to study it.
It is this desire that is responsible for your reading and my writing
this book.

How did Aristotle know that we have this desire? One does not
know the content of a desire unless one knows what ultimately
satisfies it. By its satisfaction we learn what the desire is a desire
for. That is why Aristotle speaks of the delight we take in our
senses. If the knowledge we pursued were merely a means to a further end, say, power over others or control of the environment,
then our innate desire would not be a desire for knowledge. It
would be a will to power or an obsessional drive for control. That
we take pleasure in the sheer exercise of our sensory faculties is a
sign that we do have a desire for knowledge. For though we do use
our sensory knowledge to organize ourselves in the world and to
achieve practical ends, this knowledge is also pursued for its own
sake.

[1] *Metaphysics* 1.1, 980a21–7. The Greek for 'to know' is *eidenai*.

I

Leisure was of the utmost importance to Aristotle. It was only after men had developed the arts to help them cope with the necessities of life that they were able to turn to sciences which are not aimed at securing any practical end.[2] That is why, Aristotle says, mathematics was founded in Egypt: for it is there that a priestly caste had the leisure to pursue knowledge for its own sake. But then the natural desire to know had to wait upon a historical development, the creation of societies with leisured classes, before it could find full expression. Before that time an observer might have been able to detect a delight men took in sensory experience itself, but he would not have been able to grasp that this pleasure was only a surface manifestation of a much deeper force within man's soul. One cannot help but wonder: was Aristotle himself living at a time appropriate for appreciating the true content of this desire?

Aristotle certainly thought that within an individual's history the desire to know develops in content: that is, the individual develops a richer sense of what it is he wants to know. The structures of the world and of our own souls conspire to encourage this development.[3] Man is not born with knowledge, but he is born with the capacity to acquire it. But the world must cooperate with him if he is to exercise that capacity. Man starts life with the ability to discriminate among sensory phenomena, an ability he shares with other animals. His soul retains a record of its sensory encounters. The world, for its part, offers man repetition and regularity in his sensory encounters. Through repeated encounters with items in the world, our sensory discriminations develop into memory and then into what Aristotle calls 'experience.' Experience Aristotle characterizes as 'the whole universal that has come to rest in the soul.'[4] From repeated perception of particular men, we form the concept of a man, and the knowledge *that this thing we see is a man* is experience. If the universal, or concept, were not somehow *already* embedded in the particular, we could not make the transition from bare sensory discrimination to knowledge of the individual. As Aristotle says, 'though one perceives the particular, perception is of the universal.'[5] The world, then, provides a path

[2] *Metaphysics* I.I, 981b13–25; I.2, 982b20–4.
[3] See *Metaphysics* I.I, 980a27–981a12; *Posterior Analytics* II.19, 99b35–100b3.
[4] *Posterior Analytics* II.19, 100a7.
[5] *Posterior Analytics* II.19, 100a17–b1.

2

along which man's curiosity can run. Because the universal is embedded in particulars, a person's first explorations among particulars will naturally lead him toward a grasp of the embodied universal. Having acquired experience, or knowledge of individuals, we are able to formulate more abstract forms of knowledge, the arts and sciences (*technai* and *epistēmai*).[6] Each stage of cognitive development is grounded in the previous stage and the structure of the world itself helps us to ascend from the Cave of Ignorance. It is only because the world offers a course along which man's inquiries can run that his desire to know has any hope of being satisfied.

But the world does not 'grab us by the throat' and yank us out of the Cave. There must be something in us that drives us to take advantage of the world's structure. From earliest childhood humans display an innate curiosity. Indeed the British psychoanalyst Melanie Klein once called this childhood curiosity *epistemophilia* – love of *epistēmē*.[7] But curiosity is not, I believe, the best way to conceptualize what drives men on. Perhaps it is better to think of man's natural capacity to be puzzled. We tend to take this capacity for granted. Yet it is a remarkable fact about us that we cannot simply observe phenomena: we want to know *why* they occur. We can imagine beings who simply watched the sun set and the moon rise in the heavens: they might come to expect the regular transitions, but they would lack curiosity as to why the changes occur. We are not like that. The heavenly motions cry out (*to us*) for explanation.

It is out of wonder, Aristotle says, that men first began and even now begin to philosophize.[8] That is, philosophy grows out of man's natural capacity to feel puzzlement and awe. We cannot remain content – we are literally discontented – until we have an explanation as to why the heavens are as they are. This discontent is of a piece with the desire to know: it propels us toward exploration and the formation of explanations. Even myths, Aristotle recognizes, are manifestations of man's propensity for puzzlement: they are designed to allay our unease by offering expla-

---

[6] *Metaphysics* I.1, 981a1–b10.
[7] Melanie Klein, *Love, Guilt and Reparation*, e.g., pp. 87, 188, 190–1, 227–8, 426, 429.
[8] *Metaphysics* I.2, 982b12–22.

nations of the phenomena. Of course, myths offer at best temporary relief, for the explanations they offer are unsatisfying. We are ultimately led, by our own natural makeup, to the honest pursuit of explanations for their own sake.

In searching for explanations, men inevitably encounter difficulties.[9] There are of course conflicting opinions on most serious subjects; and the opinions themselves express persuasive, though differing, accounts of the phenomena. These difficulties are, for Aristotle, the starting-point of philosophy. It is by working one's way through the puzzles or difficulties that philosophical wisdom grows. Hence Aristotle devotes an entire book of the *Metaphysics* simply to cataloguing the puzzles surrounding the question of what are the basic elements of reality.[10] As he says, 'one should have surveyed all the difficulties beforehand ... because people who inquire without first stating the difficulties are like those who do not know where they have to go.'[11] Aristotle uses the metaphor of a knot. When we are confronted with difficulties we do not know how to solve, our thought is all tied up. We are constrained, we cannot go forward in our search, the desire to know is frustrated. Hence the frustration we feel when we repeatedly return to a problem we cannot solve, and the relief and pleasure when suddenly we understand how to solve the problem and move on. According to the Oxford translation, Aristotle says that when we have solved the difficulties we enjoy the 'free play of thought.'[12] The Greek, *euporia*, literally means 'easy passage or travel.' Its opposite, *aporia*, is Aristotle's word for difficulty, but it literally means difficulty or impossibility of passage.

Aristotle typically begins a treatise by listing the difficulties which previous thinkers encountered when they first began to think about the issue at hand. To a reader fresh to Aristotle, these opening chapters can seem extremely boring. Because one is ignorant of the setting of the intellectual stage in Aristotle's time, the problems can seem obscure, lifeless and dull. However, even if the difficulties which Aristotle lists do not immediately come to life, one should not lose sight of the significance of his philosophical

[9] *Metaphysics* III.1, 995a25–b3.
[10] *Metaphysics* III.
[11] *Metaphysics* III.1, 995a33–b1.
[12] *euporesai*: *Metaphysics* III.1, 995a27 (old and revised translation – see note 24 below).

method. For Aristotle, philosophy begins with questions and puzzles. We are led to the pursuit of explanations for their own sake both by our natural makeup – the desire to know – and because it is part of our nature to find the world puzzling. It is misleading to say that the world is inherently puzzling: rather, the world presents itself as puzzling to beings like us. But as soon as we formulate questions about the world, philosophy (at least in embryonic form) is already under way. By posing and answering questions we do what we can to render the world intelligible to us: and rendering the world intelligible is what, for Aristotle, philosophical activity is.

Although it is difficult to reach the truth, in another sense, Aristotle says, the truth is easy.[13] Almost every belief is a stab at the truth. Beliefs are formed on the basis of interaction with the world, and Aristotle thinks it very rare that a belief has no drop of truth in it. Not only is knowledge accumulated by the humble efforts of many thinkers and researchers, but even false beliefs are usually formed reasonably. Aristotle describes the truth as 'the proverbial door which no one can fail to hit.' Thus there is a point to investigating men's beliefs – even the false ones – for by seeing how men have stumbled, we may gain a clearer grasp of the truth.

The reason the truth is difficult lies not in the world, Aristotle thinks, but in us: 'For as the eyes of bats are to the blaze of day, so is the reason in our soul to the things which are by nature most evident of all.'[14] What is it for things to be *by nature* most evident of all? Aristotle distinguishes that which is most understandable without qualification from that which is most understandable to us.[15] Because we begin life in ignorance and must work our way from experience of particulars to knowledge of general truths, the route we take is a tortuous one, and as we move toward these truths we are unaccustomed to them. Yet, though what is initially most understandable to us and what is simply most understandable are distinct, they are essentially related. For it is from our current state of knowledge (or ignorance) and our puzzlement that we are led along, as though on a path, toward discovering what the world is really like. And once we have grasped basic truths about

[13] *Metaphysics* II.1, 993a30–b15.
[14] *Metaphysics* II.1, 993b8–9.
[15] See, e.g., *Metaphysics* I.2, 982a30–b30.

the world and the structure of reality, we realize that there is nothing so clear as they. Our job, as systematic inquirers, is to turn that which is most clear into that which is most clear to us. It is that which satisfies the desire to know. The basic truths of reality no longer confront us like the blaze of day.

Thus, although philosophy begins in wonder, it ends in lack of wonder.[16] We may, for example, be surprised to discover that the diagonal of a square is incommensurable with its sides, but once we have learned the theory of incommensurable magnitudes, it would seem bizarre if the diagonal were not incommensurable. For the theory teaches us why the diagonal must be as it is. The man who has achieved this appropriate lack of wonder is a man who has achieved wisdom (sophia), and the pursuit of wisdom for its own sake is philosophy (philosophia) – literally, love of wisdom. The desire to know achieves its deepest satisfaction in the philosopher who understands the principles and causes of the world.

But if philosophy is the ultimate goal of our original innate desire, perhaps we have to re-think what that desire is. We are not satisfied to know, for example, that the heavens move in such a way; nor will we be satisfied to know a vast array of such facts about the phenomena. We want to know *why* the heavens move that way, *why* the phenomena are as they are. We are after more than knowledge, we are after understanding. Aristotle was, I believe, aware of this. Although 'to know' is an adequate translation of the Greek 'eidenai,' Aristotle used this term generically to cover various species of knowing.[17] One of the species is 'epistasthai' (literally, to be in a state of having epistēmē) which has often been translated as 'to know' or 'to have scientific knowledge,' but which ought to be translated as 'to understand.' For Aristotle says that we have epistēmē of a thing when we know its cause.[18] To have epistēmē one must not only know a thing, one must also grasp its cause or explanation. This is to understand it: to know in a deep sense what it is and how it has come to be. Philosophy, says Aristotle, is epistēmē of the truth.[19]

---

[16] *Metaphysics* I.2, 983a13–21.
[17] See M. F. Burnyeat, 'Aristotle on Understanding Knowledge.'
[18] See, e.g., *Posterior Analytics* I.2, 71b8–12.
[19] *Metaphysics* II.1, 993b19–20.

Aristotle uses '*epistēmē*' in two ways: first, to refer to an organized body of knowledge, like geometry; second, to refer to the state of the soul of a person who has learned this body of knowledge. This is not an equivocation or ambiguity. For a person who has learned geometry has the *epistēmē* as part of his soul. Indeed, it is because his soul has become the *epistēmē* – has actually become an organized body of knowledge – that he can be said to be a geometer. Note that what the geometer has is not just knowledge, but an organized body of knowledge. The geometer knows not merely that the interior angles of a triangle are equal to two right angles, he knows why a triangle *must* have such interior angles. For he can supply a proof. Understanding is by its nature completely general. The geometer's proof, for example, does not explain why this particular figure has interior angles equal to two right angles (except, as Aristotle would say, incidentally). The proof explains why all triangles have such interior angles.[20] As we seek understanding we move away from particular facts toward the general principles, causes, explanations which underlie them.

'*Epistemophilia*' – love of *epistēmē* – turns out to be a remarkably apt expression for the inner drive which motivates a child's first explorations of the world. But if the true content of a desire is revealed only by what ultimately satisfies it, then it is too constricting to conceive of *epistemophilia* as innate curiosity or even desire for knowledge: the desire is for *epistēmē*, or understanding.

And yet there must be more to *epistēmē* than mere understanding. For *epistēmē* binds man to the world in a much deeper and more significant relation than the concept of understanding on its own would suggest. First, the world is not merely the object of our understanding, it is the occasion for it. The world prompts us to inquiry by presenting itself (to us) as puzzling, and then it obligingly yields up its truths in response to our patient investigations. The world as such is meant to be known (by beings like us) and it invites man to fulfill his role as a systematic understander of the world. Imagine how frustrating it would be to be born with the desire to understand in a world which did not cooperate! The world would remain incomprehensible, and yet we would obsessionally keep bumping our heads against it. Aristotle had great faith

---

[20] I discuss this in detail in section 6.2 below.

in the world: indeed, his philosophy is an attempt to give the world back to creatures who desire to understand it.

Second, it is by gaining understanding of the world that man comes to understand who he is. The project of understanding the world lies at the bottom of who we are. Until we have pursued that project all the way, it is not just that we do not yet fully know what the desire to understand is a desire for, we do not yet know who *we* really are. That is, we don't yet fully understand what it is to be a systematic understander of the world. Therefore, we cannot gain self-knowledge merely by turning our gaze onto ourselves. Because we desire to understand, because we are at bottom systematic understanders, self-understanding must to some extent be indirect. When we first come to Aristotle, much of what he is doing does not seem to be anything remotely like what we would now consider to be philosophy. He seems to us a scientist engaged in earnest exploration of the natural world. But this dichotomy between philosophy and science would seem, in Aristotle's eyes, to rest on a superficial understanding of the relation between inside and outside. It is by looking out to the world that man's soul maps the structure of the world. Once he has come to understand the world, not only has he become what he most fundamentally is, a systematic understander, but he can also look to the world to see the structure of his soul mapped there. (This is not, as a modern idealist might think, because man constitutes the world in his image, but because man's nature is such that the world is able to impress its image on him.)

In any case, what we do easily recognize to be philosophy is, for Aristotle, a natural outgrowth of man's exploration of the world. *For epistēmē is by its nature reflective: one cannot understand the world unless one understands the place of understanding within it.* In a similar way, the desire to understand and the desire to understand that desire must be one. There is, therefore, no additional step required, no change in perspective needed, to move from 'ordinary' understanding of the world to an attempt to understand that very understanding – or, indeed, to understand the nature of philosophical thought itself.

What one comes to understand, Aristotle thought, is that the understanding of first principles and causes is divine.[21] No doubt the

---

[21] *Metaphysics* I.2, 982b28–983a11. See also *Metaphysics* XII.7,9, and *Nicomachean Ethics* X.7.

early discovery of basic principles underlying the disparate phenomena must have seemed so marvelous as to be a God-given gift: it is, after all, unlikely that Prometheus could have stolen all this from jealous, hoarding gods. We are such and the world is such that understanding comes to us almost as a loving bequest. But Aristotle had a more hard-headed reason for considering this understanding to be divine. God is himself thought to be among the causes of all things and a first principle. Thus in knowing first principles we come to an understanding of God. For God, this knowledge would be self-understanding. It is absurd to suppose that we mortals can have insight into God's nature while God himself remains ignorant. It is more reasonable to suppose that we are partaking of something divine.

This plausible train of thought has two very remarkable consequences. First, since God is a first principle of all things, and is (at least partially) constituted by self-understanding, it would seem that this understanding is itself a cause or principle of all things. Understanding is itself a force in the world. Second, when man acquires this understanding, he is not acquiring understanding of a distinct object which, as it turns out, is divine: the understanding is itself divine. Thus in the acquisition of this understanding – in philosophical activity – man partially transcends his own nature. Aristotle explicitly recognized this consequence:

> ... it is not insofar as he is man that he will live [a life of contemplation], but insofar as something divine is present in him ... If mind is divine, then in comparison with man, the life according to it is divine in comparison with human life. But we must not follow those who advise us, being men, to think of human things and, being mortal, of mortal things, but must, so far as we can, make ourselves immortal, and strain every nerve to live in accordance with the best thing in us; for even if it be small in bulk, much more does it in power and worth surpass everything.[22]

All men by nature have a desire which leads them to transcend

---

[22] *Nicomachean Ethics* x.7, 1177b26–1178a2. The old Oxford translation uses 'reason' as a translation for *noûs*; the revised translation uses 'intellect.' The reason I use 'mind' is given in section 4.3 below.

their own nature. Paradoxically, it is in this divine transcendence of his own nature that man most fully realizes himself:

> [Mind] would seem, too, to be each man himself, since it is the authoritative and better part of him. It would be strange then if he were to choose not *his* life but that of something else ... that which is proper to each thing is by nature best and most pleasant for each thing; for man, therefore, the life according to mind is best and pleasantest, since mind more than anything else *is* man.[23]

Man has a desire to understand which, if satisfied, pulls him right up out of human life into a divine existence. Yet man is most fully realizing himself when he does this. This is a view of human nature which is, to say the least, not easy to understand.

The aim of this book is to come to a deeper understanding of Aristotle's claim that all men by their nature desire to know. To understand this one line of the *Metaphysics* we will have to work through much of Aristotle's philosophy. For there is both a broad and a narrow sense in which one can study the desire to understand. In the broad sense, we must come to understand Aristotle's own attempt to understand the world. For only once we comprehend the world according to Aristotle can we comprehend what, for him, the desire to understand was a desire for. And, as we have seen, if one wants to appreciate man's place in nature one must, Aristotle thinks, work hard at understanding nature itself: for it is only through a serious study of nature for its own sake that man can ultimately achieve self-understanding. It is toward that goal that the desire to understand is urging us all along. That brings us to the narrow sense: we must inquire into the place the desire to understand occupies within Aristotle's world. In this book I try to keep both perspectives alive. I try to give a wide-ranging picture of Aristotle's world, but one designed to illuminate the significance of his claim that man by his very nature desires to know. If we do not know what it is to have a nature at all, we cannot understand what it is for man by nature to do anything. Therefore chapters 2 and 3

---

[23] *Nicomachean Ethics* x.7, 1178a2–7 (old translation; my emphasis).

present Aristotle's conception of nature in general. In chapters 4 and 5, I focus on Aristotle's account of *man's* nature. Chapter 4 is about the human soul: the capacity for sense perception, for thinking about and understanding the world, for desiring, and for deliberating, on the basis of those desires, how to act. Man also has the ability to organize and shape his desires, and chapter 5 is about man's ability to shape himself into a being who derives genuine happiness from an ethical life within society. Man, says Aristotle, is by nature a political animal. If we are to comprehend Aristotle's world, we must see how the natural desire to understand coexists with the natural imperative for leading an ethically virtuous life within political society. Finally, in chapter 6, I give a rather sweeping account of what the desire to understand is a desire for. Aristotle discovered the possibility of conducting a very broad inquiry into the structure of reality. He called this study 'first philosophy'; later commentators called it 'metaphysics.' I first present an introduction to Aristotle's logic, for he conceived it as an important tool for laying out the broad structure of reality. Then I present what I take to be some of the central ideas and arguments of the mature metaphysics and theology, while trying to assess the significance of the fact that *this* is where the desire to understand leads us.

I believe this dual approach to Aristotle – tracking the desire to understand in its broad and narrow senses – recapitulates the essence of his philosophy. This approach can help a reader understand what Aristotle is doing at any particular point in the exposition of his account of the world and why he is doing it. Thus this book can serve as an introduction to Aristotle's philosophy. I speak of helping a reader, for I do not think it is possible to be seriously interested in Aristotle without trying to read him. Anyone who has tried to read him will know that it is not easy. The Greek is written in a dense style (it is, I admit, an acquired taste: after a while one comes to like it), and though the English translations do a remarkable job, they are nevertheless difficult to read. Occasionally, the translators compensate for the dense style by supplying an interpretation of what they think Aristotle is saying. This can be helpful, but it can sometimes be misleading, even to an intelligent and otherwise well-educated reader. In this book I make an effort to render Aristotle's writing more accessible. Each section begins with a list of texts to be discussed, and when I quote Aristotle I regularly offer comments upon the translation.[24] My hope in writing this book is that a reader who works both with it *and* with an English translation will then be able to go on and read Aristotle for himself. My hope is that a great work which has, for many, remained almost unreadable can be transformed into a source of intellectual sustenance and joy.

Because I am trying to shed a particular light on Aristotle's philosophy as well as to provide an introduction to it, this book has certain definite limitations. For instance, this is not a comprehensive introduction. That is, I do not attempt to summarize in a step-by-step fashion all the major positions Aristotle occupied. This is, rather, a *philosophical* introduction: an attempt to work with Aristotle's concepts and arguments and bring them to life. This requires that much time and energy be spent elucidating a single concept or argument. Although I do cover a wide range of Aristotelian texts, and I do try to present a large-scale picture of Aristotle's world, this picture could not be comprehensive without losing claim either to being philosophical or to being an introduction. Moreover, I make virtually no effort to defend my interpretation of Aristotle against rivals. Aristotle may well be the most commented-upon thinker in the history of the world. The reader ought to be aware that for virtually every claim I make in this book, there is a conflicting claim by a thoughtful, serious student of Aristotle who would offer a different interpretation. Although I could defend my claims at greater length, I cannot do so here without abandoning the book's claim to be an introduction. But I do not mind. The point of this book is neither to give the reader a boiled-down summary of each of Aristotle's works nor to give him an absolutely definitive interpretation, but to enable him to go on and read these works himself.

As we begin this study, I think that we can conceive ourselves as standing in a similar relation to Aristotle's world – that is, to his

---

[24] In this book I shall rely for quotations on *The Complete Works of Aristotle, The Revised Oxford Translation*, since it is a significant improvement on the original Oxford translation, *The Works of Aristotle Translated into English*. However the original translation is nevertheless pretty good, and an abridged version of it, *The Basic Works of Aristotle*, is readily available. I shall occasionally revert to the original translation in my quotations, and I shall also make occasional emendations and translations of my own. These will be noted.

system of beliefs – as Aristotle stood to the world in which he lived. It is the desire to understand that motivates us all. In Aristotle's case it was a desire to understand the world in its entirety; in our case (at the moment) it is a desire to understand one very small part of the world: namely, Aristotle's beliefs and outlook. Thus, as students of Aristotle, we need not conceive of ourselves as engaged in a fundamentally different type of activity from that which Aristotle was himself engaged in. Aristotle endeavored to make the world intelligible and believed in its ultimate intelligibility; we are trying to render Aristotle's account of the world intelligible, and, perhaps, have even more grounds for believing in its ultimate intelligibility. For even if Aristotle was mistaken in his belief that the world was meant to be understood, surely we cannot be mistaken in our belief that Aristotle's philosophy was meant to be understood. It is therefore a mistake to think that we can learn about Aristotle only by making him an object of our study. Because our form of inquiry is not fundamentally different from his, we ought to be able to re-enact at least some of the intellectual problems which bothered him and thus gain non-observational insight into the type of activity he took philosophy to be.

Since I am primarily concerned with the truth about Aristotle, not the truth of Aristotle's views *per se*, I spend little time locating him within the history of science. I do occasionally contrast an Aristotelian concept, say of cause, with the modern conception. But the point of such contrasts is to bring to light how different Aristotle's world is from the modern, not to show how Aristotle's beliefs fall short of what we now take to be the truth. This is the price of restricting the world of our inquiry to Aristotle's world, but there are two humbler reasons why I accept this limitation. First, I am not competent to discuss Aristotle's role within the history of science: others have, can, and will make a better job of that than I could. Second, it is not my place to tell a reader of this book – perhaps a working scientist – that the Aristotelian ideas he encounters will be of no use to him. Books which do deal with the seventeenth-century scientific revolution tend to treat Aristotelianism as an *objet mort*: a specimen worthy of inspection, but certainly dead. But if science is still a living enterprise, full of problems of interpretation and conceptualization, there is no telling from what quarter a working scientist may draw inspiration. So, rather than describe in detail why, say, Aristotle's concept of final cause is (now thought to be) false, I try to present the concept in as living a form as possible: to show what within Aristotle's system motivates and sustains this concept.

One last remark. Aristotle believed that to understand ourselves we must understand the world. He also believed that to understand the world one must understand oneself. In particular, one cannot understand the world if one remains ignorant of the role the desire to understand plays in one's own soul as well as in the world at large, if one remains ignorant of the human mind and its capacity to understand, if one remains ignorant of the cost to oneself and to others of pursuing one's desire. Aristotle tried to raise himself and his students out of this ignorance. Though the modern world may have left the details of his account behind, his insistence that understanding and self-understanding are each dependent on the other is, I believe, a truth whose depth we have only begun to appreciate.

2

Nature

2.1 Nature as an inner principle of change[1]

If we are to understand what it is for man by nature to desire to understand, we must understand what it is for something to exist *by nature (phusei)*.[2] Aristotle begins *Physics* II by saying that existent things can be divided into those which exist by nature and those which exist from other causes.[3] The Greek word which is translated as 'cause' does not mean cause in the modern sense: namely, an antecedent event sufficient to produce an effect. Rather, it means the basis or ground of something. Aristotle later says that we do not understand something until we know why it is what it is: and the cause gives us 'the why.'[4] We shall discuss Aristotle's conception of cause later. For the moment, the important point is that Aristotle thinks that to say that something exists *by nature* is to cite its cause.

Aristotle thinks he can unproblematically identify the things that exist by nature. The paradigms are living organisms – animals and plants – but he also includes their parts and the 'simple bodies' – earth, air, fire, and water. The task, for Aristotle, is to find the characteristic feature which distinguishes natural items from everything else. 'Each of them,' he says, 'has *within itself* a principle of change and rest.'[5] The ability to grow is obvious in plants and animals, and animals can move about their environment, but even the simple elements have tendencies to move in fixed directions. For example, fire has the tendency to move toward the circumference of the universe, and will do so unless it is hindered. When it reaches the circumference, the fire's 'upward' motion will cease.[6]

---

[1] Appropriate reading for this section: *Physics* II.1–2.
[2] See *Physics* II.1, 192b38.
[3] *di' allas aitias*: *Physics* II.1, 192b8–9.
[4] *to dia ti*: *Physics* II.3, 194b17–20.
[5] *Physics* II.1, 192b13–14 (my translation).
[6] Cf. *Physics* II.1, 192b37.

One might wonder: if nature is an *internal* principle of change, how could nature be a cause? Nature would seem to be too much a piece of the thing itself to be its cause. One way to begin is to think of the contrast Aristotle has in mind when he divides reality into natural objects and things that exist from other causes. The paradigmatic case of a thing that exists from another cause is an artefact. Artefacts depend for their existence on an external source, a craftsman, who constructs the artefact out of certain material. Now it is obvious that the craftsman is a cause of the artefact he produces. But why should we isolate this creative principle as a cause only if it is external? The wondrous fact about natural objects is that they seem to have this creative force internalized, and thus it seems right that one should focus on it if one wants to know why something is what it is. This seems to be Aristotle's reasoning, for he concludes that 'nature is a principle or cause of change or rest *in* that to which it primarily belongs.'[7]

We as yet know almost nothing about this inner principle. One suggestion, made by some of Aristotle's predecessors, is that a thing's nature is the material stuff which constitutes it. According to Aristotle, Antiphon argued that if you planted a bed what would emerge from the rotting bed would not be another baby bed, but a shoot which would grow into wood. This, Antiphon allegedly thought, showed that the real nature of the bed was wood and that the form of the bed was merely an attribute imposed on it.[8] Given this use of the craft analogy, it is appealing to think of the form as superficial: a passing mark on a plastic and changeable reality. But, for Aristotle, this appeal depends on a misuse of the analogy between art and nature. Artefacts are of interest to him as much for their differences from natural objects as for their similarities. Precisely because an artefact has an external principle of change, the form imposed on the matter has an air of superficiality. But it is the *nature* of a young boy to grow into a man. Thus we cannot think of the manhood of a man as an incidental property superficially imposed on flesh and bones. And if you, so to speak, 'planted a man' – that is, let him go through the natural processes of generation, reproduction and decay – what would grow up would be another man, not mere flesh and bones. If we are to make correct

[7] *Physics* II.1, 192b21 (my translation).
[8] *Physics* II.1, 193a9–17.

use of the craft–nature analogy, Aristotle thinks, we must get away from thinking of the form of a bed as superficially imposed on wood. Instead, we must think of the bed as having its own integrity and ask: *what is it to be a bed?* Here the answer cannot be: to be wood. As Aristotle says, a pile of wood is at best a bed *only potentially*:[9] that is, the wood is such that it could be formed into a bed by a competent craftsman. To be a bed, the wood must actually have the form imposed on it. Thus if we are to think of a bed as having a nature at all, it is more appropriate, Aristotle thinks, to identify the bed's nature with its form. Indeed, if a bed were a natural object, then when planted it would grow up into a bed. That a bed does not reproduce other beds shows that the bed does not have a nature. For the form of a bed is not a principle internal to the bed. On this Aristotle and Antiphon agree. They disagree only to the extent that Antiphon thinks that this reveals something important about the nature of natural objects, whereas Aristotle thinks it reveals an important difference between natural objects and artefacts.

Yet if the form is internal to a natural object, how can one distinguish a natural object's form from its matter? After all, with an artefact there is a straightforward sense in which there is matter which exists before the artisan crafts it and which may persist after the artefact has broken down. But (1) if the nature of a natural object is an internal principle which makes the natural object a *natural* object and (2) the form is a candidate for being this nature, it would seem that form would have to be a part of a natural object from the beginning. The form, then, cannot be defined in terms of properties superimposed on a matter which exists before and (maybe) after the natural object exists.[10]

Aristotle, I believe, relies on the analogy between art and nature to give one some idea of the form of a natural object. A craftsman can impose a form on various bits of matter: he can make a bed from this wood and from that, he can shape a sphere in wax or in bronze.[11] In each case there is a *process* in which the matter comes to take on a particular form. Now with all living things there is a process by which each thing comes to be. This natural process of

---

[9] *Physics* II.1, 193a34–5.
[10] See J. L. Ackrill, 'Aristotle's Definitions of *Psuchē*;' and see section 4.1 below.
[11] See also *Metaphysics* VII.7–9, which is further discussed in section 6.5 below.

generation Aristotle conceptualizes as a process in which the organism comes to realize its (natural) form. Surely, we do see a level of organization in mature living organisms which is the outcome of a process of growth and maturation. It was not there before the organism grew to maturity. And we can give at least minimal sense to the idea of matter persisting through change in form. Immediately after an organism dies it lacks a principle of change and rest; what remains is the matter. However, this is at best an attenuated characterization, for the matter begins to decay simultaneously with death. The matter seems to be dependent on the form to be the matter that it is.

And, indeed, the form seems to be in some sense dependent on the matter: with natural organisms, unlike many artefacts, there is only one type of matter in which a form can be realized. Human form cannot be realized in froggy material or in iron. In short, with natural organisms we lack the clear-cut criteria which we have with artefacts for distinguishing matter and form. Yet if, as Aristotle believes, art does imitate nature, we can reason backwards from the imitation to that which it is an imitation of.[12] Aristotle would, I suspect, endorse the following counterfactual conditional: 'If there *were* a Divine Craftsman, he *would* impose the form of natural organisms on the appropriate matter.' Of course, Aristotle would deny the antecedent: there is, he thinks, no Divine Craftsman. However, since art does imitate nature, it is possible to view natural organisms *as though* they were created. From this perspective the creation consists in the imposition of form on matter.[13]

There is a, perhaps apocryphal, story about a young child asking Einstein how a radio works. Einstein asked the child to imagine a big cat which stretches from New York to Chicago. Someone in New York bites on the cat's tail and the cat yelps in Chicago. 'Radio waves are just like that,' Einstein reportedly said, 'except that there is no cat.'

Natural form is precisely that which a Divine Craftsman would

---

[12] *mimeitai*: *Physics* II.2, 194a21. For a further discussion of the idea of reasoning backward in order to determine the form/matter distinction in natural objects, see section 4.1 below.

[13] Indeed, Aristotle believes that neither matter nor form is ever created. See *Metaphysics* VII.7–9. Creation, for Aristotle, is the creation of a compound of form and matter; and the creation consists in the imposition of the form on the matter. See section 6.5 below.

impose if there were a Divine Craftsman; but there is no such Craftsman. The development of form, as an organism grows to maturity, is a process *internal* to the organism itself. But an organism's internal principle of change is its nature. An object's nature would thus seem to be a developmental force which impels it *toward* the realization of its form. How then can Aristotle identify an organism's nature with its form? The answer, which we shall investigate in detail later, is that form can exist at varying levels of potentiality and actuality. A young organism's form should not be identified with its current organization and structure. In addition to the structural articulation which the immature organism has so far achieved, it has within itself a force for future growth and development. This force is the form, though at this stage Aristotle thinks the form should be thought of as a potentiality or *power* (*dunamis*). The form in the young healthy organism is an internal force propelling it toward the realization of its form. This is not as paradoxical as it might initially appear, for when the organism has reached maturity, its form will no longer be a potentiality. In the mature organism, the form exists as a full-fledged actuality. In the growth of an organism, form is itself developing from potentiality to actuality, and it is directing this process. One cannot, therefore, identify natural forms with an organism's structure. Structure helps to constitute the form, but forms are also dynamic, powerful, active. They are a force for the realization of structure.

Form also provides the link between the mature and the immature organism. The growth of an organism is, for Aristotle, a process directed toward an end (*telos*): the mature functioning organism. The mature organism is 'that for the sake of which' the process of growth has occurred.[14] And yet Aristotle also identifies an organism's nature with the end or the 'that for the sake of which.'[15] Again there is an air of paradox. If an organism relies on its internal principle of change in order to reach its end, how could this end, which did not exist during the process of growth, be identified with the organism's nature? Aristotle's answer is that we should conceive the end as being the (*fully actualized*) form. For the form is and has been its nature throughout its development. The form is *both* that toward which the process is directed – 'that

---

[14] *Physics* II.2, 194a27 (*to hou heneka*).
[15] *Physics* II.2, 194a28–9.

for the sake of which' the growth occurs – *and* that which is directing the process. It is an immature organism's nature to grow into a mature member of the species, and it is a mature organism's nature simply to be a member of that species in the fullest, most active sense. This, for Aristotle, is one and the same nature: the active, dynamic form which, at varying levels of potentiality and actuality, is at work in the appropriate matter.

Since the seventeenth century Western science has moved steadily away from conceiving forms as part of the basic fabric of the universe. It is thought that if we understand all the properties of the matter we will see form as emerging from these properties. It is important to realize that Aristotle's world is not like that. In Aristotle's world, forms cannot be understood in terms of matter. Forms must occupy a fundamental ontological position: they are among the basic things that are.

Aristotle had, I suspect, a family of reasons for his belief in the irreducibility of form. If art imitates nature, then form must be a principle additional to the matter. A bed does not come to be from wood alone; there must be a craftsman who imposes a form on the wood. A natural object has this principle internalized, but that does not diminish the fact that the principle must be additional to the matter. No doubt Aristotle also thought he could support his belief in the irreducibility of form on the basis of empirical observation. Matter, for Aristotle, is indefinite, lacking order. As one moves toward the basic elements – earth, air, fire, and water – it appears incredible that an organized unity like flesh, let alone a living organism, should be completely explained by these elements alone. Aristotle also had theoretical reason for thinking this impossible.[16] For each of the basic elements themselves have (primitive) natures: fire to move upward to the circumference of the universe, earth to move toward the center, air and water to occupy intermediate positions. Were there no additional organizing principle, there would be nothing to hold the elements together: in the absence of external constraints, the elements would go flying off in the disparate directions of their natural places.

An organized unity, Aristotle believes, can always be dis-

[16] See Sarah Waterlow (Broadie), *Nature, Agency and Change in Aristotle's Physics.*

20

tinguished from the matter which constitutes it. For an organized unity, to be *organized* requires a principle responsible for the organization. Aristotle contrasts a heap and a syllable.[17] A heap is not really a unity at all and thus may be thought of as a mere agglomeration of its material constituents. The syllable *ba*, by contrast, cannot be thought of as a mere heap of its constituents *b* and *a*. To be a syllable rather than a mere concatenation of the shapes *b, a,* it must have been formed either in writing or in speech, by a person who also understands the language. This person – or the linguistic knowledge in his soul – functions as a principle of organization: he forms the syllable into the syllable that it is.

Matter, Aristotle says, is a relative item.[18] What he means by this is that the matter of a given thing must be understood in relation to the form that it is the matter of. The matter will always be less organized than the form, but it may itself have a certain organization. Indeed, there may be a hierarchy of matter and form. For example, Aristotle says that the matter of animals is their parts: heart, lungs, brain, liver, limbs, etc. But these parts of animals are themselves composites of form and matter: they are made up of homogeneous matter – flesh, viscera, and bone – organized in certain ways.[19] So while human lungs, liver, hands, etc., are the matter of a human being, a human is not a mere heap of liver and lungs. He is liver, lungs, etc., organized in such a way: there is thus required, in addition to the organization already manifested in the liver, lungs, and limbs, a principle responsible for organizing human organs and limbs into human form. This type of reasoning is applicable all the way down. Flesh and bones are the matter of human organs and limbs, but an arm is not a mere heap of flesh and bones. It is flesh and bones organized in such a way: there is thus required, in addition to the organization already manifested in the flesh and bones, a principle which is responsible for organizing the flesh and bones into an arm. And, to take this reasoning one step further: flesh does have a certain organization, but flesh is itself a composite of form and matter. The organization of flesh cannot be understood solely in terms of the organization already manifested in its matter, fire and earth. Flesh is not a mere heap of earth, water,

[17] See, e.g., *Metaphysics* VII.17, 1041b12–32.
[18] *Physics* II.2, 194b9 (*pros ti hē hulē*).
[19] See *Generation of Animals* I.1, 715a9–11.

and heat: this matter must be organized by an additional principle. Thus organized, the flesh can stand as matter for the limbs of a human being: that is, in need of an *additional* principle to organize it.[20]

Both Aristotle and a modern biologist would agree to the following subjunctive conditional: 'If this young child were allowed to live in a supportive environment, it would grow into a mature, healthy adult.' However, for the modern biologist the truth of this conditional would be grounded in the *already achieved material structure* of the young child. The child already has a structure which ensures that, in supportive conditions, the child will grow into a healthy adult. For Aristotle, by contrast, the actual material structure of the child is in itself insufficient to guarantee normal development. Yet Aristotle does endorse the subjunctive conditional. And he does not think that the conditional is *brutely true*: that is, true, but not in virtue of anything actual. The fact that the child *would* in a healthy environment grow to a mature adult is grounded in the *actual* presence of form in the child. This form is the additional principle, responsible both for the already achieved material structure of the child and for the child's future development. It is not merely a functional state of material structure. Nor, as it exists, is the form in the child in its fully developed state. It exists in the child as a power or potentiality for attaining this fully developed state.

However, if this power is not a functional state of material structure, how can its presence be observed? Are natural powers beyond the realm of empirical inquiry? No, they are not; but it takes some care to spell out the conditions under which they can be observed. Obviously, powers are not immediate items of sensory perception. Nor can they be seen under a microscope. If an intelligent scientist were permitted to observe only one immature natural organism in his life, having been kept in ignorance of the general facts of generation and destruction, then there would be no way he could detect the presence of a power in the organism. The first dawning of the idea that a power is present could only occur in retrospect. From the perspective of the fully developed organism we realize that there was a force present in the immature organism which directed its growth and activity toward this mature state.

[20] I discuss this further in section 2.3 below.

However, although the original idea of the presence of power is necessarily backward looking, this does not imply that powers are unobservable.

Aristotle attached much significance to the regularity of natural processes of generation and decay. If a teleological process of generation did occur only once, one would have to wait until the end to comprehend the antecedently existing powers which brought it about.[21] Because natural processes of growth occur with such dependable regularity – the exceptions can be dismissed as degenerate or crippled – there is empirical evidence for the presence of a power in an immature organism. Moreover, the form of an immature organism is not present merely as a power toward development. It is also manifest in its structure and organization. So, while the form is not merely a functional state of the young organism's material structure, it is nevertheless responsible for that structure. And, while that immature structure on its own is not itself sufficient to ensure the development of a more complex and mature structure, the immature structure is a manifestation of form which (given the proper setting) is sufficient to ensure development.

Since the seventeenth century it has been customary to treat so-called *virtus dormitiva* explanations with scorn. A *virtus dormitiva* explanation gets its name from Molière's play *Le Malade imaginaire*, in which a foolish doctor is asked how a certain powder induces sleep. He replies that it has a *virtus dormitiva* – a power of inducing sleep. The heart of the objection to *virtus dormitiva* explanations is that they are not explanations at all. To say that a powder causes sleep because it has a power to bring on sleep is to explain nothing: it is just to repeat that the powder causes sleep.

There is no doubt but that Molière's doctor is a fool and his 'explanation' a sham. But his legacy to Western culture is, I believe, a mistaken conception of adequate explanation. It is widely believed that if any explanation has the structure of a *virtus dormitiva* explanation, it must therefore be circular and non-explanatory. Thus

---

[21] Hegel believed that one such unique process was human history. Thus philosophy was, for Hegel, essentially retrospective. For the full meaning of human activity could only be fully understood from the vantage-point of the realized end. As Hegel put it, 'the Owl of Minerva spreads its wings only with the falling of the dusk' (*Philosophy of Right*, Preface, p. 13).

Aristotelian powers are viewed as inevitably suspect. This, I think, is a mistake. There may be a valid objection to certain explanations which have a *virtus dormitiva* structure, but the objection is not one of principle. Even if we do not live in Aristotle's world, it is not absurd to imagine that our world is as he described. In such a world we could not explain the organism's ability to develop in terms of its material microstructure. In such a world this ability is form, and form is one of the basic constituents of the universe: it cannot be explained in terms of anything more fundamental.

In Aristotle's world form as a potentiality or power does help to explain the growth, development, and mature functioning of living organisms. And there are empirical tests for the presence of form. Were there no structure in an immature organism or regularity in the processes of development there would, in Aristotle's eyes, be no basis for the attribution of a power, regardless of the outcome. The absurdity of Molière's doctor is manifested not merely by his *virtus dormitiva* explanation but, first, by the fact that he has not noticed that he is not living in Aristotle's world (and by that time in the history of science he should have); second, by the evident fact that he merely cites the *virtus* without having any understanding of how it might work as an explanation; third, by the fact that he has done nothing to determine whether the powder actually has the power. (He could have devised tests to distinguish accidental onset of sleep from genuine inducement.)

Each thing which has a nature is, Aristotle says, a substance (*ousia*).[22] Reality, for Aristotle, forms a hierarchy of dependencies. The color white, for example, may exist, but it can only exist as the color *of* something.[23] Substance stands at the base of the hierarchy: it is that on which the reality of other things depends, while it is not dependent on anything else. This characterization of substance is very abstract. As a result, we may know that substance is ontologically independent yet remain ignorant of what in the world fits this characterization. Indeed, *Metaphysics* VII, which represents the mature Aristotle's search for substance, is probably the most difficult text in the entire Aristotelian corpus. Fortunately we do not

[22] *Physics* II.I, 192b33. It is worth noting at the outset that Aristotle's conception of substance will develop over time.
[23] See, e.g., *Metaphysics* VII.I.

have to work our way through that text in order to understand Aristotle's claim that everything that has a nature is a substance. For Aristotle distinguished substance in the primary sense from various other things we call substance because they have some degree of ontological independence. Whatever finally emerges as primary substance, we can appreciate right now that things which have a nature enjoy at least some degree of ontological independence.

Natural organisms are loci of reality and self-determination. Because each has in itself a principle of change, there is an objective basis for distinguishing it from the rest of the environment. It is not just that we observers are minded so as to perceive certain functional organizations as salient and thus select out certain bits of a relatively homogeneous reality as objects of interest. Natural forms are ontologically basic, and each thing having a nature has such a principle within itself. Moreover, the principle which directs the growth, development, and characteristic activity of a natural organism exists in the organism itself. The environment only supplies a backdrop against which an organism acts out the drama of its life. The environment may be benign or hindering, but beyond that it plays no significant role in the development and life of the organism.[24] Further, this inner principle is not like an extra silicon chip which is plugged into an already existing computer. It is rather the clearest expression of what the organism itself is. An organism is thought to be most fully what it is when it has reached maturity: thus it is most fully what it is when its form is fully developed.[25] The principle directing the change, growth and characteristic activity expresses the organism's self-determination.

It is by virtue of its nature, then, that each natural organism is a substance.[26] Because it has a nature, an organism is relatively independent of the environment and self-directing. It provides a subject for properties to belong to, and it does not itself depend on another subject for its existence.[27] Yet there is a problem here. It seems odd to say that a natural organism is a substance *because* of its form.

---

[24] For a discussion of how the modern conception of the importance of the environment differs from Aristotle's, see Sarah Waterlow (Broadie), *Nature, Agency and Change in Aristotle's Physics.*

[25] *Physics* II.1, 193b6–7.

[26] Cf. *Physics* II.1, 192b33–4.

[27] See also *Metaphysics* V.8, 1017b13–14.

This would seem to imply that it *depends* on its form to be the substance that it is. And this would seem to threaten the idea that an organism is ontologically independent. How could a natural organism be a substance if it depends on its form? One can say that the form expresses what the organism most truly is. Form is not a property true *of* the organism; form is constitutive of the organism's very being. One can also point out that an organism does not depend on its form in the way that a property depends on a subject. But the fact remains that the organism is a composite of form and matter, and the form is ontologically prior to the composite.[28] Such reasoning will eventually convince Aristotle to dismiss natural organisms as candidates for *primary* substance – as we shall see. We can continue to call them substances, however, for within the natural world they do exercise a certain type of ontological independence.

2.2 Understanding and 'the why'[29]

We do not think we understand something, Aristotle says, until we have grasped *the why* of it.[30] The expression 'the why' is awkward even if it is a literal translation, but this is one of those cases where awkwardness is of value. For it is often thought that Aristotle is saying that a cause is anything which answers a why-question. This is anachronistic. It looks as though Aristotle is relativizing causes to our interests and curiosities. In fact the situation is the reverse. 'The why' is an objective feature of the world: it is that about which we *ought* to be curious if we wish to understand a thing. The expression 'the why' is suggestive of the intimate link Aristotle saw between man and world. Man is by nature a questioner of the world: he seeks to understand why the world is the way it is. The world for its part reciprocates: it 'answers' man's questions. 'The why' performs a curious double duty, as interrogative and indicative, suggesting both question and answer. And the world's 'answers' are not merely responses to man's probings: they manifest the ultimate intelligibility of the world. 'The why,' therefore, penetrates to the world's most basic reality.

---

[28] See *Metaphysics* VII.7–9, and section 6.6 below.
[29] Appropriate reading: *Physics* II.3, 7–8; III.1–3.
[30] *to dia ti: Physics* II.3, 194b18–19; cf. *Posterior Analytics* I.2, 71b8–12.

To grasp the why of a thing, Aristotle says, is to grasp its *primary* cause.[31] From what we have learned so far one would expect Aristotle to identify the why with a thing's nature. For the form, which is the thing's inner principle of change, provides us with the best understanding of what the thing most truly is and why it is the way it is. This expectation is, I believe, realized: Aristotle did identify the why with an object's nature or form. This will seem surprising only if you have heard that Aristotle isolated *four* distinct causes: material, formal, efficient, and final. What he actually cites are not four causes but four *fashions* in which we cite the cause.[32] Of course, Aristotle was proud to have identified the four distinct ways in which cause is cited. Nevertheless, he believed that for the generation of natural organisms and for the production of artefacts there were at most two causes – form and matter. And matter ultimately has to be relegated to a secondary position, for it is ultimately unintelligible: at each level of organization what we come to understand is the principle of organization or form. The matter provides the brute particularity of an object: it can be perceived, but not understood.[33] Unintelligible matter cannot, in a strict sense, give us the why of anything. The so-called formal, efficient, and final causes are (at least in the wide variety of events that occur within the natural world) three different aspects of form itself. Aristotle says that these three causes 'often converge on one thing.'[34] The one thing is form, and 'often' covers *all* cases of natural generation and creation of artefacts.[35] So although Aristotle can talk about the three causes which coincide, he can also talk about the *primary* cause. He is not then picking out one of four causes for special honor: he is citing the one item, form, which can be considered either as the form it is or as the efficient cause or as the final cause. The form really is the why of a thing.

---

[31] *hē protē aitia*: *Physics* II.3, 194b20.

[32] *tropoi*: *Physics* II.3, 194b23–4, b26, b29, b32.

[33] See, e.g., *Physics* III.6, 207a24–32. For the attenuated sense in which matter can be considered intelligible, see the discussion of final cause in section 2.3 below, and the discussion of the hierarchy of matter and form in section 2.4 below.

[34] *eis hen pollakis*: *Physics* II.7, 198a25.

[35] It does not cover the causal influence of an unmoved mover. It also does not cover mathematical objects like geometrical objects and numbers. Cf. *Physics* II.7, 198a28–9.

2.3 Four fashions

Aristotle does think that there are four ways in which we cite the cause of a thing. The first is the matter: or 'that out of which a thing comes to be and which persists.'[36] The paradigmatic case is the matter of artefacts: for example, bronze may be shaped into a bowl, then melted down and beaten into a sword. The bronze is the matter, first of the bowl and later of the sword. The remaining three ways in which we state the cause are three different ways of specifying the same thing, the form.

The second fashion is the form – that is, it is the form *specified as such*. Since this cause is not distinct from the ones which will follow, what we learn here is how Aristotle characterizes form. He calls it 'the *logos* of the essence.'[37] 'Essence' is a customary translation for what is literally rendered as 'the what it is to be.'[38] An organism's nature, its inner principle of change, gives us what it is to be that thing. Indeed, the fact that an organism has a nature provides a metaphysical basis for distinguishing among what we moderns would think of as the properties of the organism. Those properties which are part of an organism's essence should not be conceived as true *of* the organism. These properties express what the organism *is*. Other properties – like being pale, walking, being six feet tall – are true *of* the organism; and they depend for their existence on the organism which acts as the subject to which they belong.[39]

The Oxford translation of 'the *logos* of the essence' is 'the *definition* of the essence.'[40] While 'definition' is sometimes an appropriate translation for *logos*, in this context it cannot be correct. Aristotle is here trying to characterize the form as cause, and a cause is not a definition, but a real item in the world. *Logos* is a protean word: it can also mean proportion, ratio, order. The *logos* of the essence need not be a linguistic item; it can be the order, arrangement, proportion instantiated by the essence itself. '*Logos* of the essence' brings home that the essence – what it is

---

[36] *to ex hou gignetai ti enuparxontos: Physics* II.7, 194b24.
[37] *ho logos, ho tou ti ēn einai: Physics* II.7, 194b27.
[38] *to ti ēn einai.*
[39] I began discussing this distinction in section 2.1. It will be discussed in greater detail in sections 6.5–6.6 below.
[40] The old Oxford translation is 'statement of the essence.'

to be a thing – instantiates an order, or proportion, in the matter.

Precisely because the essence does instantiate an order, it is intelligible. Mind can grasp the order manifested in an essence, and *thus* we can give an account or definition of it. Aristotle is translated as saying that what is potentially flesh has not yet its own nature until it receives 'the form specified in the definition.'[41] A more literal rendering would be: until it receives '*the form according to the logos*'. Here again 'definition' is the wrong translation. For Aristotle does not mean that the potential flesh is in the process of conforming to a linguistic entity. It is rather that the potential flesh is in the process of realizing a certain order, and this order is the *logos*. Yet Aristotle does move from the order of a form to its definability. For example, he says that the form according to the *logos* is that 'by which we, when defining, say what flesh or bone is.'[42] This is not an equivocation. Aristotle thinks *the very same logos* present in the form and in the definition: that is why the definition is a definition. It is a *logos* which gives the *logos*: the definition states the essence. Aristotle thinks that order is ultimately intelligible: it is that which is realized over and over again in natural organisms, it is that which a single definition can capture as the essence of these organisms, it is that which the mind can apprehend. Because the form of a natural organism or artefact gives us what it is to be that thing, *the why* and *the what* converge. We tend to envision philosophical activity as concerned at least as much with essential charaterization – what there really is – as with explanation – why things are the way they are. For Aristotle, a single inquiry will reveal both, for *the why* of something is its essence.

The third way we specify the cause is as the primary source of the change or rest.[43] The father is cause of the child, in this sense, as is the craftsman of what he makes – and, generally, that which brings about a change is the cause of what is changed.[44] The Greek for 'primary source of change' is often translated as 'efficient cause.' For the primary source or principle is that which *brings about* a change. Yet this translation is misleading for two reasons.

[41] *Physics* II.1, 193b1–2.
[42] *Physics* II.1, 193b2 (my translation).
[43] *Physics* II.3, 194b29–30.
[44] *Physics* II.3, 194b30–2.

First, it suggests anachronistically that Aristotle had isolated the modern conception of cause; second, it suggests that this is a different cause from the form rather than a different way of specifying the same cause. Let us consider these reasons in turn.

Aristotle's primary principle of change differs dramatically from the modern conception of efficient cause. The most obvious difference is that on the modern, post-Humean conception, the efficient cause is an *event* which is regularly followed by its effect, whereas Aristotle tends to cite *things* – the father, the builder, the doctor – as paradigms of his primary principle. This difference is so great that it would immediately destroy any resemblance between efficient cause and primary principle were it not for the fact that Aristotle does distinguish between *the potential* and *the actual* cause.[45] The builder is the *potential* cause of the house, the builder building is the *actual* cause. Those who have wanted to assimilate Aristotle's cause to the modern conception have insisted that the actual cause – the builder building, the doctor doctoring, the father fathering – is an event; indeed, it is an event which brings about its effect, and thus it should be treated as the efficient cause. This line of reasoning fails, I believe, to capture the significance of Aristotle's insistence that it is the builder building which is the actual cause.

To see this, let us consider for a moment why the modern conception of cause focusses on events at all. Hume argued that transitive agency in nature is empirically unobservable. All one can ever observe is one event following another. One can never observe *the causing* which, as it were, glues the two events together. When there is a regular pattern of one type of event following another we tend to see the first event as causing the second; but, Hume argued, we never see the causing, we only witness the events. Hume did not think we should abandon the language of causation, but Humeans do have to reconstrue what is meant by 'cause.' To isolate an event as a cause must be construed as shorthand for claiming that the event occupies a certain place in a larger regularity of events. To say that a particular event x causes an event y is to say that x is an event of type X and y is an event of type Y and, in general, when an event of type X occurs it is followed by an event of type Y. We may even say that X-type events bring about Y-type events,

[45] *Physics* II.3, 195b4–6.

but all we can mean by this is that if an X-type event *were* to occur a Y-type event *would* follow. Strictly speaking, though, all connotation of transitive agency should be expunged. One reason why we moderns focus on events as causes is that we want to get away from appealing to anything that is empirically unobservable, and we take the actual causing to be unobservable.

Aristotle, by contrast, thought that the actual causing was clearly observable: the builder building is the actual causing and one can see his activity of building. For Hume the causing is not itself a particular event: it is that which would occur between the antecedent and the subsequent event, if anything did, but nothing (at least, nothing empirically observable) does occur. What is at issue is a disagreement not only about causes but about *what constitutes an event*. It is important to realize that events are not unproblematically given. It is easy for us to overlook that, because we think we can locate any space–time point and call what is going on there an event. But Aristotle had no such matrix to isolate and identify events. He did not have a watch, and when he specified the place of an object it was not in terms of its location in a unique all-encompassing field. The place of an object was characterized in terms of the boundary of the body which contained it.[46] The way Aristotle chose to identify events instead was via the actualizing of potentialities: the potentialities of substances to cause and suffer change.

One way to characterize the difference between Hume and Aristotle is to say that while for Hume causation must be understood in terms of a relation between two events, for Aristotle there is only one event – a change. Aristotle can pick out the single event of a change: and causation must be understood as a relation of things (or things doing their thing) to that event. A change, for Aristotle, is the actualizing of potentiality.[47] For example, a pile of bricks may be a house potentially and a builder may be able to build the house. The actualization of these potentialities is the building of the house. Indeed, Aristotle says that change can be understood as

---

[46] See *Physics* IV.4.
[47] *Physics* III.1, 201a10–11. This will be discussed in more detail in chapter 3 below.

the actualizing of the potential agent and the patient.[48] Thus we can think of a change in terms of a builder actualizing his potential by becoming a builder building and the bricks having their potential actualized by becoming a house being built. However, the actualizing of these two potentialities is not two separate events. The actualizing of the agent and the actualizing of the patient are, for Aristotle, one and the same event.

In *Physics* III.3, Aristotle argues that there is but a single activity in a given change, and it occurs in the patient. Aristotle is concerned to show that not every cause of change need itself undergo change when it acts as a cause – that there is at least a possibility of an unmoved mover. Thus when he confronts the question 'Where does one locate the agency which is the actualizing of the agent?' he is willing to bite the bullet and say, 'in the patient.' If we think of a teacher teaching and a student learning we should not, according to Aristotle, think of two activities which are related to each other: 'teacher teaching' and 'student learning' are two different ways of characterizing the very same happening. One description captures the perspective of the agent, the other captures the perspective of the patient. Although there may be various ways to characterize this activity, Aristotle argues that there is nevertheless only one activity and it is occurring in the student. It may sound odd at first to think of the teacher's teaching as occurring in the student, but for Aristotle if it is happening anywhere at all, this is where it would have to be. And, on second thoughts, the idea is not so odd: where else could *teaching* be occurring? We can imagine a teacher going through the motions in an empty classroom, or lecturing to a flock of geese, but Aristotle would deny that he was teaching. Unless a student is learning a teacher cannot be teaching.

Similarly with the builder: 'the builder building' and 'the house being built' refer to one and the same event from two different perspectives. The activity of the builder building is occurring in the bricks and mortar that are becoming a house. And, again, were the builder not performing his characteristic activity on the appropriate material, he would not be a builder building. At best, he would be a builder doing something else. Thus it is futile to specify the builder building as an antecedent event which might serve as efficient cause in the modern sense. The event which 'the builder

[48] *Physics* III.3, 202b26.

building' refers to is every bit as much the effect as it is the cause. Indeed, it is because there is only one event for Aristotle that the vocabulary of cause is ineliminable. The language of cause requires one to note that there are two distinct 'objects' involved in a change – an agent and a patient – without allowing what Aristotle must deny: that there are two distinct events. (A Humean, by contrast, can always cease using the shorthand language of cause in favor of (what for him is) a more accurate description of general regularities and of the place of particular events within those patterns.)

So far we have shown that 'the primary principle of change' should not be conceived in terms of the modern conception of efficient cause. But what reason is there for thinking that it should be identified with form? Has not Aristotle identified a distinct cause?

We have already seen that there are two features of forms which Aristotle is concerned to stress: first, that they are immanent in natural objects and, second, that they are dynamic. Forms are instantiated in natural organisms – they are the inner principles of change – and they act as a force within the organization for the realization (and reproduction) of the form.[49]

There are at least three ways in which forms are transmitted in the natural world: by sexual reproduction, by the creation of artefacts, and by teaching. The creation of artefacts remains a paradigm. The craftsman has his art or *technē* in his soul: that is, the form which he will later impose on external matter first resides in his soul. We have already seen that form can exist at varying levels of potentiality and actuality. The form of an artefact, as it resides in a craftsman's soul, is a potentiality or power. It is in virtue of this power in his soul that we can say that he is a craftsman. The full actuality of the craftsman's art is his actually making an artefact. Thus the builder building is actually the form of the house in action. And, as we have seen, this activity is occurring *in* the house being built. In short, the primary principle of change is the form in action.

When Aristotle cites the builder building or the teacher teaching as the actual cause of change it is not because he is trying to focus on an antecedent causal event – i.e. on what for us would be the ef-

[49] See section 2.1 above.

ficient cause. It is because he is trying to cite the *primary* principle of change: the form in its highest level of actualization. Aristotle identifies the agent of change with that which determines the form: '*The changer will always introduce a form ... which, when it moves, will be the principle and cause of the change.* For instance, an actual man makes what is potentially a man into a man.'[50] But he also says that if we are being more precise we must think of the cause as being the form itself: 'In investigating the cause of each thing it is always necessary to seek what is most precise ... thus man builds because he is a builder, and a builder builds *in virtue of his art of building. This last cause then is prior; and so generally.*'[51] Aristotle could not conceive the primary source of change as a mere antecedent event. It must be something – the form – which persists and determines the form in the change. Even in art there is a sense in which form is responsible for its own realization. When we specify the builder as the primary source of change we are not simply citing him as the cause: we are concerned with what eventually constitutes him as a builder. This is the form (of a house, say) which, as a potentiality, is the builder's art. It is the builder's capacity to be a builder. The art of building at its highest level of activity is the builder building. This is occurring in the house being built and is identical to the activity of the house being built. As Aristotle says, 'architecture is *in* the buildings it makes.'[52] Thus in Aristotle's world, there is no *event* antecedent to this activity which might be isolated as the efficient cause. If we are to isolate anything antecedent to this activity which might help to explain its occurring, we have to specify a thing – a builder – or perhaps a form which exists as a potentiality or power in the builder's soul.

Teaching is very much like the creation of an artefact, though the 'matter' on which the teacher imposes his form is the student's soul. A teacher, in teaching, is able to pass on his knowledge to his student: this, for Aristotle, is to impart the (relevant) forms or essences in his soul to the student's soul. The teacher teaching is the activity of form – a form which constitutes the knowledge the teacher is passing on. If the teaching is successful, the student's

[50] *Physics* III.2, 202a9–12 (my emphasis). I use the words 'changer' and 'change,' where the Oxford translation uses 'mover' and 'motion.' Aristotle does not stick to this consistently throughout the *Physics*, but it at least serves as a paradigm.
[51] *Physics* II.3, 195b21–4 (my emphasis).
[52] *Generation of Animals* I.22, 730b7–8.

mind takes on the form that is in the teacher's mind. It is as though the student's mind is the successful teacher's artefact.

Similarly with sexual reproduction. Consider, for example, the human species. It is of the essence of the human soul that members of the human species be able to reproduce their kind. To be a father is to have the power to pass on the human form to another member of the species. This power helps to constitute the human form itself. The father fathering is just the actualization of this power: namely, active human form.

Therefore, the primary source of change is form. The actual primary source is form in an active state.

The last way in which we cite the cause is the end (*telos*) or 'that for the sake of which' something is done.[53] For example, plants grow leaves in order to protect their fruit and send roots downward for nourishment, swallows build nests for protection, and spiders build webs for the sake of nourishment.[54] In each case such activities of plants and animals are for the development, maintenance, or protection of form: 'Since nature is twofold, the matter and the form, of which the latter is the end, and since all the rest is for the sake of the end, *the form must be the cause in the sense of "that for the sake of which."*'[55] The '**final cause**' is not a different cause, it is a different way of referring to nature. Aristotle concludes his discussion of final cause by saying: 'It is evident then *that nature is a cause*, a cause that operates for a purpose.'[56] Our task is to understand how nature or form can operate as a final cause.

In Aristotle's world form exists not merely as a realized state, it also exists as a *striving* toward that state. This striving is a basic ontological entity: it is an irreducible force in the young organism directed toward an end. The end, the form in its realized state, is none other than a successful striving.[57] Since a striving is not merely the expression of an actual material state, we cannot make sense of strivings unless we understand what they are strivings

53 *Physics* II.3, 194b32–3. Appropriate reading: *Physics* II.3–9.
54 *Physics* II.8, 199a20–30.
55 *Physics* II.8, 199a30–2 (my emphasis).
56 *Physics* II.8, 199b32–3.
57 Compare this to the account of human action as successful trying. Action on this analysis is not trying plus bodily movement, a successful trying is an action. See Brian O'Shaughnessy, *The Will*.

toward. We need to cite form as final cause in order to make the whole range of developmental activities – form as potentiality – intelligible.

In the twentieth century much work has been done by philosophers to show that teleological explanations are compatible with mechanical explanations.[58] For example, one can say that the spider builds its web in order to secure nourishment, but one can also explain its orderly activity via its neuro-physiological makeup and genetic inheritance. That is, actual physical structure grounds teleological behavior. It is important to realize that Aristotle does not believe in any such compatibility.[59] For Aristotle, the reason one has to cite the form in its final, realized state is that it is only by reference to that form that one can understand teleological behavior.

This comes out most clearly in Aristotle's discussion of chance and spontaneity.[60] Chance (*tuchē*) and spontaneity (*to automaton*) are important for they provide cases of *apparent* teleology. A *spontaneous event* is one which (1) might have occurred for the sake of something, (2) as it happens did not, but (3) was instead brought about by some external cause.[61] For example, the stone which struck the man did so spontaneously, for it might have been the weapon of his enemy, though in fact it just rolled off the cliff.[62] Note that a spontaneous event is not a disturbance of the causal order. The stone falls because of its own weight – or, in Aristotelian terms, because it seeks its natural place and is unhindered. An event counts as spontaneous not because it interrupts a causal chain or because it literally emerges from nowhere, but because it appears as though it is happening for an end even though it really is not. The stone did not really drop in order to strike the man, though it might appear so.

Chance, like spontaneity, is a case of apparent purposiveness,

---

[58] See, e.g., Charles Taylor, *The Explanation of Behavior*, and 'The Explanation of Purposive Behavior;' Hilary Putnam, 'Philosophy and our Mental Life,' Jonathan Bennett, *Linguistic Behaviour*.

[59] See John Cooper, 'Aristotle on Natural Teleology.' For attempts to make Aristotle out to be a compatibilist, see, e.g., Wolfgang Wieland, 'The Problem of Teleology,' and *Die aristotelische Physik*; and Martha Nussbaum, *Aristotle's De Motu Animalium*, Essay 1.

[60] *Physics* II.4–8.

[61] See *Physics* II.6, especially 197b18–20.

[62] Cf. *Physics* II.6, 197b30–2; for other examples: b15–18.

but it is restricted to men's activities.[63] For example, a man goes to the market to buy a chicken and encounters a debtor.[64] If he had known the debtor was in the market, he *would* have gone there for the sake of meeting him. An observer who was ignorant of what the creditor did and did not know might easily conclude that he went to the market in order to meet his debtor. But the observer would be mistaken. The creditor formed no such intention, for he was ignorant of the debtor's whereabouts. Thus the observer's teleological explanation, though tempting, would be false. Again, chance is not a disturbance of the natural order, it is just that in the regular affairs of men events occur which look as though they occurred for a certain purpose when they did not. They may well have occurred for another purpose: for example, both the creditor and the debtor came to the market in order to buy a chicken.

So, if an end-like state were the inevitable outcome of a process which depended solely on the material state of the organism, Aristotle would call this state spontaneous. Far from being a compatibilist, Aristotle explicitly contrasts processes which occur by necessity and genuinely teleological processes.[65] He even considers a type of natural selection only to reject it. Might it not be, he asks,

> ... that our teeth should come up *of necessity* – the front teeth sharp, fitted for tearing, the molars broad and useful for grinding down the food – since they did not arise for this end, but it was merely a coincident result; and so with all other parts in which we suppose that there is purpose? Wherever then all the parts came to be just what they would have been if they had come to be for an end, such things survived, *being organized spontaneously* in a fitting way...[66]

It is odd to a modern eye to see Aristotle link necessity and spontaneity. For one is inclined to think that if an event occurs as the outcome of an inevitable, determining process that is just what it is for the event *not* to be spontaneous. But for Aristotle a spontaneous event is one that appears to be for an end. That is why he is able to

[63] See, e.g., *Physics* II.5, 197a5–8; II.6, 197b1–6.
[64] See *Physics* II.5, 196b33–197a5, 197a15–18.
[65] See, e.g., *Physics* II.8.
[66] *Physics* II.8, 198b23–31. (I use the expression 'came to be' where the Oxford translation uses 'came about'.)

link the necessary and the spontaneous. If an organism or its functioning parts were the inevitable outcome of material processes that would be what it was to be occurring spontaneously.

Spontaneity is thus a serious threat to Aristotle's world-view. For it undermines the candidacy of form to be primary cause. If form is the inevitable outcome of necessary processes, then form would be merely supervenient upon these necessities.[67] Form could not then supply *the why*; an account of the necessary interactions would supply it. Aristotle answers his hypothesis of necessary processes and natural selection as follows:

> It is impossible that this should be the true view. For teeth and all other natural things either invariably or for the most part come about in a given way; but of not one of the results of chance or spontaneity is this true ... If then, it is agreed that things are either the result of coincidence or for the sake of something, and these cannot be the result of coincidence or spontaneity, it follows that they must be for the sake of something ... Therefore action for an end is present in things which come to be and are by nature.[68]

Aristotle's argument seems to have the following structure:

(1) natural things, like teeth, come about always or at least regularly in a certain way;
but
(2) spontaneous or chance events occur rarely;
and since
(3) things occur either for an end or spontaneously [by chance],
and
(4) natural things cannot occur spontaneously [by (1) & (2)],
it follows that
(5) natural things must be for an end [by (3) & (4)]

This argument is more powerful than it might at first appear to a modern reader. To a modern reader, the fact that teeth invariably occur in a certain pattern is testimony to the existence of necessary

[67] Aristotle does believe that certain lowly species come to be through spontaneous generation, but in general the generation of living things is dependent on form.
[68] *Physics* II.8, 198b34–199a8.

processes, not to their absence. How could Aristotle invoke invariability in an argument against necessity? Is his argument not obviously fallacious? At first it seems so. It looks as though Aristotle is relying on two distinct criteria of the spontaneous: apparent purposiveness and rarity of occurrence. Necessary processes turn out to be spontaneous because they are only apparently teleological. But then the alleged rarity of spontaneous events is used to rule out the existence of necessary processes. Might one not object that if there genuinely are necessary processes which produce apparently purposeful results, then it is simply a mistake to assume that spontaneous events are rare? That is, should we not reject premiss (2)? If the necessary processes are ubiquitous, then so too are the spontaneous events.

The argument is not that bad. But to appreciate it, one must see it against a backdrop of Aristotle's conception of order. There are two theses about order which Aristotle believed and argued for with some vigor. If one accepts these theses, this argument is a good one. The first thesis is:

(1) order is an expression of form *all the way down.*

As we have already seen, Aristotle believed that matter was a relative item. Though flesh and bone may be the matter of human limbs, once we consider flesh itself we see that it is a compound of form and matter, the form being the order and arrangement of the matter which constitutes flesh. And so on. The second thesis is:

(11) the order which exists at any level of matter is insufficient to generate the order required at the next level of organization.

What is needed in addition is form as a basic irreducible force – a developmental power – which, Aristotle believes, the statically given material structure could not possibly account for. The form of a developing organism, remember, is not merely its achieved structure, it is a force in the organism for attaining ever higher levels of organization until the organism achieves its mature form. Aristotle finds the idea of structure emerging from necessary processes incredible, because for him the necessary processes could not possibly be grounded in an actual structure. The idea that the order which exists at the level of flesh would be sufficient to generate the order required for human life was as absurd for Aristotle as the idea that the order that exists in a pile of wood would be sufficient for the pile to turn itself into a bed. If one accepts these two theses, then spontaneous events should be very rare. For there is, in general, no basis for a developmental process to occur solely in virtue of the necessary properties of the matter. Though it is not impossible for order to emerge – environmental forces may impose some sort of order – such emergence would have to be a very rare occurrence.

Since the seventeenth century teleological explanations have been in disrepute. There are so many misconceptions surrounding the idea of teleology that it is worth stressing that all Aristotle is committed to is the basic ontological reality of forms, combined with the idea that natural forms characteristically develop from potentiality to actuality. In particular, Aristotle is not committed to the (absurd) idea of backward causation: that is, that the achieved end is exerting some kind of backward causal pull on the antecedent events. This confused idea arose by taking the modern notion of efficient cause and putting it at the end of a developmental process for which it was responsible. (And when one forgets that there could be any other conception of cause than the modern notion of efficient cause, it becomes easier (though it is unjustifiable) to attribute this confusion to Aristotle.) Nevertheless, Aristotle does believe that there is *real* purposefulness in the world. And real purposefulness requires that the end *somehow* govern the process along the way to its own realization. Of course, it is not, strictly speaking, the end *specified as such* that is operating from the start: it is *form* that directs the process of its own development from potentiality to actuality. Form which exists as a potentiality is a force in the organism for the acquisition of a certain character: namely, actual form. Form as an actuality is the end or final cause.

Of course, the existence of potential form at the beginning of a developmental process is due to the antecedent existence of actual form. In natural generation, the potential form of the child is due to the actual form of (one of) the parents being passed on in sexual reproduction. In the creation of artefacts, the form in the craftsman's soul becomes actualized as he creates. Ultimately, it is actual form which is responsible for the generation of actual form. So in this extended sense the end was there at the beginning, establishing a process directed toward the end: actual form.

Nor is Aristotle committed to the idea of a conscious design in nature. Indeed, he explicitly denies that nature is the expression of some divine purpose or divine craftsman. We tend to think that if there *really* is some purpose in nature there must be some agent whose purpose it is. That is why it is so common to hear that purpose is just a projection of mind onto (mindless) nature. Aristotle would disagree. Aristotle believes in the basic reality of form, and he everywhere sees natural processes as directed toward the realization of that form. It would, however, be a mistake to conclude that his primary conception of purposefulness is *mindless*. Whether or not a teleological development is mindless or mindful depends upon what is meant by 'mind.' If mind is simply equated with consciousness, then the growth of a natural organism is certainly mindless. In realizing a developed form, a natural process achieves its goal even though no mind has directed or created the process. And yet Aristotle's world is essentially intelligible. It is a world that is so ordered, structured, saturated with purposefulness that it is meant to be understood in the sense that it is man's nature to inquire into the world's order and come to understand it. If the world were not in this extended sense so mind-like, it would be impossible for man to understand it. Our appreciation of purposefulness is not, for Aristotle, a projection of (human) mind onto nature; it is a projection of purposeful, intelligible, 'mindful' nature onto the human mind.

Indeed, the purposeful activity of minded men is an imitation of nature.[69] If a house came to be by nature, Aristotle says, it would grow in the same way that it is built. The step-wise process of building, which is for the sake of the finished shelter, is an imitation of nature. It is as though nature has taught man purposeful activity: that is, conscious purposeful activity is learned from the (unconscious) purposefulness which permeates nature. A man may consciously direct his purposeful activity, but consciousness is not an essential feature of purposefulness itself. Even man can engage in purposeful activity without consciously planning all the steps: 'It is absurd to suppose that purpose is not present because we do

---

[69] *Physics* II.8, 199a8–20, b26–30.

not observe the agent deliberating. Art does not deliberate.'[70] A craftsman who has learned his art has internalized the form of a house in his soul. When the craftsman goes to work the form of the house becomes active. The craftsman need not deliberate or spend much time engaged in conscious thought: his purposeful activity is more or less automatic. This is the activity of form.

Kant argued that our teleological judgements attribute a *conceptual causality* to nature.[71] He was impressed by the fact that the parts of the organism are in the service of the whole organism and that the disparate activities of the organism are directed toward maintaining its life and reproducing its kind. For example, when a spider builds its web the entire web-building activity seems to be directed toward the end of keeping the spider in existence. And all the parts of the spider seem to be subjugated to this goal. But the goal is the existence of an organism, a spider. It is as though the concept *spider* were exerting a causal influence. The question for Kant then became, 'how could a mind-like entity like a concept have a causal influence in nature?'

Aristotle accepted the reality of forms, so under some construal he did believe in conceptual causality. That is, he believed that the form of a spider really does exert a causal influence. However, this does not mean that he thought the causality was dependent on our minds or that it was a projection of our minds onto nature. One may think of forms as conceptual in the sense that they are what render the world intelligible. They are what project themselves onto our minds when we study the world and *only thus* are what our minds contemplate when we are contemplating. But then one must get away from thinking that concepts only have existence in a mind. Indeed, it is because concepts are really there in the (unconscious but mind-like) natural world – that is, that forms are instantiated in natural objects – that we humans can think with concepts at all. For it is only by encountering these forms in our journey through the world that we pass from the ignorance in which we are born to a state where we can contemplate at will. The forms in the world give man the concepts to contemplate.

---

[70] *Physics* II.8, 199b26–8.
[71] Immanuel Kant, *Critique of Judgement*.

2.4 The hearts of animals[72]

If form is a basic force in nature, then its development and emergence cannot be due to necessary processes which occur in the matter. The natural process of generation is in this respect similar to the process of making an artefact.[73] It is absurd, Aristotle thinks, to explain the structure of a house by saying that the foundation comes to be as it is – heavy, thick, and made of stone – because heavy material is naturally carried downward, while the roof comes to be as it is – light and wooden – because light material naturally rises to the top. If this were the case, then matter would be dictating form. In Aristotle's view the situation is almost the reverse: form is disciplining matter. The house-builder who, as we have seen, has the form of a house in his soul, aims to impose that form on suitable material. That is, his project is to build a shelter, and his actions can be seen as organizing the available material so as to form the best shelter that he is capable of building. Thus, as Aristotle says, although the house cannot come to be *without* matter, it is not *due* to the matter.[74] The reason the foundation is made of heavy stone is not because stone naturally sinks to the bottom, but because a good shelter ought to have a solid foundation. The matter of the artefact is subservient to the form.

Aristotle says that a similar situation holds for '*all* other things which have a final cause.'[75] Natural organisms and artefacts are composed of matter, and matter does have certain limited necessary properties, but the generation and organization of organisms and artefacts cannot be a manifestation of material necessity. The important type of necessity that is operative in natural generation and artistic creation Aristotle calls *hypothetical necessity*.[76] Hypothetical necessity is a necessity which flows backward from the achieved end to the process directed toward that end or to the structure of the parts that constitute that end. *If* a saw is to cut wood, it *must* be made of a material capable of cutting wood,[77] and that material, the iron, must be shaped in a certain way. The

---

[72] Appropriate reading: *Physics* II.9; *Parts of Animals* I–IV; *Generation of Animals* I, II, IV.
[73] *Physics* II.9.
[74] *Physics* II.9, 200a5–6.
[75] *Physics* II.9, 200a7–8.
[76] *to anankaion ex hupotheseōs*: cf. *Physics* II.9, 200a13.
[77] *Physics* II.9, 200a10ff.

iron itself lacks any properties which would of brute necessity turn it into a saw. Now it is a mistake to conceive hypothetical necessity as a mysterious backward-working efficient cause. It is not that the finished saw brings about its own production. An artefact like a saw is produced by a person capable of making tools, a toolmaker. It is the toolmaker's ability to make a saw – the form of a saw in his soul – that is the antecedent efficient cause. Hypothetical necessity is represented in the toolmaker's deliberation about how to make a saw. Or it may be represented in the deliberation he *would* engage in if he engaged in any deliberation at all.[78] For, as we have seen, an artisan need not actually deliberate when he engages in his craft.

So hypothetical necessity is ultimately the necessity of rationality. *If* a saw is to have this function, it *must* have this structure and makeup. Sometimes this rationality is explicit, as when a man reasons about how to make a saw; often the rationality is implicit, as when a trained craftsman simply makes a saw. But the reasoning *we* go through when we work out what is necessary for there to be a saw puts the rationality of the saw – its structure and makeup – on open display.

When we leave the realm of artefacts and turn to nature, there is no longer any explicit reasoning which we need to recreate. For there is no Creator who reasons about how it is best to construct a man or a frog. And yet if form is a basic force in the natural world, that world ought to be one in which the reasoning based on hypothetical necessity is valid. For if natural processes are genuinely occurring for the sake of an end, then we ought to be able to reason backward from the end to be achieved to the process directed toward it. We also ought to be able to render intelligible the structure manifested in the end. Aristotle says that the best course of study is to begin with the phenomena presented by each group of animals and only then proceed to the causes of those phenomena.[79] The rationale for this strategy is that we must have an understanding of the final cause, the fully achieved forms of living animals. For it is only from an understanding of the achieved form that one can reason backward and determine why it had to be achieved in *this* way.

The presence of form as a basic force in the natural world thus

[78] For an account of Aristotle's theory of deliberation, see section 4.5 below.
[79] *Parts of Animals* I.1, 640a13–19.

legitimates reasoning based on hypothetical necessity. This in turn secures the rationality of the natural world. If, for example, the parts of a man are there in order that he be a man – that is, achieve his form, engage in his characteristic activities – then it is only in the light of what it is to be a man that the parts of men can be made intelligible.

> The fittest mode of treatment is to say a man has such and such parts *because* the essence of man is such and such, and *because* they are necessary conditions of his existence, or, if we cannot quite say this, then the next thing to it, namely, that it is either quite impossible for him to exist without them, or at any rate, that it is good that they should be there. And this follows: because man is such and such, the process of his development is necessarily such as it is; and therefore this part is formed first, that next; and after a like fashion should we explain the generation of all other works of nature.[80]

Although the natural world is to a significant degree rational, that does not mean one can dispense with empirical observation of it. Far from it. It is only by engaging in detailed observations of, say, frogs or men that one can learn what the form of a frog or a man is. One must observe their development and characteristic activities; one must dissect them and inspect their parts. The rationality of the natural world is manifested not in the ability to dispense with empirical observation, but in the kind of theorizing which occurs when one does engage in such observation. One's theorizing will be based on the hypothesis that the parts of the animal must be (more or less) the way they are in order for that animal to achieve its form. This hypothesis allows a researcher to reason in two directions: from reality to its rationality and from rationality back to its reality. From one's observations of a frog one comes to understand what it is to be a frog; but once one understands what it is to be a frog one can reason backward to the type of functions the frog's various parts must perform.

Aristotle's zoological works, the *Parts of Animals* and *Generation of Animals*, are exercises in the type of reasoning needed in a world in which hypothetical necessity reigns. Having provided the

[80] *Parts of Animals* I.1, 640a33–b4 (my emphasis).

theory of hypothetical necessity, Aristotle, in his biological studies, engages in its practice. And it is in studying his biological works that we can, I think, resolve a puzzle that must confront any student of Aristotle. On the one hand, Aristotle insists that the true subject of natural philosophy is form and not matter.[81] Not only is form not built up out of necessary material processes, matter is in itself unknowable and unintelligible. On the other hand, Aristotle seems to devote an enormous amount of time and energy to the study of the matter of living things: the parts of animals, and the flesh, bone, and visceral tissues which compose them. Indeed, one might well wonder how Aristotle could avoid such study. For how could one come to understand the form of man if one did not understand the matter in which that form is realized? Do we not need to know the parts and composition of a man if we are to understand what it is to be a man?

The resolution of this dilemma lies in the fact that there is a hierarchy of form and matter. The matter of animals, Aristotle says, is the heterogeneous parts that compose it – head, arm, heart, liver, lungs, etc.[82] However, these parts are not brute matter; they are flesh, bone, and visceral tissue organized in certain ways.[83] That is, they are themselves composites of form and matter. By studying the principles of organization of, say, the heart, one can come to understand why the heart must be as it is if it is to perform its function in the living animal. So, to put it paradoxically, there is a way to study matter while all along studying form. 'No part of an animal,' Aristotle says, 'is purely material or purely immaterial.'[84] What one is really learning about the matter (the heart) is its form (or principles of organization). Of course, one can carry this reasoning a step further: one can inquire, say, into the visceral tissue which constitutes the heart. But, again, the homogeneous matter – the flesh, bone, and visceral tissue which constitute the heterogeneous parts of animals – is itself a composite of form and matter. Each is constituted out of the elements – earth, air, fire, water – according to a certain *logos*.[85] And, again, we can under-

[81] See, e.g., *Parts of Animals* I.1, I.5, 645a31–b4; *Generation of Animals* I.1, II.1; *Physics* II.2.
[82] *Generation of Animals* I.1, 715a8–11.
[83] See, e.g., *Parts of Animals* II.1.
[84] *Parts of Animals* I.3, 643a24–6.
[85] *Parts of Animals* I.1, 642a18–24; II.1.

stand the structure or form of visceral tissue by understanding the function of the heart which the visceral tissue constitutes. In this way rationality is transmitted from the form of the living animal all the way down. If man is to be such an animal, he must have an organ structured to perform such a function, but to perform such a function it must be constituted of tissue so structured ... As our inquiry delves into the matter, our understanding never encounters anything but form.[86]

Since form emerges at each level of the hierarchy, there are two ways in which Aristotle can conceive of the form of an animal. One way is to abstract as much as possible from all material aspects of the animal. Man, for example, is essentially a rational animal; and Aristotle can state this essence without specifying exactly how rationality happens to be realized in this animal. The other way is to conceive of form as revealed by the concrete manner in which it is realized. On this approach we more fully understand what it is to be a man when we understand just how rationality can be realized in an animal with such functioning organs and parts. Aristotle uses each approach at various places in his work, but it is clear that in his biological works the second approach is dominant. That is why he can engage in the detailed study of animals with such enthusiasm:

> Having already treated of the celestial world, as far as our conjectures could reach, we proceed to treat of animals, without omitting, to the best of our ability, any member of the kingdom, however ignoble. For if some have no graces to charm the sense, yet nature, which fashioned them, gives amazing pleasure in their study to all who can trace links of causation, and are inclined to philosophy. Indeed, it would be strange if mimic representations of them were attractive, because they disclose the mimetic skill of the painter or sculptor, and the original realities themselves were not more interesting, to all at any rate who have eyes to discern the causes. We therefore must not recoil with childish aversion from the

[86] Indeed, even when one gets to the four elements one can keep going. For the so-called elements are themselves compounds of more elementary forces: see *Parts of Animals* II.1, 646a15; *On Generation and Corruption* II.2; *Meteorology* IV.10. Earth is composed of the cold and solid, air of the hot and fluid, fire of the solid and hot, water of the fluid and cold.

examination of the humbler animals. Every realm of nature is marvellous: and as Heraclitus, when the strangers who came to visit him found him warming himself at the furnace in the kitchen and hesitated to go in, is reported to have bidden them not to be afraid to enter, as even in that kitchen divinities were present, so we should venture on the study of every kind of animal without distaste; for each and all will reveal to us something natural and something beautiful. Absence of haphazard and conduciveness of everything to an end are to be found in Nature's works in the highest degree, and the resultant end of her generations and combinations is a form of the beautiful.

If any person thinks the examination of the rest of the animal kingdom an unworthy task, he must hold in like disesteem the study of man. For no one can look at the primordia of the human frame – blood, flesh, bones, vessels and the like – without much repugnance. Moreover, when any one of the parts or structures, be it which it may, is under discussion, it must not be supposed that it is its material composition to which attention is being directed or which is the object of the discussion, but rather the total form. Similarly, the true object of architecture is not bricks, mortar, or timber, but the house; and so the principal object of natural philosophy is not the material elements, but their composition, and the totality of the substance, independently of which they have no existence.[87]

There is, in fact, good reason for Aristotle to take this second approach. For there is reason to conceive of the formal aspect of the matter – the forms, that is, of the animal's parts and of the flesh, bone, and visceral tissue which compose the parts – as themselves manifestations of the form of the animal. No bone in the body, says Aristotle, exists as a separate thing in itself: each bone is what it is partly because of its relation to the whole organism in which it is functioning.[88] Even as material an item as a blood vessel gains its existence as a blood vessel by functioning within the con-

[87] *Parts of Animals* I.5, 645a4–37.
[88] *Parts of Animals* II.9, 654a34–b6.

text of a living organism. As Aristotle puts it, 'no blood vessel is anything in itself.'[89] So it would seem that, even at this very material level, the matter of a living organism is the matter it is by virtue of its being a manifestation of form. And when we move from bones and blood-vessels to the organized parts of animals, the same reasoning holds.

The form of man, for example, is responsible for the human hand being the way it is. That is why we can reason, on the basis of hypothetical necessity, from man's being a certain type of animal to his having a hand.[90] It is a mistake, Aristotle thinks, to suppose that man gained his superior intelligence through his hands: that is, that because he was gifted with hands his mind was able to develop so as to use them in ever more resourceful ways. Rather, nature acts 'as any prudent man would do': man is endowed with hands because he has the practical intelligence to employ them in their myriad uses. Indeed, the hand is the organ *par excellence* by which man manifests practical reason. He can make and use tools with it, and thus Aristotle calls it an instrument for further instruments. Nature, Aristotle says, allots a specific organ, limb, etc., only to those animals which can use it.[91] That is why one will never find hands on an unintelligent animal and why one must find hands on a being whose essence it is to display superior intelligence and practical rationality.

Therefore, it is from man's capacity for practical rationality that one can deduce the presence of a hand. However, although the form of man necessitates the presence and structure of a hand, the hand is part of the matter of a human being. So the form of a human being is responsible for the matter being the matter that it is: that is, the form of man is responsible for a hand being a hand. Since the hand is itself a composite of form and matter – flesh and bones organized in *this* way – the form of man must be responsible for the form of a hand. This is borne out by Aristotle's remarks on death. The hand of a dead man, Aristotle says, is no longer really a hand: it is a hand in name alone.[92] For a hand to be a hand, it must

[89] *Parts of Animals* II.9, 654b2–3 (my translation).
[90] *Parts of Animals* IV.10, 687a9–b4. See also *Generation of Animals* II.6; and cf. *Politics* I.4, 1253b33.
[91] *Parts of Animals* III.1, 661b23ff. (Thus one will never find an animal that has both sharp teeth *and* tusks: for nature does not make anything in vain.)
[92] *Parts of Animals* I.1, 640b34–641a21.

not only be shaped in a certain way and made of certain stuff, it must be capable of functioning as a hand. But if the hand is part of the matter of a living human being, then this matter is destroyed at the moment of death. Even the flesh, bone, and visceral tissue start to break down into their material components at death: they lose their organizing principles at the moment of death, even though the ensuing decomposition is relatively slow. This would again suggest that the organizing principles of flesh, bone, and visceral tissue are themselves manifestations of human form.

Aristotle does not think that any strict procedures can lay bare the rationality of the natural world. This comes out most clearly in his discussion of the classification of animals. Plato had proposed a method of division, and one might have hoped to use it to classify the species. But any such strict division will, Aristotle thinks, lead to unnatural groupings.[93] For example, suppose one began a division:

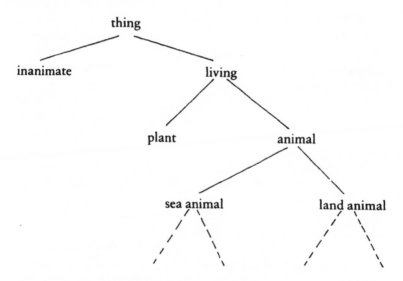

Such a division would unnaturally separate the class of birds into two classes (sea-bird and land-based bird) which were not sub-classes of the unified class of birds. On this division there would be no unified class of birds.

[93] *Parts of Animals* 1.3.

Aristotle is skeptical of any strict procedure of classification. So, rather than formulate a precise algorithm, Aristotle simply counsels man to rely on his own instincts.[94] That is, when man investigates the physical world he is naturally led to see certain similarities and differences among the phenomena. It is by using his innate sense of similarity that man originally classified the disparate types of birds into a unified genus, and similarly for fishes and other animals. So although a strict procedure of classification is impossible, it is also unnecessary. Man need only rely on his own sense of sameness and difference, based of course on careful observation, to divide up the world correctly.

It is important to realize that Aristotle is not making a merely pragmatic claim. He is not saying, as a pragmatist might, that if man carves up the world according to his interests and perceptions of similarity, that is all that can matter to him. It is, for Aristotle, only because man has a certain place in the world that there is any basis for relying on his judgements. Since nature is, for its part, a manifestation of rational structure, and man, for his part, is a being who by nature appreciates and understands rational structure, man can follow his own instincts and judgements in his quest to lay bare the rationality of nature. Here again we see what might be called an argument from the possibility of philosophy. Because man is by nature a systematic understander of the world, he can (more or less) rely on the systematic judgements he makes as he investigates the myriad phenomena of nature. Of course, these systematic judgements are the products of two-way reasoning: one is always reasoning forward from the phenomena one encounters in empirical inquiry toward general organizing principles; and one is reasoning backward, on the basis of hypothetical necessity, from one's understanding of species-form to the phenomena one expects to encounter in empirical investigation.

One example of this two-way reasoning is Aristotle's discussion of the hearts of animals.[95] It is, Aristotle says, *both* a rational inference *and* evident to the senses that the heart must be the primary source of sensation.[96] First, the source of sensation must be a

94 *Parts of Animals* I.3, 643b10–16 (my emphasis).
95 See, e.g., *Parts of Animals* III.3–5; *Generation of Animals* II.4, 6.
96 *Parts of Animals* III.4, 666a18–20; cf. 666a3–8.

unified, single organ, because the faculty of sensation is unified.[97] That is, a person does not have several distinct consciousnesses, one of touch, another of sight, another of sound, another of smell. Our perceptions of sight, sound, and smell form a unified perceptual awareness of the world. One would thus expect to find a unified organ which is the seat of this consciousness. One would also expect to find this organ located near the center of the animal, for it would then be (almost) equally in reach of every part of the body. For a person's ability to perceive stretches out to encompass all the extremities of his body. And in empirical investigation one does find such an organ, the heart. Of course, the heart is a bit off center, but that too is to be expected. For there is a tendency in nature to place the most noble organ in the most noble place: and above and front are more noble than below and back.[98] Further, sensation and motion are directed forward, so there is again reason to expect the primary source of sensation and motion to be located above and at the front.[99] And since sensation requires heat, one would expect that the primary source of sensation would also have to be the source of heat.[100] This would also have to be the source of blood, for it is from the source of heat that blood derives its warmth and fluidity.

The embryological development of animals also provides evidence of the primary importance of the heart.[101] It is evident to empirical investigation – at least, so Aristotle thinks – that the heart is the first organ to develop in the embryo. However, Aristotle is not content to rest with empirical observation. He says that it is clear not only to the senses, *but also on theoretical grounds*, that the heart is the first principle of development.[102] For, he says, just as a young animal which has been separated from its parents must be able to manage for itself, so the embryo (when it has become sufficiently separated from the parents to constitute itself as a distinct embryo) must have its own first principle of develop-

[97] *Parts of Animals* III.4, 666a13–15. See also *On the Soul* III.2.
[98] *Parts of Animals* III.3, 665a21–6; III.4, 665b18–21.
[99] *Parts of Animals* III.3, 665a11–15. Indeed, one can further understand the location and organization of the lungs and windpipe, since air must be transmitted from the lungs to the heart: see *Parts of Animals* III.3; *History of Animals* I.16–17.
[100] *Parts of Animals* III.5, 667b22–31.
[101] See *Parts of Animals* III.4, 666a20, a34–b1; *Generation of Animals* II.4, 6.
[102] *Generation of Animals* II.4, 740a1–23 (my emphasis).

ment. Reason tells us that the first developed organ ought to be the principle which directs the further development of the embryo. Therefore the heart must be that organ. And this reasoning gains further corroboration from the following thought. Animals distinguish themselves from the rest of nature by their capacity for sensation and (in many cases at least) self-movement. Therefore, one would expect that the principle of sensation and of movement would appear first in animal development: this principle is the heart.[103]

This is a paradigm of the two-way reasoning which Aristotle thinks justified by the nature of the world and man's place in it. Since the world is rational, one may reason from the phenomena one encounters in sensory experience toward general principles which would render those phenomena intelligible. Conversely, one may reason from general principles of intelligibility toward the sensory phenomena which ought to manifest them. Man can reason in both directions, and, ultimately, all his reasonings ought to fit together to form a harmonious, intelligible whole. Of course, there is no doubt but that Aristotle uses his method to draw false conclusions. The brain, not the heart, is the seat of sensation, but Aristotle thinks this impossible. The brain, he thinks, is an organ for cooling the blood[104] (that is why it is located at a bodily extremity), yet the source of sensation must be located at the source of heat. But though Aristotle formulates a false theory about the heart and brain, it is not his method as such that forces him to these false conclusions. His mistake lies in the specific reasoning, based on hypothetical necessity, by which he deduces the primary role of the heart. The method itself only encourages one to conceive of the parts of an animal as contributing in definite ways to the functioning of the whole animal. In the light of the characteristic activities of an animal, the parts are rendered intelligible. Aristotle is thus not wrong in his belief that the organization and development of animals manifests a certain rationality (though of course he does not understand the basis for this rationality).

It is this intelligibility that is preserved through the change of generations. The reason for the generation of animals, Aristotle

[103] *Generation of Animals* II.6, 742b33; *Parts of Animals* III.4, 666a34.
[104] *Parts of Animals* II.7.

says, is that no individual animal can live an eternal life.[105] Animals, therefore, strive for immortality in the only way open to them: by reproducing their kind. In this way the species exists eternally. Now, while the parents may pass on a family resemblance between one generation and the next,[106] what primarily remains through the continuing change of generations is the formal, intelligible structure of each species. It is the intelligibility of each species that is truly eternal.

[105] See *Generation of Animals* II.1, 731b24ff. Cf. *On the Soul* II.4, 415a26–b7.
[106] See *Generation of Animals* IV.3, for Aristotle's account of the inheritance of family resemblance.

3
Change

3.1 The Parmenidean challenge[1]

Nature, for Aristotle, is an inner principle of change. If we are fully to understand what it is for man to have a nature, we must understand Aristotle's conception of change. This is no trivial matter. For in the intellectual climate in which Aristotle grew up it was not obvious that change was possible at all. As Aristotle said,

> The first of those who studied philosophy were misled in their search for truth and the nature of things by their inexperience, which as it were thrust them into another path. So they say that none of the things that are either comes to be or passes out of existence, because what comes to be must do so either from what is or from what is not, both of which are impossible. For what is cannot come to be (because it *is* already) and from what is not nothing could have come to be...[2]

The reference is obviously to the pre-Socratic Parmenides, and his followers, who argued that change was impossible. For a change to occur, Parmenides argued, something would have to come into existence from a state of non-existence. But from nothing nothing could come to be. But nor can something come to be from something, for something already exists and thus cannot come to be.

Aristotle's response to Parmenides provides a paradigm of his philosophic method. On the one hand, Aristotle is convinced that no sound theoretical argument can lead to a conclusion which we can see to be evidently false. As he says,

> To maintain that all things are at rest, *and to disregard sense-perception in an attempt to show the theory reasonable, would be an instance of intellectual weak-*

[1] Appropriate reading for sections 3.1–3.3: *Physics* 1.7–8; III.1–8.
[2] *Physics* I.8, 191a24–31.

ness, it would call into question a whole system, not a particular detail: moreover, it would be an attack not only on the physicist but on almost all sciences and all received opinions, since change plays a part in all of them.[3]

Nature is an inner principle *of change*, and Aristotle thinks we should simply accept that it exists:

That nature exists it would be absurd to try to prove: for it is obvious that there are many things of this kind, and to prove what is obvious by what is not is the mark of a man who is unable to distinguish what is self-evident from what is not.[4]

Parmenides would clearly not be satisfied by Aristotle's approach. Parmenides' argument is designed to undermine our confidence in sensory perception as a guide to the nature of reality. Thus it is futile to point out the evident instances of change we see all around us. Once we have worked our way through his argument we are supposed to discard the testimony of the senses as being essentially illusory. It would be absurd in Parmenides' eyes to draw from the well of the illusory in order to quench our thirst for the real. But this is just what Aristotle is doing – at least, so it would seem to Parmenides.

Aristotle, for his part, has little patience with skepticism.[5] The truth, he is convinced, must *harmonize* with the reality we evidently see around us. The point of philosophy is not to undermine our pre-theoretical beliefs, but to help us make sense of them. Philosophy gives us deeper insight into *why* our ordinary beliefs are true. Our ordinary beliefs about the world thus become a starting-point of philosophical activity which may be modified but which can never be completely abandoned. It is therefore an axiom of his philosophic method that an argument to a conclusion radically at odds with ordinary beliefs about the world, no matter how compelling, must have a flaw in it.

However, though Aristotle is quick to dismiss the possibility

[3] *Physics* VIII.3, 253a32–b2 (my emphasis). (I use 'change' instead of the Oxford translation's 'motion' for *kinēsis*.)
[4] *Physics* II.1, 193a3–6.
[5] See, e.g., G. E. L. Owen, 'Tithenai ta phainomena.'

that such radical arguments are true, he nevertheless takes them very seriously. For if the truth does harmonize with our ordinary beliefs, a compelling but disharmonious argument must stand as an obstacle to our understanding of the truth: 'Thought is bound fast when it will not rest because the conclusion does not satisfy it, and cannot advance because it cannot refute the argument.'[6] Not only does the truth harmonize with ordinary belief, the truth forms a harmonious whole. We are stuck in exile, removed from the truth, so long as theoretical argument and evident testimony of the senses pull us in opposite directions. Moreover, we find such exile discomfiting. When thought is tied up in a knot, we are ill at ease: our natural desire to understand is frustrated.[7] It is, Aristotle thinks, by untying the knot that our desire to understand gains genuine satisfaction. By coming to understand why an apparently compelling argument is only *apparently* compelling we both free our thought from the constraint of *aporia* and come to a deeper understanding of *why* our ordinary beliefs are true. By working through difficult puzzles, like Parmenides' challenge, we move from knowledge to understanding, from ordinary belief to philosophic wisdom. Thus, while Aristotle does not for a moment entertain the possibility that Parmenides is right, he treats Parmenides' argument with the greatest respect.

Another hallmark of Aristotle's philosophic method is to find some truth in the view he is opposing. The truth, we have seen him say, 'seems to be like the proverbial door, which no one can fail to hit.'[8] There must, after all, be some reason why a compelling argument appears compelling. We will not understand this appearance, the appearance of truth, until we understand the genuine truth which lies hidden within the (ultimately false, but initially compelling) argument. Aristotle agrees with Parmenides' principle that nothing comes from nothing.[9] Indeed, that agreement is grounded in their mutual adherence to an even more basic principle: the principle of sufficient reason. If something came to be *from nothing*, there would be no reason why it came to be now rather than earlier or later, no reason why it came to be here rather than somewhere

---

[6] *Nicomachean Ethics* VII.2, 1146a24–7.
[7] See *Metaphysics* III.1, and chapter 1 above.
[8] *Metaphysics* II.1, 993b4–5.
[9] See, e.g., *Physics* I.8, 191b13–15.

Change

else. Both Parmenides and Aristotle would agree to the following conditional:

If there is such a thing as change, we must be able to understand it.

Both Parmenides and Aristotle believe in a deeply intimate relationship between thinking and being. It is because Parmenides thinks change incomprehensible that he dismisses its reality. He believes himself entitled to move from the *unthinkability* of change to its *unreality*. Aristotle basically accepts this inference. His task is to show that the idea of change is coherent and can be understood. That change exists Aristotle took to be obvious. What is needed is an analysis of change which, as it were, gives the world back to us in intelligible form. In an extended sense this does secure the reality of change, for the reality of the world must be intelligible.

Change, Aristotle believes, requires a certain blend of reality and unreality. If literally nothing existed, nothing could come of it. But this is not the situation which prevails before a change. Change, for Aristotle, is always change *of* a subject which exists prior to, during, and after the change.[10] For example, a man who learns to play a musical instrument changes from being unmusical to being musical. This fact, Aristotle believes, can be described in various ways.[11] For example, consider the following two claims:

(1) the man becomes musical
and
(2) the not musical becomes musical.

While both these descriptions are true, the latter may be metaphysically misleading. For (2) does not make it evident that there is something which remains throughout the change. One might mistakenly interpret it as saying that being can simply come to be from not-being – that no further qualification is required. Sentence (1), by contrast, allows us to see that there is an enduring subject of change. *Musical* is a property *of* a subject, a man, and the man existed before and he endures after he acquired musical ability. So

[10] *Physics* I.7, 190a14–16, a33–b5.
[11] See *Physics* I.7 189b32–190a13.

58

Aristotle agrees that a musical man cannot come into existence from nothing, but he denies that this is what happens. A musical man comes into existence from something: from a man (who prior to learning lacked the ability to play a musical instrument at will). Aristotle also agrees that a musical man cannot come to be if the man is *already* musical. Although there must be something which is the subject of change, there must also be something which that thing is not: namely, that toward which the change is directed.

Yet this analysis hardly seems to solve the problem. Even if the man exists, if he is not musical, then from the point of view of becoming musical, he would seem to be just another type of non-being. The question seems to arise again: how can being (musical) arise from not-being (not musical, though a man)? Aristotle is aware of the problem, and he solves it via his theory of potentiality and actuality.[12] There is more to say of the unmusical man than that he is unmusical. The unmusical man actually has the *capability* of learning music. There is, then, one sense in which being comes from non-being – the musical comes to be where once there was the non-musical – and thus there really is a change. However, there is also a sense in which being comes from being – the man who is *potentially* musical comes to be musical (actually). One needs to keep both these senses alive in one's mind if one is to grasp both the reality and the possibility of change.

Once one realizes the crucial role potentiality and actuality play in Aristotle's account of change, an otherwise puzzling remark falls into place. Aristotle says that even the generation of natural organisms, which qualify as substances, requires an underlying substratum.[13] The generation of substances presents a problem, for the substance which comes to be cannot be thought of as a property which comes to be true of an enduring subject. A substance is not a property of anything. Nevertheless, Aristotle says that in the generation of plants and animals there is something which underlies the change: the seed from which the organism comes to be. This seems odd. Surely, the seed does not survive the generation of the substance. The seed was not substance, the (generated) substance is not seed. Where then is the underlying substratum which endures through the change? To answer this

12 He mentions the theory at *Physics* 1.8, 191b27–9, and develops it at III.1–3.
13 *Physics* 1.7, 190b1–3.

question, one must realize that the seed is itself a composite of form and matter. The form of a man, say, comes from the male parent, and in virtue of the possession of this form we can say of a seed that it is a man (potentially). What we mean by this is that if the seed is implanted in a female's womb it will in ordinary conditions develop into a human being. The form exists antecedently to the generation of the natural substance and endures to become the form of that substance. In the process, though, it changes from being potentially the form of a substance to being actually the form. The matter too persists through this change, yet it cannot be regarded as the subject of change on its own. If the matter which existed in the seed antecedently to the generation were not informed by human nature (as a power or potentiality) it could not change into a human being.

3.2 The analysis of change

For change to be possible, then, there must be something which exists before the change which has the potentiality to become what emerges in the change. This potentiality should not be thought of as a bare possibility. The potentiality is real: it exists in the world. For example, the form of a seed is a real power in that seed to develop into a natural substance. As we have seen, this power is not a material state of the seed: the form is what it is and not another thing.

When Aristotle comes to define change, he focusses on this antecedently existing potentiality. *Change*, he says, *is the actualizing of potential being as such.*[14] This definition can be confusing. One might well think that the actualization of a potentiality would be the finished product: for example, the actualization of what is potentially a man would be a man. But to speak of the actualiz*ing* of a potentiality *as a potentiality* is to isolate the process by which the potentiality turns into an actuality. Aristotle remains fond of using artefacts as examples. When the build*able* (*to oikodomēton*) is actualized, he says, it is *being built* (*oikodomeitai*) and this is *the process of building* (*oikodomēsis*).[15] Once the house is built there

---

[14] *Physics* III.1, 201a10–11 (*hē tou dunamei ontos entelecheia, hēi toiouton, kinēsis estin*), cf. 201a27–9, and III.2, 202a5–6.

[15] *Physics* III.1, 201a16–18; cf. 201b5–15.

is an actual house, and in this sense the potentiality has developed into an actuality. But there is no longer an actualizing of the potentiality *as such*, for the potentiality no longer exists to be actualized.

From Aristotle's definition of change, a number of consequences flow pretty directly about how to conceptualize it. First, change, for Aristotle, is fundamentally directional. Because change is the actualizing of a potentiality, the entire change will be directed toward its fulfillment. And the change will cease as soon as the potentiality has developed to an actuality. As Aristotle says, change is from something and to something.[16] Second, if we do not know what the change is directed toward, we do not understand what the change is. Since potentialities are basic items in the world – they cannot be reduced to the actual material state of the object – they cannot be fully understood except by reference to end states for which they are potentialities. Since change is the actualizing of a potentiality, it cannot be fully understood except by reference to the terminus of change. Third, it is at least natural to suppose that everything that changes is caused to change by a distinct cause of change, a changer. For if change is the actualizing of a potentiality, there must be some reason why the potentiality is actualized now rather than earlier or later. The potentiality has, after all, existed in the object for some time, so the explanation of the beginning of the change cannot be found within the potentiality itself. It would violate the principle of sufficient reason and render change incomprehensible to suppose that, although the change could have occurred at any time that the potentiality existed, there is no reason why it began now rather than at another time. If, by contrast, a change begins when the object comes into contact with a changer, then we have the beginning of an explanation of why the change occurred when it did.[17] To complete the explanation we need to know more about the changer: what it is about the changer that makes it a changer. Aristotle's answer is that the changer, or agent of change, always introduces a form.[18] The paradigm remains the creation of artefacts. The builder is a distinct cause of change. The wood may be potentially a house, but there could be no explanation of the actualization of this potentiality if there were no builder who

---

[16] E.g., *Physics* V.1, 224b35–225a1 (*pasa metabolē estin ek tinos eis ti*).
[17] See *Physics* III.2, 202a5–12. Cf. VIII.4, 255a34–b1.
[18] *Physics* III.2, 202a9–11. Cf. VIII.5, 257b10.

began to impose the form of a house on this wood. And the builder is a builder — an imposer of form on matter — in virtue of the possession of form in his soul. As a builder, a man who has the capability of building, this form remains a potentiality in his soul; but when, in the presence of the appropriate materials, he exercises his capability and becomes a builder building, the form moves from a state of potentiality to an active state. Thus it is form as embodied in a distinct cause, the builder, that causes the change to occur in the matter.

With natural organisms the situation is slightly more complex since organisms have an inner principle of change. There is thus some case to be made for the claim that such organisms change themselves, and Aristotle does call them 'self-movers' or 'self-changers.' Nevertheless, it remains the case that there ought to be some ground for the actualizing of a potentiality, and that ground cannot be found within the potentiality itself. Aristotle argues on a number of occasions that, although organisms ought to be regarded as organized unities, they should not be thought of as homogeneous. Within a self-mover one can distinguish a part which is moved from a part which causes the motion.[19] It is easy to become confused about Aristotle's claim, in part because it is discussed at such an abstract level. One might, for instance, wonder: if the form of a developing organism is a potentiality, does it require a distinct cause within the organism to get it moving? If so, does not this undermine the candidacy of form to be the inner principle of change? But if form does not require a distinct cause — and thus retains the title of inner principle of change — does not this undermine the principle that every potentiality requires a distinct cause for its actualization?

Form can retain its title of inner principle of change. For natural organisms are composites of form and matter. The potentiality which is relevant to account for the change which is the development of an organism is a potentiality which resides in the matter. It is the potentiality of the matter to take on the form. It is the organism's form that is the distinct cause of the change which is the actualization of the matter's potentiality. Of course, the form also can be characterized as a potentiality or power of the organism to achieve a fully developed form, but that does not impugn its ability

[19] See *Physics* VII.1; VIII.4–5, especially 258a1–27.

to function as the distinct cause of change. Moreover, the form which is a potentiality or power in the developing organism does in fact depend for its existence on a distinct and prior actuality: the actualized form in the male parent who passed on the form to his seed.[20]

Some interpreters have objected that Aristotle's principle that everything which undergoes change requires a distinct cause of change is an *ad hoc* addition to his physical system. The principle is invoked, it is argued, only in order to get to the desired conclusion that there must be an Unmoved Mover of the physical world as a whole.[21] It is Aristotle's theological concern that there should be a divine cause of the physical world that leads him to posit the principle requiring a distinct cause of change. So the objection goes – and it is, I believe, ultimately unpersuasive. The principle requiring a distinct cause is dictated by Aristotle's decision to analyze change in terms of the actualization of a potentiality. This decision having being made, one need only recognize that potentialities exist for long periods when they are not being actualized, and believe that there ought to be an explanation for when change does occur, to be led to posit a distinct cause which initiates the change.

The final consequence of Aristotle's definition of change is that there is a single actualization of cause and subject of change.[22] Aristotle is here trying to isolate the cause not of a finished product, like a house, but of an event, a change. Since a change is defined as the actualization of a potentiality, he cannot specify the cause of change as an antecedent actualization of a potentiality. If he did, there would be an infinite regress: for any given change, an antecedent change would be required to bring it about. So although the cause must be distinct from the subject of change, there is a single activity which is an actualization of them both. 'The builder building' and 'the house being built' refer to one and the same activity, though they describe it in different ways. Thus if one needs to specify a distinct cause of a change, as Aristotle does, one must specify a thing, a substance, and not an event. In Aristotle's world there is no antecedent event which could possibly serve as the cause of a change. The only available antecedently existing

---

[20] See, e.g., *Physics* III.2, 202a9–12.
[21] See *Physics* VIII.
[22] See *Physics* III.3. This has already been discussed in section 2.3 above.

candidate for a cause is a *thing* which has the power to bring about the change. The exercise of this power is the change itself.

Although this single actualization thesis is buried in the heart of Aristotle's physical system, it has had a profound influence in Western philosophy. In Hegel's famous master–slave dialectic, there is a life and death struggle between two agents, each demanding recognition from the other. To escape death, the vanquished agent opts for enslavement to his newly created master. Ironically, the slave triumphs through hard work. Although his toil is supposedly in the service of his master, and thus alienated and forced, in fact in his work he objectifies his soul. Because the builder building and the house being built are one and the same activity, the slave finds in his toil an outer expression of his inner soul.

Hegel intended the master–slave dialectic as an implicit criticism of Aristotle's defense of slavery and the master class. According to Aristotle, philosophy began only when men had the leisure to pursue inquiry for its own sake.[23] It is only then that the desire to understand could gain full expression, for only then were men not tied down to inquiring into the means to attain certain set and necessary ends. Freed from the need to secure the necessities of life, they could pursue understanding for its own sake. Thus Aristotle sets theoretical understanding above practical ability, the knowledge of a craft. Theoretical understanding is, for Aristotle, something altogether divine, and it is only a member of the master class who is in a position to attain it. Hegel, by contrast, portrays the master as slothful and degenerating. Precisely because he is 'free' from the slave's honest toil, he is deprived of the opportunity to realize his soul in the world. But Hegel uses a basically Aristotelian physical principle in his critique of Aristotle's political theory. Hegel also believes, in contrast to Aristotle, that the slave's labor represents a necessary moment of self-alienation. Before he can achieve genuine self-recognition, he must objectify himself in his labor, thus preparing the way for a later reconciliation in which the slave can find himself in his works. For Aristotle, by contrast, it seems that there is no alienation in the process of creation at all. The craftsman never becomes other in the process of building, because the craftsman expressing himself as a craftsman and the

---

[23] See, e.g., *Metaphysics* I.1, 981b13–982a3.

creation of something apart from the craftsman are one and the same activity.

Marx, as is well known, offers his own critique of Hegel's master–slave dialectic. The industrial worker does not achieve the same triumph under his capitalist employer as Hegel's slave does under his mythical master. In Marx's world, it is labor that gives value to things. Therefore, if the capitalist employer is to make a profit, a significant portion of a laborer's life and energy must be alienated from him. The value which the laborer pours into his creation by his own toil must be the property of the capitalist, if capitalism is to work. Because the builder building is the same activity as the house being built, the capitalist laborer is alienated from himself. The house being built is not merely something he brings about, it *is* his labor objectified. Since a laborer in capitalist society is essentially that, by being alienated from his own labor he is alienated from what he most fundamentally is. Again, an Aristotelian principle about the relation of a craftsman's soul to the artefacts he produces is at play.

3.3 The media of change I: the infinite

All change, for Aristotle, is the change of an enduring subject. A physical object – the paradigm subject of change – can increase or decrease in size; it can acquire or lose a property; it can change its spatial location. All these changes occur in space and time. To understand change we must understand the media – space, time, and physical magnitude – in which it occurs. But, Aristotle argues, if we are to understand space, time, and matter, we must understand the infinite. 'The infinite,' Aristotle says, 'presents itself first in the continuous'[24] – the continuous structure of space, time, and matter. All changes occur in time, which is infinitely divisible; those physical changes which occur in a natural object occur in infinitely divisible matter; and those changes in which a physical object changes location are changes in which an object traverses an infinitely divisible portion of space. Aristotle cannot render change fully intelligible, and thus cannot secure the reality of change, until he makes comprehensible the idea of infinite divisibility.[25] Since 'the science of nature is concerned with magnitudes and change

[24] *Physics* III.1, 200b17–18.
[25] Aristotle argues for their infinite divisibility in *Physics* VI.1–2.

and time ... it is incumbent on the person who treats of nature to discuss the infinite.'[26]

But it is not at all clear what Aristotle could mean by his claim that the media of change are infinitely divisible. One would expect him to treat infinite divisibility as a potentiality: that is, to ascribe infinite divisibility to a magnitude is to say that the magnitude is capable of being divided in a certain way. However, when Aristotle says that something is potentially Φ he usually means that it is possible that it should become actually Φ. But what could possibly be the appropriate actualization here? It could not be a physical process of actually cutting a finite physical magnitude; for, obviously, any physical cut we make in such a magnitude will have finite size, and thus the magnitude will be completely destroyed after only finitely many cuts. Nor could it be a process of theoretical division: that is, a mental operation which distinguishes parts of the magnitude;[27] for no mortal could carry out more than a finite number of theoretical divisions. And even if, like Aristotle, we believed in the permanence of the species and the eternity of the world, there is no way in which a theoretical divider of the present generation could pass on his work to a divider of the next generation.[28] We seem to lose grip on the idea that the magnitude has this potentiality. For it seems that not only can the potentiality never be fully actualized, but no process of division can even be considered a manifestation of this potentiality.

Aristotle himself recognizes that there is a problem. One need not assume, he says, that all potentiality must be understood along the lines of the potentiality of bronze to be sculpted into a finished statue.[29] For 'to be' is an expression with various senses. To say that the infinite exists is more like saying 'it is day' or 'the Olympic games are occurring' in the sense that one thing is always coming after another.[30] There is no moment at which the Olympic games exist as a completed entity. Rather, one contest occurs after another. And one can even distinguish between the potential and

---

[26] *Physics* III.4, 202b30–5. (Again, I translate *kinēsis* as 'change.')

[27] See David Furley's account of theoretical division in *Two Studies in the Greek Atomists*, Study I, 'Indivisible Magnitudes.'

[28] I deliberately ignore those who are able to perform supertasks. See Paul Benacerraf, 'Tasks, Supertasks and the Modern Eleatics.'

[29] *Physics* III.6, 206a18–25.

[30] *aei allo kai allo gignesthai: Physics* III.6, 206a22.

actual existence of the games: when they are occurring, one event after another, the games actually exist, for this is all that it could mean for them to be. This would suggest that when we say that a magnitude is infinitely divisible we are saying that it is capable of undergoing a certain process of division and that when it is being divided this capability is being actualized.

However, there is an important asymmetry between the Olympic games and an infinite division. Though there is no moment at which either the games or the division will result in a completed entity, there at least comes a time in the passage of the games when they are over. By contrast, any process of division will terminate after only finitely many divisions. Aristotle is aware of this asymmetry, for he does not leave his analysis of the infinite with an analogy to the Olympic games. He continues: 'For generally the infinite has this mode of existence: one thing is always being taken after another, and each thing that is taken is always finite, but always different.'[31] In general, the infinite *exists* in the sense that there is *always* another to be taken. The essence of Aristotle's interpretation of the way in which the infinite is said to exist is that there will always be possibilities that remain unactualized. A magnitude is infinitely divisible, and in virtue of this it is possible to begin actually dividing it. Of course, any such actual process will terminate after only finitely many divisions. But that does not mean that the process does not bear witness to the magnitude's being infinitely divisible. Whether it does or not, though, depends not on the process of division, but on whether after the termination of that or any other division there remain divisions which could have been made. For whatever reason the division terminates, as terminate it must, the reason will not be that all possible divisions have been exhausted. The important point is that the infinite divisibility manifested in change is something which we as philosophizing human beings can comprehend. We do not, impossibly, have to witness an infinite division; we have only to recognize the (ever present) possibility of unactualized divisions. We come to recognize that the impossibility of an actual infinite division of matter is not ultimately a fact about the matter, but a fact about ourselves: we are the dividers, and we are capable neither of carrying out nor of witnessing an actual infinite division.

[31] *Physics* III.6, 206a27–9.

Aristotle must therefore distinguish between a process bearing witness to the existence of the potential infinite and a process bearing witness to the existence of the actual infinite. No process of division could bear witness to a length's being actually infinite by division. However, an actual process of division which terminates after finitely many divisions, but before all possible divisions are made, is all that a witness to the existence of the potential infinite could be. While such a process is occurring one can say that the infinite is *actually coming to be*, one division occurring after another. The contrast is with a process that might be occurring but is not.[32] But even as he says this, Aristotle can insist that the infinite by division is potential and not actual because the process of division can only reveal the length to be potentially infinite.[33]

It is tempting to suppose that a magnitude is potentially infinite because there could be a process of division which continued without end.[34] In fact, the situation is just the reverse. It would be more accurate to say that, for Aristotle, it is *because* the magnitude is potentially infinite that there could be such a process. The physical magnitude is potentially infinite not because of the existence of any process, but because of properties of the magnitude. The structure of the magnitude is such that any division will have to be only

[32] *Physics* III.6, 206a23–5, 206b13–14.
[33] *Physics* III.6, 206a16–18, 206b12–16. See also *Metaphysics* VIII.6, 1048b14–17. I discuss the translation and interpretation of these lines in 'Aristotelian Infinity,' pp. 192–3.
[34] In the twentieth century a distinguished school of mathematicians, known as Intuitionists, have attacked the notion of the actual infinite. They have tried to reconstrue all talk of infinity in mathematics in terms of the potential infinite: that is, in terms of the ability to carry out unending processes. It is worth noting how different Aristotle's conception of the potential infinite is from the Intuitionist conception. Both Aristotle and the Intuitionist would agree that a magnitude is infinitely divisible, and both would interpret this as a claim that no matter how many divisions of a magnitude have been made another could be made. But each is claiming a different possibility. Aristotle is claiming that the magnitude *is* such that if there *were* a divider who *could* continue to divide the length, then no matter how many divisions he made he *could* always make another. Only the last 'could' is fundamental to Aristotle's claim, for it is a claim about the structure of the magnitude, not the existence of a process. The Intuitionist, by contrast, is primarily concerned with the ability of the creative mathematician. He is trying to reconstrue mathematics to reveal it to be a human creation. The fact that humans are unable to perform infinitely many divisions is what motivates the Intuitionist denial of the actual infinite. The Intuitionist, unlike Aristotle, does ground the potential infinite in the existence of a process: a process such that, no matter how many steps the mathematician has carried out, he could *in principle* carry out another.

a partial realization of its infinite divisibility: there will have to be possible divisions which remain unactualized. On reflection it seems that Aristotle must install the infinite as a permanent potentiality of matter. For if change relies upon the continuous structure of space, time, and matter, there must be something about the world that manifests its continuity to us.[35] Otherwise change would become unintelligible. Since we are beings who could not possibly perform or witness an infinite division, the world must be such as to guarantee that any process of division need not terminate. And we must be such as to be able to appreciate this fact about the world: we must be capable of recognizing the existence of unactualized possibilities. In this way change is secured as both real *and* intelligible.

For Aristotle, then, it is because a magnitude is infinite by division that certain processes are possible. A problem with this theory might be thought to arise with Aristotle's considered response to Zeno's paradox of division.[36] Zeno, a student of Parmenides, put forward a number of paradoxes designed to show that change was impossible. In one paradox it is alleged that it is impossible for Achilles to run a race from A to B: for before reaching B he would first have to reach 1/2AB, but before reaching 1/2AB he would have to reach 1/4AB ... and so on. It looks as though Achilles cannot even get started: for before reaching any point along his journey he would already have had to traverse infinitely many points, and this, it is alleged, is impossible. In response, Aristotle distinguishes between the potential and actual existence of a point.[37] A point on a line may be actualized if one stops at it, or reverses one's direction at it or divides the line at it. According to Aristotle, Achilles would indeed be unable to traverse the finite length AB if in the course of his journey he had to traverse infinitely many actually existing points. However, continuous motion along a length is not sufficient to actualize any point along the length. Aristotle would thus be among those who think that, while it may be possable for Achilles to traverse AB in one minute by moving continuously across it, it would be impos-

---

35 For Aristotle's definition of continuity, see *Physics* v.3. See also *Physics* iii.6, 206a14–16.
36 *Physics* viii.8, 263a4–b9.
37 *Physics* viii.8, 262a12–263a3.

sible for him to traverse it in two minutes if he went in the first thirty seconds to the midpoint (1/2AB) and then rested thirty seconds, in the next fifteen seconds to the three-quarter point (3/4AB) then rested fifteen seconds, and so on. For such a 'staccato run' to be successful, Achilles would have had (by the end of two minutes) to actualize infinitely many points on the length AB, and this Aristotle held to be impossible.

The important issue for the present discussion is that Aristotle appears to make the existence of infinitely many points on a line depend upon the existence of a process. Aristotle does deny the actual existence of infinitely many points on a line, and he does this because he takes certain kinds of processes – for example, a 'staccato run' – to be impossible. But he does not deny the potential existence of infinitely many points, and he does not make this potential existence dependent upon the existence of any type of process. Although Aristotle denies the actual existence of infinitely many points on a line, this is not as odd as it might at first appear. For he denies that a line is made up of points. A line is continuous, and nothing continuous can be made up of points.[38] Since we need not, in fact should not, think of a length as composed of points, we need not, in fact should not, think of the points as actually existing.

Points, for Aristotle, do not actually exist independently of our 'probing' for them, yet they are not of our own making.[39] A point, for Aristotle, exists only in a derivative sense: it is, so to speak, a permanent possibility of division. But these are possibilities which cannot all be actualized. In *On Generation and Corruption* Aristotle considers the problems that arise from supposing that an infinitely divisible magnitude has actually been divided 'through and through.'[40] The situation Aristotle is envisioning is that all possible divisions of a magnitude have actually been made. What then will remain? No magnitude could remain, for magnitudes are divisible, and this would contradict the assumption that the division has been carried out through and through.[41] Nor could there be points without magnitude remaining. A division divides a whole into its

[38] *Physics* VI.I, 231a20–b6; V.3, 227a10–12.
[39] Cf. Michael Dummett, *Truth and Other Enigmas*, p. 18.
[40] *On Generation and Corruption* I.2, 316a15–317a18.
[41] For the Atomist critique of Aristotle's argument, see David Furley, *Two Studies in the Greek Atomists*, Study I.

constituents, yet one cannot without absurdity think of points without magnitude as the constituents of a length.

Aristotle overcomes this dilemma by distinguishing two senses in which a line may be said to be divisible 'through and through.'[42] A length is divisible through and through in the sense that it could be divided *anywhere* along the length. But it is not divisible through and through in the sense that it could (even potentially) be divided *everywhere* along the length. One can thus actualize *any* point but one cannot actualize *every* point; for any process of division, there must be divisions which could have been made which in fact were not made.

Aristotle is attempting a revolution in philosophical perspective: he wants to remove the infinite from its position of majesty. The infinite traditionally derived its dignity from being thought of as a whole in which everything is contained.[43] But the view that the infinite contains everything arises, Aristotle argues, from a conceptual confusion.

> The infinite turns out to be the contrary of what it is said to be. It is not that of which *nothing* is outside it that is infinite, but what *always* has something outside it ... [That which] has nothing outside it is complete and whole. For thus we define the whole – that from which nothing is wanting, as a whole man or a wooden box ... On the other hand, that from which something is absent and outside, however small that may be, is not 'all'. *Whole* and *complete* are either quite identical or closely akin. Nothing is complete (*teleion*) which has no end (*telos*) and the end is a limit (*peras*).[44]

To appreciate the ingenuity of this argument, one must realize that the Greek word for 'infinite' is *apeiron* and that the alpha which is the first letter in the word is a prefix which functions as a type of negation, like the English prefix 'un.' It is known as the alpha privative. 'The infinite' in Greek is literally the *un*limited. Aristotle's argument is designed to show that the infinite is imperfect and incomplete. Its structure is as follows:

[42] *On Generation and Corruption* I.2, 317a3ff.
[43] *Physics* III.6, 207a15–21.
[44] *Physics* III.6, 206b33–207a15.

Suppose

> (1) the infinite is that which has nothing outside;
> but
> (2) that which has nothing outside is said to be complete and whole.

The examples Aristotle gives are paradigms of finite, self-contained objects; they are individual entities, natural substances, or artefacts.

> (3) The whole = the complete;
> but
> (4) every complete thing has an end,
> and
> (5) an end is a limit.
> The reader is left to draw the conclusion from (3)–(5) that
> (6) the whole has a limit (*peras*).
> But
> (7) The infinite is that which has no limit.
> Therefore, the original supposition is false:
> (8) The infinite is that from which it is *always* possible to take something from outside.

The infinite 'turns out to be the contrary of what it is said to be' because of the absurdity of equating the infinite and the whole. It would be absurd to equate the whole and the infinite, for that would be to say that the *unlimited* had a *limit*. The claim that the infinite must lack a limit would appear to Aristotle to be an analytic truth: a truth established by the meaning of the words alone.

Having dethroned the infinite, Aristotle can argue: '[The infinite] does not contain, but in so far as it is infinite, is contained. Consequently, also, it is unknowable, *qua infinite*: for matter does not have form.'[45] Aristotle often draws an analogy between the infinite and matter.[46] It is this assimilation of the infinite to matter that lies at the heart of the conceptual revolution he is trying to achieve. For certain pre-Socratic thinkers, notably Anaximander, the infinite is something grand and mysterious. It is an enveloping, eternal principle which governs the change and transition found in the world. For Aristotle, by contrast, the world is finite and unenvel-

---

[45] *Physics* III.6, 207a24–6.
[46] See, e.g., *Physics* III.6, 206b14–15, 207a21–6, a35–b1, b34–208a3.

oped, eternal and ungenerated. What Aristotle does need, how-ever, is an underlying stuff from which things are formed: thus the infinite is, if with rough justice, pressed into service as the material principle.

The infinite, for Aristotle, is immanent in nature, not a transcendent principle: thus he can say that we first encounter the infinite in the continuous.[47] The infinite, like matter, does not contain the world but is contained. That which contains is form.[48] Most importantly, matter as such is merely a potentiality: the only way it can exist actually is as *informed* matter.[49] The infinite exists only potentially, as matter does.[50] Due at least in part to its potentiality, the infinite, like matter, is unknowable.[51] Matter as matter is unknowable because it lacks a form and it is form that is knowable. The infinite is unknowable both because that which is indeterminate is unknowable and because that which the mind cannot traverse is unknowable.

Here we encounter a thread that runs to the core of Aristotle's philosophy. Were the chain of causes of a given thing infinite we would not be able to know the explanation of that thing, because the mind cannot traverse an infinite series, that is, a series that has no limit (*peras*). But we can know the causes of a thing, therefore they must be finite in number.[52] If the features which make a substance what it is were infinite, then substance would be unknowable. But we can know what a substance is, therefore there are only finitely many features in its essence or definition.[53] Throughout Aristotle's work this theme recurs: the possibility of philosophy – the possibility that man can satisfy his desire to understand – depends on the fact that the world is intelligible, accessible to man's inquiring mind. The world must therefore be a finite place containing objects that are themselves finite. This is an argument from the possibility of philosophizing. Aristotle argues from the necessity of the world's being a certain way *if* we are to understand it, to the world's actually being that way. If we are to understand

[47] *Physics* III.1, 200b17.
[48] *Physics* III.7, 207a35–b1.
[49] Cf. *Metaphysics* V. 1050a15, 1049b13; *On the Soul* 430a10. See also *Metaphysics* XIII, 1078a30ff.
[50] *Physics* III.6, 206b14ff.
[51] Cf. *Physics* III.6, 207a24–6, a30–2.
[52] See, e.g., *Metaphysics* I.2.
[53] See, e.g., *Posterior Analytics* I.22.

such arguments, we must understand what, for Aristotle, makes philosophy possible. It is not that we make the world in our own image: it is not a question of reducing the world's possibilities down to ours. The world *is* such that it can be known, and our capacity for understanding it is itself a real component of the world. At least, we are a part of the world and our capacity to know lies at the bottom of what we are. Understanding, therefore, is not something we project upon the world in order that it should smile back at us knowably. Understanding is itself a constitutive factor in the world's basic makeup.

3.4 The media of change II: the infinity of time[54]

Aristotle develops his theory of the infinite in order to account for three apparently distinct phenomena: the infinite divisibility of magnitudes, the infinity of numbers, and the infinity of time.[55] But the claim that time is potentially infinite amounts to more than the claim that a period of time is infinitely divisible. For although a stretch of time is continuous, Aristotle also wants to emphasize the idea of process: time flows on and on. Time, he believes, has no beginning and no end.[56] Yet how can Aristotle account for the infinite duration of time? He can do so, but only by invoking the role the human mind plays not just in the measurement, but in the very existence, of time. Aristotle's account of time operates at two levels. First, he gives a theoretical understanding of the nature of time. Second, he wishes to account for our experience of time. These two levels are related. For time, as Aristotle conceives it, is partially constituted by our experience of it. Aristotle's project is thus to arrive at an understanding of time itself derived from our experience of it. Again we have an argument about reality based on the possibility of our experience of it.

Certain early thinkers identified time with change.[57] This cannot be quite right, Aristotle says: first, because change occurs in a particular location, in a changing object, yet it is the same time everywhere; and, second, because change can occur at different speeds, faster and slower, but time cannot. Indeed the speed of a change is

---

[54] Appropriate reading *Physics* IV.10–14.
[55] *Physics* III.4; III.6, 206a9–12.
[56] See also *Physics* VIII.1–2.
[57] *Physics* IV.10, 218b9–20.

defined by reference to time: a fast change, for example, is one which occurs in little time.

Though time is not change, Aristotle does find a significant truth in this common belief:

> Neither does time exist without change; for when the state of our minds does not change at all, or we have not noticed its changing, we do not think that time has elapsed, any more than those who are fabled to sleep among the heroes in Sardinia do when they are awakened; for they connect the earlier 'now' with the later and make them one, cutting out the interval because of their failure to notice it. So just as if the now were not different but one and the same, there would not have been time, so too when its difference escapes our notice the interval does not seem to be time. If, then, the non-realization of the existence of time happens to us when we do not distinguish any change, but the mind seems to stay in one indivisible state, and when we perceive and distinguish we say time has elapsed, evidently time is not independent of movement and change. It is evident then that time is neither movement nor independent of movement.[58]

Aristotle is here arguing from the nature of our experience of time to the nature of time itself: we do not think time has passed when we are oblivious to change, therefore time is dependent upon change. Aristotle is not here claiming that time is subjective: those who sleep beside the heroes in Sardinia connect two distinct 'nows' – a prior 'now' and a later 'now' – and make them one. Though it seems to them that no time has passed, they are making a mistake. So not any subjective judgement regarding the passage of time is correct. Yet Aristotle does believe that one cannot give an account of the objective reality of time without including in the account an enduring soul which *could* experience the change. The challenge, then, is to understand how, for Aristotle, it is possible to arrive at an understanding of the objective nature of time based on our apprehension of it.

Mind enters Aristotle's theory of time via his treatment of 'the now':

[58] *Physics* IV.11, 218b21–219a2.

We apprehend time only when we have marked change, marking it by before and after; and it is only when we have perceived before and after in change that we say that time has elapsed. Now we mark them by judging that one thing is different from another, and that some third thing is intermediate to them. When we think of the extremes as different from the middle and *the mind pronounces that the nows are two*, one before and one after, it is then that we say that there is time, and this that we say is time. For what is bounded by the now is thought to be time – we may assume this.

When therefore we perceive the now as one ... no time is thought to have elapsed, because there has been no change either. On the other hand, when we do perceive a before and an after, then we say that there is time. *For time is just this – a number of motion in respect to before and after.*[59]

It is only when we have perceived a before and after in change that we say time has elapsed. It is that perception that enables us to number it. But the number of change or motion is just what time is.[60] But is that number itself objective? Usually when Aristotle talks of numbering, he is concerned with the enumeration of discrete items of a certain sort. It is a plurality of discrete things which are numerable.[61] This would suggest that Aristotle had in mind that one pick out a certain unit of time – say the passage of a day as marked by the heavenly movements – and then 'pronounce a now.' The number of days will be measured by the pronouncement of the nows.[62] It is change, then, as well as our recognition of it that

---

[59] *Physics* IV.11, 219a22–b2; cf. IV.11, 220a24–6 and 12, 221a13–14, b2, b7, b11, b22–3, b25–6. (Again, I translate *kinēsis* as 'change' rather than as 'motion.')

[60] *Physics* IV.11, 219b1–2; cf. 220a24–6, 221b2, b11.

[61] *Metaphysics* V.13, 1020a7–12, cf. *Categories* 6.

[62] Aristotle also says that time is a *measure* of motion (*Physics* IV.11, 220b32–221a1, 221b7, 221b22–3, 221b25–6), and he often speaks of measuring time (cf., e.g., *Physics* IV.12, 220b14–222a9; there are by my count twenty references to measuring time in this passage alone). One is naturally led to wonder whether Aristotle is distinguishing between time as a measure of motion and time as a number of motion. One could, for example, measure incommensurable periods of time, but one could not number them. I do not think that Aristotle does have any such difference in mind. He uses the verbs *anametreō* and *katametreō* (to measure out precisely) when describing measuring (220b32–221a4), and he

grounds our recognition of a before and after and the interval which the distinct nows mark. This recognition – the marking of distinct nows – itself recognizes the reality of time and is also a *realization* of time itself. For time is nothing other than a number or measure of change.

We are aware that time has passed when the soul 'pronounces the nows as two': what does such a pronouncement consist in? A soul enduring through time is one that exists in the present: it is able to specify past and future by reference to its own existence. For the soul to pronounce a now is for it to be aware of the present moment as present. Such a pronouncement has a certain irrefragable quality: it is not liable to error. For the only time at which a soul can pronounce a now is in the present: it may have pronounced a now in the past and it may be that it will pronounce a now in the future, but when it actually pronounces a now, it must be at (what is then) the present moment. For a soul to pronounce the nows as two is either for it to be aware that at two distinct times it has pronounced a now or that at a previous time it pronounced a now which is distinct from the now it currently pronounces. The soul is not dependent on external changes to be aware of the passage of time. It can record the changes in its own states. We can, for example, lie in a quiet dark room and be aware that time is passing. It is only 'when we ourselves do not change our thought or do not notice the changing' that 'it does not seem to us that time has passed.'[63] One might like to say that pronouncing the nows is like starting and stopping an internal mental stopwatch. But the analogy with a stopwatch can be misleading: for it suggests a watch with its own units of measurement. For Aristotle, the nows we pronounce are the primary units: they mark the interval as an interval of time. (We may, of course, choose to pronounce the nows according to certain natural signs which we take to signify a uniform passage of time: for example, the sun's position in the heavens.) The analogy of a mental stopwatch is tempting because

characteristically uses these expressions for measurements in which a whole is divided into aliquot parts. (For *katametreō*, cf. *Physics* VI.7, 237b27; VI.10, 241a13; for *anametreō*, cf. *Physics* VI.7, 238a22; see also *Metaphysics* V.25, 1023b15.) For passages in which Aristotle seems to run numbering and measuring together, see *Physics* IV.11, 220a24–6, a32–b3, 220b14–24, 221b7–23, 223b12–20.

[63] *Physics* IV.11, 218b21–3.

one naturally wants the measure to have a more objective basis than our pronouncing nows: one is tempted by the idea that in pronouncing nows we are merely keeping time to an antecedently existing objective measure. In the figure of the mental stopwatch we have already presupposed all that there is to time. For Aristotle, by contrast, time is the outcome of a peculiar interaction between ourselves and the rest of nature. In nature there are changes, many of them displaying a certain type of regularity. Our recognition of this regularity – as manifested by the soul pronouncing the nows – is both a recognition and a realization of time. Time is that which exists in between the nows that the soul pronounces.[64]

Aristotle explicitly acknowledges the dependence of time on the soul:

> It is also worth investigating how time can be related to the soul; and why time is thought to be in everything both in earth and in sea and in heaven ... Whether if soul did not exist time would exist or not, is a question that may fairly be asked; for if there cannot be some one to count there cannot be anything that can be counted either, so that evidently there cannot be number; for number is either what has been, or what can be, counted. But if nothing but soul, or in soul mind, is qualified to count, it is impossible for there to be time unless there is soul, but only that of which time is an attribute, i.e. if change can exist without soul.[65]

Time is a measure and, as such, could not exist were there no soul or mind of soul which could measure. This does not mean that the measurement is subjective or that any measurement a soul makes is correct: it only means that we cannot give an adequate account of time without including in the account a soul which is measuring the changes. It is from the perspective of a soul which endures through time, which lives in the present, remembers the past, and anticipates the future, that change is measured. And yet, though the reality of time is in some sense dependent both upon the existence of a soul which measures change and upon the independent

---

[64] Cf. *Physics* VI.6, 237a5–6, a9, a10–11.
[65] *Physics* IV.14, 223a16–28 (my emphasis). (I translate *noûs* by 'mind' instead of 'reason' and *kinēsis* by 'change' instead of 'movement'.)

reality of change itself, time provides the ground of the possibility of making sense of change. As the medium in which change occurs, time provides the soul with the opportunity of rendering change intelligible.

If, however, we are to render *time* intelligible, we must come to understand the constitutive role we play in the objective order of time. We cannot have any understanding of what time is like 'in itself,' totally independent of our apprehension or experience of it. For the reality of time is partially constituted by the soul's measuring activities. Time can still be the measure of change, but it requires our being in time to effect its measurement. One way to appreciate the depth of this conception is to consider what it is for an event to occur at some time. For an event to occur *at some time* it is necessary for that event to stand in a determinate relation to the now: that is, to the moment at which the soul presently pronounces the now.[66] From, say, the fall of Troy until now the heavens have revolved continuously a finite number of times. A soul could measure the time elapsed by counting the revolutions.

But what if one should consider the entire previous history of the world? Aristotle's world is uncreated and eternal. So if one were able to measure a stretch of time encompassing all events in the history of the world, that stretch would have to be infinitely extended. But how could there be an infinitely extended stretch of time? When one tries to combine Aristotle's belief in the infinity of time with his belief that magnitudes can be of only finite size, his natural philosophy seems to verge on incoherence. First, time is supposed to be a measure of change. One measures the change by picking out a motion which is uniform and letting that be a standard against which the time of a given change is measured. The paradigmatic measure of change is, for Aristotle, the regular circular motion of the heavens, which he takes to be eternal.[67] But, second, a body in motion traverses a spatial magnitude.[68] So if time is infinite and time is measured by motion, why does not the infinity of time bear witness to the existence of an infinitely extended magnitude?

The obvious response is that the only motion which Aristotle

---

[66] *Physics* IV.13, 222a24–9.
[67] *Physics* IV.14, 223b12–21; cf. *Physics* VIII.8–9.
[68] Cf., e.g., *Physics* VI.1, 231b18–232a22.

thought could be regular, continuous, and eternal was circular motion.[69] And circular motion is not truly infinitary.[70] While traversing the circumference of a circle, one can always continue one's motion, but one cannot properly call the circle infinite. For the circle to be infinite, it would be necessary that each part traversed be different from any part that had been traversed or could be traversed again. And this necessary condition is not fulfilled. So although the heavens have always moved and always will move in a regular circular motion, and thus provide a measure against which the time of other changes can be measured, they do not themselves traverse an infinitely extended magnitude.

This response is not fully satisfying. For although the sphere of the heavens may be finite, the *path* the heavens describe through all time must be infinite. Aristotle himself admits that if time is infinitely extended then length must be infinitely extended.[71] He circumvents this problem by restricting the measurement of time to particular events. *Each event* is in time, but *all events* are not in time.[72] An event is *in time* only if it is encompassed by time: that is, if there were events that occurred before and after it. So although each event in the history of the world is in time – and one can thus measure the time elapsed from that event until now – one cannot treat all events in the previous history of the world as being in time: one *cannot measure* the time elapsed in the previous history of the world.

How, then, can Aristotle even *say* that the world is eternal? For the world to be eternal it must have existed at all times, always. What, for Aristotle, can such a claim consist in? To say that the world must always have existed is to say that there is no time at which the world did not exist. But since time is the measure of change, and the motion of the heavens provides the standard measure, were there no world and thus no change, neither would there be any time. The claim that the world is eternal seems in danger of collapsing from its vaunted position as a metaphysical claim about the nature of the world into an obvious analytic truth – based on the meaning of the concepts alone. *Of course* there was

[69] *Physics* VIII.8–9.
[70] *Physics* III.6, 206b33–207a8.
[71] *Physics* VI.2, 233a17–20.
[72] *Physics* IV.12, 221a1–222a9.

no time at which the world was not, for if the world were not there would be no time and *a fortiori* no time at which it was not. It does not help to claim that 'there always was change and always will be change throughout all time.'[73] For to claim that there *always* was change is to claim that there is no previous time at which there was no change; but that is trivially true. For were there no change there would be no time, since time is the measure of change. Similarly, the claim that there always will be change seems to be no longer a metaphysical discovery about the future, but an analytic truth. Nor will it help to claim that time is a measure of rest as well as of change, for all rest is in time, and thus time must extend in both directions beyond any given rest.[74] One can say, for example, that a given animal has temporarily ceased its motion, but during this interval, as during the entire period of the animal's life, the animal's change and rest can be measured. One cannot thus think of a stationary heaven as resting and so as being in time. Nor will it help to claim that the world is ungenerated.[75] For to claim that the world is ungenerated is to claim that there is no time at which it came into being, and this may be trivially true.

Aristotle does provide us with an argument which enables us to break out of this circle. In *Physics* VIII.1, he argues that the supposition that there was a first change leads to absurdity:

> Change, we say, is the actuality of the changeable insofar as it is changeable. Each kind of change, therefore, necessarily involves the presence of the things that are capable of that change ... Moreover, these things also must either have a beginning before which they had no being, or they must be eternal. Now if there was a becoming of every changeable thing, it follows that before the motion in question another change must have taken place in which that which was capable of being changed or of causing change had its becoming. To suppose, on the other hand, that these things were in being throughout all previous time without there being any motion appears unreasonable on a moment's thought, and still more unreasonable, we shall find, on further

[73] *Physics* VIII.9, 266a6ff.
[74] *Physics* IV.12, 221b7–14.
[75] Cf. *On the Heavens* I.10–12.

> consideration. For if we are to say that, while there are
> on the one hand things that are changeable, and on the
> other hand things that cause change, there is a time when
> there is a first changer and a first thing undergoing
> change, and another time when there is no such thing
> but only something that is at rest, then this thing must
> previously have been in the process of change; for there
> must have been cause of its rest, rest being the privation
> of motion. Therefore before this first change there will
> be a previous change.[76]

Aristotle is arguing that given any purported first change, there
must have been a change which existed before it. (In a similar vein
he argues that given any purported last change, there must be a
change which occurs after it.)[77] Thus we can understand his claim
that there has always been change as being more than an analytic
truth, if we interpret him as claiming that it is absurd for there to
have been a first change. Similarly, Aristotle's claim that the world
is eternal should not be interpreted in terms of an infinitely extended length of time, but only as a claim that no moment could be
the first (or last) moment of the world's existence.

Aristotle's argument establishes no more than the *potential*
infinity of time: time *is* such that for any moment in time it is possible to find an earlier and a later moment. In fact, there is a serious
question as to whether it even establishes the potential infinity of
time. It is, for example, absurd to suppose that any given heartbeat
was the first or the last of my adolescence, yet that only shows that
the heartbeats of my adolescence constitute a *vaguely* determined
totality.[78] Aristotle never considered the possibility that the
moments of time constitute a vague totality, so let us simply
assume that they do not.[79] The fact that infinity of time is only
potential is intimately bound up with the role that mind plays. An
actual infinite extension of time would, in Aristotle's eyes, do nothing for us: for we are beings who cannot possibly comprehend an
actual infinite extension. But it is the very essence of time to be

[76] *Physics* VIII.1, 251a9–28. (I translate *kinēsis* as 'change' rather than 'motion.')
[77] *Physics* VIII.1, 251b28–252a5.
[78] See Michael Dummett, 'Wang's Paradox', in *Truth and Other Enigmas*, and Crispin Wright, 'Language Mastery and the Sorites Paradox.'
[79] Though David Sanford has made a fascinating case for treating time as vague: see his 'Infinity and Vagueness.'

comprehensible to us. Since the very reality of time is manifested in the soul's measurements, the infinity of time can be grounded in nothing more than the fact that, given any change, it will always be possible to measure an earlier and a later change. Nothing more needs to be said – and that is just as well, for in Aristotle's world nothing more can be said. Because our experience of time partially constitutes its reality, Aristotle can infer from our experience of time to the very nature of its existence.

Aristotle's theory of time thus seems to slip through the net of Kant's First Antinomy. Kant thought he had constructed two equally valid arguments, one to the conclusion that the world had no beginning, the other to the conclusion that the world had a beginning in time. The proof that the world had no beginning is similar in structure to Aristotle's. To prove that the world did have a beginning, Kant supposes that the world had no beginning and then infers that an (actually) infinite extension of time must have passed before the present moment, which he takes to be impossible. Aristotle would accept both that the world had no beginning and that it is incomprehensible and therefore that it is impossible that an actual infinity of time should have elapsed, but he would reject Kant's argument as invalid. From the fact that the world had no beginning all that follows, according to Aristotle, is that there can be no measurement of a first change. Given any measurement of a change which a mind makes, the mind could always make a measurement of an earlier event. It is to the importance of so understanding our temporal claims that Aristotle is drawing our attention when he says that time is *potentially* infinite.

3.5 A paradox of change: Zeno's arrow[80]

Aristotle's conception of change was, as we have seen, formulated in the shadow of Parmenides' attack on the very reality of change. It is worth seeing how the developed theory copes with one of the great challenges to the possibility of change: Zeno's paradox of the arrow. The paradox is reconstructed from two condensed passages in Aristotle. *Physics* VI.9 begins:

Zeno's reasoning, however, is fallacious, when he says

[80] Appropriate reading: *Physics* VI.

that if everything when it occupies a space just its own size is at rest, and if that which is in locomotion is always in a now, the flying arrow is therefore motionless. This is false; for time is not composed of indivisible nows any more than any other magnitude is composed of indivisibles.[81]

Later on he says:

[Zeno's paradox of the arrow] is that already given above, to the effect that the flying arrow is at rest, which result follows from the assumption that time is composed of nows: if this assumption is not granted, the conclusion will not follow.[82]

The paradox, I conjecture, had the following form:

(1) Anything that is occupying a space just its own size is at rest.

(2) A moving arrow, while it is moving, is moving in the present.

(3) But in the present the arrow is occupying a space just its own size.

(4) Therefore in the present the arrow is at rest.

(5) Therefore a moving arrow, while it is moving, is at rest.

One aspect of the reconstruction deserves mention. The phrase 'in the now' is a familiar Aristotelian expression, but it captures a concept, crucial to Zeno's argument, which has been overlooked by many students of ancient physics: the concept of the *present* instant.[83] Commentators tend to interpret Zeno as saying that in a

---

[81] *Physics* VI.9, 239b5–9. I have interpreted the phrase 'is against what is equal' (*kata to ison*) as 'occupies a space just its own size.' (The Oxford translation says: 'it occupies an equal space.') The Greeks had difficulty working out a conception of space, and the interpretation preserves the sense of the Greek while sparing us its artificial ring.

[82] *Physics* VI.9, 239b30–3. (I use the literal translation 'time is composed of *nows*' where the Oxford translation has 'time is composed of *moments*.' As we shall see, the difference is important.)

[83] Some commentators have tried to use this as evidence for thinking that 'the now' is foreign to Zeno's argument. See, e.g., Vlastos, 'A Note on Zeno's Arrow,' pp. 187, 192, and Owen, 'Zeno and the Mathematicians,' p. 165, note 38. These arguments are I believe unconvincing. See, e.g., Parmenides, Diels–Kranz 28B8:5, which mentions the present (*nun*).

moment the arrow occupies a space its own size.[84] Yet much of the strength of the paradox – and of Aristotle's response – depends on the fact that the moment of travel with which Zeno is concerned is the present moment.

Aristotle attacks the paradox on two broad fronts. First, as one can see from the quoted passage, he denies that time is composed of nows. The now is simply a division of past and future, itself having no duration. When he talks of a collection of nows (*ta nun*), he is speaking of durationless instants, each of which either is, was, or will be present. Since each now has no temporal magnitude, a collection of nows cannot together compose a temporal magnitude.[85] Therefore, even if Zeno was right in saying that in each now the moving arrow is stationary, it does not follow that the arrow is stationary throughout the duration of its flight. For the duration should not be thought of as composed of nows. So even if all the premises are true, there is no paradox, for the argument is invalid. The argument depends on the assumption that if a property P holds of an object at every present instant of a given period of time, then P holds of the object throughout the period. This assumption, according to Aristotle, is not valid. The appearance of validity depends on a misconception of the nature of time.

Second, Aristotle also denies the truth of the premises. He argues that it is a mistake to speak of the arrow either as moving *or* as being at rest in a now. For motions occur at different speeds or velocities. And velocity is determined by dividing the distance traveled by the amount of time it takes to travel that distance. So for an object to be moving at any given velocity, it must be moving over a certain distance in a given *period* of time.[86] It follows that it does not make sense to speak of an object moving in a now:

> We will now show that nothing can be in motion in a
> now. For if this is possible, there can be both quicker and
> slower motion. Suppose then that in the now the quicker
> has traversed the distance AB. That being so, the slower
> will in the same now have traversed a distance less than

[84] See, e.g., G. E. L. Owen, 'Zeno and the Mathematicians,' p. 157; Gregory Vlastos, 'A Note on Zeno's Arrow,' p. 192; Jonathan Barnes, *The Presocratic Philosophers*, vol. I, pp. 276–85.
[85] See *Physics* IV.10–14.
[86] *Physics* IV.14, 222b30–223a15.

AB, say AC. But since the slower will have occupied the whole now in traversing AC, the quicker will occupy less than this in traversing it. Thus we shall have a division of the now, whereas we found it to be indivisible. It is impossible, therefore, for anything to be in motion in a now.[87]

The idea is that moving objects move at varying speeds, so that if objects could be moving in a now, one could use the varying speeds to divide the indivisible now. For, as in the above example, one could ask how long it took the faster object to move the distance AC (the distance traveled by the slower object in the now) and the answer would have to be some time that is less than the now.[88]

But, Aristotle continues, neither does it make sense to speak of an object being at rest in a now:

> Nor can anything be at rest; for we assert that, that only can be at rest which is of such a nature to be in motion but is not in motion when, where, or as it would naturally be so; since, therefore, nothing is of such a nature as to be in motion in a now, it is clear that nothing can be at rest either.
>
> Moreover, inasmuch as it is the same now that belongs to both the times, and it is possible for a thing to be in motion throughout one time and to be at rest throughout the other, and that which is in motion or at rest for the whole of a time will be in motion or at rest in any part of it in which it is of such a nature as to be in motion or at rest: it will follow that the same thing can at the same time be at rest and in motion; for both the times have the same extremity, viz. the now.
>
> Again, we say that a thing is at rest if its condition in

---

[87] *Physics* VI.3, 234a24–31. See also VI.5, 237a14; VI.8, 239b1; VI.10, 241a24–6.

[88] An atomist need not be bothered by this argument, for it assumes that the motion that occurs in a now is continuous motion, and this an atomist could deny. Treating the now as a temporal atom, he could allow two objects to move at different speeds in the sense that in the next now one object was two spatial atoms removed from where it had been in the previous now, whereas the other object was only one spatial atom removed. One could not divide the now by asking when the faster object was one spatial atom removed; for, according to the atomist, there was no such time. Of course for Aristotle such discontinuous motion was not motion at all: see *Physics* VI.1, 231b18–232a22, and D. J. Furley, *Two Studies in the Greek Atomists*.

whole and in part is uniform now and before; but the now contains no before; consequently, there can be no rest in it. It follows that the motion of that which is in motion and the rest of that which is at rest must occupy time.[89]

Rest, like motion, must occur over a period of time: for just as motion requires that an object be at different places at different times, so rest demands that the object be at the same place at different times.

So on this front Aristotle attacks the premisses of Zeno's argument. Premiss (1) is false because in a now an object will occupy a space just its own size and yet neither be in motion nor at rest.[90] Indeed Aristotle denies that one can precisely locate a moving object, in the sense of saying exactly what it is up against.[91] One can locate the object precisely and thus be able to say that the object occupies a space just its own size only if the object is resting or if one is speaking of its position in a now.[92]

Premiss (2) is false if by 'the present' Zeno meant, as Aristotle takes him to mean, the present *instant*. For the arrow is not moving in the present instant. If however one should interpret 'the present' to be a stretch of time, so that (2) becomes uncontentiously true, then premiss (3) becomes false: during a present period of time, the moving arrow is not occupying a space just its own size.

Aristotle's argument appears compelling. Ironically, there is probably no other of his arguments that has come in for such heavy criticism. The most popular objection – perhaps inspired by the development of calculus – is to Aristotle's belief that an object cannot

---

[89] *Physics* VI.3, 234a31–b9. There might seem to be a tension between this position and Aristotle's claim that there is a first moment at which a change *has* occurred (*Physics* VI.5, 235b6–236a7). For suppose that the change that is occurring is one in which a moving object is coming to a halt (cf. *Physics* VI.8). Then one might expect that there must be a first moment at which the object is at rest. Indeed under the pressure of such an argument Aristotle does talk about an object resting in a moment (*Physics* VI.5, 236a17–20); but his full reply would, I think, be that there is a first moment of the period that the object is at rest, and if one wishes to say that this is the 'first moment of the object's being at rest' that is all right as long as one is not misled into thinking that the object is resting in an instant. Aristotle does explicitly deny that there can be a first instant of rest, and the reason he gives is that rest, like motion, cannot occur in an instant (*Physics* VI.8, 239a10–14).
[90] See *Physics* VI.8, 239a23–b3.
[91] *kata to ison*: *Physics* VI.8, 239a23–b26.
[92] *Physics* VI.8, 239a26–b1.

be moving in an instant. We can say that an object is moving at an instant if that instant is part of a period of time in which the object is moving.[93] Indeed, one should distinguish, so the objection goes, the notion of an object moving *in* an instant from the notion of an object moving *at* an instant.[94] To say that the object is moving *in* an instant is to say that the object actually traverses some distance during the instant; that is, it is to construe the instant as a very small stretch of time. Aristotle correctly dismisses as absurd the notion of an object moving *in* an instant. But this does not show that an object cannot be moving *at* an instant. For to say that an object is moving *at* a moment is only to say that that moment is contained in a period during which the object is moving.

However, this objection does not do justice either to Zeno or to Aristotle. The arrow is alleged to be moving *at* an instant if and only if it is moving in a period that contains the instant. But Zeno would not be at all happy about our simply helping ourselves to the assumption that there exists a period in which the arrow is moving. 'Surely,' he would say, 'if the arrow is moving at all, there is no time it could be moving *other than the present*. And yet you have admitted that the arrow is not moving *in* the present, in the sense that it is not actually traversing any distance in the present. You want to say that the arrow really is moving *at* the present, in the sense that the present is part of a period of time in which the arrow does move some distance. However, you should have admitted that there is no time the arrow could be moving other than at the present. So it is absurd for you to say that the arrow is moving at the present in virtue of its moving in some other time!'[95]

---

[93] For a classic formulation of this objection, see G. E. L. Owen, 'Zeno and the Mathematicians,' pp. 157–62. He argues, against Aristotle, that the question of whether or not time is composed of nows is irrelevant.

[94] G. E. L. Owen ('Zeno and the Mathematicians') makes this point (p. 161), as does Vlastos ('A Note on Zeno's Arrow').

[95] For evidence of Zeno's Parmenidean bent, see Plato, *Parmenides*, 127A–128E. For Parmenides' attachment to the present and rejection of the past and future, see Diels–Kranz 28BA, especially lines 5–6. Vlastos has denied that Zeno's arrow can have anything to do with the notion of the present. He argues that 'the now' is a favorite Aristotelian technical term which Aristotle anachronistically used in his description of Zeno's paradox. This argument is unconvincing. For it does not matter if a particular technical use of 'the now' was not in evidence before Aristotle's time. Zeno's paradox, as I have construed it, does not depend on any technical use of 'the now,' but on a highly general notion of the present – which perhaps by its very generality makes it difficult to see how to refute the paradox.

By construing the claim that the arrow cannot be moving 'in the now' as the claim that the arrow cannot be moving *at an instant*, modern commentators have unwittingly blunted Zeno's arrow. For then it is too easy to go on to say, perhaps invoking concepts derived from calculus, that the arrow can be moving at an instant in virtue of its moving in a period that contains the instant. But since Zeno was concerned with the special case of the present, one cannot answer him with the notion of motion at an instant. Indeed, such a notion will be either inapplicable or superfluous. If we do not assume the existence of a *period* of time in which the arrow *is moving* – a period that can be divided such that some of it is past, the rest is future – then the notion of motion at an instant is inapplicable. For one can only say that the arrow is moving *at* an instant if it is moving in a period of time that contains the instant. If, however, one follows Aristotle by assuming the existence of a period of time in which the arrow is moving, 'the now' merely being an instantaneous division of this period, then the appeal to the notion of motion at an instant is superfluous: one has already assumed all that is needed to show that the arrow is moving.

Another modern approach to Zeno is simply to deny premiss (1): that is, deny that if an object occupies a space just its own size, then it is at rest.[96] Objects occupy a space exactly equal to their size at every instant of their temporal careers, even if they are constantly moving. One can imagine oneself, say, on an airplane from New York to London: at every instant of the journey one occupies a space just one's own size – after all, one only had to buy a ticket for a single seat – and yet one is moving throughout the entire journey. Once one begins thinking in these terms it becomes difficult to see why anyone could have thought that premiss (1) is plausible. However, the paradox now looks so unappealing that one might become suspicious that one's victory over Zeno has been too easy.

The suspicion is justified. If one cannot uncontentiously assume the existence of a period of time in which an object is moving, then one cannot go on to say that the object is moving at any instant

---

A general notion of the present certainly was in evidence in Zeno's time. Parmenides, Zeno's alleged mentor, says: 'Nor was it ever, nor will it be: since *now* it is, altogether' (Diels–Kranz 28BA:5). It is precisely the Parmenidean assumption that something can only be in the present that gives Zeno's arrow its point.

[96] See Jonathan Barnes, *The Presocratic Philosophers*, vol. 1, p. 283.

contained in that period. Zeno's use of the present is designed to make contentious our assumption that there exists a period of time which both contains the present instant and is a period in which the object *is moving*. For, as Aristotle points out in the very first problem about time, of any period of time that contains the present instant, some is past, the rest is future.[97] 'How,' Zeno might ask, 'can one say that the arrow *is moving* in virtue of things that *have* happened to it or *will* happen to it?'

Of course, *if* we can say we are on an airplane traveling from New York to London, then we can also say that we are moving at any instant during our journey; even though at that instant we occupy a space just our own size. But, Zeno wants to ask, how can we say there is any time during which the plane is moving? Have we not helped ourselves to the notion of a period of time when an object is moving? And yet we have already conceded both that the only time an object can be moving is in the present (premiss (2)) and that in the present it does not actually traverse any distance (premiss (3)). There does not seem to be any time during which we can say that the plane – or the arrow – is moving, in virtue of which we can say that it is moving at an instant. Premiss (1) looks obviously false only if one begs the question by assuming that there is a period of time in which the object is moving.

One response that does not beg the question is to deny premiss (2): that is, deny that for an object to be moving it needs to be moving in the present. One can say that an object is moving during a stretch of time solely in virtue of its being at different places at different times in that stretch. Then one can go on to say that an object is moving *at* the present instant if that instant is contained in a stretch in which the object is moving. To Zeno's incredulous question, 'So you think that an object can *be moving* solely in virtue of positions it has occupied in the past and will occupy in the future?', one would simply answer, 'yes.'[98] This would be the response of someone who did not wish to incorporate the notion of a present duration into his scientific theory of time. Theorists of

---

[97] See *Physics* IV.10.

[98] This would be the position of one who wished to deal with Zeno's paradoxes via what Sellars has called the scientific image. See Wilfred Sellars, *Science, Perception and Reality*. See also Bertrand Russell, *The Principles of Mathematics*, pp. 347, 350.

time who do not wish to give the present a special status may prefer this solution to Aristotle's.

However, it is worth noting that this strategy gives a victory to Zeno. For we primarily use the continuous present tense 'x is moving' to talk about an event that requires a duration of time all of which is considered present. We may also talk about an object moving at an instant, but this use is derivative of the primary use. But the theorists we are considering deny that any period of time can, strictly speaking, be treated as present. So these theorists ought to concede to Zeno that, *as we ordinarily use the terms*, the arrow is not moving during the course of its flight. One can concede this and nevertheless maintain that the arrow is at a different position at any moment from its position at any other moment.

Zeno has scored a victory on this analysis which is more than verbal. For anyone who adopts this analysis will come to think that some of his previous beliefs about motion were merely perspectival: that is, dependent on the human point of view. From the human perspective, an arrow seems to be moving because of changes that are occurring in a period of time which can legitimately be conceived to be present. Advocates of this analysis urge that on the impersonal scientific conception of the world there is no period of time that is present. The flight of an arrow consists solely in its being at different positions at different times.

To Aristotle, this approach to Zeno's arrow would be absurd. The idea that time could be completely purged of reference to the present, of reference to a soul measuring changes, would be incoherent. And if one does not wish to grant any victory to Zeno, the first line of attack should be premiss (3): that in the present the arrow is occupying a space just its own size. One can do this not by pointing out any obvious fallacy, but by developing a theory of time in which the present can be conceived of as a period of time. That this is part of Aristotle's strategy is revealed by his doctrine that time is not composed of nows. Any period of time can only be thought of as composed of smaller periods of time. Having developed a theory of time that construes the present as a period of time, one can then proceed, as Aristotle did not, to give a sense to the notion of an object moving at an instant or at the present instant. It is only then that one is entitled to say that an object can be moving at an instant even though it only occupies a space its own size. This is a far from trivial truth, depending as it does upon a theory of time that treats the present as a period of time.

It is often said that Zeno's paradox was puzzling to the Greeks only because they lacked the modern concepts of the calculus, in particular the notion of motion at an instant. By now it should be clear that such a claim is unjustified. It is also commonly said that Aristotle's argument that there cannot be motion at an instant dramatically retarded the development of dynamics. Of course it is possible for a good argument to have stultifying effects, and this may have been Aristotle's legacy. But it is commonly thought that Aristotle presented a fallacious argument which badly influenced all those who believed it. This belief is unjustified: Aristotle's argument is valid, and there is no intrinsic reason why it should have had any negative influence on the progress of dynamics.

Aristotle's argument, as we have seen, is that a moving object must be moving at some velocity; and velocity is a matter of distance traveled over time elapsed. It would therefore be absurd to ask the velocity of an object at an instant; for an instant is not a duration of time and *a fortiori* not a duration of time in which any distance can be traveled. But since it is not moving at any velocity at an instant, it is not moving at an instant.

No discovery of the calculus or dynamics reveals any flaw in this argument. Rather, it has been discovered that there is a use in dynamics for taking the limit of those velocities at which an object is moving during successively shorter periods of time which converge on a given instant. Each of the achieved velocities of which one is taking the limit is calculated by dividing the distance covered in a period of time by the length of the period of time. Traditionally this limit has been called the 'instantaneous velocity' of a moving object or the velocity at which the object is 'moving at an instant.' This does not show that there is any mistake in Aristotle's argument, only that there is a use of the expressions 'instantaneous velocity' and 'moving at an instant' that he did not envision: namely, as designating the limit of velocities. Of course, modern dynamics surpasses Aristotelian dynamics in part owing to the fact that we understand the concept of a limit much better than he did; but this admission differs significantly from the claim that Aristotle fallaciously argued that there cannot be motion in an instant.[99]

[99] It might be objected that one cannot think of motion as occurring only over

Since the calculus does not automatically render Zeno's arrow obsolete, there is reason to go back and re-examine Aristotle's proposed solution. This will shed some light both on what constitutes a reply to a skeptical argument and on why Zeno's paradox continues to fascinate. Aristotle, as we have seen, attacks both the validity of the argument and the truth of the premises. The argument is invalid, he says, because even if one grants that the arrow is stationary in each present instant, it does not follow that the arrow is stationary throughout the period of its flight. The reason is that a period of time is not composed of present instants, or nows.

But Aristotle does not *prove* that time is not composed of nows. Rather, in *Physics* IV.10–14 he develops a theory of time in which a period of time can be said to be composed only of smaller periods of time and not of instantaneous nows. While he does argue that the premises of Zeno's argument are false, his argument depends upon his theory of the structure of time, which is not so much proved as rigorously presented. Of course, every proof must rely ultimately upon premises that are not themselves proven, so Aristotle is hardly at fault for not proving every assumption. Indeed he repeatedly insists that one must distinguish that which needs proof from that which does not, and prove the former by the latter.[100]

Aristotle, I think, began with the belief that an arrow obviously does move during the course of its flight, a belief based on the testimony of sensory experience. Aristotle and Zeno agreed on the testimony of the senses but differed on its significance. Zeno, the

---

periods of time. For if one considers an object that is constantly accelerating, the most natural way to express this phenomenon is to say that at every moment the object is moving at a different velocity. And if the object is at each moment moving at a different velocity from at any other moment, this means that there is no period of time during the acceleration when the object is traveling at any fixed velocity. This objection will not stand up to scrutiny. For the instantaneous velocity of an object at time t is calculated by determining the velocities of the object during temporal intervals which converge on t. So in order to determine any instantaneous velocity, one must be able to determine the velocities of the object during certain periods of time. During a period of constant acceleration the following phenomenon will occur: if one takes any two instants during that period, no matter how close together, and calculates the respective limits of the velocities achieved over periods which converge on those instants, the results will be different. If one wishes to describe the phenomenon by saying 'at every instant the object's velocity is different' that is all right, *provided* that one is not led to believe that something special is happening in an instant. For that is to be misled by one's vocabulary.

[100] Cf., e.g., *Physics* VIII.3, 253a32–b6.

true follower of Parmenides, took his argument to show that sensory experience must give a misleading picture of the nature of reality; Aristotle, by contrast, took the sensory experience to show that there must be something wrong with any argument that leads to such a drastically conflicting conclusion. In *Physics* III–VI he constructs a theory of space, time, and change which purports to describe abstractly how the motion he evidently saw to occur actually does occur. The problem is that arguments in physics may depend on assumptions that even upon mature consideration do not appear self-evident or forever beyond reproach. For example, Aristotle took time to be a measure of change. The existence and nature of time were taken to be derivative of the existence and nature of change. Further, as we have seen, Aristotle reasoned that, since time is a measure of change, it depends for its existence upon the existence of a soul or mind which does the measuring.

We, like Aristotle, tend to begin with the belief that objects do actually move and that there must be some theory which explains how such motion is possible. That time is not composed of nows seems plausible enough in the context of Aristotle's overall theory of time, and if we are gripped by that theory we will know how to answer Zeno. But it is important to be aware that it is we who have been persuaded of Zeno's fallacy, not Zeno.[101] Zeno would think that Aristotle's theory begs the question by assuming that there is a period of time, a period which can be represented either as divided into past and future, with the present a durationless instant, or as a period that is entirely present.

Yet this does not reveal a fundamental flaw in Aristotle's response. To assume that it does is to assume that one must always be able to answer the skeptic with no assumptions at all or assumptions that are blindingly self-evident and incontrovertible. For most interesting skeptical arguments, such as Zeno's arrow, no such refutation is available. At best one can follow Aristotle's strategy and answer Zeno with arguments based on premises one sincerely believes to be true. Given that one does sincerely believe the premises, the skeptical paradox will cease to be problematic for oneself: it will no longer be a genuine difficulty. That is the best, indeed the only, way to meet as ingenious an argument as Zeno

[101] For a fuller discussion of this approach to skeptical arguments, see my *Aristotle and Logical Theory*, chapter 6.

offers. The skeptical puzzle is not refuted in the sense of being dismissed on the basis of absolutely incontrovertible assumptions; it goes away. However, sincere beliefs, no matter how sincerely believed, are not guaranteed to be stable over time for an individual or a community. Should the assumptions of a theory used to answer a skeptical paradox come into question, the puzzle which one may have thought buried forever will be resurrected. One may be able to construct another theory which will answer the paradox; but there is no theory which can guarantee that one will forever be able to keep a good puzzle down. Thus one can both believe that time is not composed of nows and also believe that that belief could be seriously undermined. Because of this basic doubt, one must admit that Zeno's arrow may again emerge as a serious challenge to those – Aristotle and ourselves – who believe in change.

4

Man's nature

4.1 Soul[1]

Soul was traditionally thought to be a principle of living things. Soul was invoked above all, Aristotle says, to explain two remarkable features of animal life: the capacity for movement, and the capacity for cognition – perception and thinking.[2] However, previous thinkers treated soul as an independent item, which they joined to a body without explaining how the two could be related.[3] Aristotle thinks he can give an adequate account of soul and its relation to body by relying on his distinction between form and matter. He defines soul as 'the form of a natural body having life potentially within it.'[4] Since the form of a living body is its nature, it turns out that soul is the nature of living things: the inner principle of change and rest.

Form is the actuality of a body, the matter a potentiality, so soul is the actuality of a living organism. However, Aristotle distinguishes different grades of actuality.[5] Aristotle uses the distinction between having learned an organized body of knowledge (an *epistēmē*) and actually exercising that knowledge. It is fitting to think of one's knowledge as an actuality: for one has passed beyond the stage of merely being capable of learning, one has actually acquired the knowledge. There is nothing that is left which remains to be done in order to be able to exercise it at will. Nevertheless, this does not seem to be as high a level of actuality as the exercise of one's knowledge. When one is contemplating, one's knowledge is active, whereas when one is not, one's knowledge is an ability to become active – to contemplate – if one wishes. By analogy, organisms live at differing levels of activity. When awake

[1] Appropriate reading for sections 4.1 and 4.2: *On the Soul* I.1–2, II.1–12.
[2] *On the Soul* I.2, 403b25–7; III.3, 427a17–19.
[3] *On the Soul* I.3, 407b13–26.
[4] *On the Soul* II.1, 412a20–1.
[5] *On the Soul* II.1, 412a10, a22; cf. II.5.

they are actively living, when asleep they remain alive but are only minimally exercising the powers of life. Soul, Aristotle says, is the *first actuality* of a living body.[6]

Because soul is form, Aristotle thinks he has solved the problem of how soul and body fit together. Form and matter are not two distinct ingredients which, when mixed, constitute a living organism. An organism is itself a unity which, in philosophical reflection, can be seen to have formal and material aspects:

> That is why we can dismiss as unnecessary the question whether the soul and the body are one: it is as though we were to ask whether the wax and its shape are one, or generally the matter of a thing and that of which it is the matter. Unity has many senses ... but the proper one is that of actuality.[7]

Soul is not a special ingredient which breathes life into a lifeless body; it is a certain aspect of a living organism, and a living organism is a paradigm of a functioning unity.

That is one reason why the organism is thought to be a substance. Indeed, when Aristotle wrote his early work, *The Categories*, an individual organism provided the paradigm: 'substance, most strictly, primarily, and most of all.'[8] For an organism is itself a subject: properties are predicable of it and thus dependent on it for their existence; the organism itself provides a locus of reality. 'All substance,' Aristotle said there, 'seems to signify a "this something." '[9] Aristotle used the expression 'this something' as a term of art for a definite, ontologically independent bit of reality. The organization of an individual organism gave it its definiteness; the fact that it was a subject of properties and not itself a property of an underlying subject gave it ontological primacy. However, when Aristotle wrote the *Categories* he had not yet discovered the distinction between form and matter.[10] Once

---

[6] *On the Soul* II.1, 412a27–8, b5.

[7] *On the Soul* II.1, 412b6–9; cf. II.1, 413a3–7, and II.2, 414a19–28.

[8] *Categories* 5, 2a11.

[9] *Categories* 3b10. I translate *tode ti* literally as 'this something,' while the Oxford translation simply has 'this.' I prefer the literal translation, even though it is awkward, for, as will become clear, this phrase is a metaphysical term of art for Aristotle. See section 6.6 below.

[10] See Alan Code, 'Aristotle: Essence and Accident,' and 'On the Origins of some Aristotelian Theses about Predication.'

armed with this distinction, though, he cannot help but re-think what counts as primary substance. For if the individual organism is a compound of matter and form, it would seem to depend upon its form, or soul, to be the organism that it is. Let us leave the question of what counts as primary substance hanging. By the time he wrote *On the Soul* Aristotle at least recognized that there is *some* sense in which soul is substance.[11] For, he says, it is in virtue of its form or essence that an individual organism is a 'this something.' Uninformed matter lacks all definition and cannot exist on its own, so it cannot count as a 'this something.' It is the presence of form, essence or soul which lends to the organism whatever degree of definiteness and independence it has.

Yet it is precisely because soul and body must form a unity in a living organism that it is difficult to distinguish them.[12] Artefacts provided the original model for the form–matter distinction; and there is a clear sense in which a craftsman imposes form on distinct matter. With living organisms, by contrast, matter and form are intimately bound up with each other: there is no distinctly existing and persisting matter on which soul can, from time to time, be imposed. Indeed, the matter of a living organism seems to depend on being ensouled to be the matter that it is. And a given type of soul, say human soul, seems to require a particular type of matter.[13] The living organism is such a unity that the real challenge for Aristotle is not to show how soul and body can form a unity, but to show how this unity can legitimately be conceived as having two aspects, soul and body.

Aristotle was aware of this problem. He did not simply transfer a distinction from a realm in which it makes sense to a realm in which it does not, insensitive to what he was doing. He had cogent reason for thinking that the distinction between form and matter could be made out within the realm of the living. Soul is substance, Aristotle says, in the sense of the essence – or 'what it is to be' – of the body.[14] This is substance according to the *logos*. The essence or *logos* of something is, as we have seen, an order – an order which is intelligible. As we shall see later, the mind comprehends a thing by

---

[11] *On the Soul*, II.1, 412a8, b10–11.
[12] See J. L. Ackrill in 'Aristotle's Definitions of *Psuchē*;' and see section 2.1 above.
[13] *On the Soul* II.2, 413b25–7.
[14] *On the Soul* II.1, 412b10–11.

taking on its *logos*. Thus there is a route backward, from mind to world, which will lend content to the idea of the form, or soul, of a living organism. By studying a living, functioning organism one's mind eventually takes on the form realized in the organism. By reflecting philosophically on what one has learned about the organism one gains insight into what the form of the organism is.

Aristotle thought that one could at least get started with the analogy between art and nature. We are invited to imagine that an artefact, an axe, is a living organism.[15] Its essence would be the power to chop. If it should ever irrevocably lose that ability, it would no longer be an axe – except, perhaps, in name alone. Similarly, if we take an individual organ, say an eye, its essence is the ability to see. The eye is a good example, for we can imagine the matter of an eye remaining more or less intact even after the eye had lost the power of sight. (Imagine the eye of a blind man or an eye floating in a jar of formaldehyde.) The eye is a certain material organ which has the power of sight: once it has lost this power it is no longer an eye. The question is whether Aristotle can extend this analogy so as to cover the living organism as a whole. The soul, he says, is an actuality in the sense that sight or the power of a tool is:[16] so if we can learn the characteristic activity of the organism as a whole, the soul will be the power to engage in that activity.

But how can one investigate a *power*? There is no substitute, Aristotle thinks, for investigating as carefully as possible the various exercises of the power and seeing how they occur. From Aristotle's point of view the problem with all the characterizations of soul given so far is that they are all too abstract. One can say that the soul is the form of a living body, but if we do not yet understand how to distinguish clearly the form from the matter of living organisms, this characterization will be of minimal help. Aristotle, however, does not rely on this characterization. His strategy is the reverse: to engage in a detailed investigation of soul – the power of living things to live their lives – in order to shed light on what constitutes the form of a living thing. It is absurd, he says, to state an absolutely general definition of what soul is.[17] We must look instead to the workings of the different types of living organisms –

[15] *On the Soul* II.1, 412b12–413a7.
[16] *On the Soul* II.1, 413a1.
[17] *On the Soul* II.3, 414b25. See also I.1, 402a10–22, b21–403a2.

plants, animals, and man. What we find is that the powers which constitute soul form a hierarchy: the capacity for nutrition, growth, and reproduction is shared by all living things; animals distinguish themselves from plants by having sensation in addition; some animals distinguish themselves from the rest by the ability to move; and man distinguishes himself from other animals by his abilities to engage in practical and theoretical reasoning. It is by investigating the workings of all these abilities that, Aristotle thought, we would gain insight into man's nature.

We shall concentrate on the higher faculties of soul: sensation, power of movement, and cognition. However, it is worth noting that in the most basic of life functions, nutrition and reproduction, Aristotle saw a trace of the divine:

> ... for any living thing that has reached its normal development ... *the most natural act* is the production of another like itself, an animal producing an animal, a plant a plant, in order that, as far as its nature allows, it may partake in the eternal and divine. That is *the goal towards which all things strive, that for the sake of which they do whatsoever their nature renders possible* ... Since then no living thing is able to partake in what is eternal and divine by uninterrupted continuance (for nothing perishable can for ever remain one and the same), it tries to achieve that end in the only way possible to it, and success is possible in varying degrees; so it remains not indeed as the self-same individual but continues its existence in something *like* itself – not numerically one, but *one in form*.[18]

Aristotle is positing within the form of living things a force for the preservation of form. Though an individual organism is mortal, it will be deeply motivated to keep its form in existence via that 'most natural' act: the reproduction of its kind. Wherein lies the divinity? It is true that, for Aristotle, eternality is a mark of the divine, but it is not sufficient for divinity. Matter is eternal in the sense that it is neither created nor destroyed, but Aristotle does not think matter divine. We need a deeper reason for thinking that the preservation

---

[18] *On the Soul* II.4, 415a26–b7 (my emphasis). (I translate *eidei d'hen* as 'one in form' while the Oxford translation says 'specifically one.')

of form is divine. I am not going to give that reason just yet. I mention it only as a challenge to our understanding of Aristotle: we have not worked our way into Aristotle's world until we understand how in the most basic of life activities, reproduction, an organism, insofar as its nature allows, partakes of the divine.

4.2 Perception

Aristotle's strategy is to shed light on the form of living organisms by a study of their characteristic activities, most notably perception and movement. And yet when he summarizes what occurs in an act of perception he again refers to form:

> A sense faculty is that which has the power of receiving into itself the sensible forms of things without the matter, in the way in which a piece of wax takes on the impress of the signet ring without the iron or gold; what produces the impression is a signet of bronze or gold, but not qua bronze or gold: in a similar way the sense is affected by what is colored or flavored or sounding, not insofar as each is what it is, but insofar as it is of such and such a sort and according to its *logos*.[19]

It seems as though Aristotle is trying to explain form by appeal to form: the form of a living animal – at least, its capacity for perceptual experience – is characterized by its ability to take on forms. This is the second time Aristotle has used the analogy of the wax tablet and its impressions. The first was designed to show the unity of a composite of form and matter. So here the analogy suggests the unity of a sense faculty with the sensible form it has taken on. But we are not going to have insight into the form that is soul unless we have insight into what it is for the sense faculty to receive the sensible forms of things.

It is important not to confuse the *sensible* form of a thing with its form. The sensible form of, say, a tree is manifested, first, in the tree's appearance as a tree; second, in the tree's ability to cause appropriately situated perceivers to perceive it as a tree. The form of

---

[19] *On the Soul* II.12, 424a17–24. (I translate *aisthēsis* here as 'sense faculty' rather than the Oxford translation's 'sense,' and I leave *logos* untranslated, while the Oxford translation gives 'form.')

a tree, by contrast, is its nature or essence. Of course, sensible form is itself an expression of form: part of what it is to be a tree is to appear like a tree. But the reality of a tree is not exhausted by its appearance. There is more to being a tree than meets the naked eye. Now if perception is to provide an accurate awareness of the world, there must be structural similarities between physical objects on the one hand, and the conscious states of perceivers of those objects on the other. If a tree bore no structural similarity to the perceptual state of a person looking at it, there would be no reason to call that person's mental state a *perception* of a tree. It is this structural similarity, guaranteed by the very idea of perception, that Aristotle is trying to capture with the notion of sensible form.

Aristotle is obliged to give an account of sensation in terms of his overall theory of change. The reason is twofold. First, when we become sensorily aware of some part of the world we experience a change in our cognitive state: for example, when we see a tree, we become aware that we are seeing a tree. Second, when we try to account for this change of state it seems that we must assign an external cause, namely the object we are perceiving. On Aristotle's general theory of change, that which *potentially* has a certain form is caused to go through a process of taking on that form by an external agent which already has the form. Since Aristotle thinks perception to be an accurate awareness of features that exist in the world, it is natural for him to conceive the perceptible object as having a form which the sense faculty is capable of taking on. The tree which we see has the perceptible form of a tree, and it causes our faculty of sight to take on its visible form.

However, in Aristotle's general theory of change, there is a *single activity* of agent and patient and this activity occurs in the patient. The builder has the form of a house in his soul, but it represents a mere potentiality or capacity for engaging in building activity. The activity of the builder building occurs in the house being built, not in the builder. And the activity of the builder building is itself the form of a house at its highest level of actuality. With perception, by contrast, the causal direction is reversed: the world makes a causal impact upon the perceptual faculties of suitably placed perceivers. But if perception is to be conceived as a change, then the causal impact of world on perceiver ought to be a single activity which is occurring in the sense faculty of the perceiver.

Now the activity which occurs in a perceiver when he, say, sees a tree is a *perceptual awareness* of a tree. The tree causes the perceiver to be perceptually aware of a tree. If perception is conceived in terms of the sense faculty taking on the sensible forms of things, then the perceptual awareness ought to be the sensible form at the highest level of activity. The sensible form of a tree *as it exists in the tree* is a capacity for causing a perceptual awareness of the tree in a suitably placed perceiver.[20] And the perceptual awareness of the tree is the very same sensible form as exists in the tree, only at a heightened state of actuality. For although the tree has the sensible form of a tree, the tree is not perceptually aware of itself. The tree has no perceptual awareness at all, for it has no sense faculties. An act of perceptual awareness is the outcome of a causal interaction between two distinct items, a physical object and a sense faculty. The perceptible object and the corresponding sense faculty stand to each other as two potentialities which have a *single* actualization. The perceptible object has the capacity to be perceived, the sense faculty has the capacity to perceive. The single actualization is the act of perceiving – and this occurs in the perceiver.

But how can Aristotle conceive of the perceptible form of an object as a potentiality? Is not form an actuality? Aristotle's answer is that one must distinguish between *levels* of potentiality and actuality. The sensible form of an object is its appearance, the appearance it *actually* has. Let us then consider the sensible form of a tree as it exists in the tree a *first-level actuality*. However, when one considers what it is for the tree to have this appearance, one realizes that its sensible form is a capacity for causing a certain perceptual awareness in suitably situated perceivers. The sensible form of the tree, though an *actuality of the tree*, is a *potentiality for being perceived*. The actual perceiving of the tree is itself the sensible form of a tree at a higher-level actuality. This higher-level actuality of sensible form can only occur in a sense faculty. Thus the highest level of actuality of perceptible form occurs not in the perceptible object, but in the sense faculty of a being who is perceiving that form.

[20] Note the analogy with the builder: the form of a house as it exists in the builder's soul is his capacity for causing a house to be built. But this causing, should it ever occur, would occur in the house being built.

Similarly, an animal's sense faculty is part of the animal's soul or form; and soul, of course, is an actuality of the animal. But, again, it is a *first-level* actuality. When one considers what it is to be a sense faculty, one realizes that it is a *potentiality* for taking on sensible forms. Aristotle recognizes that it is a potentiality of a very special sort. For although he characterizes perception in terms of the sense faculty receiving the sensible forms, perceptual awareness of the world is such a remarkable and special event that it cannot be characterized in terms of a merely passive sense faculty. Again, Aristotle makes this point by distinguishing levels of potentiality and actuality.[21] The analogy he uses is with the acquisition and exercise of knowledge or understanding. We can call even an ignorant young man a knower, for he is a member of a species capable of acquiring knowledge.[22] But he is a knower only in the sense of having a *first-level potentiality*: he is made of the right stuff to acquire knowledge given suitable interactions with the world.[23] Once he has learned a body of knowledge, for example geometry, we can say that he is a knower in a more developed sense. His soul has taken on a certain stable condition:[24] he can construct and follow geometrical proofs at will. But even this developed state of the soul must be thought of as a potentiality. For his geometrical knowledge consists in an ability to engage in active geometric practice. His knowledge, then, can either be conceived as a *second-level potentiality* – which emphasizes the ability of a knower to think actively – or as a *first-level actuality* – which emphasizes the developed state of the soul.[25] In virtue of possessing this knowledge the person may be called an *actual or active knower*, but this actuality is exhausted by his *ability* to contemplate when he wants.[26] Thus the state of his soul represents a first-level actuality. This state is contrasted with that of the man actively contemplating a geometrical proof: he is actively exercising his knowledge.

Now the transition from having knowledge to actively using

---

[21] See *On the Soul* II.5.
[22] *On the Soul* II.5, 417a21–4.
[23] *On the Soul* II.5, 417a27.
[24] A *hexis*.
[25] For the potentiality, see *On the Soul* II.5, 417a24–b19; for the activity, see III.4, 429b5–9.
[26] *ho epistēmōn, ho kat' energeian: On the Soul* III.4, 429b6–7.

one's knowledge is, Aristotle thinks, a very special sort of change.[27] When one is learning, one's soul is undergoing a straightforward change of state. A state of ignorance is being replaced by a state of knowledge. But when one already has knowledge, the active exercise of this knowledge is not a change of state of the soul. Indeed, Aristotle says that the active use of knowledge helps to *preserve* the knowledge which one already has. If this is to be thought of as a change at all, it is a change of a very special sort. What is so special about this change is that the outcome, active contemplating, is itself an *activity*.[28] An activity (*energeia*) differs from a change (*kinēsis*) in that it is not directed toward any external end, and thus may serve as an end in itself. An ordinary change, like building or learning, is directed toward an end (a finished house, knowledge) and will cease when the end is achieved.[29] Contemplating, by contrast, need not be directed toward an as yet unrealized goal: it can be engaged in for its own sake, and it need not cease at any particular point.

Perception, too, is a very special sort of change. On the one hand, the process of transmission of the sensible form from the object to the perceiver is a change. A tree causes me to see a tree. Sensory perception depends on an external cause which somehow activates the medium between perceiver and object, and the end state of this process is the sensory awareness. On the other hand, the product of the change, sensory awareness, is itself an activity. Seeing, Aristotle says, is complete at every moment, and we engage in it for its own sake, not just for its usefulness. Indeed, as we have seen, Aristotle thinks that the sheer delight we take in the active exercise of our sense faculties is evidence for there being a desire to know in our souls.[30]

Now the reason we can engage in this special sort of change – that is, have perceptual awareness of the world – is that we have in-

27 *On the Soul* II.5, 417b2–7, b14–16.
28 See especially *Metaphysics* IX.6.
29 Aristotle offers the following test for distinguishing activities from changes: if at any time during a period in which something is φ-*ing* it is also true to say that it *has* φ-*ed*, then φ-*ing* is an activity. For example, at any time at which a person is seeing, it is also true that he has seen; but it is not true that at any period of time at which a person is building that he has built. For a person is building only when he is building something; and he has built only when that something is completed and the process of building has ceased.
30 *Metaphysics* I.1, 980a21–7.

herited the *developed* capacity to perceive from our parents.[31] It seems, then, that we are born with the second-level potentiality for perception – our sense faculty. The first-level potentiality – the ability to become a perceiver – is located in the seed that is passed on by the male parent. So the transition from having the ability to perceive to perceiving is like the transition from having knowledge to exercising it: a very special sort of change.[32] However, since knowledge has been internalized, it can be exercised at will. Perception, by contrast, depends upon an external object which causes the sense faculty to shift into an active state. Thus perception is able to retain a certain similarity with an ordinary case of change. In an ordinary change, an active possessor of form (a builder building say) causes the form to be taken on by something which was capable of receiving it (the wood). The activity of the form as cause occurs in that which is undergoing change. For example, the activity of the builder building is occurring in the house being built, not in the builder. Similarly with sensory perception: the perceptible form as it exists in the perceptible object is a *potentiality* for being perceived. A sense faculty is a (developed) *potentiality* for taking on perceptible forms. But the activity of the perceptible form of the object and the activity of the sense faculty, are, Aristotle says, one and the same, though the accounts which one would give of each differ.[33] This activity occurs in the sense faculty. Thus the highest level of actuality of perceptible form occurs not in the perceptible object, but in the sense faculty of a being who is perceiving that form.

Perception, then, is a single activity which has a subjective and an objective aspect. The sense faculty is a 'subjective' potentiality: a potentiality for becoming aware of sensible forms that exist in the world. The perceptible form of a physical object is an 'objective' potentiality: a potentiality for making a perceiver aware of this form. This perceptible form is clearly what the active perceiving is a perceiving of. The perceptible object may really exist, even when it is not being perceived, but if we are to understand what it is for it to be a *perceptible* object, we must recognize it as having a potentiality the actualizing of which occurs in the perceptive

---

[31] In particular, from the male parent.
[32] *On the Soul* II.5, 417b16–19.
[33] *On the Soul* III.2, 425b26.

faculty of a perceiver who is actually perceiving it. That potentiality is the enmattered perceptible form. This may initially appear paradoxical, since we think of form as being a type of actuality, but the physics of perception requires that the form which the perceptive faculty 'receives' represents a higher-level actuality than the perceptible form embodied in the object. And the oddity is diminished when we think of the enmattered perceptible form as a first-level actuality, the second-level actuality of which is an activity: the active sensory perceiving of the perceptible form without the matter.

The perceptible form as it occurs in the sense faculty of the perceiver can thus be ranked in relation to the form as it is embodied in the perceptible object: the activity in the sense faculty is a higher level of actualization. Now in some cases we have words to mark this distinction. For example, the Greek word for 'sound' – *psofos* – is used ambiguously to refer both to the potentiality that is located outside and the activity that is located within the perceiver. That is, one can use *psofos* to refer to the sound that occurs out in the world when, say, a tree crashes to the ground; and one can also use *psofos* to describe the activity that occurs within a listener when he hears that sound. But if we wish to refer unambiguously to the activity that occurs in the listener, we can use the word 'sounding' (*psofēsis*).[34] Sounding, according to Aristotle, can *only* occur in the hearer. However, he thinks that those who held, say, that there could not be sound without hearing were misleading: for though the claim may be true of sound *as an activity* and hearing *as an activity*, it was interpreted as a claim about sound in the world – that is, about sound as a potentiality for being heard – and as such the claim is false.[35] To do full justice to the situation, though, we must distinguish levels of potentialities or actualities. One must thus distinguish three states: for example,

(i) a tree standing in the woods
(ii) a tree crashing in the woods unheard
(iii) a tree crashing in the woods and being heard by a suitably placed perceiver.

In state (ii) one can say, according to Aristotle, that the tree makes

---

[34] *On the Soul* III.2, 426a7–13.
[35] *On the Soul* III.2, 426a20–6.

a sound, in the sense that it creates a sound in the world. This is a second-level potentiality: a potentiality for being heard. But one should deny that it is sounding. It is only in state (iii) that the true activity of sound – sounding – occurs. And this activity occurs in the sense faculty of the person who hears the sound. This may seem odd to modern readers, but for Aristotle sound that occurs unheard must be understood as a potentiality for active perceiving.[36]

The vocabulary we have been using so far describes what is going on from the perspective of the world's impact on the perceiver. The vocabulary of 'sound' and 'sounding' is that of the world impinging on the perceiver. But one can also describe the activity of perceiving from the perspective of the hearer. Like the Greek word for 'sound,' the Greek word for 'hearing' – akoē – is ambiguous. It may be used to refer to the capacity to hear, the sense faculty. (To give a fanciful example: 'After listening to all those loud concerts, my hearing isn't what it used to be.') Or it may be used to describe the actual hearing of a sound. ('I am hearing voices.') However, if one wishes to designate the actual hearing of a sound unambiguously, one may use the expression 'actively hearing' (akousis).[37] Thus the very same activity may be called either 'sounding' or 'actively hearing.' This is no more mysterious than the fact that we can call the very same activity either 'the builder building' or 'the house being built.' One describes the activity from the perspective of the agent, the other describes the activity from the perspective of the patient, but it is a single activity that is being described.

The activity of hearing can thus be referred to from both a subjective and an objective perspective: we may call it actively hearing – thus characterizing it from the point of view of the perceiver – or we may call it sounding – thus paying homage to the external sound which is its potentiality; but in both cases we are referring to one and the same state. Thus one might say that actively hearing *is* a sound and that it *is of* a sound. It *is* a sound in the sense that it is an active form of sound – a sounding. And it *is of* a sound, for

[36] Indeed, according to Aristotle, we can even say of a silent solid object that it 'has sound' because it has the capacity to make a sound when struck: On the Soul II.8, 419b4–9.
[37] On the Soul III.2, 426a12.

Aristotle is clearly providing the physics of perception. In perception the highest level of activity – perceptible form in its highest actualization – does occur in the perceiver, but this activity is the perception of an external phenomenon.

If, in Aristotle's world, form which exists as a potentiality is in part a force toward the realization of form at the highest level of actuality, then *one ought to conceive of perceptible forms embodied in physical objects as forces directed toward the awareness of form.* For it is only in the awareness of a perceiver that perceptible form achieves its highest level of actuality. The sensible form of a tree is a real force in the tree toward being perceived as a tree. The perceiving of the tree must occur in the sense faculty of a perceiver, but the perceiving itself is nevertheless the highest realization of sensible form.

However, there is a serious question as to how sensible form undergoes the transition from existing in a physical object, like a tree, to existing in the sense faculty of a perceiver of the object. For it is in that transition that the sensible form becomes a part of consciousness. The tree has the sensible form of a tree, but it has no awareness of its appearance as a tree; but, for a perceiver, to have that sensible form in his sense faculty is just what it is to be perceptually aware of the tree. How can sensible form bridge that gap? The task is to show how some part of the world – ourselves and other animals – can become conscious of the rest of the world. The danger is that we make the account of the transition from world to mind either too material or too spiritual. If, on the one hand, we give a purely material account, of, say, the physical change that a certain visual scene (a tree) forms in the eye of the perceiver, we seem to leave consciousness out of the account. It remains unclear how, by such a physical change, one is meant to get out of the non-conscious physical world. On the other hand, if we give a totally spiritual account, it is not clear that we have given an account of a *transition*, for it is not clear that we have begun in a thoroughly non-conscious world.

In fact, Aristotle's notion of sensible form is ideally suited to bridging the gap between the non-conscious and the conscious parts of the world. When considering his general account of form, we have already seen that form is neither purely physical nor purely non-material. Form cannot be fully understood as a functional or structural state of matter, but structural organization is a *partial* manifestation of form. This is the account of form I offered earlier: the form of a young organism is manifested in its achieved organization, but it *also* exists as a power in the organism for further growth and higher structure. This power cannot itself be understood as a manifestation of the achieved organization and must simply be accepted as a basic reality. When we come to perception we might expect an analogous situation: namely, that sensible form is in part an organization of the matter of the perceptible object, and that perception involves the transmission of this form from the perceived object to the sense organ. The transmission of this form would be physical, and thus one would expect *On the Soul* to have an account of physical transmission of organization. However, if form is not exhausted by organization of physical matter, one would expect there to be some aspect of the taking on of sensible form which could not be understood as being a property of matter. This aspect, I believe, is the awareness involved in perception.

One way to grasp this is by seeing what is wrong with a purely material or a purely spiritual account of sensible form. On a *material account*, sensible form can be understood as a property which the sense organ acquires. On the most vivid account, the perception of a red rose consists in the eye jelly turning red.[38] The eye does not absorb any rosy matter from the rose, but the redness of the rose causes the eye to change to the same color. Less dramatically, any account which says that sensible form is solely a certain organized state of the matter is a material account. When the eye perceives a red rose it need not actually turn red, it need only acquire an organization structurally analogous to the organization instantiated in the red rose. A *spiritual* account, by contrast, is one that insists that all that is involved in the sense faculty's taking on the sensible form is the person's becoming aware of the perceptible quality.[39] To be aware that one is seeing a red rose is what it is for the faculty of sight to take on the sensible form.

One can, I think, show conclusively that the eye's taking on the

---

[38] See, e.g., Richard Sorabji, 'Body and Soul in Aristotle.'
[39] The most recent defender of this view is M. F. Burnyeat, 'Is Aristotle's Philosophy of Mind Still Credible?'; but past defenders include John Philoponus, Thomas Aquinas, and Franz Brentano.

sensible form of a red rose cannot consist in its turning red. Ironically, one can do this by seizing on the inadequacies of the Greek language. For Greek is not sufficiently rich to capture all the aspects of perception. The Greek word for color – *chrōma* refers unambiguously to a perceptible state of the perceptible object. That is, *chrōma* refers unambiguously to the potentiality for being perceived that exists in the red rose. And if we want to capture the activity of color – the perceiving of color that occurs in a perceiver – we have to leave the 'objective' vocabulary of color behind. For there is no word in Greek which respects the fact that the activity of color is an activity *of color*. That is, Greek lacks a word like 'coloring' (**chrōmēsis*). Now we can capture the activity of perceiving color, but we must do so by resorting to the 'subjective' vocabulary of sight. The Greek word for 'sight' – *opsis* – can be used ambiguously to refer either to the sense faculty ('he has sight') or to the activity of seeing. We may also refer unambiguously to the activity of seeing by using the Greek word for 'seeing' (*horasis*). Of course, 'seeing' names the activity of color, but it does not capture the 'objective' perspective on this activity. It captures the activity of color from the 'subjective' perspective of the perceiver. 'Color' is thus a potentiality word: we may say that objects are actively colored, but this means that they are able (in suitable conditions) to contribute to a higher-level actualization which is seeing.[40] The color of an object is a perceptible form whose highest level of activity is not a color but an activity of seeing a color.

But if 'color' must be used unambiguously to refer to the perceptible form in the object, then the sense faculty's taking on the perceptible form cannot consist in the eye's becoming colored. If Aristotle actually thought that an eye that is seeing red turned red, he would have said that 'color' can be used ambiguously both to refer to the perceptible form in the object and to refer to the higher-level actuality, the form in the sense faculty. Moreover, if the eye were caused by a red rose to turn red, then perception would be an ordinary case of change, but Aristotle, as we have seen, is at great pains to stress that, if we are to think of perception as a change at

[40] *On the Soul* III.5, 430a16–17. Thus when Aristotle says, for example, that 'light makes things that are potentially colored actively colored,' he does not mean that light raises colors to the level of seeing. He means rather that light is a condition of the transparent medium such that colored objects are able to affect appropriately located perceivers.

all, we must treat it as a change of a very special sort.[41] Indeed, the
fact that perception involves a change of a special sort is enough, I
think, to rule out any purely material account of sensible form. For
if the sensible form of a tree merely caused a purely physical or
structural change in the eye, there would be no reason for thinking
this change to be anything more than an ordinary sort of change.
What makes the change special is that the outcome of the change is
seeing: an awareness that is an activity.

Nevertheless, when a sense faculty takes on a sensible form, the
perceiver does undergo some physical change. So a purely spiritual
account of sensible form cannot be correct. In general, when form
is the form of a physical body it makes some difference to the body
itself that it has the form. Form may not be fully explicable in terms
of material structure, but the presence of form does make some difference to that structure. A sense faculty and a sense organ are,
Aristotle says, one and the same, though they differ in being.[42]
What Aristotle means is that the account one would give of each
differs in that the account of a sense faculty is purely formal, while
the account of a sense organ must state that a form is realized in a
certain type of matter. For example, the faculty of sight is simply
the power or capacity to see, while an eye is a certain type of
material object in which the capacity to see is realized. Since the
eye and the faculty of sight are the same, when the faculty takes on
the perceptible form without the matter, so, *a fortiori*, does the eye.

Aristotle believed in the existence of a transparent medium
(found in air, water, certain solids, and the outer sphere of the universe) which itself could exist in active or potential state.[43] Light,
Aristotle thought, was the active state of the transparent. Color is
that which has the power of setting the actively transparent – light
– in motion.[44] Now Aristotle is clearly interested in the physical
transmission from the object to the perceiver: the movements
which color induces in the light make a physical difference to the
transparent medium itself. And Aristotle stresses that it is only on
the basis of such a physical transmission that color can be seen. If,
for example, one puts a colored object directly on one's eye, one

[41] For other criticisms of the materializers, see M. F. Burnyeat, 'Is Aristotle's Philosophy of Mind Still Credible?'
[42] *On the Soul* II.12, 424a24–8.
[43] See *On the Soul* II.7.
[44] *On the Soul* II.7, 418a31–b2, 419a9–10.

will not see the color. Rather there must be physical contact between the eye and the excited, moving light. It is unlikely that Aristotle would give such a physical account of this transmission if he
did not think it made any physical difference to the eye. And he
clearly does seem to notice a physical change that the eye
undergoes: '... the air modifies the pupil in this or that way and
the pupil transmits the modification to some third thing (and similarly with hearing) ...'[45] Aristotle obviously noticed what it is very
hard to ignore: that the pupil of the eye varies in diameter according to the brightness of the light in which a see-er is seeing.

In the case of hearing, he clearly describes a physical change in
the aural sense organ.[46] The crashing of a tree in the woods sets in
motion a single mass of air which extends continuously from the
tree to the aural sense faculty.[47] The sense faculty or, more properly, the organ of hearing has air in it, and the motions of the air
outside the ear set up motions in the air within.[48] This is a physical
description of what is occurring when the aural sense faculty takes
on the perceptible form without the matter. The physical description does not exhaust what is going on in the act of perception: for
one is caused to hear not by the movement of air alone, but by a
sound, and sound is a perceptible form, an irreducible reality. But
clearly the transmission of sound does involve a physical change in
the environment, and the perception of sound – active hearing –
does involve some physical change in the sense organ. Aristotle
does insist that sound, strictly speaking, can only affect that which
is capable of hearing.[49] It is not the sound of thunder that splits the
tree and makes it crash in the wood, but rather the air in which the
sound of thunder is. And yet though the sound is not the air, nor is
it the movement of the air, it cannot be transmitted without movement of the air in the environment causing movement of air in the
aural sense organ.

Aristotle insists that the sense *organs* must be potentially such as
the perceptible object is actually.[50] This does not mean that the eye

[45] *On the Soul* III.7, 431a17–19.
[46] *On the Soul* II.8.
[47] *On the Soul* II.8, 420a3–4; see also 419b20, b25, b35, 420a8, a23–6, b14–16.
[48] *On the Soul* II.8, 420a4–5.
[49] *On the Soul* II.12, 424b9–12.
[50] See, e.g., *On the Soul* II.11, 423a30–424a15; II.12, 424a24–32; III.4, 429a25–
b3; cf. II.10, 422a34–b2.

should actually be able to turn red. It need only imply that the eye takes on the same sensible form as is instantiated in the red rose and, at the higher level of activity, the same perceptible form might be manifested as an *awareness* of red. At this higher level of actuality, the sensible form need not actually *be* red. However, if Aristotle thought that perceiving made no physical difference to the sense organ, one would expect him to say that the sense *faculty*, not the sense organ, was potentially such as the perceptible object is actually. And the potentiality of the sense organ does have a certain physical manifestation, even if the physical state does not exhaust the potentiality. The organ of touch, for example, can be neither hot nor cold if it is to perceive both extremes; the organ of sight is colorless, the organ of hearing is soundless. The sense faculty, Aristotle says, is a mean between the extremes which determine the field of that sense.[51] Sight, he says, can see both black and white because it is actually neither but potentially either. But if Aristotle really thought that the sense organ underwent no physical change, why would he at least partially characterize the mean state of a sense faculty – the ability to take on both dark and light perceptible forms – in terms of the actual property of the sense organ, namely being colorless? The fact that the sense faculty is in a mean state is, for Aristotle, partially manifested in the sense organ's actual physical state. This mean state is disturbed by extremes: very bright light or loud sound can disturb the ability to see or hear.[52] Given that the mean state is at least partially manifested in an actual physical state of the organ, one would expect a disturbance of the mean state to imply some physical change in the organ. That is why when Aristotle comes to discuss mind – *noûs* – he denies that it has any physical organ.[53] The seeing of brilliant sights may disturb the ability to see, but the thinking of brilliant thoughts only improves mind's acuity. But there would be no need to deny mind a physical organ if he did not think that there was *some* physical manifestation to cognitive awareness. His reasoning seems to be that if mind did have a physical organ then the thinking of brilliant thoughts would have a disturbing effect on the ability to think. This reasoning only makes sense if Aristotle also thinks

[51] *On the Soul* II.11, 424a4–6.
[52] *On the Soul* II.12, 424a28–32; III.4, 429a31–b3; III.2, 426a30–b7.
[53] *On the Soul* III.4, 429a29–b5.

that the disturbing effect would be manifested by a change in the physical state of the organ. The analogy Aristotle offers for the disturbance of a sense faculty is that of the lyre whose tone is destroyed by violent twanging of the strings.[54] Clearly the lyre undergoes a physical change as well as a change in ability to produce certain harmonious sounds. A sense faculty is not itself a physical magnitude, but a certain *logos* of a physical magnitude, a sense organ.[55] This *logos* – the order, arrangement, or proportion – as well as the disturbance of the *logos*, does have physical manifestations.[56]

What, then, is it for the sense faculty to take on the sensible form without the matter? The claim is not to be understood solely in

---

[54] *On the Soul* II.12, 424a30–2.

[55] *On the Soul* II.12, 424a26–8.

[56] Toward the end of his discussion of sensation, Aristotle asks whether things which do not have sense faculties can be affected by sensible forms (*On the Soul* II.12, 424b3–18). His first answer is 'no': if a smell is just a potentiality to be smelled, a color is just a potentiality for being seen, then these items cannot have any effect on what cannot perceive them. Then he changes his mind: for something smelly does make the surrounding air smelly. And yet, although the air is affected by the smell, it does not perceive it. So Aristotle then asks: *what more* is perceiving smell beside a certain affection? His answer has provoked a debate between those who wish to give a spiritual and those who wish to give a material account of taking on the sensible form. The materializers rely on the Oxford Classical text which reads: '... *ē to men osmasthai kai aisthanesthai* ...' (II.12, 424b17), which might be translated as '... or is it that there is smelling *and* awareness ...': see Richard Sorabji, 'Body and Soul in Aristotle' (pp. 69–70). Aristotle is saying, according to the materialists, that for perceiving smell there is both a physiological affection *and* an awareness of smell. Although Aristotle may believe this, it is unlikely that he is saying it here. For the first verb, *osmasthai*, itself means 'to smell' in the sense of *to perceive* smell. So it is doubtful that Aristotle would use it to mark out a physiological affection in contrast to awareness. To smell (*osmasthai*) is just one way to perceive or to be aware (*aisthanesthai*). The spiritualizers, for their part, argue that the Greek text is corrupt and the word 'and' (*kai*) ought to be deleted (Myles Burnyeat, 'Is Aristotle's Philosophy of Mind Still Credible?', and A. Kosman, 'Perceiving that We Perceive'). In most Greek manuscripts, it reads: '... *osmasthai aisthanesthai* ...'; but in one manuscript tradition a scribe wrote '*ai ai ai*' three times, and a nineteenth-century editor took the middle *ai* to be a remnant of *kai*, meaning 'and' or 'also.' The spiritualizers argue that the middle *ai* should not be there at all. Then the line might read: '... or is it that smelling is awareness ...?' But even if the spiritualizers are right about this line, even if smelling is an awareness of smell, it might still be true that this awareness makes some physical difference to the olfactory sense organ. Accepting the spiritualizer's case for this line will not itself settle the case in their favor. And even within these few lines there is reason to reject their case. For, remember, Aristotle asks *what more* there is to perceiving than a certain affection. One might well expect that the certain affection would itself have physiological ramifications even if there were also an awareness.

terms of awareness, so how is it to be understood? I suggest that it be taken quite literally. For a sense faculty to take on the sensible form is for it to become like the perceptible object with respect to sensible form. This is partially manifested by a perceptual aware-ness and it is partially manifested by the sense organ's taking on a certain *logos*, or order. Because the sensible form in the sense faculty is at a higher level of actuality than it is in the perceptible object there is no need to assume that the organ actually takes on the very same perceptible quality. Likeness in form need not con-sist in that. It is just that for any *logos* which in a rose makes it such as to look red, that very *logos* is instantiated in the eye when the person sees the red rose. For the organ not to take on the matter is just that: when seeing the rose the eye does not absorb any rosy matter. This interpretation is confirmed later in *On the Soul*, when Aristotle says that the sense faculties are potentially the sensible objects. He continues: '[The sense faculties] must be either the things themselves or their forms. The former alternative is of course impossible: it is not *the stone* which is present in the soul but its form.'[57] The rejected alternative is just what it would be for the sensible form and the matter to enter the soul: one would have somehow to take the stone as well as its perceptible form into one's soul. It is precisely because this is absurd that Aristotle insists that perception involves taking on the perceptible form alone, not the matter.

4.3 Mind[58]

Man not only has the ability to perceive the world: he distinguishes himself from all other animals by his ability to understand it. The world, for its part, is not exhausted by what it yields up to sensory perception. There is a reality which underlies sensory appearances. We may, for example, see frogs jumping around a pond; we may even touch, smell, and taste them. But these sensory experiences on their own do not tell us what froggy life is *really* like. We do not, as it were, get to the bottom of froggy life until we study frogs in detail: understand how they reproduce and feed themselves, understand the principles which are responsible for organizing

---

[57] *On the Soul* III.8, 431b27–432a1.
[58] Appropriate reading: *On the Soul* III.2–4.

froggy matter into a mature functioning frog. There is something definite that it is to be a frog, and man, alone among the animals, has the ability to inquire, on the basis of his sensory experience, what frogs are really like. The question to be addressed in this chapter is: what happens to a man — what change occurs within his soul — when he moves from a state of ignorance to a deep understanding of what the items he encounters in nature are really like?

We are not, then, interested in frogs *per se*. We are interested in the intelligibility of the world and the impact of the world's intelligibility on man. Frogs are merely an example of an item in the natural world which yields up its truth in response to man's inquiries. Intelligibility and truth are intimately bound in Aristotle's world. For what the world offers in response to inquiry is *the essence* of frog life. It is the ultimate reality of frog life — what it is to be a frog — that is ultimately intelligible. Man has the generalized ability to get to the bottom of things he encounters in the world: to find out what they are really like. It is the desire to understand that prompts man to engage in such inquiry, and it is the deep understanding of the world that satisfies that desire.

There is, then, a single activity — contemplating the world — which at once manifests the world's intelligibility and also reveals what man most truly is. If the reality which underlies the appearances did not yield itself up to man's probing inquiries, there would be no basis for thinking the world intelligible. The intelligibility of the world is its ability to be understood. Understanding, for its part, is man's capacity to grasp how things really are, not just how they immediately present themselves. And as man does come to understand the world, he comes to understand something fundamental about himself: namely, that understanding the world lies at the bottom of what he is. Man is by nature a systematic understander of the world. By rendering the world intelligible to himself, he gains a deep understanding of what he himself is really like.

Man is the only animal who can understand the things he encounters in the world. Frogs may embody the principles of froggy life, but comprehension of those froggy principles will forever escape an embodied frog. Frogs cannot penetrate to the bottom of themselves. Man is the only animal who can truly understand a frog. Man can also understand himself. Unlike his froggy neighbor, man not only embodies the principles of human life, he has the ability to understand the very principles which govern his life. Indeed, it is part of man's very nature to understand his nature. How does he do this?

Aristotle, as we have already seen, uses the different levels at which one can be said to understand to illuminate the relationship of soul to body.[59] Since we began with the study of soul, perhaps we can reverse the direction and use what we have learned about the development of soul to shed light on how man comes to understand the world and how he comes to contemplate it. Consider, for example, the various stages in the life of Kermit the frog:

(1) Kermit as an embryo
(2) Kermit the tadpole
(3) Kermit the mature frog (asleep).
(4) Kermit actively living his mature life: catching flies, jumping into the pond, looking for mates, etc.

At each of these stages, Kermit embodies the form of a frog, but at varying levels of potentiality and actuality. As an embryo, Kermit is a frog, but only as the barest of potentialities. The embryo has the capacity – given a suitable environment – to develop into something (a tadpole) which itself is capable of developing into a frog. The tadpole too is potentially a frog. But the potentiality of the tadpole to be a frog is at an altogether *higher level* than the potentiality of the mere embryo to be a frog. So at the first two stages of his career, Kermit does embody the form of a frog, but the form is a force or power in the embryo or tadpole for the acquisition of a more developed organization. By the later two stages of Kermit's life, however, form has achieved actuality. But, as we have seen, there are different levels of actuality. Soul is merely the *first-level* actuality of Kermit's living body: it is a developed capacity to live which he has even when asleep. By contrast, when he actively uses this capacity, this activity is form as a *second-level* actuality: it is the exercise of his developed capacity to live. Because form can exist at these varying levels, one can make sense of the idea that the same form is present throughout. Kermit's embryo has the capacity to become a living frog, and Kermit has the more highly developed capacity to live a fulfilling life. The active living of this life

[59] *On the Soul* II.1, 412a10, a22, II.5; cf. section 4.1 above.

is the same form as was present earlier at lower levels of actuality and potentiality.

There are, we have seen, two senses in which form may be an actuality: in one sense it is like understanding, in the other it is like contemplating. The two senses are clearly related to each other. For the man who understands is *able* to contemplate whenever he wants.[60] Contemplating is thus an activity which represents a *higher-level* actuality than the understanding whose exercise the thinking is. Therefore, one might expect a similar set of stages in Aristotle's mental development:

(i) As a young man he might be called a psychologist, because he is a human being and humans are a species capable of acquiring knowledge of the soul (*psuche*) of animals.

He is now a psychologist in virtue of possessing a *first-level* potentiality: the ability to learn about living things and their principles of life.

(ii) Having talked with his father about medicine, studied with Plato, carried out extensive biological research (including detailed observation of frogs), and written *On the Soul*, Aristotle is now a psychologist in the sense of actually having knowledge or understanding of the soul.

He is now able to think about the soul whenever he wants (just so long as there is no external interference).[61] This state too is a capacity, but it represents a *higher-level* potentiality than the capacity to acquire knowledge. He now has a developed state of his soul which he can exercise at will.[62] In virtue of his possessing this capacity we may call him an active or actual understander, but this actuality is exhausted by his ability to think when he wants.[63] Thus it is a *first-level actuality*. By contrast, consider

(iii) Aristotle actively contemplating what it is to be a frog.

This activity is the higher-level actuality of which the capacities of the two previous stages represent varying degrees of potentiality.[64]

---

[60] *On the Soul* II.5, 417a27–8; III.4, 429b5–7.
[61] *On the Soul* II.5, 417a24–8.
[62] A *hexis*: *On the Soul* II.5, 417a21–b2.
[63] *On the Soul* III.4, 429b5–9.
[64] *On the Soul* II.5, 417a28–30.

There do, therefore, seem to be corresponding stages in Kermit's physical and Aristotle's mental development. But the relationship is even more intimate than these remarks might suggest. For when Aristotle's studies lead him to the bottom of froggy life, his mind has taken on the very same form as is embodied in Kermit: frog soul. To acquire psychological knowledge about froggy life, Aristotle's mind must become frog soul. His mind must become the substance he was seeking to comprehend.

But how can Aristotle's mind become frog soul? Aristotle thought that the mind worked analogously to the sense faculty. As the sense faculty stands with respect to *perceptible* objects, thus mind stands with respect to *intelligible* objects.[65] The sense faculty is receptive of the *perceptible* forms of things without the matter, and mind is receptive of the *intelligible* forms of things without the matter.[66] It is the essences of things that are intelligible, so mind contemplates essences. When one sees a frog, the perceptive faculty receives the perceptible form; when one has studied froggy nature and is able to think about what it is to be a frog, one's mind has taken on the intelligible form.

Aristotle argues that there must be a special faculty of the mind which is able to understand form or essence. In general, Aristotle discriminates the various sensory and cognitive faculties by the different types of objects each is able to apprehend or by the different types of functions each is able to perform. Sight, for example, is distinguished from the other sense faculties by the fact that its objects are visible. Sight is simply that faculty which is able to see visible things, hearing is that faculty which is able to hear noises, smell is that faculty which is able to smell smells, etc. The same principle holds true in the higher cognitive realms. Essences themselves are a distinct type of object, Aristotle argues, so if man is able to grasp essences there ought to be a distinct faculty of the soul which enables him to do this:

> Since we can distinguish between a magnitude and what
> it is to be a magnitude, and between water and what it is
> to be water, and so in many other cases (though not in
> all: for in certain cases the thing and its form are identi-
> cal), flesh and what it is to be flesh are discriminated

[65] *On the Soul* III.4, 429b17–18.
[66] *On the Soul* II.12, 424a17–19; III.4, 429a15–16; III.8, 431b26–432a3.

either by different faculties, or by the same faculty in two different states; for flesh necessarily involves matter and is like what is snub-nosed, a *this* in *this*. Now it is by means of the sensitive faculty that we discriminate the hot and the cold, i.e. the factors which combined in a certain *logos* constitute flesh: the essential character of flesh is apprehended by something different ...[67]

Aristotle is arguing that there must be a special faculty of mind which is able to grasp essences. He calls this faculty *noûs*, though he also uses *noûs* widely to cover the faculty which engages in a wide range of thinking activities. I shall thus translate *noûs* as 'mind', though we ought to be aware that we are here concerned with the activity of man's highest cognitive faculty.[68]

Mind is able to grasp essences. But essences are the *forms* of composites of form and matter. Thus what mind understands has no material aspect at all: it grasps that which might exist in matter. Flesh, as Aristotle says, is a *'this* in *this'*: that is, it is *this* (fleshy) form embodied in *this* matter. It is because flesh is composite of form and matter that flesh differs from the essence of flesh. When mind comes to understand the essence of flesh it, as it were, lifts the form right out of its material instantiation. Now Aristotle's example might at first be confusing. For Aristotle tends to treat froggy flesh as *the matter* of a frog, while treating frog soul as a frog's essence or form. And yet we must remember that matter is a relative item.[69] Although froggy flesh will be the matter *of a frog* – it is that which is organized by the active formal principles of frog life – we must remember that this flesh is itself a composite of form and matter. Flesh is earth, air, water, and heat organized according to certain formal principles. At each level of organization it is the formal organizing principles that tell us what the flesh or what the

[67] *On the Soul* III.4, 429b10–18. (I leave *logos* untranslated, where the Oxford translation uses 'ratio.')
[68] In a similar vein Aristotle used the verbs *theorein* and *noein* widely to cover a whole range of cognitive activities, much as we use 'to think.' However, he also used the verb narrowly to designate the exercise of man's capacity for theoretical understanding: the highest activity of mind. Translators often use 'contemplating' for this activity, and I shall follow their use, at least to some extent. If the context is clear, I think it is also permissible to follow Aristotle's example and use 'to think:' but one should be aware that we are concerned with the special exercise of man's capacity to understand.
[69] See sections 2.1, 2.3, and 2.4 above.

frog is *really* like. Aristotle is insistent that at each stage the essence of the thing will be purely formal. It is only because Aristotle has identified the essences of things with their forms that it is possible to conceive of mind, when inquiring into what things are really like, as lifting forms right out of their material instantiation.

To emphasize this point Aristotle contrasts essences with the abstract objects found in mathematics.[70] It is tempting to think of a geometrical object, like a straight line, as a purely formal object, but Aristotle denies this. A straight line, Aristotle says, is like a snub (nose): a this (shape) in this (matter). A geometrical straight line, for Aristotle, is just an ordinary physical straight line (embodied, say, in the side of a door). The reason a geometrical straight line appears to be purely formal is that it is *considered* in abstraction from its material instantiation.[71] If we wish to arrive at something truly formal, we must ask *what is it to be* a straight line? Here the answer might be: the shortest distance between two points. This is the form embodied in any straight line.

Aristotle allows that there are some things which are identical with their essences.[72] One would expect these 'things' to be things without matter: for it is material objects that are conceived of as essences embodied in distinct matter. The 'things' which are identical with their essences are forms. For example, the form frog soul is identical with its own essence. Since there is no matter in the form, frog soul is just what it is to be a frog. When man in his inquiries gets to the bottom of froggy life, it is the form of a frog that his mind contemplates. This form is identical to its own essence. The question is: what happens to the human mind when it engages in such contemplating?

Aristotle approaches this question, as is his wont, through a series of difficulties about the nature of thinking or contemplating. The solutions to these difficulties will shed light on how mind works. The first problem is to explain how mind can possibly think about the world. Aristotle has already argued that, since mind is able to think *all* things, it must be completely pure and without affections: unlike the sense faculties, mind has no bodily organ, for

---

[70] *On the Soul* III.4, 429b18–20.
[71] For a fuller discussion of this, see section 6.2 below.
[72] *On the Soul* III.4, 429b12. See also *Metaphysics* VII.6 and the discussion of this chapter in section 6.6 below.

such a material realization would hinder and distort its ability to think.[73] Seeing brilliant sights disrupts the *logos* of the eye, but the thinking of brilliant thoughts improves mind's ability to think. Thus he claims that mind is *nothing actual* before thinking. Before thinking it has no nature other than to be a potentiality for thinking. But if mind is simple and unaffected, how can it possibly think about the world? For thinking is a (special type of) being affected by the world, and such an interaction between world and mind seems to require that there be something common between world and mind.[74] In general, when an agent causes some effect in a patient there is something common between agent and patient: namely, that the patient be potentially what the agent is actually. For example, the pile of wood must be potentially a house if a builder is to be able to impose the form of a house on it. Now Aristotle accepts this general principle, even for mind. Although mind is nothing actual before thinking, it is nevertheless potentially all intelligible things. But since before thinking mind is able to become the intelligible forms of things, this ability ought to have something in common with that by which it is affected – the intelligible forms of things – for it ought not to be problematic that thinking should occur.

If, however, we try to specify what this something in common is that binds man's ability to understand with the world's ability to be understood, we are led to an even greater difficulty. This difficulty is raised by asking whether mind can contemplate itself.[75] The problem is to explain how mind can think *both* about the world *and* about itself. For faculties of the soul are discriminated according to the types of thing they apprehend.[76] For example, sight is the faculty that sees colors, hearing is the faculty that hears sounds. It would seem that mind is the faculty that thinks intelligible objects. But then, if the mind is distinguished as the faculty that can apprehend *a certain type of thing,* and if mind can contemplate *both* the world *and* itself, it would seem that mind and the world must be the same sort of thing.[77] Aristotle thus poses the di-

[73] *On the Soul* III.4, 429a15–b5.
[74] *On the Soul* III.4, 429b22–6.
[75] *On the Soul* III.4, 429b26–9.
[76] *On the Soul* III.2, 426b9–12.
[77] Aristotle confronted an analogous problem when he tried to give an account of how we can be aware that we perceive (*On the Soul* III.2). If it is the sense faculty

lemma: either things in the world are themselves mental, or mind is after all mixed with physical things. It is the solution to this dilemma that begins to shed light on how mind works:

> Have not we already disposed of the difficulty about interaction involving a common element, when we said that mind is in a sense *potentially* whatever is thinkable, though *actually* it is nothing until it has thought? What it thinks must be in it just as characters may be said to be on a writing table on which as yet nothing actually stands written: this is exactly what happens with mind.
>
> *Mind itself is thinkable in exactly the same way as its objects are.* For *in the case of objects which involve no matter*, what thinks and what is thought are identical; for understanding and its object are identical. (Why mind is not always thinking we must consider later.) *In the case of those which contain matter* each of the objects of thought is only potentially present. It follows that while they will not have mind in them (for mind is a potentiality of them only in so far as they are capable of being disengaged from matter) mind may yet be thinkable.[78]

Aristotle solves his dilemma while all along insisting that mind is in no way physical. Before thinking, mind is nothing actual: it is a pure potentiality for thinking and understanding. But even in contemplating mind remains completely unmixed with the physical. Contemplating consists in mind *becoming* the objects of thought. These are the 'objects which involve no matter' or, literally, 'things without matter'; the forms or essences. Therefore, mind is thinkable just as any object of thought is thinkable. For since mind,

---

that is responsible for this awareness, then it would seem that sight can perceive both colored objects and itself. But if sense faculties are discriminated according to the type of object they apprehend, it would seem that the sense faculty of sight would itself have to be colored in order to be perceived by sight. Aristotle concludes that *in an extended sense* it is: in the act of perceiving, the faculty does take on the perceptible form of the object. And it is only in the act of perceiving that we are aware that we are perceiving. Thus the taking on of the perceptible form seems to involve reflective awareness. The very same activity which is a seeing of red is also an awareness that one is seeing red.

[78] *On the Soul* III.4, 429b29–430a7. (I translate *noûs* as 'mind' rather than as 'thought', and *epistēmē* as 'understanding' rather than as 'speculative knowledge.')

when contemplating, is *identical* to the object being contemplated, in contemplating any object at all mind must be contemplating itself. For that is all that mind, in thinking, is. Thus in all thinking mind is thinkable – indeed, mind is thought. For understanding and the object of understanding are the same.

But what about enmattered things – is mind not able to think about them? Is mind able to think about the natural world? Aristotle says that enmattered things are *potentially* intelligible, so they must stand in some relation to the 'things without matter' which are actually thought. The 'things without matter' are essences or forms, the non-material aspect of a composite of form and matter. It follows that mind – which in thinking simply is the objects of thought – does stand in some relation to the physical world; and Aristotle endorses this when he says of physical things that 'each of the objects of thought is only potentially present.' So physical things are not themselves mental, but they bear a sufficient relation to things which are mental for us not to need to think of the physical world as totally opaque to reason. But what is this relation, the relation which ensures that the natural world is at least potentially intelligible?

To begin with, physical things are the same in form as the 'things without matter' which mind, in thinking, becomes. Frog, for example, is a composite of a certain form in a certain type of matter – a *this* (form) *in this* (matter).[79] As such, frog is only potentially intelligible. Mind cannot grasp the matter which is part of the composite; but it can grasp frog soul, which is the form of frog and identical with its essence.[80] The problem is determining the content of the claim that for these 'things without matter' mind and its object are the same. At the very least they are the same form. Given that all Aristotle is here concerned with are forms – he has isolated the 'things without matter' for special treatment – one might think that there is nothing more which could be said. For the identity conditions for forms are exhausted by determining whether they are the same or different in form. And yet if form can exist at varying levels of potentiality and actuality, it seems that there must be more that can be known about the relation of mind and its object

[79] See also *Metaphysics* VII.10, 1035b27–30.
[80] See also *Metaphysics* VII.11, 1037a5–7, a27–30, a33–b4; and cf. 6, 1031a28–b14, a18–21, 1032a4–6.

than that they are the same form. Kermit's embryo and the mature Kermit have the same form, but Aristotle does not end the story there. He develops a theory of levels of potentiality and actuality which makes it plausible that the young and the mature Kermit embody the very same form.

But what about the frog soul which Aristotle's mind has become when he has understood what it is to be a frog? In what relation does this frog soul stand to the frog soul embodied in frogs like Kermit? Further, what is the relation between the frog soul which Aristotle's mind has become when he has gotten to the bottom of froggy life and the frog soul which his mind is when he is actively contemplating what it is to be a frog?

One way to sharpen this question is to ask whether there is any relation between stages (1)–(4) of Kermit's physical development and stages (I)–(III) of Aristotle's mental development. Each set of stages may be ranked in terms of ascending levels of potentiality and actuality, but can one similarly rank frog soul as the form of Kermit in relation to frog soul as the form of Aristotle's mind? The question I am asking concerns the relation between the soul which mind becomes in thinking about what it is to be a frog, and the soul which is the object of thought. There ought to be an answer to this question, for the presence of frog soul in Aristotle's mind is the outcome of his various interactions with frog soul in the world: the frogs he has observed living their lives, the instruction he has received in psychology and zoology (from instructors whose minds had already become frog soul), etc. Aristotle, like other humans, was born with a bare capacity to understand, and he depends on interaction with forms found in the world if he is to understand them. If one knows how to characterize this interaction, one ought to be able to rank frog soul as mind in relation to frog soul as the form of a living body.

Let me mention two models of this interaction which yield different relations of mind to world. First, there is the model of *natural reproduction*. A human couple are able, conjointly, to pass on human soul to their offspring. One might think of human mind becoming frog soul as the outcome of an extended process of reproduction. The frog soul which human mind becomes would then exist at the same level of actuality as the frog soul of a living froggy body. The activity which is Aristotle actively contemplating what it is to be a frog would be frog soul existing at the same level of actuality as Kermit actively living his life. There are of course disanalogies with reproduction. Aristotle's mind cannot go on to produce a tadpole. But Aristotle can teach others about the principles of froggy life, thus producing frog soul in their minds.

Second, there is the model of *artistic creation*. This is the inverse of the process by which a craftsman imposes the form in his soul on material in the world: the forms in the world impose themselves on our minds. Though coming to be an active understander or knower is not a typical case of being affected, it is sufficiently similar to be considered a special type: being affected by that which is intelligible in the world.[81] And though this special type of change lacks a special name, Aristotle compares the transition to the builder who begins actively building.[82] The builder, as we have already seen, has the form of a house in his soul.[83] It is a 'thing without matter,' the possession of which in the soul enables the builder to impose the form on suitable material. The builder's art exists for the sake of the building, rather than vice versa, and this active building is substantially prior to the builder's art.[84] The active building occurs because the builder has the form in his soul, but the activity of building is not something other than the form; it is the form at a higher level of actuality: an activity occurring in the house being built.[85] The building is an activity which is occurring because of the form (in virtue of the form within the builder's soul), is for the sake of the form (a house), and is the form. The active understander, like the builder, is able to move from having his knowledge to exercising it, but unlike the builder's, the active understander's activity occurs within him.[86] There is clearly a transition from the possession of the understanding, which is a condition of the soul, to its exercise. And this may be how we can grasp what it is for the form in the mind to move to a higher-level actuality.

The analogy which Aristotle draws between contemplation and

---

[81] *On the Soul* III.4, 429a13–15, b24–6; II.5, 417b7, b14–15. See the discussion in section 4.2 above.

[82] *On the Soul* II.5, 417b7–12, b14–16; III.4, 429a14–15, b24–6, b29–30.

[83] *Metaphysics* VII.7, 1032a32–b2, b12–14.

[84] *Metaphysics* IX.8, 1050a4–12.

[85] *Metaphysics* IX.8, 1050a25–34; *Physics* III.3. See sections 2.3 and 3.2 above.

[86] *Metaphysics* IX.8, 1050a28–b1.

perception supports the creation model. Thinking, like perceiving, is a special type of suffering, in this case by the intelligible rather than the perceptible.[87] Indeed, Aristotle sometimes compares the understander actively contemplating to sight seeing a color.[88] And, as we have already seen, Aristotle says that mind stands in a relation to its objects analogous to that in which the perceptive faculty stands to the objects of perception.[89] The activity of the perceptible and the activity of the sense faculty are one and the same, though the accounts one would give of the two differ.[90] That activity, as accords with Aristotle's general principles of change and creation, occurs in the sense faculty. Thus the perceptible and the perceptive faculty stand to each other as two potentialities which have a single actualization. The actualization of these potentialities is the actual receiving of the perceptible form without the matter. As we have seen, corresponding to the 'subjective' potentiality which is the sense faculty, there is an 'objective' potentiality which is what we think of as the perceptible form of an object.

If the analogy between thinking and perceiving is to hold, one would expect there to be a single activity – contemplating – which is the joint product of two distinct potentialities: mind on the one hand, and the forms or essences of things on the other. Of course the analogy cannot be exact, for perception requires the presence of an external perceptible object on each occasion of perception, whereas an active understander can think whenever he chooses.[91] Yet one might envision a two-step process. First, in actively studying froggy life one finally comes to understand what it is to be human: this activity is the mind taking on the intelligible form. This first step does require an external object: form as it is embodied in frogs out in the world. Having come to understand human life, the mind of the thinker acquires a stable condition (a *hexis*) such that he is now *able* to think about the principles of frog life whenever he wants. This condition of the (human) mind is frog soul at a lower-level actuality than it exists when the thinker is actively contemplating what it is to be a frog.[92] It is in virtue of this

[87] *On the Soul* III.4, 429a13–14.
[88] *Metaphysics* XIII.10, 1087a19–21.
[89] *On the Soul* III.4, 429a17–18; cf. II.5, 417b18–19.
[90] *On the Soul* III.2, 425b26–7.
[91] *On the Soul* II.5, 417b19–28.
[92] *On the Soul* III.4, 429b5–7.

developed ability to think that he is an actual or active understand-er.[93] The mind of the actual understander has become each of the things it can contemplate, but before thinking it remains potential. So the actual understander differs from the potential understander in virtue of the type and level of potentiality he has. The actual understander's potentiality is the understanding – the *epistēmē* – he has. Second, whenever the understander again wants to think about frog life, the form of frog in his mind undergoes a transition from (what in the mind is) a first-level actuality to a second-level actuality.

However, the high-level actuality which is frog soul actively being contemplated must be an even higher actuality than the high-level actuality of frogs actively living their lives. For it is from studying the active lives of frogs (as well as the developmental and quiescent periods) that one comes to understand froggy life. The intelligible form which mind actually thinks or becomes represents a higher-level actuality than the form to which mind, before think-ing, is receptive. The activity of frogs living their lives is an actu-ality of frog form; but, from the (higher) perspective of mind, frog form as it is embodied in active frog life is a potentiality for being understood. And understanding frog life is itself a potentiality for the active contemplating of what it is to be a frog. If thinking is to be understood on the model of creation, as I believe it is, then the active thinking of what it is to be frog is frog soul at a *higher* level of actuality than it exists as the activity of a living frog body. Aris-totle's mind, when he is actively thinking about frog life, is frog soul at a higher level of activity than it is as the form of Kermit's body when he is actively living his life.

Generally speaking, the forms or essences embodied in physical objects and natural organisms must exist at a lower level of actu-ality than the same forms or essences as they exist in a mind which is actively contemplating them. This may at first seem odd, for the essence of a natural object is an actuality, the actuality of that object. However, the essence of a natural object can also be con-sidered under a different aspect: it is that aspect of the object which is intelligible. Essence gives us not only the reality – what it is to be that thing; it also gives us what is intelligible about that thing. We must therefore treat the enmattered essence as a *first-level* actual-

---

[93] *ho epistēmōn ho kat' energeian: On the Soul* III.4, 429b6.

ity. The intelligible form to which mind is receptive is the essence of the thing, which mind is able to think. The intelligible form which mind, in thinking, becomes is a second-level actuality.[94]

The single actualization which from the 'subjective' perspective is mind actively contemplating is less easy to describe from the 'objective' perspective. One could characterize it as the intelligible form of an object rising from a first- to a second-level actuality, but the transition is still being described by implicit reference to the intellect. The problem is that 'essence,' at least when used to refer to physically instantiated essences, is not something we comfortably describe as *rising* from a physical first-level actuality to a mental second-level actuality. In this respect, 'essence' bears at least some resemblance to a 'potentiality word' like 'color.' Remember that 'color' can only be used to refer to the potentiality for being seen which resides in the object; there is no word in the vocabulary of color which captures the actualization of this potentiality – though the actualization can be described from the 'subjective' perspective as 'seeing.'[95] Similarly, although 'essence' is the actuality of the object, it strains the vocabulary of 'essence' to speak of the activity of thinking as a higher actualization *of essence*. Perhaps the best Aristotle could do was to call essences 'things without matter.' Things with matter, like frogs, are intelligible – thus they are not totally opaque to reason – but as enmattered their intelligibility is only a potentiality. That which mind grasps, and in grasping is, are the things without matter. These are essences. But it is precisely because the essences are things without matter that they are capable of rising to a mental second-level actuality. And it is because 'things without matter' can rise that the physical world is potentially intelligible. The mental second-level actuality has both a 'subjective' and an 'objective' aspect: subjectively speaking, it is mind actively contemplating; objectively speaking, it is an essence, a form, or a thing without matter. The first-level actuality, by contrast, has only an objective aspect: the physically instantiated essence.

But it is the essence or form of a physical object that is intelli-

[94] Since mind is receptive of the intelligible forms of things, it is tempting to identify the intelligible forms as the second-level actuality of which the embodied essence is the first-level counterpart. But in fact 'intelligible form,' like 'perceptible form,' can be used to refer to both first- and second-level actualities.

[95] See *On the Soul* III.2, 426a11–15, and section 4.2 above.

gible. So the form which is, from one perspective, the actuality of the object is, from another perspective, a potentiality which is actualized in active contemplating. *The active contemplating of that form is the form itself at its highest level of actuality.* An embodied form might thus be conceived as striving to be understood. Of course, from an 'objective' perspective an embodied form is not doing anything more than being the form of that object. The form of a frog, for example, is not doing anything more than being the inner principle which directs the frog's growth and characteristic activity. However, by engaging in such a froggy life, the frog is doing all it can do to be understood. And when Aristotle in his biological studies comes to understand what it is to be a frog, his mind takes on the form of frog. There is no doubt but that Aristotle thought that he had such experiences: that he was capable of understanding animal life. Thus he must have had a conception of *what it is like* for his mind to take on the frog form. Phenomenologically speaking, it must seem that one has understood the principles of frog life. However, this very same experience can also be described as the *self*-understanding of *the frog form*! For in active thinking there is no difference between mind and object: mind simply is the form it is thinking. So the mind that is actively thinking what it is to be a frog is, otherwise described, frog form thinking itself. And, in general, a form which has reached the level of actuality where it is mind thinking the form has achieved self-understanding. All embodied forms are thus potentialities for their own self-understanding. Aristotelian essences, one might say, are a force for their own self-understanding. The achieved self-understanding is the form itself in a disembodied state.

We moderns tend to think that mind must be distinct from its objects. When we apply a locution like 'the understanding of ...' to a subject-matter *S*, we think that the outcome, 'the understanding of *S*,' cannot be identical with *S* itself. But in Aristotle's world, when *S* is an essence or form, the understanding of *S* is just *S* itself at its highest level of actuality.

Aristotle knew that thinking involves reflective awareness. Just as when we perceive we are aware that we perceive, so when we contemplate we are aware that we are contemplating.[96] This reflective awareness does not require a separate mental faculty which

[96] See *Nicomachean Ethics* x.9, 1170a29–b1; and cf. *On the Soul* III.2 and 4.

has mind actively thinking as its object. The reflective awareness that one is contemplating is itself part of mind actively contemplating. Thus, as Aristotle says, mind is thinkable just as the object of thought is thinkable.[97] For in thinking an object of thought one is also aware that one is thinking, and both the thinking of the object and the awareness that one is thinking are none other than the object of thought itself at its highest level of activity.

There is, however, one exception to the claim that contemplating form is always form at a higher-level actuality than is found in the natural world. The exception is found when a human being contemplates what it is to be human. Let us first consider the following transitions in Aristotle's own development:

> (1*) Aristotle's embryo has human soul as a (first-level) potentiality. The embryo has the capacity to develop into a human being.
> (2*) The embryo having developed into a human being, soul is substance in the sense of being the form of Aristotle's physical body potentially having life.

Aristotle's soul is the first-level actuality of his living body. By contrast, the actualization of this capacity is

> (3*) Aristotle actively living his life: engaging in research, arguing with Plato, thinking about what it is to be a frog, thinking about what it is to be a human being, etc., teaching Alexander, giving orders to his slaves: actively living the life of which he is capable.

Now stage (3*) represents human soul at its highest level of actuality. It is not merely a potentiality to be understood. For understanding what it is to be a human being is itself a part of Aristotle's active life. To see this, let us consider the corresponding stages in Aristotle's mental development:

> (I*) As a young man we may call him a psychologist, because he is a human being and humans are a species capable of acquiring knowledge of the soul (*psuchē*) of animals.
> (II*) Having talked with his father about medicine, studied with Plato, carried out extensive biological research

[97] *On the Soul* III.4, 430a2–3.

(including detailed observation of humans), and written *On the Soul*, the *Nicomachean Ethics*, etc., Aristotle is now a psychologist in the sense of actually having knowledge or understanding of the soul.

(III*) Aristotle actively contemplating what it is to be human.

At stage (III*) Aristotle's mind must be human soul at the highest-level actuality. And yet this human soul realized at stage (III*) cannot be a higher level of human soul than is manifested in Aristotle actively living his life (stage 3*). For stage (III*) is an ingredient in stage (3*): Aristotle actively contemplating what it is to be human is itself an active part of Aristotle's active life. However, although contemplating human soul may itself be an expression of an active human life, it need not be. Let us consider the successful, active, but on the whole non-contemplative, general Nicias at the height of his career.

(III**) Nicias actively leading his army, engaging in strategic debate, etc.

Nicias leads an active, successful, rich human life. But because his life is relatively devoid of contemplation – in particular, of contemplation of what it is to be human – Nicias' life is an embodiment of human soul at a lower level of actuality than is found in the mind actively contemplating human soul. Since the mind actively contemplating human soul (and thus being human soul) is itself an ingredient of the human soul of the person who understands and actively contemplates the human condition, this would suggest that the person who has come to understand human soul is himself an embodiment of human soul at an altogether higher level of actuality than the person who has led a successful but non-contemplative human life. The active contemplating of human soul is a higher-level activity of human soul than the other activities of living a human life. Purely physical considerations of the interaction of mind and world would suggest that contemplating is a higher form of activity than the non-contemplative active living of a human life.[98]

And so it should be: for man is by nature a systematic

---

[98] See *Nicomachean Ethics* x.7, 1177b26–1178a8. I shall discuss this in detail in section 6.8 below.

understander of the world. In the non-contemplative life, the innate desire to understand never gets fully satisfied. But when man does turn his attention onto himself, when he gets to the bottom of human life, he learns that he is a being whose nature it is to transcend his own nature, at least in the following sense. Man is the only being in the natural world for whom the highest expression of its form may be found within that being itself. The highest form of a frog will not be found in a frog, for frogs are incapable of understanding themselves. But the highest level of human soul will be found in the mind of the person who is actively contemplating the essence of human life. Indeed, the highest-level actuality of *any* form found embodied in the natural world will be that form actively being thought by a mind which understands it.

Since man is by nature a systematic understander of the world, when he comes to understand his own role as a systematic understander, he must realize that within the natural world he is the highest repository of forms found in the natural world. As man comes to understand the world, his mind comes to mirror it: that is, it becomes the forms which, through his inquiries, he has come to understand. But we should not think of this 'mirroring' of the world as a *mere* reflection of it. For although man must first encounter the forms in the world before his mind is able to become them, the forms found in his mind are at an altogether higher level of reality than the forms he has encountered. Mind is not just a repository of forms, it is the highest expression of the forms themselves.

However, if man is a *systematic* understander of the world, there remains a question about how the world makes systematic understanding of itself possible. The forms found embodied in natural objects are, as we have seen, potentially intelligible. But if man is to come to a systematic understanding of the world, he must do more than apprehend the separate forms as though they were discrete atoms of intelligibility. To be a systematic understander, he must come to see the world as forming an intelligible whole. And for this to be possible, the world itself must constitute an intelligible whole. The question then arises: is there any reason why the world constitutes a systematically intelligible whole? Aristotle will not be able to answer this until he considers the relation of the natural world to God. But it is worth noting that the issue has already arisen when man comes to understand himself as a systematic understander of the world and wonders what success he may achieve in fulfilling his nature.

4.4 Active mind[99]

Aristotle did not believe that contemplating could be accounted for solely in terms of the ability of mind to receive the intelligible forms and the intelligibility of informed objects. In the story told so far, there is too much potentiality around to explain how active contemplating occurs. There is the potentiality for contemplating and the potentiality for being understood, but how can one get an actuality, active thinking, from these two potentialities alone? One cannot. Aristotle believed that actuality was both ontologically and temporally prior to potentiality.[100] There may be processes in the natural world in which a potentiality develops into an actuality, but the very existence of this potentiality must be grounded in a prior actuality. For example, the soul of an embryo is a potentiality for growth and development, but its existence is dependent upon the active, actual form of the male parent who passed on the form as a potentiality in his seed.[101] But what in the case of mind can serve as the prior actuality? It cannot be form as it is found instantiated in physical objects: for no matter how active and developed a physical thing is, its form must, from the perspective of mind, remain a potentiality. Nor can the prior actuality be mind, at least mind as it has been characterized so far: for being thinking mind is *nothing actual*; it exists as a bare potentiality for thinking. Thus if there is to be a prior actuality, it must be something other than we have encountered so far. Form at the highest level of actuality must somehow be responsible.

Aristotle offers us his answer in *On the Soul* III.5 – a chapter which is so fraught with problems of interpretation, that it is worth quoting in full:

> Since in every class of things, as in nature as a whole, we find two factors involved, a matter which is potentially all the particulars included in the class, a cause which is

[99] Appropriate reading: *On the Soul* III.5.
[100] *Metaphysics* IX.8.
[101] *Metaphysics* VII.7, 1032a24ff.

productive in the sense that it makes them all (the latter standing to the former, as e.g. an art to its material), these distinct elements must likewise be found within the soul.

And in fact mind, as we have described it, is what it is by virtue of becoming all things, while there is another which is what it is by virtue of making all things: this is a sort of positive state like light; for in a sense light makes potential colors into actual colors.

Mind in this sense of it is separable, impassible, unmixed, since it is in its essential nature activity (for always the active is superior to the passive factor, the originating force to the matter).

Actual knowledge is identical with its object: in the individual, potential knowledge is in time prior to actual knowledge, but absolutely it is not prior even in time. It does not sometimes think and sometimes not think. When separated it is alone just what it is, and this alone is immortal and eternal (we do not remember because, while this is impassible, passive mind is perishable); and without this nothing thinks.[102]

Aristotle seems to be introducing another mind to explain how our minds come to be thinking. Generations of interpreters have called this Active Mind (*noûs poiētikos*) (though Aristotle himself never uses this expression) to distinguish it from Passive Mind (*noûs pathētikos*). Passive Mind, it seems clear, is the mind we have already described: it is our ability to receive the intelligible forms of things. But what, then, is Active Mind? What is the mind which 'makes' all things? The wrong way to begin, I think, is to assume that Aristotle is describing two distinct faculties of the soul, Active Mind and Passive Mind. One is then forced to consider the relation between them. One might begin instead by querying Aristotle's very first contention. Just because we find the distinction between matter and cause in nature, why should it follow that we find this distinction in the soul? After all, the soul is the form of the living body, the body is the matter: why should there, how could there, be a distinction between matter and cause within the form itself?

---

[102] *On the Soul* III.5. (I translate *noûs* as 'mind.' The revised Oxford translation translates *monon* in the last quoted sentence as 'above' rather than as 'alone.')

The distinction that we have found to exist within form is between levels of potentiality and actuality. This would suggest that the distinction to be found in the soul is not between different faculties, somehow related to each other, but between levels of actuality. If this is so, then Active Mind is active mind (that is, *noûs poiētikos* is none other than *noûs energeiai*).

Active Mind makes all things: that is, it makes all things intelligible. This 'making' is not to be understood as Active Mind engaging in some type of productive activity. The 'making' is explicable in terms of the causal responsibility of form at the highest level of actuality for form at lower levels of actuality and potentiality. If form as it exists in a natural object, even a mature organism or well-formed object, is not form at the highest level of actuality, it cannot simply be accepted as basic. It must in some way be dependent on form at the highest level. But form as it exists in a natural object is, from the perspective of mind, no more than a potentiality to be understood. In being actively understood the form rises to its highest-level actuality: it now is mind thinking the form. One should expect, then, that form as it is found in the natural world must be somehow dependent on mind. For mind, when actively thinking, is none other than the highest activity of form. Ultimately, as we shall see, another way to describe this active thinking is to call it 'God.' The 'making' of Active Mind can be understood in terms of God's causal influence on the world.

But Aristotle's God does not engage in any kind of productive activity. The world is not His artefact. One analogy used to elucidate the claim that Active Mind makes all things is the relationship between art and matter. It is this analogy that most tempts us to conceive of Active Mind as engaging in productive activity. For there is no better example of producing than the craftsman imposing his craft on unformed matter. However, the analogous relationship is not that between a *craftsman* and *unformed* matter, but between art and matter. Art just is the form as it exists as an actuality in the craftsman's soul, the form which is responsible for form's existing in artefacts: 'From art proceed the things of which the form is in the soul. By form I mean the essence of each thing and its primary substance.'[103] The form of each thing seems to be that which Aristotle isolates as *primary* substance: it is that in virtue of

[103] *Metaphysics* VII.7, 1032a32–b2.

which the artefact is the artefact that it is. But the form which is primarily responsible is not the enmattered form of the artefact, but the form as it exists in the craftsman's soul. In a certain sense, Aristotle says, a house comes to be from a house, the 'thing having matter' comes to be from the 'thing without matter,' for the builder has the form of the house in his soul.[104] This form or essence in the soul Aristotle calls 'substance without matter.'[105] The matter is that which is capable of receiving the form. So the relation of art to matter is just the relation of (actual) form to (potential) form. Now our minds are capable of receiving the intelligible forms of things, but before they do they are nothing actual. This bare potentiality to receive the form invites the metaphor of matter to describe it. Of course there is nothing genuinely material about the mind – when it has received the form it is pure form – but its receptivity to form and its original complete absence of actual form invite the vocabulary of matter to describe it.

Aristotle also uses light to elucidate Active Mind's way of 'making.' Light does not engage in any productive activity; it is a condition (hexis) of the transparent medium. Indeed, it is the transparent's actualized state. Now colors are only movers of the actualized transparent: so light is the condition in which colors can be actual movers. In that sense, 'light makes things that are potentially colored actually colored.' Of course, to be an actual color is still to remain in a state of potentiality: the fullest actualization does not have a name in the objective vocabulary of 'color,' but can be referred to subjectively as seeing (horasis). If the analogy is to hold, Active Mind must be a condition of a 'transparent medium' which allows the intelligible forms of things actually to make an impression on inquiring minds. Natural organisms which are, from the point of view of nature, trying to realize their forms are, from the point of view of mind, trying to become intelligible. But unless there were some further cause of our coming to understand these forms, they would be like colors in the dark. For we are beings who can come to contemplate forms only after a journey through the world in which we encounter and experience forms embodied in composites of form and matter. With an ignorant individual and a physically embodied form, there remains too much

[104] *Metaphysics* VII.7, 1032b11–14.
[105] *Metaphysics* VII.7, 1032b14.

potentiality around to explain how the person comes to be actively contemplating. For the mind we are born with is a bare capacity to think, and enmattered things are only potentially intelligible. A prior and present actuality is needed. That is why the distinction between cause and matter must be found within soul, given that it is found within nature. Our coming to understand the world is based on our interaction with nature, an interaction which occurs according to basic natural principles of causal interaction. But there is no way to explain this interaction on the basis of our (passive) mind and physically embodied form alone. Active Mind is the prior actuality needed to explain how thinking occurs in the individual.

But what is the transparent medium? Since the distinction between Active Mind and passive mind is one that occurs within the soul, the transparent ought to be a condition of the soul, a heightened state, that makes it especially susceptible to the influence of forms found embodied in nature. Toward the end of *On the Soul*, Aristotle describes the transmission of the shape and color of an object through the transparent medium as like an impression in wax being transmitted all the way through the wax.[106] The visible object is, as it were, located at one end of the wax, the eye is located at the other. The wax takes on the 'impression' of the form and transmits it all the way through from object to eye. Here the metaphor of a wax tablet is being used to describe the transparent medium, whereas before it was used to describe the sense faculty's or mind's receptivity to form. I suspect that this dual use of the metaphor allowed Aristotle to conceive of the transparent as mind in a heightened state: for example, the mind in a state of active inquiry, ready to be influenced by that which is intelligible in the world. Light is a condition (*hexis*) of the transparent medium. Aristotle occasionally used *hexis* as a synonym for 'form.'[107] Both are positive states which stand opposed to privation. Although light is a condition of the transparent, in that condition the transparent is saturated with (visible) forms. And when a person actually learns a subject like biology or geometry, his mind assumes a certain con-

[106] *On the Soul* III.12, 435a5–10.
[107] Here I am indebted to R. D. Hicks, *Aristotle, De Anima*, p. 501. Among the references he cites are *Metaphysics* XII, 1070a11, 1069b34, 1070b11; VIII, 1044b32.

dition, the condition in virtue of which he is an actual knower. This condition simply is the mind having become the relevant forms. The condition is the form. Thus I think we should think of the mental transparent as mind in a state of active readiness and inquiry, the state in which intelligible forms can make an impression on it.

However, when we move from having learned biology to actively contemplating soul, the form or soul which our mind has become rises to its highest-level actuality. It is not easy for Aristotle to distinguish 'this' active mind from any other mind actively contemplating – or being – that form. Indeed, it is not easy for him to distinguish it from Active Mind itself. For Aristotle standardly differentiates things by form or by matter or by both. But mind has no material instantiation, and once the mind is actively thinking a form it should be identical (in form) to all other minds which are thinking that form. There is, it would seem, only one active mind and that is Active Mind. Of course, Aristotle could fashion criteria for distinguishing 'my active mind' from yours and for distinguishing our active minds from Active Mind. You and I have no doubt had different routes (of perceptual experience, teaching, etc.) by which we came to be able to contemplate essences. And although our minds are completely immaterial, they seem to have *some* relation to matter: the consciousness which at times is contemplating forms is at other times having perceptual experiences, and these are tied down to our bodies. Active Mind can be distinguished from our minds by its causal relation to our minds: because form exists antecedently as Active Mind we are able to understand the forms we encounter in the world. Yet if we abstract from the causal dependencies and routes of learning and concentrate solely on the active thinkings of a certain form by your mind, my mind and Active Mind, there would seem to be no difference between them. When I actively contemplate an essence, my contemplating has no particularity at all. I leave behind the concrete circumstances in which my body is located; I even leave behind the causal history that enabled me to think this form. The active thinking would seem to be occurring at no location at all. Aristotle says that mind is a divine element in man, and I think that we should take him literally.

Even if Active Mind helps to explain how we come to be contemplating, there remains a question of why we ever stop. Active Mind is not at some times contemplating, at other times not. It would seem that Active Mind is always lighting up the world; why then are we not always contemplating? Aristotle does not have much to say on the subject, but I think his answer is that we are not God; we are human beings. Part of what it is to be human is, paradoxically enough, to have a non-human element in us: mind, which is divine. However, the life of active thinking, the life of active mind, is a life we can live for only short periods of time. And when we die, of course, our ability to contemplate goes with us, and thus Aristotle can say that 'passive mind is perishable.'

4.5 Mind in action[108]

Man, says Aristotle, is a principle or source of actions.[109] Things do not just happen to man, he is capable of doing things. Human action is as mysterious as it is commonplace. On the one hand, our lives are permeated with our activities: we have no conception of what it is to live except in a life saturated with action; on the other hand, human action is a very special type of event. Only some of the arm-risings that occur in the world are arm-raisings. What more has to occur in the world beyond an arm-rising for it to be an arm-raising? There does not seem to be any difference in the physical motion of the arm itself. It would seem natural, then, to look to the causal antecedents of the motion. An arm-raising is distinguished from a mere arm-rising by the fact that it flows from man as a source. In his actions man distinguishes himself from soulless nature. So it seems that we must look to the soul to find out how man does the things he does.

Human action is a species of animal movement. All animal movement, Aristotle argues, must flow from desire. Lesser animals have basic appetites as well as sense perception, and imagination based on their sensory awareness. But their movements would be incomprehensible on the basis of sensation and imagination alone. The mere seeing of food cannot provoke an animal to move toward it. There must be something which moves animals to move,

---

[108] Appropriate reading: *On the Soul* III.9–13; *Nicomachean Ethics* III.1–5; VI; *On the Movement of Animals* VI–VII.
[109] *Nicomachean Ethics* III.3, 1112b32.

and this motive force is desire. Desire and animal movement have a similar structure: desire is desire for an object which the animal is lacking, and animal movement is directed toward the object of desire. It is in animal movement that desire finds tangible expression. One might think of animal movement as desire in action.

Humans distinguish themselves from other animals by their ability to think and by the fact that in addition to the appetites they have more sophisticated desires – for example, the desire to understand. Human action cannot be understood merely as an attempt to satisfy basic appetites. But once one admits that man has 'higher-order' as well as 'lower-order' desires, that he is able to think about what he wants and how to obtain it, that his actions are often the outcome of complex cognitive processes, it becomes much more difficult to see how action results. Aristotle distinguishes different faculties of the soul by their different functions – and yet desire seems to cut right across the various 'parts' of man's soul.[110] For, as Aristotle says, we find wishes in the part of the soul which reasons about how to act, and we find desires in the 'irrational' part of the soul: for example, the basic appetites for food and sex.[111] However, if the basis for distinguishing parts of the soul is by the function of each part, but the source of movement seems to be located in both the rational and the irrational parts, what reason is there for thinking that the soul has parts at all? It seems that either Aristotle must give up the idea that the soul has parts, or he must find a way of conceiving the source of movement to be a single part of the soul. He chooses the latter option. There appear, he says, to be two sources of movement, practical mind and appetite.[112] Practical mind differs from theoretical mind in that it is concerned with considering how a desire can be satisfied. It is that part of the mind with which an agent considers what he

[110] On the Soul III.9–10. (I regret to report that both the new and the old Oxford translations are misleading in these chapters. I shall try to explain the problem for those who do not know Greek. Basically, the translator uses 'appetite' as a translation both for a word that is standardly translated as 'appetite' (epithumia) and for a word that is standardly translated as 'desire' (orexis). Thus the translation makes it look as though appetites cut right across the parts of man's soul. This is not Aristotle's point. Aristotle recognizes that there are many different sorts of desire: there are basic appetites for food and sex, there are also 'higher-order' desires for understanding, for virtue, etc. It is desire, not appetite, that cuts across the parts of man's soul.)

[111] On the Soul III.9, 432b5–6.

[112] On the Soul III.10, 433a9–30. (Here he does mean appetite.)

should do. Aristotle locates both practical mind and appetite within a single faculty of the soul responsible for movement: the desiring part of the soul.[113] For, although a desire which finds explicit expression in a mental process may appear very different from an unconsidered innate drive toward food, both have a similar structure: both are motivating forces for the achievement of an (as yet) unattained goal through action.

If the desiring part of the soul is a single faculty which contains both a mental part (practical mind) and an a-rational part (the basic appetites) one wants to know how these disparate parts fit together. And if practical mind is to be subsumed under the desiring part of the soul, we ought to be able to conceive of this mind as an expression of desire. How does practical mind work? It does not seem odd to suppose that we can employ our ability to reason *in the service of* satisfying our desires, but it does at least initially seem odd to suppose that reason is itself an element in the desiring part of the soul: *that reason itself motivates us to action*. To see how reason can motivate, one must look to Aristotle's theory of deliberated choice *(prohairesis)*.[114] 'Choice' and 'decision' are often used as translations for Aristotle's concept of *prohairesis*, but these translations suppress the fact that at least in the paradigm case one makes a *prohairesis* only *after* a process of deliberation.[115]

Aristotle's theory of deliberation *(bouleusis)* is a theory of the transmission of desire. The agent begins with a desire or wish *(boulēsis)* for an object.[116] The object of wish appears to be a good to the agent. But the appearance helps to constitute the wish itself. So a wish is something which both has motivating force – an agent is motivated to obtain an object of wish – and is a part of consciousness. That is, an agent's awareness that he wishes for a certain end is itself a manifestation of that wish. The wish motivates the agent to engage in a process of deliberation whereby he considers how to

---

[113] *to orektikon*: *On the Soul* III.10, 433a21. (The Oxford translation wrongly calls this part of the soul 'the faculty of appetite.' Aristotle's point is that both appetite and practical mind – though they appear so disparate – should be conceived of as contained in a single desiring part of the soul: for both practical mind and appetite are motivating forces, and Aristotle believes that all motivating forces within an animal are species of desire.)

[114] *Nicomachean Ethics* III.2–4.

[115] *Nicomachean Ethics* III.2, 1112a15; III.3, 1113a2–7.

[116] *Nicomachean Ethics* III.4.

obtain his desired goal. Aristotle describes deliberation as a process of reasoning backward from the desired goal, through a series of steps which could best lead to that goal, until the agent reaches an action which he is or will be in a position to perform.[117] One description Aristotle gives of this process is the reasoning a doctor engages in when he is considering how to cure a patient:

> ...health is the *logos* and the knowledge in the soul. The healthy subject, then, is produced as the result of the following train of thought; since *this* is health, if the subject is to be healthy *this* must first be present, e.g. a uniform state of the body, and if this is to be present, there must be heat; and the physician goes on thinking thus until he brings the matter to a final step which he himself can take. Then the process from this point onward, i.e. the process towards health, is called a 'making.'[118]

Aristotle makes an analogy between this process of reasoning and the method of analysis in Greek geometry.[119] Ancient Greek geometrical practice comprised two methods, analysis and synthesis, of which we are much more familiar with synthesis. In a synthesis, a complex geometrical figure is constructed from simple elements by iterations of basic constructions: for example, the drawing of a line between two points or the drawing of a circle of a certain radius around a fixed center point. Most of the proofs in Euclid's *Elements* are examples of synthesis. Analysis was designed to help one get to a position in which one could begin a synthesis. One begins an analysis with the finished product: a complex geometrical figure which one would like to be able to construct in a stepwise, rigorous fashion. One then breaks the figure down in a series of orderly steps. At each stage one resolves or analyzes the figure into the immediately more simple figures which constitute it. One continues this stepwise analysis until one reaches the basic constructions which a geometer is allowed to make. An analysis is therefore a deconstruction, and once it is complete one can simply

---

[117] See *Nicomachean Ethics* III.3; VII.3; *Metaphysics* VII.7; *On the Movement of Animals* VII.

[118] *Metaphysics* VII.7, 1032b5–10. See also *Parts of Animals* I.1, and the discussion of hypothetical necessity in section 2.4 above. (I leave *logos* untranslated; the Oxford translation uses 'formula.')

[119] *Nicomachean Ethics* III.3, 1112b20–4.

reverse direction in order to carry out a synthesis. Similarly with deliberation and action. The deliberation starts with the desired goal and analyzes it into a series of steps which lead from the goal right back to the deliberating agent. Once the deliberation is complete the agent can begin the 'synthesis': he can begin acting so as to attain his desired goal.

Often the deliberation will culminate in a decision to act in a certain way. For example, the doctor may decide to warm the patient by wrapping him in blankets. This deliberated decision is a *prohairesis*. Suppose that the doctor is also aware that he has blankets in his nearby closet. Then, as Aristotle would say, *straightaway* he will move toward the closet. Aristotle represented an action as being the conclusion of a piece of practical reason. The idea is that once one has decided to act in a certain way and believes that one's current circumstances allow one to act in that way, nothing more is needed to explain the occurrence of the action. A deliberated decision is therefore the last step the mind takes before it extends itself outward into action:

> The same thing is deliberated upon and chosen except that the object of deliberated choice is already determinate, since it is that which has been decided upon as a result of deliberation that is the object of deliberated choice. For everyone ceases to inquire how he is to act when he has brought the moving principle back to himself and to the ruling part of himself; for this is what chooses.[120]

Deliberation is not merely an intellectual process by which an agent realizes how to act; it is a transmitter of desire. The doctor begins both with medical knowledge and with a desire to cure his patient. As Aristotle points out, a doctor who has medical knowledge alone need not cure anybody.[121] The desire to bring the patient back to health itself motivates the doctor's deliberation, and the deliberation transmits desire to each of the stages of the deliberation. For example, the doctor has no independent desire to heat the patient's body. He obtains this desire by realizing that, if

---

[120] *Nicomachean Ethics* III.3, 1113a2–7. (I use 'deliberated choice' as a translation for *prohairesis*, rather than simply 'choice,' for I wish to emphasize that at least in the paradigm case a *prohairesis* is the outcome of a deliberation.)

[121] *On the Soul* III.9, 433a4–6.

he is to bring the patient back to health (which he does desire), then he must produce a uniform state of the body, which he can do by heating it. Having realized this, he now desires to heat the body. And, again, the doctor lacks any independent desire to wrap the patient's body in blankets: it is only because he realizes that this is the best way for him to heat the patient's body that he desires to wrap it up. Deliberation is thus the way the mind transmits desire from the wished-for goal to an action the agent can perform.

Some philosophers have complained that Aristotle has too narrow a conception of deliberation: in particular, that he insists that we can only deliberate about means and not ends:

> We deliberate not about ends but about what contributes to ends. For a doctor does not deliberate whether he shall heal, nor an orator whether he shall convince, nor a statesman whether he shall produce law and order, nor does anyone else deliberate about his end. Having set the end they consider how and by what means it is to be attained; and if it seems to be produced by several means they consider by which it is most easily and best produced, while if it is achieved by one only they consider how it will be achieved by this and by what means this will be achieved, till they come to the first cause, which in the order of discovery is last. For the person who deliberates seems to inquire and analyze in the way described as though he were analyzing a geometrical construction ... and what is last in the order of analysis is first in the order of becoming. [122]

Do we not, it is objected, deliberate about what are to be the ends in our lives – for example, whether to become a doctor or a statesman? In response, supporters of Aristotle have pointed out that the things which *contribute* to an end may include *constituents* of the end: for example, one may deliberate about whether being a doctor or being a statesman is to be a constituent of the good life which one hopes to lead. One does not deliberate whether or not to have a good life, but one may deliberate about what the good life is going to consist in.

Although this 'Aristotelian' response is consistent with Aris-

---

[122] *Nicomachean Ethics* III.3, 1112b11–24.

totle's claim that we deliberate about things which contribute to
the end, it is doubtful that Aristotle himself included this type of
thinking within the compass of what he called 'deliberation' (*bouleusis*). 'Deliberation' is a term of art which Aristotle used to describe a very special sort of practical reasoning: that in which
desire is transmitted from premises to conclusion. So we should
not think that everything we are willing to call a deliberation
counts as a deliberation in Aristotle's sense of the term. The paradigm of an Aristotelian deliberation is when one begins with a desired goal and considers how to achieve it. While it is not
inconceivable that the consideration of what should be the constituents of the end will involve the transmission of desire, it is unlikely. Consider, for example, Plato's decision to turn away from
politics and become a philosopher. He did not reason: 'I have a
desire to live a good life. Given the current political climate I shall
probably be frustrated in a political life; philosophy might be a
way of living a good life ... [straightaway he starts to philoso-
phize].' The problem with this model is that it portrays the desire
to philosophize as *derived from* the desire to lead a good life. It is
unbelievable that Plato's reasoning took that shape. It is more
plausible to suppose that he found he derived deep satisfaction
from doing philosophy and that his desire to philosophize survived
reflective testing when he considered whether the philosophical life
was worthwhile. He also judged that the political climate of
Athens made it impossible to have an acceptable political career.
This reasoning is not *transmitting* desire from the goal to live a
good life to the constituent of philosophizing. It is better conceived
as *forming* the desire for an end, the philosophical life. It is more
like falling in love than it is like deliberating.

There do seem to be some cases where one can deliberate in Aristotle's sense about the constituents of an end, but they are rather
peculiar pieces of reasoning. Imagine, for example, a contemporary college student, Paul, considering whether to apply to law
school or to medical school. Paul has no intrinsic desire to be either
a lawyer or a doctor: he only desires a professional life of financial
security. This is what he considers the good life to be. He reasons:

> I would like to live a good life. This is a professional life
> of financial security. The available options are law and

medicine. I know that I have certain verbal skills and
have always had the ability to persuade people. This
would be an advantage to me if I were a lawyer. I also
hate blood, am squeamish, and get nervous when I get
close to sick people. Thus I would be uncomfortable
being a doctor. Since, for me, there is no other reason for
choosing between law and medicine, I shall choose law.
Therefore, I'll apply to law school.

This reasoning does count as an Aristotelian deliberation: for the
desire to be a lawyer is derived from the desire to live a life of
financial security. But for this to be a deliberation, there must be a
peculiar relation between means and ends. Although the lawyer-ly
life is, for Paul, a *constituent* of the end of living a life of financial
security, *Paul treats it as a means* to the end. The crucial point
about an Aristotelian deliberation is that it is meant to cover only
those forms of practical reasoning in which desire is transmitted
from the end to the means – or to those constituents which can
derive desire from the desire for the end.

But if a deliberation is a transmitter of desire and a deliberated
choice is the last step of a deliberation, this would suggest that deliberated choice is itself a desire. Aristotle accepts this suggestion:

> The object of deliberated choice being one of the things
> in our own power which is desired after deliberation,
> *deliberated choice will be deliberated desire* of things in
> our own power; for when we have decided as a result of
> deliberation, we desire in accordance with our deliber-
> ation.[123]

Elsewhere Aristotle says that deliberated choice is either *thoughtful desire* or *desiring mind*.[124] and that it shares in reason and
desire.[125] So it is not just that deliberation transmits desire from the
agent's goal to his deliberated choice; the deliberated choice is
itself a desire. But it is a desire with very special features. First, it is
a desire about which we can have absolute certainty: unlike many
other desires, one cannot have a deliberated choice unless one is

[123] *bouleutikē orexis: Nicomachean Ethics* III.3, 1113a9–12.
[124] *dio ē orektikos noûs hē prohairesis ē orexis dianoētikē: Nicomachean Ethics*
VI.2, 1139b4–5.
[125] *hē de prohairesis koinon dianoias kai orexeōs: On the Movement of Animals*
VII, 700b23.

aware that one has it. Second, the awareness of this desire is part of the desire itself. Modern philosophers tend to think of consciousness as being distinct from the objects of consciousness. So, for example, if one has a desire for food, one's awareness that one has a desire for food is distinct from the desire itself. But with an Aristotelian deliberated choice one's awareness of the desire to act in a certain way is part of the desire itself. There is in this case no distinction to be made between thought and object of thought. Third, a deliberated choice is an essentially reflective desire: it is of the essence of a deliberated choice that one be aware of it. And the reflection is part of the desire itself. For the self-conscious thought – say, 'I shall wrap him in blankets' – both is a manifestation of self-consciousness and *is* the deliberated choice. Thus deliberation, for Aristotle, should not be conceived as supervenient upon given desires and motives, as though it is occurring in a different part of the mind. Deliberation is itself an expression of desire: it is motivated by a wish, it is a transmitter of desire, and its conclusion is either a desire – that is, a deliberated choice – or an action immediately motivated by the deliberation. And deliberation is not just expressive of desire; it helps to constitute our desire. The doctor's desire to make this man healthy is, through deliberation, transformed into the desire to make this man healthy by wrapping him in blankets. Deliberation helps to make our desires concrete: to render them into a sufficiently specific form that we can begin to act on them. Deliberation thus brings our abstractly given desires back to us: it presents our desires to us in a form in which we can begin to satisfy them.

That a deliberated choice is both a desire and a piece of self-conscious reasoning is of philosophical significance. For there is a distinguished tradition in Western philosophy that says that human freedom consists in the exercise of self-conscious control over one's desires; but it remains unclear what the relation is between self-consciousness and one's desires. Freedom is important to us not as one value among others, but as that which constitutes our very being. Other animals may have beliefs and desires, but humans distinguish themselves from the rest of nature by the ability to become consciously aware of their beliefs and desires, to consider them and to decide what to do on the basis of that consideration. A human agent need not merely be caused to act by his desires: by his reflecting on his desires and deciding which to satisfy and how, the desires become reasons for him. In acting for these reasons, an agent manifests his freedom and humanity; but, unfortunately, we have little understanding of what this manifestation of freedom consists in. Since this freedom helps to constitute our humanity, in being ignorant of its workings we are ignorant of our essence. We lack an understanding of what it is, fundamentally, to be us.

According to Kant, a free agent must reflect on his desires from a standpoint outside the desires themselves. The deliberation will not be truly free, free of determination by desire, unless it is carried out from a perspective which can view the desire, and so consider it as one factor among others, but which remains independent of its causal sway. On this conception reflection is a manifestation of freedom precisely because it is a form of *detachment*. The moral agent, for Kant, is one who in thought detaches himself from his desires, particular interests and circumstances and considers solely what a purely rational will would will. Hegel, a devoted student of Aristotle, criticized Kant's conception of free will. Such a will, Hegel argued, would be so detached from its own desires and from the circumstances of deliberation and action that it would be empty: it would never be able to determine what to will. Though this criticism of Kant is widely accepted by contemporary philosophers, there is no alternative analysis of freedom which has won widespread agreement. I am concerned here not with the minimal conditions for ascribing responsibility to an agent for his actions, but with a higher notion of freedom. There is an intuitive notion of freedom, which has had various formulations in Kant, Spinoza, and others, which requires more of us than that we be able to do what we want to do, more of us than that our desires not be a product of coercion, more of us even than that we be able to reflect on our desires and deliberate on the basis of them. The intuitive notion requires that our reflection be *effective* in the formation and structuring of our desires. We need to give content to the idea of freedom manifested in effective reflection.

If our goal is a conception of reflection that is at once not detached from the desires it is considering and a manifestation of human freedom, we would do well to go back to Aristotle's conception of practical mind. His conception of deliberation is of a mental activity that is both a reflection and a process by which desire is both transmitted and formed. The doctor's deliberation is itself a manifestation of his desire to cure, and in the process desire is transmitted to the means. It is also the process by which the desire to wrap the patient in blankets is formed. Of course, much more needs to be said if we are to show that any piece of Aristotelian practical reasoning is also a manifestation of human freedom. But the way is at least left open to consider reflection as an expression of desire rather than as an activity carried out in complete detachment from desire. This is important for anyone who wants to *naturalize* human freedom: that is, to give an account of freedom that makes it plausible that a certain type of animal, a human being, can enjoy it. Reflection is an activity we engage in, and, if Aristotle is right that all our activities are products of desire, then reflection too must be motivated by desire. What we wish to understand is how a single peculiarly human activity can be at once a product of desire, a manifestation of desire, an effective reflection, and a manifestation of freedom.

Aristotle's ethical outlook gives us the tools with which to naturalize human freedom. We have already seen how his account of practical mind allows a single activity to be a product of desire, a manifestation of desire, and a *certain* type of reflection. It is in the *Nicomachean Ethics* that we see how desire can be organized so as to issue in an effective reflection which is also a manifestation of freedom. If we are to gain insight into the nature of human freedom, we must *extract* the account from Aristotle's ethical writings. For Aristotle was not directly concerned with specifying the conditions sufficient for human freedom: he was concerned with the conditions for living a good life. The good life, for Aristotle, was a life of happiness (*eudaimonia*), and happiness partially consists in the desires within our soul having taken on a certain organization. Ethics is, among other things, a study of the organization of human desire. When we look to the motivational structure of a good man, it becomes possible to see how a single activity can be both a manifestation of human freedom and the triumph of a desire.

5
Ethics and the organization of desire

5.1 The point of the *Nicomachean Ethics*[1]

One reason for going back to Aristotle's ethics is to study how profoundly different his ethical outlook is from our own. It is fair to say that we live today without a coherent and compelling morality.[2] There are various moral strands which pull in various directions, but when pushed for a justification we find it hard to explain why we should hold the moral beliefs we do hold. Much of what constitutes the Western moral outlook is inherited from the Judaeo-Christian tradition, and if 300 years ago one were asked, for example, why you should do unto others as you would have them do unto you, one would have undoubtedly given a religious answer. In the past 300 years there has been a dramatic loss of confidence in the ability of religious belief to ground a moral outlook. In part this loss is due to a growing conviction that moral beliefs ought to be justifiable other than by appeal to divine authority: they ought to appear reasonable to a moral agent.[3] But with the loss of confidence in religion's ability to ground morality, no other form of justification has come to take religion's place. There are other forms of justification, to be sure, but none commands universal or deep respect.

One way in which we differ from the Greek world in which Aristotle lived is that we place more emphasis on intention than on act. In the Christian outlook, it does not matter ultimately if one is born well or poorly, or whether one actually has an opportunity in life to do good deeds. What matters is that one has a good heart, lives purely, intends to do well by others, and obeys Biblical and

---

[1] Appropriate reading for sections 5.1–5.3: *Nicomachean Ethics* I–II.
[2] For an extended discussion of this issue, see Bernard Williams, *Ethics and the Limits of Philosophy*, and *Moral Luck*; and Alasdair MacIntyre, *After Virtue*.
[3] Of course, this idea goes back at least to Socrates: see Plato, *Euthyphro*. See also Kant, *Groundwork of a Metaphysics of Morals*, and *Critique of Practical Reason*.

Church injunctions. One can love one's neighbor even if by chance of birth one can do nothing for him. For the ancient Greeks, by contrast, if one were deprived of the opportunity to live well, nothing could compensate for that. They were thus obsessed by the notion of fate or chance, since it seemed possible that some accident of position or circumstance could prevent one from living well in the world.[4] Even the Greeks who believed in an afterlife in Hades did not believe that there was any compensation to be received there. Far from it. One continued in the afterlife to endure the shame of not having been able to lead a good life. The prospect of chance or fate thwarting their intentions terrified the Greeks, and much of their literature and philosophy reflects that.

Christianity tried to compensate for chance. It promised an afterlife in which virtue would be rewarded. But here the meaning of the word 'virtue' had to change dramatically to make this promise possible. For the Greeks, 'virtue' (*aretē*) meant *excellence*: to be virtuous was to be excellent at doing something. Achilles was a virtuous man for he was an excellent warrior, he provided for his family and friends, etc. For Christians, 'virtue' came to denote a quality of the *inner* spirit that may have no or few outward manifestations. If one lived this inward life of virtue, then even if the world was unjust – if it did not recognize or reward one – one's virtue would ultimately be recognized. This would be all but impossible for a Greek to understand, but so long as people believe in the Christian religion this belief compensates for chance and fate in this world.

However, whether or not one believes in a Christian afterlife, if one accepts that morality should not require a specifically religious justification, then if the life of inward virtue is to be commended it must appear in its own terms to be a good life for man to lead. Kant tried to formulate a justification for the life of inward virtue which did not depend upon the reward of an afterlife, not because he had lost religious faith, but because he wanted to provide an independent justification for morality. The appeal of Kantian morality is that it directly links morality to a dignified conception of man as a rationally free agent. Kant severed the tie between morality and the pursuit of happiness because, he argued, morality cannot be bind-

---

[4] For a discussion of this issue, see Bernard Williams, *Ethics and the Limits of Philosophy*, and Martha Nussbaum, *The Fragility of Goodness*.

ing on an agent in virtue of desires he just happens to have. The agent might have lacked those desires, and, Kant argued, it is intolerable that an agent should be bound to morality by so contingent a thread. Morality should bind an agent solely insofar as he is rational; thus morality, for Kant, should be constituted by the formal laws of rationality alone. In regarding himself as a purely rational agent, for the purpose of making a moral judgement, a man treats himself as free of the casual sway of particular desires, passions, and interests that might otherwise engage him. In morality, as Kant conceived it, man can realize his highest freedom.

Although Kantian morality does not offer the divine compensation of an afterlife, it does offer *some* compensation for the life one finds oneself living. What matters, from the perspective of Kantian morality, is not the concrete ways and circumstances in which one actually lives one's life, but whether one has a good will. If one genuinely wills that one should act according to the (self-legislated) moral law, then one has the compensation of knowing that one is a good person regardless of how one actually acts, regardless of the circumstances in which one is forced to act, and regardless of the consequences of one's acts.

Kant and Aristotle would each see the other's project as fundamentally flawed. Kant, for his part, would not recognize Aristotelian ethics as a system of morality.[5] Aristotelian ethics is an attempt to answer the question: what is the good life for man? Since Aristotle's man is by nature a political animal, he attains the good life within society, and thus the question of what is a good life cannot be answered for an individual in abstraction from the society in which he lives. Society provides much of the context and opportunity for living a good life. Thus the question of what is a good life for man must be answered by political science.[6] The aim of political science, according to Aristotle, is the highest good achievable by action.[7] It is generally agreed, he says, that this is happiness – *eudaimonia*. The aim of the *Nicomachean Ethics* is to give one a reflective understanding of how one can achieve happiness by living an ethical life within society. This reflective understanding is

---

[5] For the difference between ethics and morality, see Bernard Williams, *Ethics and the Limits of Philosophy*.
[6] *Nicomachean Ethics* I.2, 1094a24–b11.
[7] *Nicomachean Ethics* I.4, 1095a15–20.

itself supposed to be of practical value:

> If there is some end of the things we do, which we desire for its own sake (everything else being desired for the sake of this) ... clearly this must be the good and the chief good. Will not the knowledge of it, then, have a great influence on life? Shall we not, like archers who have a mark to aim at, be more likely to hit upon what we should? If so, we must try, in outline at least, to determine what it is...[8]

This ethical outlook would be disqualified by Kant as a system of morality. Morality, for Kant, had to be self-legislating or *autonomous*: it must be what a purely rational will would legislate for itself. Any attempt to achieve a merely given end – like human happiness – would, for Kant, count as *heteronomy* and thus be disqualified as morality.

Aristotle, for his part, would not recognize Kantian morality as an ethical outlook. He would find bizarre the idea that human happiness was a merely given end which ethics tried to achieve as an external goal. Happiness is not based on the satisfaction of desires which a person just *happens* to possess. According to Aristotle, man has a nature: there is something definite and worthwhile that it is to be a human being. Happiness consists in living this noble life: in satisfying the desires that are *necessary* for man to have in order to live a full, rich life. However, although these desires are necessary for man to lead a fully human life, they cannot be discovered by *a priori* reasoning. The Greek word which is being translated as 'happiness' – *eudaimonia* – is also translated as 'human flourishing' or 'well-being.' So when Aristotle asks

> Why should we not call happy the man who exercises his abilities according to the highest standards of virtue and excellence in a context which affords him sufficient resources and not merely for a brief moment but throughout his life?[9]

the answer cannot be: because a man's happiness depends upon the satisfaction of his desires which may or may not bear any re-

[8] *Nicomachean Ethics* I.2, 1094a18–25.
[9] *Nicomachean Ethics* I.10, 1101a14–16 (my translation).

lation to his living a virtuous life. The genuine pursuit of happiness and the virtuous life are, for Aristotle, one and the same. The happy life is, for Aristotle, one in which man deeply fulfills his nature. And this realization of man's nature is the virtuous life. Any system of thought which ignored this could not, for Aristotle, count as an ethical system.

One of the most serious criticisms that has been made of Kantian morality is that it lacks content. Interestingly enough, this criticism was first made by Hegel, a philosopher who was himself deeply influenced by Aristotle.[10] He argued that from a purely formal principle of rationality one cannot derive any substantial conclusions about how to act. A purely rational will would be so divorced from the concrete circumstances of action that it would have no basis for making any decisions about how to act. Such an impoverished will, in Aristotle's eyes, could not possibly form the basis of an ethical outlook. The charge of emptiness continues to be made against Kantian morality, and it is a charge that ought to be investigated seriously. For there remains widespread agreement that Kantianism describes what the objective stance in morality is. We have already seen that Kantian morality encourages one to take a detached perspective with respect to one's desires. This encourages the idea that in viewing the world objectively I reflectively detach myself from my present concerns, interests, and situation and conceive of myself simply as one agent among others.[11] But if Hegel's Aristotelian criticism is correct, then if one actually succeeds in viewing the interests and concerns of all agents, including oneself, from a genuinely detached perspective, there will be no motivation left for acting in any particular way at all.[12]

[10] See G. W. F. Hegel, *Phenomenology of Spirit*, sections 599–671; *Philosophy of Right*, sections 105–40; *History of Philosophy*, vol. 3, pp. 457–64.
[11] See, e.g., John Rawls, *A Theory of Justice*, and 'Kantian Constructivism in Moral Theory'; Thomas Nagel, *The Possibility of Altruism*, 'The Limits of Objectivity,' and *The View From Nowhere*.
[12] This Aristotelian criticism has had more recent exponents: see, e.g., Bernard Williams, *Ethics and the Limits of Philosophy*, 'The Presuppositions of Morality,' and 'Persons, Character and Morality,' in *Moral Luck*. There has also been a neo-Kantian response. Neo-Kantians have argued that the aim of the detached perspective is not to generate motivations to act, but only to endorse motivations which already exist, from a standpoint outside of these motivations. But it remains enigmatic how the detached point of view is supposed to accomplish this, and one suspects that either it will be impotent to endorse any motivations or that it will endorse some by being covertly guilty of heteronomy: of smuggling into the 'detached' perspective the very motivations it ends up endorsing.

There seems then to be philosophical as well as historical reason for going back to Aristotle's ethics. With decline in confidence that Kantian morality can give us any guidance as to how to act, there is reason to go back to an ethical system based firmly in the study of human motivation. The hope is that an ethical system grounded in human motivation will not only answer questions about how to act, but will also be justifiable by reference to life as it is lived in this world. Ethics, Aristotle believed, was grounded in the study of human desire. We have already seen that, for Aristotle, all human action is grounded in desire. It is of the greatest interest to see whether any study of human desire could have recognizably ethical conclusions about how humans should act.

The point of the *Nicomachean Ethics* is not to persuade us to be good or to show us how to behave well in the various circumstances in life: it is to give people who are already leading a happy, virtuous life insight into the nature of their own souls. The aim of the *Ethics* is to offer its readers self-understanding, not persuasion or advice. Of course, as we have seen, Aristotle thinks that self-understanding will be of practical value: those who understand what human happiness is will, like the archers who have a mark to aim at, be more likely to hit their target.[13] However, this understanding can be of practical value only for those for whom it is *self-understanding*: namely, for those who are already living a virtuous life. There are two reasons for this.

First, ethics is not an area in which it is possible to spell out precise rules about how to act:

> Our discussion will be adequate if it has as much clearness as the subject matter admits of, for precision is not to be sought for alike in all discussions, any more than in all the products of crafts ... We must be content then in speaking of such subjects ... to indicate the truth roughly and in outline ... In the same spirit, therefore, should each type of statement be *received*: for it is the mark of an educated man to look for precision in each class of things just so far as the nature of the subject matter admits; it is evidently equally foolish to accept

[13] *Nicomachean Ethics* I.2, 1094a18–25.

157

probable reasoning from a mathematician and to demand
from a rhetorician demonstrative proofs.[14]

Ethics cannot properly be conceived as a moral computer which
one feeds information about the current circumstances as input
and which churns out instructions about how to behave as output.
The way to find out what to do is to seek the judgement of a good
man, for he will be a good judge of how to behave. The good man
will be sensitive to what the circumstances require and will be motivated to act in the right way. But if ethics is not a set of rules, then
a treatise on ethics cannot be treated as a piece of software which
one ingests in order to become a good person. One cannot become
a good person by internalizing a set of rules, for there are no rules
to internalize.

Second, human happiness is not something which can be adequately understood from an external perspective. Among the
ends toward which human actions are directed, Aristotle distinguished between ends that are distinct from the actions which
produce them and ends that are the activities themselves.[15] This is
the distinction we have already seen between a change (*kinēsis*)
and an activity (*energeia*). House-building, for example, is directed
toward the production of a house, which is distinct from the process of building. By contrast, one may jog in order to be healthy,
but jogging is part of what it is to be healthy. Health is not some
end-state that is produced after all the jogging, swimming, eating
well, sleeping well. Being healthy is the state in which all those activities are carried out. This distinction is central to Aristotle's
ethics, for acting virtuously is not a means to a distinct end of living
a happy life. Acting virtuously *constitutes* a happy life. This cannot
be adequately understood by a non-virtuous person. From the perspective of a bad man a virtuous act will appear onerous, painful
or silly. From the perspective of the immature, the idea of a virtuous act may have some appeal, but his soul will not be sufficiently
formed for this to be the strongest desire within him. He will feel
the pull of contrary desires and he will not understand in any but
the most superficial sense that acting virtuously is the way to be
happy.

[14] *Nicomachean Ethics* I.3, 1094b11–27; cf. 1.7. 1098a20–b8.
[15] *Nicomachean Ethics* I.1.

That is why Aristotle did not want the young to attend his lectures.

> A young man is not a proper hearer of lectures on political science; for he is inexperienced in the actions that occur in life, but its discussions *start* from these and are about these; and, further, since he tends to follow his passions, his study will be vain and unprofitable, because the end aimed at is not knowledge but action. And it makes no difference whether he is young in years or youthful in character; the defect does not depend on time but on his living and pursuing each successive object, as passion directs. For to such persons, as to the incontinent, knowledge brings no profit; *but to those who desire and act according to the logos, knowledge about such matters will be of great benefit.*[16]

Aristotle's *Ethics* are not designed to persuade anyone to become a good person. There is nothing in them designed to be compelling to someone who is not already living an ethical life. The argument is internal in the sense that it is directed toward those who have good natures, good temperaments, who have already been brought up to live virtuously. The lectures are intended to help them to develop a self-conscious and coherent ethical outlook: to reinforce reflectively the lives they are already inclined to lead. Of course, the transition from unreflectively living a virtuous life to understanding the virtues and the life one is living is itself of practical value. For this self-understanding helps to constitute the good life for man. Thus Aristotle can say that 'we are inquiring not in order to know what virtue is, but in order to become good, since otherwise our inquiry would have been of no use.'[17] Although Aristotle's inquiry does investigate what virtue and happiness are, the inquiry is essentially practical: it is aimed at helping a good person understand and thereby increase and solidify his goodness.

It is here that the desire to understand and the desire to lead an ethical life in society are in greatest harmony. The inquiry into a justification for the ethical life should be undertaken, according to Aristotle, by those who are already living an ethical life. They seek

16 *Nicomachean Ethics* 1.3, 1095a2–11. See also 1.4, 1095b3–13 (I leave *logos* untranslated; the Oxford translation gives 'rational principle.')
17 *Nicomachean Ethics* II.1, 1103b27–9.

a deeper understanding of the life they are already motivated to live. However, the outcome of this inquiry is not merely a theoretical understanding of one's life – it is not merely that the desire to understand is satisfied – it is a reflective endorsement. One comes to see that there is good reason to live the ethical life, for the ethical life is, quite literally, the good life. So one's understanding of the ethical life reinforces one's motivation to live it.[18]

5.2 Happiness and man's nature

If there is some end of the things we do, which we desire for its own sake, Aristotle says, this must be the chief good.[19] Notice that Aristotle's claim is hypothetical: he does not just assume that there is one good toward which all our actions are aimed. He does argue that there must be at least one end which is not subordinate to other ends and which we pursue for its own sake. For if we did X for the sake of Y and Y for the sake of Z and Z for the sake of ..., we would never do anything. There would be an infinite regress and our wills would never engage. *If* there is some one good, then knowledge of it will have a great influence on our lives.

What would life be like if there were not? There would be various ends which we pursued for their own sakes and which were not themselves subordinate to any other ends. Life would potentially be ultimately neurotic. For if the various ends-in-themselves called for conflicting actions in a given situation, we would be pulled this way and that. There would be no way of acting that satisfied our conflicting desires, so *any* way we ended up acting would leave grounds for regret and remorse. Of course, people may be neurotic. But the hope is that the world is such and man's nature is such that there is at least a possibility of living a non-neurotic life. The hope is that it is at least possible for a man's motivational structure to form a harmonious whole. However, if there were at the end of the line disparate ends-in-themselves, there would be no guarantee that it was even possible for the healthiest among us not to be neurotic.

Aristotle does believe that there is a highest good of human

[18] I discuss this further in section 5.5 below. As we shall see, the desire to understand and the desire to live an ethical life in society do not always have such a symbiotic relation. See section 6.7 below.

[19] *Nicomachean Ethics* I.2, 1094a18.

action: this is happiness.[20] Aristotle identifies the good in any sphere of action with the end toward which the action is directed.[21] In medicine the good is health, in building the good is a house. So if there is an end of all the things we do, this will be the chief good attainable by human action. There is, Aristotle says, general agreement that happiness is the chief end of human action, but there is disagreement about what happiness is.[22] The most vulgar of men identify happiness with pleasure.[23] This, Aristotle says, is a slavish life, suitable for beasts. The life is beastly because a man who gives his life over to satisfying his basic appetites has done nothing to distinguish himself from the 'lower' animals. One reason that man ranks above the rest of animal life is that he has the capacity to organize his soul. He is able to organize himself so as to derive satisfaction from activities other than securing the basic pleasures. The hedonistic life ignores this quintessentially human ability. The life is slavish because it is controlled by these basic pleasures. Since the pleasure-seeker has done nothing to organize the state of his soul, thus remaining at the level of a beast, the basic appetites are in an important sense external to him, directing his activities. For he has done nothing to identify himself with his appetites; they remain forces within him pulling him toward this pleasure and that. In this sense the pleasure-seeker lives a life of compulsion.

If we are to discover what happiness is, we must focus on what is distinctive of human life. Only in the peculiar activities of human life will we discover the peculiarly human ability to be happy:

> ...to say that happiness is the chief good seems a platitude, and a clearer account of what it is is still desired. This might perhaps be given, *if we could first ascertain the function of man.* For just as for a flute player, a sculptor, or any artist, and, in general, for all things that have a function or activity, the good and the 'well' is thought to reside in the function, so would it seem to be for man, if he has a function. Have the carpenter, then, and the tanner certain functions or activities, and man has none? Is he naturally functionless? Or as eye, hand,

---

[20] *Nicomachean Ethics* 1.4, 1095a14–30; 1.7, 1097a30–b6.
[21] *Nicomachean Ethics* 1.7, 1097a15–24.
[22] *Nicomachean Ethics* 1.4, 1095a15–17.
[23] *Nicomachean Ethics* 1.5, 1095b13–22.

foot, and in general each of the parts evidently has a function, may one lay it down that man similarly has a function apart from all these? What then can this be? Life seems to be common even to plants, *but we are seeking what is peculiar to man*. Let us exclude, therefore, the life of nutrition and growth. Next there would be a life of perception, but *it* also seems to be common even to the horse, the ox, and every animal. *There remains then an active life of the element that has a logos* (of this, one part has such a principle in the sense of being obedient to it, the other in the sense of possessing it and exercising thought) ... Now *if the function of man is an activity of soul in accordance with, or not without, a logos* – and if we say a so-and-so and a good so-and-so have a function which is the same in kind, e.g. a lyre-player and a good lyre-player, and so without qualification in all cases, eminence in respect of virtue being added to the name of the function (for the function of a lyre-player is to play the lyre and that of a good lyre-player is to do so well): if this is the case and we state *the function of man to be a certain kind of life, and this to be an activity or actions of the soul implying a logos, and the function of a good man to be the good and noble performance of these,* and if any action is well performed when it is performed in accordance with the appropriate virtue: if this is the case, *human good turns out to be activity of the soul in accordance with virtue,* and if there are more than one virtue, in accordance with the best and most complete. But we must add 'in a complete life.' For one swallow does not make a summer, nor does one day; and so too one day, or a short time, does not make a man blessed and happy.[24]

In this translation, I have left the Greek word *logos* untranslated. The Oxford translation translates it as 'rational principle.' So the function of man, on that translation, is an activity of soul which is according to a rational principle. The advantage of this translation is that it emphasizes a distinctively human ability, one which separates man from the rest of nature. However, although

---

[24] *Nicomachean Ethics* 1.7, 1097b22–1098a20. See also *Parts of Animals* 1.5, 645b14.

'rational principle' is one possible translation for *logos*, we have already seen that *logos* may also be translated as 'order,' 'arrangement,' or 'proportion.' It seems to me that Aristotle is alluding *both* to order *and* to reason in his use of the protean word *logos*. The function of man is an activity in accordance with a certain arrangement or order in the soul. That is why Aristotle can conclude that the human good is an activity of soul in accordance with virtue: for virtue is a certain organization of the soul.[25] How this order is instilled in man's soul is a central issue for ethics. Of course, the exercise of the virtues will often involve man's practical reason. But if the practical reasoning did not flow from a certain organization of the soul, it would be empty. In fact it is because a man's life has a certain order that he is able to reason about it: the *logos* in his mind will reflect the *logos* in his soul.

It may at first seem odd to a modern reader to suppose that man has a function. And the inference – each of the parts of the body, eye, hand, and foot, has a function, therefore the whole man has a function – looks weak. If that argument provided the only reason for thinking that man has a function, Aristotle's ethics would rest on a shoddy foundation. But, as so often with Aristotle, we must look to his overall philosophical outlook to understand the argument in a particular passage. If we accept that Aristotle has *already* argued that every natural organism has a nature, and that man has a distinct nature, a unique inner principle of change and rest, it follows obviously that man's function is to live an active life which expresses his nature. The end of human life is for man to realize his form to the fullest possible extent – and this Aristotle has identified with the chief good for man.

There are two questions, though, which need to be answered. First, for man to realize his nature it seems he must somehow transcend the basic desires with which he is born: for a life given over to seeking pleasure and satisfying the primary appetites is, as we have seen, no better than animal existence. It seems, then, that it is part of man's nature to transcend the nature with which he is born, and one wants to know: how is this possible? Second, even if Aristotle has shown that man has a function, which is to live an active

---

[25] I have also translated *aretē* as 'virtue' rather than giving the new Oxford translation of it as 'excellence.' For Aristotle, as we have seen, the virtues simply are excellences.

life according to his nature, and that this is the chief good, why should we think that this life will bring him happiness? The answers to these two questions are related: for if man can organize his desires so as to desire to live a distinctively human life, then he will be motivated to act so as to live a full human life; and the living of that life will satisfy his organized desires and thus can plausibly be considered a happy life.

5.3 Virtue

The organization of desire which enables man to live a truly happy life Aristotle calls virtue. Remember, a virtue for the ancient Greeks was an excellence. So the virtues, for Aristotle, are states of the soul which enable a person to live an excellent life: to fulfill his function to the fullest extent:

> We must not only describe virtue as a state, but also say what sort of state it is. We may remark, then, that every virtue or excellence both brings into good condition the thing of which it is the excellence and makes the work of that thing be done well; e.g. the excellence of the eye makes both the eye and its work good; for it is by the excellence of the eye that we see well. Similarly the excellence of the horse makes the horse both good in itself and good at running and at carrying its rider and awaiting the attack of the enemy. Therefore, if this is true in every case, the virtue of man also will be the state which makes a man good and which makes him do his own work well.[26]

The virtues are stable states of the soul which enable a person to make the right decision about how to act in the circumstances and which motivate him so to act. It is these stable states of the soul that we think of as constituting a person's character. We do not ordinarily think of character as being organized desire, but character does motivate us to act in certain ways, and, in Aristotle's world, desire is the only motivating force for human action. Aristotle actually says that 'the virtues are certain deliberated decisions or

[26] *Nicomachean Ethics* II.6, 1106a14–24.

are not without deliberated decision.'[27] Later he says that virtue is a 'deliberative deciding state' of the soul.[28] But a deliberative decision, as we have already seen, is a special type of desire: a deliberative desire.[29] That is why Aristotle says that 'deliberative decision is either desiring mind or thoughtful desire.'[30] If this seems odd to modern readers it is probably because we are working with a much narrower conception of desire than Aristotle had. If we think of desire as a bare force in the individual urging him toward some goal, then the idea of a thoughtful desire or of virtue as an organized desire will be all but incomprehensible. But in Aristotle's man the desires encompass a much richer set of motivational states. The appetites are bare forces, but there are other desires, like deliberative decisions, in which thought and desire are of a piece. Desires in Aristotle's world are sufficiently rich to be shaped, organized, and impregnated with reason.

The ethical virtues are instilled in man by habit.[31] None of the ethical virtues arises in us by nature,[32] and yet man has not achieved his highest good, not fully realized his nature, until he has developed the virtues and can lead a happy life. It seems part of man's nature to transcend nature: to organize his soul into a shape which would not arise by nature. Thus Aristotle says that man is *by nature* a political animal: he can fully realize his nature only within a political society that promotes human happiness.[33] Indeed, human happiness consists in part in an active life within political society. And yet, though man is by nature a political animal, though he has the capacity to form a sense of justice, an ethical sensibility, none of the political or ethical virtues arises in him by nature. We become just by doing just acts, brave by doing brave acts, temperate by doing temperate acts.[34] The virtues are states of character, and they are acquired by doing the acts that one

[27] *Nicomachean Ethics* II.5, 1106a3. (This quotation and the next two in the text are my translation.)
[28] *hexis proairetikē*: *Nicomachean Ethics* II.6, 1106b36; VI.2, 1139a22.
[29] *hē de proairesis orexis bouleutikē*: *Nicomachean Ethics* VI.2, 1139a22ff.
[30] *ē orektikos noûs hē prohairesis ē orexis dianoētikē*: *Nicomachean Ethics* VI.2, 1139b3.
[31] *Nicomachean Ethics* II.1.
[32] *Nicomachean Ethics* II.1, 1103a19.
[33] See *Politics* I.2. I discuss man's status as a political animal in more detail in section 5.6 below.
[34] *Nicomachean Ethics* II.1, 1103b1–2.

would do if one already had the state of character:

> ... by doing the acts that we do in our transactions with
> other men we become just or unjust, and by doing the
> acts that we do in the presence of danger, and being ha-
> bituated to feel fear or confidence, we become brave or
> cowardly. The same is true of appetites and feelings of
> anger; some men become temperate and good tempered,
> others self-indulgent and irascible, by behaving in one
> way or the other in the appropriate circumstances. Thus,
> in one word, states [of character] arise out of like activi-
> ties. This is why the activities we exhibit must be of a cer-
> tain kind; it is because the states correspond to the
> differences between these. It makes no small difference,
> then, whether we form habits of one kind or of another
> from our very youth; it makes a very great difference, or
> rather *all* the difference.[35]

That is why Aristotle thought his lectures would be of no use to
people who were not already well brought up. Excellence arises
from habit, not from lectures.

Habits, in Aristotle's view, do not merely instill a disposition to
engage in certain types of behavior: they instill a sensitivity as to
how to act in various circumstances. One of the reasons we must
rely on habit as a mode of educating a person to virtue (not just getting him to act virtuously) is that there are no rules which prescribe
how a virtuous person should act. One aspect of the problem goes
back to Socrates and his search for definitions. He asked, for
example, 'What is courage?'; and to any non-question-begging
answer – say, 'Standing steadfast in front of the enemy' – he came
up with a counter-example: a case of standing fast that was fool-
hardy and not courageous. Part of the problem is that he would not
allow an answer that itself contained an evaluative term, for it too
would lack a definition. Thus 'acting bravely' would be counted as
a question-begging answer. Socrates' lesson, as Aristotle understands it, is that there are going to be no rules as to how to act. At
best there would be the mock rule, 'Act courageously,' but a man
would not know how to follow that rule unless he was already

---

[35] *Nicomachean Ethics* II.I, 1103b14–25.

courageous.[36] But a person who is already courageous will have no need for rules. He will not only be motivated to act courageously; he will have a sensitivity to the particular circumstances in which he finds himself. He will be able to judge whether in these circumstances it is appropriate to stand fast or to retreat: and having made that judgement he will be inclined so to act.

Habits also organize the desires in one's soul. It is a sign of a state of character, Aristotle says, that one derives pleasure from performing certain acts:[37]

> For pleasure is a state of the soul and to each man that which he is said to be a lover of is pleasant; e.g. not only is a horse pleasant to the lover of horses, and a spectacle to the lover of sights, but also in the same way just acts are pleasant to the lover of justice and in general virtuous acts to the lover of virtue. Now for most men their pleasures are in conflict with one another because these are not *by nature pleasant*, but the lovers of what is noble find pleasant the things that are *by nature pleasant*: and virtuous actions are such, so that these are pleasant for such men as well as *in their own nature*. Their life, therefore, has no further need of pleasure as a sort of adventitious charm, but has pleasure in itself. For besides what we have said, the man who does not rejoice in noble actions is not even good; since no one would call a man just who did not enjoy acting justly, nor any man liberal who did not enjoy liberal actions; and similarly in all other cases. If this is so, virtuous actions must be *in themselves pleasant*. But they are also good and noble, and have each of these attributes in the highest degree, since the good man judges well about these attributes ...[38]

The virtuous man is promised a certain harmony in his soul. He is never torn this way and that by conflicting desires, and thus he is free of neurotic conflict. That is because, as Aristotle puts it, his pleasures are all pleasant *by nature* and *in themselves*. To be

---

[36] Cf. *Nicomachean Ethics* II.2, 1104a20ff.
[37] *Nicomachean Ethics* II.3, 1104b3–28; cf. I.8, 1099a7–25.
[38] *Nicomachean Ethics* I.8, 1099a7–23. (Again, I translate *aretē* as 'virtue' rather than as 'excellence.')

pleasant *by nature*, a pleasure must be that derived by a person living an excellent life: the pleasure of someone who is fulfilling his nature to the fullest extent. Aristotle's view of man is optimistic at least to this extent: someone who is able to realize his nature will lead a rich, full, happy life, and he will experience a certain unity and harmony among his desires. For an act to be pleasant *in itself* it must be just that: one that gives pleasure not as a means to some other end, but an act that is pleasurable in the doing of it for its own sake. The temperate man, for example, does not abstain from bodily pleasures in order to be a good man. It is a mark of his temperance that these so-called 'bodily pleasures' would not for him in these circumstances be pleasurable.[39] 'Ethical virtue,' Aristotle says, 'is concerned with pleasures and pains: it is on account of pleasure that we do bad things and on account of pain that we abstain from noble ones.'[40] The task of ethical education, though, is not to get us to perform noble acts even though our desires pull us toward bad things, but rather to reorganize our desires so that we get pleasure from doing noble acts and pain from doing bad ones.

From a modern, post-Freudian, perspective this picture of a unified soul may seem overdrawn. We moderns are inclined to believe that even a good man will feel the pull of, say, illicit bodily pleasures, though he will refrain from succumbing to them. By contrast, Aristotle's temperate man feels *no* pull toward the illicit pleasures: in these circumstances his whole body and soul pull him in a single direction, toward restraint. Indeed, in these circumstances he derives pleasure from his abstinence. Can such a person be a model for us? Who, for example, do we think is more deserving of our praise: the person who has to overcome temptation in order to do the right thing, or the man who does so effortlessly? Can we conceive of this effortlessness as more than insensitivity? For Aristotle, the effortlessness is a sign of the temperate man's sensitivity. Although bodily pleasures might in other circumstances be extremely pleasurable for him, he is sufficiently sensitive to the circumstances he is actually in to know he would derive no pleasure from them.[41] This is the person, in Aristotle's eyes, who is truly de-

---

[39] *Nicomachean Ethics* II.3, 1104b2–13.
[40] *Nicomachean Ethics* II.3, 1104b8–11.
[41] See John McDowell, 'Are Moral Requirements Hypothetical Imperatives?'

serving of our praise. When we praise the person who refrained from temptation we are trying to compensate him for his loss. We appreciate the effort to act for greater goals than the immediate gratification of appetite. Though Aristotle does recognize that praise can be used as a tool of ethical encouragement, our highest praise is, for him, not bestowed as a reward at all: it is a recognition of a man who is truly happy. It is part of our admiration of him. The truly happy man is one whose pleasures and pains fit well with the actions of a virtuous man: he gets pleasure out of acting bravely, temperately, generously; and we admire that precisely because he is truly happy. A flourishing human being attracts our admiration.

Human pleasures and pains are not, as we have seen, rigidly fixed by nature: they can be distributed and organized by habit and training. By being brought up from early youth to act bravely, considerately, temperately, we will grow to find pleasure in so acting. Thus a person's entry into the ethical is inherently non-rational. We do not get a child to act considerately by giving him the reasons for doing so – or, if we do give him reasons it is only a secondary part of the process. A child is not in a position to appreciate the reasons for acting considerately; indeed, these reasons cannot really be appreciated from outside the perspective of a considerate person. Instead, we give a child encouragements and rewards for acting considerately and discourage him from acting inconsiderately. This system of encouragements and discouragements will, ideally, respect the child's integrity, but it will not make essential appeal to his rationality. The child will typically begin acting considerately in order to gain the reward or encouragement: that is, for an external pleasure. But, through repetition, the child begins to derive pleasure from the considerate acts themselves. In this way the child grows into the ethical world.

It is on account of pleasure and pain that, Aristotle says, men act badly. However, the pleasures of a bad man are badly distributed. For the virtues are those states of character which contribute to our flourishing as human beings. So in acting badly we are literally acting against our nature: we are acting so as to diminish our chances of living fully. Take, for example, smoking. A person may derive great satisfaction from smoking, but it is clear that such a person's pleasures are badly distributed. They encourage self-destruction. For Aristotle *all* vices are like this. The opposed virtues are virtues only because they encourage and help to constitute a full rich life. Thus acting ethically is ultimately in one's own best interest. Acting ethically may involve acting well toward others, but that is because acting well toward others – friendship, citizenship – is part and parcel of human flourishing. However, although being virtuous is in one's best interest, one cannot 'sell' the virtuous life to a non-virtuous person: it does not constitute a non-ethical lure to the ethical point of view. It is only the person who is already inside the ethical point of view who can see that acting ethically is part of human flourishing.

In a certain way, Aristotle says, we acquire the virtues just as we acquire the arts. We are born neither with the virtue of temperance nor with the art of house-building, and neither of them arises in us by nature.[42] We learn an art, like house-building, by the repeated practice of building houses. So too we become brave by performing brave acts. However, there is also an important disanalogy between art and virtue.[43] In art what ultimately matters is the finished product. The goodness of a house exists in the house itself, but the virtuousness of an act does not exist in the act itself. A man may act in accordance with courage without acting courageously. To act courageously one must not only act in certain ways; the act must flow from a certain state of character.

There are, Aristotle thinks, three conditions of acting virtuously. The agent must (1) have practical knowledge. For example, for a given act to be courageous (not merely done in accordance with courage) a person must know that in these circumstances taking a stand would be the right thing to do. He must be aware that this is not a case of foolhardiness, bravado, or silliness. (2) He must choose the act and choose it for its own sake. He must be doing it because, in these circumstances, it is the courageous thing to do. (3) The act must flow from a firm character. It should not be a chance event, as it would be, for example, if a man fought fiercely because in those circumstances he happened to find no way to flee. Such a person may have a strong survival instinct, but he is not courageous.

While the arts require only condition (1), practical knowledge –

---

[42] *Nicomachean Ethics* II.1, 1103a31–b2.
[43] *Nicomachean Ethics* II.4.

a builder need only know how to build a house – choice and character are essential to virtue:

> ... as a condition of the possession of the virtues knowl-
> edge has little or no weight, while the other conditions
> count not for a little but for everything, i.e. the very con-
> ditions which result from often doing just and temperate
> acts.
>
> Actions, then, are called just and temperate when they
> are such as the just or the temperate man would do; but
> it is not the man who does these that is just and tem-
> perate, but the man who also does them *as* just and tem-
> perate men do them. It is well said, then, that it is by
> doing just acts that the just man is produced, and by
> doing temperate acts the temperate man: without doing
> these no one would have even a prospect of becoming
> good.
>
> But most people do not do these but take refuge in
> theory and think they are being philosophers and will
> become good in this way, behaving somewhat like
> patients who listen attentively to their doctors, but do
> none of the things they are ordered to do. As the latter
> will not be made well in body by such a course of treat-
> ment, the former will not be made well in soul by such a
> course of philosophy.[44]

And yet, though Aristotle has isolated three conditions of acting virtuously, it is far from clear that we can find these conditions in isolation. Since there are no rules which will prescribe the virtuous act in a given set of circumstances, since ethics is not a precise science, the only way to determine how to act in a given situation is to ask a virtuous man how he would act (unless, of course, one is virtuous oneself, in which case one will have a sensitivity to the situation that will enable one to judge accurately what action is appropriate). Thus the practical knowledge of a virtuous man does not exist independently of his character, and it is because of his character that he chooses the virtuous action for its own sake.

The practical knowledge of a virtuous man Aristotle calls practical wisdom (*phronēsis*).[45] The decisions of a virtuous man do not

[44] *Nicomachean Ethics* II.4, 1105b1–18.
[45] *Nicomachean Ethics* VI.5.

flow automatically from him; they are a product of reasoning and thought, of conscious sensitivity to the demands of a situation. Ethical virtue, as it were, flows through the mind. But this is a different part of the mind from that which is able to contemplate essences and basic philosophical truths.[46] Aristotle distinguished parts of the soul by the different functions performed, and the exercise of the ability to contemplate basic truths performs a dramatically different function from the exercise of the ability to decide how to act. Aristotle is clear that philosophical wisdom (*sophia*) is a higher form of knowledge than practical widsom:

> It would be strange to think that the art of politics or practical wisdom is the best knowledge since man is not the best thing in the world ... But if the argument be that man is the best of animals, it makes no difference; for there are other things much more divine in their nature even than man; e.g. most conspicuously, the bodies from which the heavens are framed. From what has been said it is plain, then, that wisdom is knowledge [*epistēmē*] combined with comprehension [*noûs*] of the things that are highest by nature. This is why we say Anaxagoras, Thales and men like them have wisdom but not practical wisdom, when we see them ignorant of what is to their own advantage, and why we say that they know things that are remarkable, admirable, difficult and divine, but useless: namely because it is not human goods they seek. Practical wisdom on the other hand is concerned with things human and things about which it is possible to deliberate.[47]

Indeed, practical wisdom and philosophical wisdom help to constitute two fundamentally different types of life.[48] The ethical or political life is the active life within society which the bulk of the *Nicomachean Ethics* is devoted to describing. This is a life in which

---

[46] *Nicomachean Ethics* VI.1.

[47] *Nicomachean Ethics* VI.7, 1141a20–b9. (Aristotle believed that mind simply grasped first principles: *Posterior Analytics* II.19; *Metaphysics* IX.10.) It is this activity that the translator calls 'comprehension.' 'Knowledge' (*epistēmē*) is that which one learns from the grasped first principles by rigorous reasoning. See section 6.1 below.

[48] *Nicomachean Ethics* I.5, 1095b17–19; X.7–9; *Politics* VII.2, 1324a24–34. I discuss this further in section 6.7 below.

practical mind and the *ethical* virtues are at the forefront.[49] The contemplative life, by contrast, is one that is given over to philosophy: to contemplating essences and basic truths about the broad structure of reality. It is a life in which the *intellectual* virtues, like theoretical mind, rather than the ethical are at the forefront: it is a life relatively withdrawn from the political life within society.[50] But if the ethical and contemplative describe two fundamentally different types of life, a serious question arises about the possibility of a coherent and harmonious life for man. It would seem that there are too many different things for man to be. For if all men *by nature* desire to understand and this is a desire that motivates man to contemplate the world, it would seem to be a desire which pulls him out of the ethical. And yet the ethical life is supposed to describe the good and happy life for man. It would seem that if a man is firmly within the ethical, then he must have a conflicting desire in his soul: the desire to understand. But the virtuous life was supposed to be free of such conflicts among desires. On the other hand, if a man gives in to the desire to understand and dedicates himself to a contemplative life, it would seem that he thereby forfeits the good life for man. We shall return to this problem later.[51]

The important point for the moment is that practical mind is a motive force in the individual.[52] The highest state of practical mind, that of the virtuous person, is practical wisdom. This is a developed ability to judge the good and bad ends for man and to choose the actions appropriate for securing those ends in the particular circumstances of life.[53] The practically wise man has the ability to decide what are the truly good actions for him, but these actions are not just means to ends, they are themselves ends. For these actions help to constitute a well-lived life, and living well is itself an end. And yet it would seem that practical wisdom involves deliberation; but we have already seen that Aristotle insists that we deliberate about means, not ends.[54] How could the same action be both a means and an end? Perhaps it could not: perhaps Aristotle is just being inconsistent. However, I would like to suggest that Aristotle's apparently disparate claims can be reconciled. The same

[49] *Nicomachean Ethics* II.1, 1103a14–18.
[50] Cf. *Nicomachean Ethics* VI.7; X.7–9, especially 1177b4–25.
[51] See section 6.8 below.
[52] See *Nicomachean Ethics* VI.2, especially 1139a22–b5.
[53] See *Nicomachean Ethics* VI.5, especially 1140b4–7, b20–1.
[54] *Nicomachean Ethics* III.3, 1112b11–24; cf. section 5.4 below.

action can be viewed both as a means and as an end. From the perspective of a deliberation which has proceeded from a desire for a certain goal, down through the ways to achieve that goal, to a deliberated decision about how to act, the ensuing action is a means. However, from the perspective of a well-lived life, that same action helps to constitute that life, and that life is itself an end. In fact, Aristotle does include ends in his account of what it is to deliberate well.[55] The man who is able to deliberate well is one who is *both* able to choose the best things attainable by action *and* to reason about how to attain them. Thus while deliberation *per se* may be concerned with means and not ends, deliberating well is concerned both with means and with ends.

It is the practically wise man who is able to deliberate well.[56] But how does a good deliberation motivate one to act? One might do well to go back to Aristotle's conception of deliberation and deliberated decision (*proairesis*).[57] A deliberation begins with a wish for a certain end. That wish is itself both a desire and a piece of consciousness. The wish motivates a deliberation in which the agent reasons back from the desired goal to the steps necessary to achieve it. The deliberation is both a conscious reasoning and a manifestation of the desire for the end. It is also a transmitter of desire from the wished-for goal to the means. The last step in the deliberation is a deliberated decision to act in a certain way. The decision is at once a desire and a state of consciousness. Indeed, it is essentially a self-conscious state: for the awareness that I have decided to act in a certain way partially constitutes the deliberated decision. This entire process is at once a manifestation of practical mind and a manifestation of desire. Thus Aristotle can speak of desiring mind. Practical wisdom is just what the desiring mind of a virtuous person exhibits: he wishes for the best goals and reasons well how to achieve them.

5.4 Incontinence[58]

Aristotle was interested not only in the practical wisdom of the vir-

---

[55] *Nicomachean Ethics* VI.7, 1141b8–14; VI.9, 1142b21–22; cf. VI.12, 1144a20–9.
[56] *Nicomachean Ethics* VI.7, 1141b8–10.
[57] See section 5.4 below.
[58] Appropriate reading: *Nicomachean Ethics* VII.

tuous man, but also in the practical failures of the non-virtuous. One form of failure particularly fascinated him: that in which a man decides that a certain course of action would be best for him, and then acts against his own judgement. Such a man is, for whatever reason, unable to live as he thinks he should. I speak of *such a man*, for Aristotle did not think that acting against one's best judgement was an isolated event that might occur once in an otherwise virtuous life. Acting against one's judgement was, for Aristotle, a defect of character – a defect which has come to be known as incontinence.

One reason that incontinence is of interest to philosophers is that it is not clear how it is even possible. Socrates famously argued that no man can knowingly not do what is best.[59] In broad outline his is a conceptual argument designed to show that we cannot make sense of a man's knowingly choosing a course of action when he considers an alternative action both available to him and better for him. For if he genuinely considered an alternative action to be better, how could we explain his not doing it? Thus, Socrates concluded, a bad act must be done in ignorance, under the false belief that it is for the best.

And yet Socrates, who is responsible for formulating the philosophical problem of incontinence, is also responsible for getting the issue sidetracked. For he formulated it specifically as a problem about knowledge or understanding (*epistēmē*): '...it would be strange – so Socrates thought – if when knowledge was in a man something else could master it and drag it about like a slave.'[60] In this way, a very general question about how one could act against one's judgement was transformed into the rather specific and technical question of how one's soul could be in a particular state – having knowledge or understanding – without that state ruling. This is the form of the problem which Aristotle inherited from Socrates, and much of *Nicomachean Ethics* VII is given over to answering it – to showing how the knowledge in one's soul can be temporarily shut down by strong passions. Ironically, in trying to answer this question, Aristotle widens the concept of incontinence to include ordinary cases of succumbing to temptation where we

[59] Plato, *Protagoras* 352B–353A.
[60] *Nicomachean Ethics* VII.2, 1145b23–4. See *Protagoras* 352B–C.

might say that the agent 'knew better.' Though this will be of interest to any student of the human condition, there is a peculiarly philosophical problem about incontinence that is in danger of being overlooked.

Let us call **incontinence** a situation in which (a) an agent performs an action intentionally, (b) the agent believes that an alternative action is open to him, and (c) the agent judges that all things considered it would be better to do the alternative action rather than the one he performs.[61] The concept of **incontinence** will help us to focus on what is of enduring philosophical interest about incontinence. On the one hand, there is no mention of any specific state of the soul, like knowledge or understanding, so the problem is freed from any particular conception of the soul (Socrates' or Aristotle's) which might seem peculiar to the ancient Greeks. On the other hand, the concept of **incontinence** is not so general that the philosophical problem gets lost. An ordinary case of succumbing to temptation counts for Aristotle as incontinence, but it need not be a case of **incontinence**: for there need be no evidence that at the time of his action the seduced agent judges that all things considered it would be better to do another action. Every case of **incontinence** is a case of incontinence, but not vice versa.

Incontinence poses a peculiarly philosophical problem, for it is hard to see how it is even possible. A psychologist or a novelist might tell us how humans work themselves into the tangled temptations that life presents, but there does not seem to be any way in which a person can behave **incontinently**. The reason is that an agent's beliefs, desires, values, and actions are intrinsically related to one another. We can see a being as an agent, as acting intentionally, only insofar as we can see his behaviour within the schema of beliefs and desires that we attribute to him. It is among his beliefs and desires that we must find a reason for his acting as he does. But we are able to identify his beliefs and desires only via his intentional actions: by what he says and otherwise does.[62] It is in these actions that what is of value to him is revealed; there is in principle no independent access to his values. One thus does not qualify as

---

[61] This formulation is due to Donald Davidson: see 'How is Weakness of Will Possible?'

[62] See Donald Davidson, *Essays on Actions and Events*, especially essays 1 and 11; and *Inquiries into Truth and Interpretation*, essays 9–16.

an **incontinent** merely by judging 'I ought not to X,' where X is some communal moral injunction, and then disobeying. In such a circumstance, the command 'thou shalt not X' has gotten some hold on one's conscience, but there is as yet no evidence that one has judged that *all* things considered it would be better not to X. The reason for the intrinsic relation of belief, desire, value, and action is the holistic nature of the mental. Each belief and desire is conditioned by indefinitely many others. Given any belief–desire pair on its own, we can have no idea of what action, if any, will result from it. One might at first think that if an agent is very thirsty and believes a glass of water is in front of him, he will proceed with drinking activity. But he will not if he also thinks that he will be shot by his captor for doing so. Unless, of course, he does not care about his thirst but does want to end his life. Given any action in isolation, we can, in like fashion, have no idea of the belief–desire pair which provides the proper explanation.

To see any action as intentional, it thus seems we must construct a rather complex, teleological conception of an agent, with a mutually conditioned web of beliefs and desires, acting purposefully in an environment which he more or less understands. Lying at the heart of the concept of intentional action is the presupposition of rationality. An intentional action, by its very nature, must look reasonable in the light of an agent's beliefs and desires. Any explanation of an intentional action must be part of a story which portrays the agent as a rational animal. **Incontinence** threatens this structure, and that is why it is philosophically interesting. Given the holistic nature of the mental, an agent's action may appear odd in the light of any particular belief–desire pair he has. But in an **incontinent** act, an agent has purportedly taken all his beliefs and desires into consideration. The outcome of his deliberation is supposed to be an act which, on the one hand, is intentional and, on the other, contradicts his judgement of what it would be better to do.

There is no straightforward way to determine what Aristotle thought about **incontinence**. His extended discussion in *Nicomachean Ethics* VII is about incontinence, not **incontinence**, and Aristotle was interested in all its forms. Given an ethical outlook based on the idea that human nature was such as to be able to acquire the virtues, the exercise of which would be constitutive of happiness, the general problem of loss of control would be of great interest to him. And it is in his discussion of incontinence that Aristotle explicitly adopts his well-known methodological principle: a philosophical theory must *save the appearances*:

> We must, as in all other cases, set the phenomena before us and, after first discussing the difficulties, go on to prove, if possible, the truth of all the reputable opinions ... or, failing this, of the greater number and the most authoritative; for if we both resolve the difficulties and leave the reputable opinions undisturbed we shall have proved the case sufficiently.[63]

Among the appearances are how people act – the way they apparently do act against their better judgement – and what people say about how they act. A philosophical theory need not leave all the appearances intact, but the theory must make it at least plausible that these appearances appear as they do to pre-philosophical consciousness. Aristotle mentions Socrates' argument that incontinence is impossible, and then comments that his argument 'contradicts the plain phenomena.'[64] Aristotle does not thereby disagree with Socrates' claim or fault any step of the argument. Even if he had accepted the Socratic position, Aristotle would have made this criticism: Socrates was willing to bequeath a paradox, whereas an adequate philosophical theory should go on to show why the many apparent cases do appear to be incontinence even though they are not. An adequate philosophical theory dispels paradox. One might say, roughly, that Socrates tries to show that incontinence is impossible by assimilating all cases of incontinence to **incontinence**, while Aristotle tries to save the appearances by showing that the apparent cases of incontinence are not generally cases of **incontinence**. Certainly, both Aristotle's general interest in loss of control and his conception of philosophical method commit him to considering a wide range of cases whose relation to incontinence is remote. So, if we are to find out what Aristotle thought about **incontinence**, we must extract it from his writings.

Incontinence presents a problem for self-consciousness. First, **incontinence** is an obstacle to our reflective understanding of man

---

[63] *Nicomachean Ethics* VII.1, 1145b2–7.
[64] *Nicomachean Ethics* VII.2, 1145b22–8.

and his position in the world, **incontinence** blocks our progress. On the one hand, we have a philosophical argument that **incontinence** is impossible; on the other, there are many apparent cases of incontinence: 'Thought is bound fast when it will not rest because the conclusion does not satisfy it, and cannot advance because it cannot refute the argument.'[65] Incontinence, Aristotle was well aware, is primarily a problem for those of us who are trying to understand the world and man's place in it – whether or not we are also **incontinent**. Indeed, one might think that it is *only* insofar as we are philosophers that **incontinence** presents a problem: that if we were **incontinent** the experience of **incontinence** 'from the inside' would be no more problematic than any other experience of loss of control. In fact, Aristotle suggests that this is not so. **Incontinence**, insofar as it is a possibility, could only be the experience of a highly self-conscious being: one who has actively considered his position and judged that he should act in a certain way. The experience of **incontinence** (if it is possible) must differ from other forms of loss of control, succumbing to temptation, etc., by its highly wrought self-conscious ingredient. So, second, there must be an element of surprise for the self-consciousness of an **incontinent**: self-consciousness must, in the action, experience disharmony between itself and the agent of which it is purporting to be the self-consciousness: 'That the man who acts incontinently does not, before he gets into this state, *think* that he will so act is evident.'[66] Aristotle intends this as a general claim: that all incontinent acts involve a certain degree of ignorance of how one will act. Ironically, though, the highly developed self-conscious consideration required for **incontinence** suggests that there will be a greater degree of ignorance in an **incontinent** act than in a mere case of loss of control.

Aristotle, like us, thought there was a necessary connection between judgement and action. Of course, we would give different accounts of this necessity. We are more concerned with the conceptual constraints on interpretation: that is, we believe that the

---

[65] *Nicomachean Ethics* VII.2, 1146a24–7.
[66] *Nicomachean Ethics* VII.2, 1145b30–1. (The Oxford translation has 'think that he *ought* to act so.' The Greek will allow either translation, and I prefer mine, because the incontinent's most surprising mistake is not about what he ought to do but about what he will do. A bad man may say to himself, 'I ought to help the old lady, but I won't.' This is not incontinence, but badness.)

judgements which can legitimately be ascribed to an agent must somehow be reflected in his actions. Aristotle was more concerned with judgements as the mental ingredients of the soul which necessitate an action. In one version of Aristotle's practical syllogism, one judgement is universal, recommending that one perform a certain type of action: for example,

Everything sweet ought to be tasted.

The other judgement is particular, grounded in perceptual experience, saying that this is an action of the recommended type: for example,

This is sweet.

Whenever one believes these two judgements and self-consciously considers them together, one must *straightaway* perform this action. The action itself is the conclusion of the syllogism.[67] Just as for us the necessary connections between judgement and action make **incontinence** problematic, so for Aristotle the practical syllogism as a model of deliberated action makes a pure case of **incontinence** problematic. For if the judgements were actively and self-consciously made, the chosen action would have to follow.

It is sometimes said that Aristotle does not allow room for ethical conflict. The problem is that, once one has the relevant premisses in mind, it seems one must act, regardless of what beliefs and desires one has. I do not think that this criticism is entirely fair. Aristotle explicitly recognizes the possibility of conflicts,[68] and one can accommodate the practical syllogism to this possibility, if one treats the premisses as the outcome of the conflict-ridden deliberative process. By the time the premisses are asserted, the conflict has already occurred, and the judgement one now proceeds to make (and act upon) is of the form 'all things considered.' It is true, though, that Aristotle does not tell us how we go about considering all things. But however we do go about considering, Aristotle is aware that the world in all its particularity may present us with a conflict which did not exist at the level of universal judgements. For example, one may adhere to a general injunction forbidding

[67] *Nicomachean Ethics* VII.3, 1147a24–32. Compare this with the model of deliberation we have already encountered in section 4.5 above.
[68] *Nicomachean Ethics* VII.3, 1147a32–5.

one to eat pork. But when, at the latest nouvelle restaurant, the waiter brings a complimentary hors d'oeuvre of chocolate-covered bacon, one may find oneself eating it. This is not **incontinence**, for there need not have been any consideration of what to do. When the unforeseen conflict does arise, one's desire for sweets overrides or shuts down the countervailing judgement. One moves closer to a case of **incontinence** when the contingent conflict is one that one ought to have foreseen and taken account of in one's antecedent deliberations. If, for example, the judgement forbade eating highly calorific foods, then one should have foreseen that the presence of sweets would cause conflicts. One may, of course, be ignorant about even the most likely course of experience, but the more interesting case is that in which one is ignorant about oneself.

Aristotle's intricate discussion of the various ways one's knowledge or understanding can be shut down sheds almost no light on how **incontinence** might be possible. This is not a failure of the discussion, because Aristotle is not here concerned with showing how **incontinence** is possible, only how incontinence actually occurs. Given that the premisses of a practical syllogism necessitate the action-conclusion, Aristotle needs an account of how the premisses might on occasion be blocked, rendered inoperative. He distinguishes various senses in which one can have knowledge or understanding: there is the sense in which one possesses the knowledge though one is not at present exercising it, and the sense in which one is actively contemplating.[69] Aristotle accepts that a man actively exercising his knowledge could not act incontinently with respect to it, so he concentrates on those cases in which a man may possess the knowledge but somehow be prevented from exercising it.[70] Strong angers or appetites may actually change the condition of the body, and, though in this condition one may still be able to state the arguments that a man who was genuinely exercising his judgements would state, this has no more significance than the case of drunks who are able to recite verses of Empedocles.[71] The strong passions work like a drug which shuts judgement down, just as does wine or sleep.[72] The man overcome with passion has

[69] *Nicomachean Ethics* VII.3, 1146b31–5. Cf. *On the Soul* II.5; and section 4.3 above.
[70] *Nicomachean Ethics* VII.3, 1147b9–17, 1146b34–5, 1147a11–14.
[71] *Nicomachean Ethics* VII.3, 1147a20, b12.
[72] *Nicomachean Ethics* VII.3, 1147a11–14.

knowledge in a more attenuated sense than the healthy man who is not contemplating: only the healthy man can exercise his knowledge at will. The passion-ridden man has knowledge only because when he recovers from his state he will then be able to exercise it. And, Aristotle says, one should look to the physiologist and not the philosopher for an account of how this recovery occurs.[73]

It would be disappointing were Aristotle to assimilate **incontinence** to drunkenness, but that is not what he is doing. He is trying to explain one form of drunkenness – being drunk with anger – in terms of another – being drunk with alcohol. This cannot be **incontinence**, for the drunk has little or no idea what he is doing. Nor is this a plausible model of how a man who has ethical virtue may be led to act against his judgement. For a virtuous man would not allow himself to get into a condition in which he could not exercise his judgement. This is merely an account of how a man may be overcome with passion, even though he ordinarily knows better: it is a case neither of **incontinence** nor of the breakdown of ethical virtue.

Aristotle does, however, drop a hint about a more serious form of practical failure:

> For even men under the influence of these passions utter scientific proofs and verses of Empedocles, and those who have just begun to learn can string together words, but do not yet know; *for it has to become part of themselves*, and that takes time; so that we must suppose that the use of language by men in an incontinent state means no more than its utterance by actors on the stage.[74]

Those who are first learning a subject are different from the alcoholic and emotional drunks whose judgement is shut down. The students may be performing at the peak of their mental capacities, and they may be making sincere assertions, but they have not yet learned enough to know what they are talking about; and they are mistaken in thinking that they have. Aristotle says that it is necessary for the knowledge to become a part of them. Aristotle means this literally, for the literal translation of the Greek is that one must become 'like-natured' (*sumphuēnai*) to that which one is saying.

[73] *Nicomachean Ethics* VII.3, 1147b6–8.
[74] *Nicomachean Ethics* VII.3, 1147a19–24 (my emphasis).

182

Being like-natured consists, I believe, in the *logos* that one asserts being the same as the *logos* in one's soul. In the case of the learner, he may be able to state an appropriate *logos*, but his soul has not yet taken on the appropriate form. Although a man who has knowledge will be right about what he knows, one who is trying to acquire knowledge – or who sees himself as doing so – may suffer a peculiar form of ignorance: he may (mistakenly) suppose himself to know. The possession of knowledge guarantees at least the possibility of awareness of that knowledge, but one form of ignorance is the false sense of that awareness. When Aristotle likens the **incontinent** to the actor, the analogy is not, I suspect, meant to be that neither is serious about what he is saying. That would be a plausible construal if the analogy immediately followed the example of the drunken man reciting Empedocles. But, coming as it does after the example of the learner who does not yet know, and the requirement of being like-natured, the analogy between the **incontinent** and the actor is most likely to be this: neither the *logos* of the actor nor the *logos* of the **incontinent** expresses the true condition of his soul. There is no implication that the **incontinent** is aware of this or that he does not take his assertion seriously.

With respect to ignorance of the state of one's soul, the ethical virtues pose a special problem. A student of geometry, in a self-critical mood, could in principle carry out a thought experiment to determine whether he knew geometry as well as he thought he did. He could, for example, try to prove the Pythagorean theorem and derive consequences from it; and if he succeeded this would improve his confidence that he knew what he was talking about when he said that $a^2 + b^2 = c^2$. Of course, he might make a mistake in the proof and erroneously think he had proved the theorem when he had not. But we can easily imagine him discovering that he cannot prove the theorem, and in so doing he would discover that the *logos* he spoke did not reflect the *logos* of his soul. With ethical virtues, by contrast, there is no analogous thought experiment one could even in principle carry out. The ethical virtues, as Aristotle repeatedly stresses, are taught not by verbal argument, but by habituation. One develops them through good ethical upbringing; and it is only after one has already acquired them that one is in a position to appreciate the reflective philosophical arguments which can be marshaled in their favor. That is why Aristotle does not think that lectures in ethics should be wasted on the young.[75] So, although a man who has acquired the ethical virtues will have a healthy sense of who he is and what he is like, it is relatively easy for the man who has not acquired the virtues to suppose he has. He will mouth the words of the virtuous man, and he will do so sincerely: for, insofar as he is capable of believing what he says, he does believe what he says. However, this capability does not run very deep. He will have heard a *logos* commending ethical virtue which he found compelling. But, according to Aristotle, a mere *logos* will not teach ethical principles.[76] For the soul cannot acquire the *logos* simply by hearing it and assenting to it. The *logos* of ethical virtue can be instilled only through repeated actions, through a sustained and thorough ethical upbringing.

Aristotle says: 'Badness escapes notice, but **incontinence** does not.'[77] What he means, I think, is this: even a bad man will be pursuing ends which he takes to be good – that is, good for him. That his ends are bad, even for him, will not be something he will appreciate. If he did, he would not pursue them. The **incontinent**, by contrast, will be brought face to face with his ignorance when he is put in a situation in which he must act on his purported beliefs. Here I think Aristotle is talking about **incontinence**, and not an ordinary loss of control, for there is no reason to suppose that the emotional drunk has any awareness of what he is doing. The **incontinent**, though, must confront the inescapable fact that what he says, however sincerely, is not like-natured with what he does. He is brought up short by his own action.

It was intolerable to Socrates that knowledge should be 'dragged about like a slave.' In a qualified fashion, Aristotle agrees: if one's knowledge is active, it is impossible to act **incontinently** with respect to it. However, that does not imply that Aristotle thinks **incontinence** impossible: for he recognizes that one should not restrict the question as to whether **incontinence** is possible by conflating it with the question of whether it is possible to act against

---

[75] *Nicomachean Ethics* I.3, especially 1095a3–11.

[76] *Nicomachean Ethics* II.1–6.

[77] *Nicomachean Ethics* VII.8, 1150b36. (I here give a literal translation of the Greek. The Oxford translation offers the gloss: 'vice is unconscious of itself, incontinence is not.' This is misleading, for in an important sense incontinence is unconscious of itself: the incontinent act is possible only because to a certain extent the incontinent is unaware of the true motivational state of his soul.)

one's knowledge. At the beginning of the discussion he notes that some people agree with Socrates that nothing can rule over knowledge, but they hold that the man who simply has beliefs (a less prestigious mental state) can be ruled by pleasures.[78] Later, he explicitly recognizes that the problem of **incontinence** can arise even if one's mental condition is only that of belief:

> As for the suggestion that it is true opinion and not knowledge against which one acts **incontinently**, that makes no difference to the argument; for some people when in a state of opinion do not hesitate but think they know exactly. If, then, it is owing to their weak conviction that those who have opinion are more likely to act against their belief than those who know, there will be no difference between knowledge and opinion; for some men are no less convinced of what they think than others of what they know...[79]

The problem of **incontinence** is ultimately that of acting against one's considered judgement. For Aristotle **incontinence** is possible when one's judgement is a sincerely held false conscious belief. This false belief is not a belief about the world but about oneself. An **incontinent** may, for example, truly believe that in *these* circumstances *this* is the right thing to do. His mistake lies in thinking that this is what he wants to do and this is what he will do. So the **incontinent** may well be right in his judgements about the world or about what is good. His mistake is about himself. A person can acquire such false beliefs about himself if he has not been well brought up. If one has not acquired the ethical virtues, it is easy to suppose one has. One will then assert an ethical *logos*, but one's actions will reveal to oneself and others that one's soul is not like-natured to what one says. **Incontinence** represents a failure of self-consciousness. Aristotle says that beasts are incapable of incontinence because they are incapable of formulating the universal judgement which would then be violated in action.[80] As one moves from ordinary cases of incontinence to **incontinence**, the degree of self-conscious awareness becomes more acute, for one must have one's judgement actively in mind when acting against it.

[78] *Nicomachean Ethics* VII.2, 1145b31–5.
[79] *Nicomachean Ethics* VII.3, 1146b24–30.
[80] *Nicomachean Ethics* VII.3, 1147b3–5.

But that implies that the discrepancy between thought and action must be all the greater. An **incontinent** is a stranger to himself: it is in his actions, not in his assertions, that he may discover who he is.[81]

5.5 Freedom and virtue

The virtuous person, in contrast to the incontinent, knows who he is and what he wants. He is able to judge the right thing to do in a given set of circumstances and to take pleasure in doing it. In acting as he thinks he should, he leads a full, rich, flourishing life. The virtues are motivated dispositional states which aim at their own exercise: and the exercise of the virtues is constitutive of the good life for humans. But however sensitive a person's ability to act well may be, if he has not yet reflected on his character there is an aspect of well-being which eludes him: self-knowledge. If the self-knowledge of a virtuous person is constitutive of a good life, and if the virtues are motivated dispositional states which promote and constitute a person's ability to lead a good life, one should expect the virtues to motivate a virtuous person to reflect on the virtues.

One of the high-water marks of ethical activity is a particular exercise of human freedom: that in which a person who has absorbed ethical values consciously acknowledges and endorses his own character. The ethical virtues, remember, are instilled by habituation: thus they can arise in an agent relatively un-self-consciously. In ethical reflection, a person develops from being a person capable of doing the right thing in the right circumstances to being a person who has a conscious understanding of who he is and what he is doing. Reflection on one's own character, and the ensuing self-acceptance or self-criticism, may be an activity which is at once motivated by the virtues, an expression of the virtues, *and* a manifestation of human freedom. One might thus say that the ethical virtues motivate their own self-understanding. And, in acquiring self-understanding, they achieve a legitimation. The

[81] I take that haunting phrase from Timothy D. Wilson, 'Strangers to Ourselves: The Origins and Accuracy of Beliefs about one's own Mental States,' J. H. Harvey and G. Weary, eds., *Attribution in Contemporary Psychology*.

highest state of the ethical virtues is one in which the person possessing them understands and endorses them. It is the aim of the *Nicomachean Ethics* to help the virtuous person make the transition from merely having a good character to consciously understanding and accepting his character. These lectures are intended for virtuous people. An intended member of the audience will be motivated to work through the thoughts expressed in the lectures for himself, and in so doing he will be reflectively endorsing his own character. But the lectures are themselves a manifestation of the virtues. They are motivated by Aristotle's own desire to live an excellent life, and they are themselves an instance of the transition from the mere possession to reflective understanding and legitimation of the virtues. In this sense, the *Nicomachean Ethics* is itself among the highest expressions of the ethical virtues.[82]

And yet, if this process of reflection and endorsement is an expression of human freedom, it is also a manifestation of desire. For consider how this reflection arose. In Aristotle's world there is already an ethical community which embodies the values associated with the virtues and which has virtuous members in its midst. The community has ways of educating its youth; and if the community has any ability to survive, it will be able to pass on its values to the next generation. This education, as we have seen, will to a significant extent be non-rational: there will be habituation and training, encouragements and discouragements, which do not essentially appeal to a child's rationality, but rather, say, to his desire for love and encouragement. But if the outcome of this process is to be a manifestation of freedom, the education cannot be overly coercive or brutalizing. It must respect the child's integrity: in fact, I believe, it must be a form of education which the child himself, when he later grows to be a virtuous person reflecting on his life and education, can endorse. In an ideal case, a well-brought-up person will develop a character and self-conception which will embody to a significant degree the ethical values of the community. Suppose these values are ones which we could envision as embodied in a person capable of living a full human life, and suppose we could see them as instilled by non-coercive means.

---

[82] In *Ethics and the Limits of Philosophy*, Bernard Williams asks how it is possible for ethical reflection to find a place within an Aristotelian ethical outlook. I think that the interpretation offered here gives the outline of an answer.

Then when this person reflectively decides to act on those desires which are conducive to or expressive of his character, I think we would conceive of him as exercising his freedom. Yet his character is also a cultural artefact whose production is motivated by the very same desires as the person ends up endorsing! It is because the community values the values which the person's character embodies that it sets itself to educate the agent so as to embody them.

But how can the triumph of a desire simultaneously be an expression of the human freedom manifested in effective reflection? We tend to think of reflection as a manifestation of human freedom precisely because we use reflection to exercise some *control* over our desires. In reflection we criticize some of our desires and then take steps to diminish their force; we endorse others and then takes steps to satisfy them. That is why some philosophers have thought that the self-consciousness which engages in critical reflection must be somehow detached from the desires which it subjects to critical survey. Otherwise, it is thought, the reflection could not be a manifestation of the person's freedom: the reflection would be under the sway of some desire or other and thus not truly free. The problem with this conception of reflection, as we have already seen, is that it is mysterious how such a detached self-consciousness could make any decisions at all.[83]

Instead of solving this problem, Aristotle's conception of the virtues offers us an alternative account of reflection and its relation to desire. Perhaps one reason Aristotle's account is appealing is that he has a much richer conception of desire than do many modern philosophers. If one thinks that desires must disrupt or distort a process of rational thought, then it will be mysterious how a single process could be both a triumph of desire and an instance of the freedom manifested in effective reflection. Certainly, some desires do disrupt or distort. Let us call a desire *overwhelming* if it is partially constitutive of having it that one cannot consider it — one is too busy trying to satisfy it. For an overwhelming desire, one must genuinely detach oneself from it if one is to consider it at all. Overwhelming desires provide the paradigm of unfreedom: they happen to one, and they take over. A *distorting* desire is one which disrupts the rationality of a deliberation. Cer-

[83] See section 4.5 above.

tain temptations, for example, may be distorting. With a distorting temptation, the 'deliberation' about whether to give into the temptation will be a sham, a self-deceptive exercise in dismissing countervailing reasons. Only if we conceive of all desires along the lines of the overwhelming or distorting desires does it seem that one must detach oneself from all of them if one is to consider them freely.

But not all desires are like that. If a single activity is to be both a triumph or desire and a manifestation of human freedom, there must be desires which are capable of a genuine legitimation, and the legitimation must itself be a manifestation of the desire. Within the soul of Aristotle's virtuous man there are desires which motivate the agent to embark on a reflection which seeks to legitimate those very desires. Let us call such desires *legitimating*. A person does not stand in relation to his legitimating desires as a mere conduit for their satisfaction: in commending themselves to the person, they are not merely using him as a means to their selfish ends.[84] First, by becoming transparent to consciousness, they seek endorsement by what, from the point of view of rational deliberation, are thoroughly fair means. Thus it is that their endorsement can simultaneously be an expression of the person's freedom. Second, some of these legitimating desires reveal themselves to be constitutive of the person's very being. Far from the agent's being the mere tool of a selfish legitimating desire, the desire gains its greatest force by encouraging the agent to pursue a line of reflection which culminates in the realization that the possession and satisfaction of that desire are constitutive of who he is. The ethical virtues are like that. They are organized states of desire that motivate a virtuous person to reflect that the virtues constitute who he is and who he wants to be. And the reflection itself is a manifestation of the virtues.

For the virtuous person's reflective endorsement of his own character also to be a manifestation of freedom, certain conditions must be met. First, the person's character cannot be a product of coercion. A virtuous person's character is instilled by non-rational means of encouragement and discouragement. He did not choose from some independent standpoint to become the person he now

---

[84] This is an important disanalogy between the legitimating desires and the purportedly selfish gene. Cf. Richard Dawkins, *The Selfish Gene*.

is: he was cajoled into it. He thus became a virtuous person unwillingly, not in the sense that the transition to virtue occurred against his will, but in the sense that he did not freely will to become the person he has become. Some philosophers have thought that this non-rational indoctrination alone disqualifies the person's reflective endorsement from being an act of freedom. But this disqualification seems absurdly strong: it makes it mysterious how the human animal could ever manifest the freedom of effective reflection. For Aristotle's point is that it is part of human nature that a child is in no position rationally to will the person he will become. What is important is that the non-rational encouragements and discouragements be just that: encouragements and discouragements. They should respect the child's dignity and integrity and not be coercive or brutalizing. Of course, there is no absolutely foolproof test to distinguish coercion from benign forms of non-rational training. Aristotle thought he could distinguish benign training because he grounded his theory of moral education in a view of human nature.

This brings us to the second condition: the reflective endorsement must be something more than a desire urging itself forward. Aristotle's virtuous person is able to meet this condition, for what he learns in studying the *Nicomachean Ethics* is that humans have a nature. There is something definite and worthwhile that it is to be a human being, and the virtues enable a person to live a full, rich, happy life. Thus the virtuous person's endorsement is more than a desire commending itself: it is a (organized state of) desire commending itself *for a reason*.

Third, the reflection must be accurate and sensitive to the truth. Because the virtues are commending themselves for a true reason they achieve a genuine legitimation, not just a sham endorsement. Compare, by way of an extreme example, a reflective Nazi torturer who became the insensitive, cruel man that he is by a process of intimidation, brutalization, and bullying in SS training camp. As he is about to turn on the gas, he reflects that he is glad to be the person he is in the position he is in: for the Jews, he reasons, are not really human, but parasites which weaken and degrade the human race. In ridding the world of them, he is helping man to achieve his highest nature. He even reflectively endorses his education: it was necessary, he thinks, to become hardened and develop antibodies to the pernicious undermining influence of the Jewish race. The torturer's reflective endorsement is structurally analogous to that of the virtuous man, and yet the torturer's reflective endorsement is a manifestation of his *un*freedom. For his character is a product of coercion and his reasoning is bogus, a product of ideology and propaganda.

There is no absolute standpoint from which one can judge that one endorsement is true and constitutes a genuine legitimation and that another is false and constitutes a sham legitimation. The virtuous person's endorsement of his own character is carried out from within the perspective of a virtuous person. The endorsement counts as a legitimation only if it is true, but there is no detached perspective from which to judge its truth. Some modern philosophers have complained that Aristotle's ethics rests on an outdated metaphysical biology: men do not have essences or natures, and so ethics cannot be founded on the fulfillment of one's nature.[85] The virtuous person's endorsement therefore is false and not a legitimation. This complaint is, I believe, too strong. Both the stampede away from Aristotelian science which has marked scientific development since the Enlightenment, and the development of certain philosophical theories of language in the twentieth century,[86] have encouraged philosophers to accept the idea that Aristotelian essentialism is simply an antiquated theory. This, I believe, overlooks what is essential to Aristotelian essentialism, at least for an ethical theory. An ethical theory that is at least Aristotelian in inspiration need only believe that there are ways in which human beings can flourish which are recognizably ethical. One need only believe that human life is distinctive and potentially worthwhile; that there are certain ways of life that are fulfilling and rich and others that are degrading and deprived; that there are ways of living a cooperative, ethical life within society that are fulfilling and rich. This much it is possible to believe, for this much, I believe, is true.

---

[85] See, e.g., Bernard Williams, *Ethics and the Limits of Philosophy*, and *Morality: An Introduction*.

[86] I have in mind both Quine's attack on the analytic–synthetic distinction (in 'Two Dogmas of Empiricism') and Wittgenstein's development of the idea of family resemblance (in *Philosophical Investigations*).

5.6 The master–slave dialectic[87]

There is, however, one complaint against Aristotle's virtuous man which does deserve serious examination: he lacks the ability to engage in a certain type of self-criticism. For example, though Aristotle praises the noble man, might we not think today that the very concept of nobility, as Aristotle understood it, depends for its life on a social context of masters and slaves? If Aristotle is praising a way of life available only to a master class, should he not subject to scrutiny the very idea of a way of life which is dependent on there being a class of masters? If an ethical agent's reflective endorsement of his character is truly to be a manifestation of his freedom, it seems he should engage in some sort of reflective criticism of the values of the society into which he was born. If he simply ends up endorsing the virtues of his day, no matter how good the society in which he lives, it would seem that he is to that extent unfree. For such a person, the values of his day are merely laid down *for* him, they are not freely chosen *by* him.

In fact, Aristotle did engage in a critical reflection on the values of his day. This is not obvious: in part, because *we* are not clear as to what critical reflection is or what we can expect of it; in part because there is a certain misconception about the history of political thought which misleads us. According to many histories of philosophy, the ancient Greeks did not engage in critical reflection.[88] They were uncritically 'sunk in the *polis* life,' accepting the values of their day. This cliché is simply not true.[89] Indeed, even Aristotle's praise of nobility – which, at least prima facie, seems to accept uncritically the institution of slavery – is an implicit critique of an earlier conception of nobility: namely, that of the warrior hero in Homer's *Iliad*. What is distinctively modern is not the engagement in critical reflection, but the self-conscious fascination with reflection as a tool of inquiry. If we have become more self-conscious, that is manifested not by a deeper involvement in reflection itself, but by a deeper involvement in reflecting on the nature of reflection.

It is because we have not yet fully understood what one can and

---

[87] Appropriate reading: *Politics* I, III, IV, VII.

[88] The seminal work for this view is Hegel's *History of Philosophy*.

[89] For a fascinating account of ancient Greek reflections on democratic political theory, see Cynthia Farrar, *The Origins of Democratic Thinking*.

cannot expect to emerge from a process of critical reflection that it is all too easy for us to read Aristotle as uncritically accepting the institution of slavery. It is tempting to think that in critical reflection one must somehow *step outside* one's beliefs and subject them to critical survey. Yet Aristotle self-consciously refuses to take any such step. His ethical and political arguments are directed toward people who are already virtuous, and are designed to show them that (from their own perspective) the virtuous life makes sense. This marks a radical departure from Plato. Plato thought that one had not fully secured the ethical life unless one could formulate an argument for it which would be compelling even to a person who stood outside it. Socrates thus engages in dialogues with ethical skeptics like Thrasymachus, Glaucon, and Callicles, in which he tries to show them that being ethical is in their own best interests.[90] Indulging in a cooperative virtue such as justice is, according to Callicles, an unmitigated hindrance to human flourishing. Socrates' attempt to show him that he is mistaken is among the most unconvincing arguments in the Platonic corpus.

One great advantage of Aristotle's method is that it offers a new approach to ethical skepticism. Aristotle does not think it important to convince the man who stands outside the ethical that he has made a mistake. He is concerned to show people who already live inside the ethical that it is a good idea to be there. He thus abandons a belief held by Plato and by many modern philosophers: that to attack skepticism effectively one must begin with premises the skeptic would himself accept,[91] that the only way to criticize skepticism is to engage with a skeptic. Such an engagement seems to demand an a priori proof that the ethical life is always in one's best interest. For a skeptic only holds out *the possibility* that a non-ethical life might be better for those who are able to live it. Justice, for example, is not held to be bad for everyone: the weak might profit from living in a just society. Justice is only held to be bad for the strong: for the man who can flourish without it. But if one has to rule out even the possibility of a flourishing non-ethical life, it would seem that one needs an a priori argument to do it. For an a

---

[90] See especially *Republic* 1, and the *Gorgias*.
[91] Incidentally, this belief has led to a serious misunderstanding of what Kant meant by a transcendental argument. See my article, 'The Disappearing "We".'

priori argument would abstract from the actual conditions of one's life and show one that, no matter what the conditions of one's life might be, the ethical life would always be in one's interest.

The problem is that, as far as we know, there is no a priori proof that Callicles' conception of flourishing is mistaken. That is why Socrates' debate with Callicles leaves the reader with the uncomfortable feeling that Socrates has not gotten the best of the argument. Aristotle's insight was that failure to construct a convincing a priori argument need not imply that one cannot answer a skeptical challenge. Whether or not one can depends on what one takes the role and function of skepticism to be. Skeptical challenges, in broad outline, seek to undermine the reflective justifications one gives for a set of beliefs or practices. If one takes the reflective justification for acting ethically to be a proof which eliminates all alternative possibilities for acting in one's interest other than acting ethically, then the mere construction of an alternative possibility will be sufficient to undermine the justification. The skeptic has to do relatively little to undermine us, precisely because we have set ourselves such a big task. Plato's arguments failed because they were overly ambitious. The key to an ethical outlook that is resistant to ethical skepticism is, as Aristotle saw, to sacrifice ambition. If one abandons the search for such a strong proof, one will not necessarily be undermined by the mere construction of an alternative possibility. If one can formulate a justification for a certain social and ethical practice that is at once weaker than the Platonic proof but nevertheless satisfying, one will simultaneously have forced the skeptic to do more if he is to be undermining.

The appropriate strategy is, therefore, to prove a posteriori that the ethical life is a life of human flourishing. One does this, as Aristotle did, by showing that the ethical life, *as it is actually lived* is a flourishing life.[92] An a posteriori proof that the ethical life is a flourishing life has certain distinctive features. It does not establish more than an actuality – that *this life* which we can observe and live is a flourishing one – so it does not eliminate the *possibility* of there being other less cooperative forms of flourishing. The proof will thus not necessarily be undermining to those who genuinely

[92] For further discussions of a posteriori proofs, see my *Aristotle and Logical Theory*, chapter 5, and 'Moral Objectivity.'

believe that they should live their lives in some non-ethical way.[93] But that is not the point of the proof. The proof is intended reflectively to reinforce those who are living this form of flourishing life. It does so in two ways. First, since the proof is inwardly directed – aimed at those who are already living (or, perhaps, almost living) an ethical life – it helps to make them reflectively aware that *this is* a form of flourishing and one which it is possible *for them* to live. Second, the strategy of the proof makes it difficult to pose a skeptical challenge. One reason that Callicles is such an interesting figure is that for thousands of years he has been mocking anyone who tries to prove that there is no possibility of acting in one's interest other than by acting justly. He stands for the durable, exuberant possibility that neither Socrates nor anyone since has been able to eliminate. But a self-consciousness of what constitutes flourishing which is induced by actual example – which does not seek to eliminate every alternative possibility – will not be undermined by the mere construction of a possible alternative. One can admit that a Calliclean figure, if ever there should be one, might have reason to live outside the ethical. Of course, Aristotle would never make such an admission, because he believed that Callicles was making a mistake. But the important point for now is that, even if one does make this admission, it need not be undermining to those who are already living within the ethical. Aristotle's *Ethics* is designed to show them that they are already living a satisfying, rich life.

Since Callicles is no longer reflectively undermining, he becomes a much less interesting figure.[94] For to be a skeptic one must threaten reflective stability. One will thus have to be different from Callicles: not even an actual alternative example of flourishing need be undermining. We may, for example, recognize that certain forms of artistic life do pose actual examples of alternative, uncooperative forms of flourishing.[95] Yet that recognition need not be

[93] Of course, it may be undermining: people who are living frustrating lives, divided in part by their pursuit of inappropriate goals, are susceptible to influence by people who are simply exemplifying a flourishing life. Ethical flourishers can thus serve as unmoved movers.

[94] In this regard, it is worth comparing the devastating nature of Nietzsche's negative critique of Judaeo-Christian morality with the pathetic positive conception of flourishing, the superman, which he commends.

[95] See Bernard Williams, 'Moral Luck,' in *Moral Luck*.

undermining to those whose flourishing partially consists in living an ethical life. To pose a skeptical challenge one would have to embody a genuinely alternative form of flourishing that by its very existence induced self-doubt among those who had, until now, taken flourishing partially to consist in an ethical life. By his very existence he would not merely establish an alternative actuality; he would impugn our purported a posteriori proof, by casting doubt on whether we had in fact succeeded in identifying and living an actual life of flourishing. Perhaps neither Aristotle nor we can prove a priori that there cannot be such a skeptic, but in the light of the work Aristotle has done to commend the flourishing ethical life, we have reason to be skeptical of the possibility of there being such a skeptic.

One advantage of Aristotle's approach to ethics, then, is that it defuses skepticism in a completely novel way. Instead of stepping outside of the ethical and trying to convince a skeptic in his own terms that he has reason to be ethical, Aristotle shows those who are already living an ethical life that they have good reason to be doing so. However, such an approach also has its pitfalls. The main danger is that one will be insufficiently critical. In commending the ethical life by pointing to the ethical life that is actually lived, there is the danger that one will end up defending the status quo. For if one does not step outside the society in which one lives, how can one subject any aspect of it to criticism?

There is, of course, a danger that one will be living so deeply in the midst of a social injustice that one will lack the perspective to see it as an injustice; and there is no absolutely foolproof method for determining that one lacks the required perspective. But if there is no foolproof method, then it is unrealistic to criticize Aristotle for failing to engage in a deeper form of critical reflection. Perhaps this will become clearer if one asks what one can legitimately expect of critical reflection. One cannot legitimately hope or expect to stand outside all one's values and survey them from an absolutely detached perspective. If Aristotle is to naturalize human freedom, reflection ought to be an activity in which the human animal can plausibly engage. There is no substitute for moving around critically within one's values: investigating, say, the value of nobility and its dependence on a society of masters and slaves; testing this against one's commitment to justice and equality; learning about other societies and other ethical systems; using one's imagination. Perhaps, too, one should display a certain *openness*: be open to criticisms of (some of) one's values, open to the power of a good argument, open to the suggestions of one's conscience and imagination. If this is all that critical reflection *can* be, then I think we can envision both Aristotle and his virtuous man as engaging in it. Certainly, I do not think it is stretching Aristotle's conception of a virtuous man unduly to see him maintaining this sort of openness while reflectively endorsing his own character. And Aristotle, for his part, investigated all the forms of social organization and constitution known to man. He treated them rather like a biologist investigating the habitats in which the human species might flourish. If he failed to uncover an injustice in his society, this tells us more about the limitations inherent in critical reflection than it does about Aristotle's limitations as a critic.

I should like to consider the most difficult case for my thesis: Aristotle's defense of slavery.[96] When one first reads the *Politics*, it is easy to think that Aristotle uncritically defends one of the most unjust institutions of his day. This, I believe, is a mistaken impression. It arises from ignoring the social context in which the *Politics* is written. The *Politics* provides a serious critique of democratic society, and yet it is written in one of the greatest democracies in the history of the world. So the *Politics* cannot be an uncritical legitimation of the values of the day. Moreover, Aristotle was the first political thinker to realize that slavery *needed* a defense. In fact, his defense of slavery is a critique of the institution of slavery as it existed in Athenian society. For Aristotle argues that the mere fact that someone is a slave does not make it right that he *should be* a slave.[97] Nor does the fact that the law sanctions that a certain class of people be slaves – even if that law is the democratic expression of the majority's will – justify their enslavement. Nor is it right to enslave a conquered people: that is the mere exercise of brute strength by one people over another.[98] Since Athenian slaves were, to a significant degree, either conquered peoples or their offspring, Aristotle must be criticizing the slavery of his day. In terms of the ancient antinomy of nature versus convention – *phusis* versus *nomos* – Aristotle thinks that all slavery that was founded *only* in *nomos* (law or convention) was unjustified.

[96] See *Politics* I.4–7.
[97] See *Politics* I.6.
[98] See also *Politics* VII.14, 1333b38–1334a2.

The only type of slavery he thought was justified was *natural* slavery. Some people are by their nature born to be slaves. A slave, Aristotle said, is a living possession: a piece of property used by the master as an instrument for maintaining his life.[99] Hence to be a natural slave one must be 'by nature not his own but another's man.'[100] But what kind of a person could this be? For Aristotle, it must be someone who is by nature a deficient human being:

> ... in all things which form a composite whole and which are made up of parts, whether continuous or discrete, a distinction between the ruling and the subject element comes to light ... A living creature consists in the first place of soul and body, and of these two, the one is by nature the ruler, and the other the subject. But then *we must look for the intentions of nature in things which retain their nature, and not in things which are corrupted*. And therefore we must study the man who is in the most perfect state both of body and soul, for in him we shall see the true relation of the two; although in bad or corrupted natures the body will often appear to rule over the soul, because they are in an evil and unnatural condition. At all events we may firstly observe in living creatures both a despotical and a constitutional rule; for the soul rules the body with a despotical rule, whereas the intellect rules the appetites with a constitutional and royal rule. And it is clear that the rule of the soul over the body, and of the mind and the rational element over the passionate, is natural and expedient; whereas the equality of the two or the rule of the inferior is always hurtful. The same holds good of animals in relation to men; for tame animals have a better nature than wild and all tame animals are better off when they are ruled by man; for then they are preserved. Again, the male is by nature superior, and the female inferior; and the one rules and the other is ruled; this principle of necessity extends to all mankind. Where then there is a difference as that between soul and body, or between men and animals (as in the case of those whose business it is to use their body, and who can do nothing better), the lower

[99] *Politics* I.4, 1253b25–1254a13.
[100] *Politics* I.4, 1254a14–15.

sort are by nature slaves, and *it is better for them* as for
all inferiors that they should be under the rule of a
master. For he who can be, and therefore is, another's,
and he who participates in rational principle enough to
apprehend, but not to have, such a principle, is a slave by
nature.[101]

A natural slave, for Aristotle, is a naturally deficient human being.
He is born without a rational principle in his soul to rule over his
appetites, passions, and emotions, though he is capable of appre-
hending and obeying a rational principle. The failure of rationality
to arise and rule within his own soul justifies the imposition of
such rule from without. By subjugating the natural slave, the
master is imposing a rule which by nature ought to have arisen
within the slave's soul. That is why it is better for the natural slave
to be a slave. The master is, as it were, completing nature: helping
nature along with one of its deficient products.

But if natural slaves are deficient human beings, there ought not
to be very many of them. For natural slaves are not fully human:
they lack the capacity to develop into beings who can live a full,
rich human life. How could they come into existence at all? Aristotle recognized that nature occasionally throws up a deficient
member of the species. It would seem that the only justification of
slavery that Aristotle endorses is one that relies on nature's occasional imperfections. But if we look to Aristotle's biological
works as well as his treatise on nature, the *Physics*, it appears that
Aristotle thought that nature threw up imperfections only occasionally. This would suggest that Aristotle thought that only few
people ought to be slaves.

But if few people ought to be slaves, it is equally true for Aristotle that few people are fit to be citizens. This is genuinely puzzling. Man is by nature a political animal, and yet very few people
are capable of leading a full political life. To say that man is by
nature a political animal is not, for Aristotle, to say that he is good
at winning votes. It is to say that man is by nature a creature who
can only flourish within the context of civil society. The expression
'political animal' is a literal translation: one might say instead that
man is by nature a citizen. The value of the literal translation,

---

[101] *Politics* I.5, 1254a28–b23 (my emphasis).

though, is that it preserves the sense of animality in man's nature. Man is by nature a citizen; but, in Aristotle's eyes, man is an *animal* who is by nature a citizen.

The thesis that man is by nature a political animal cuts through the ancient antinomy of nature versus convention. It is man's nature, Aristotle thinks, to establish conventions or laws according to which he can live. Indeed, Aristotle thought that the state was a creation of nature.[102] One can see this, Aristotle thinks, if one looks at how the state developed from more primitive human societies. If humans were to survive, there had to be unions of male and female, and the needs of men brought them together into larger communities, villages, and tribes. The state developed out of these associations, but its formation allows for more than securing the bare necessities of life: the state provides an environment in which man can live a good life. The state is thus the end or *telos* of the development of human organizations:

> Hence it is evident that the state is a creation of nature
> and that man is by nature a political animal. And he who
> by nature and not by mere accident is without a state is
> either a bad man or above humanity. He is like the 'tribe-
> less, lawless, heartless one' whom Homer denounces –
> the natural outcast is forthwith a lover of war: he may be
> compared to an isolated checkers-piece.[103]

The man living outside the state is like an isolated checkers-piece. This is a remarkable comparison, for an isolated checkers-piece is not, strictly speaking, a checkers-piece at all. A checkers-piece gains its very identity, and thus in a sense its existence, by its relation to the game of which it is a part. No checkers-piece can, so to speak, live outside the game of checkers. Aristotle is clearly willing to accept that an analogous relation exists between man and political society. The state, for Aristotle, is like a functioning organism; and he argues that it is metaphysically prior to, more substantial than, the individual who lives within it.[104] Just as the parts of a functioning organism gain their identity and role in relation to the

---

[102] *Politics* I.2, especially 1253a2. Of course, the word that is being translated as 'state' is *polis*: Aristotle was not talking about a nation-state like the United States; he was talking about a city-state like Athens.

[103] *Politics* I.2, 1253a1–7. The reference to Homer is to *Iliad* IX.63. The Oxford translation uses the expression 'isolated piece of draughts.'

[104] *Politics* I.2, 1253a18–29.

whole functioning organism – being a severed hand or the hand of a dead man is not a way of being a hand, it is a way of not being a hand – so a man's function is defined by his relation to society. This is made evident, Aristotle thought, by the fact that an individual separated from society can not be self-sufficient (*autarkēs*).[105] Aristotle's praise of self-sufficiency can at times appear exaggerated to a modern reader – as though if only an individual could shed the regrettable necessity of depending on others he would be truly happy. So it is worth noting that Aristotle conceived self-sufficiency as a *political* virtue.[106] Self-sufficiency is expressed in one's relations with one's family, friends, and fellow-citizens. It is taken to be 'that which makes life desirable and lacking in nothing,' and so Aristotle identifies it with human happiness.[107] The self-sufficient life, the happy life, can only be lived within the state, and thus Aristotle contrasts it with the solitary life, in which one cannot flourish.[108] 'He who is unable to live in society or who has no need because he is sufficient for himself, must be either a beast or a god: he is no part of the state.'[109]

Man by nature has a social instinct.[110] This is reflected in the fact that man is by nature a gregarious animal, endowed with speech which binds him to his fellow-man:

> ... the power of speech is intended to set forth the expedient and the inexpedient, and therefore likewise the just and the unjust. And it is a characteristic of man that he alone has any sense of good and evil, of just and unjust, and the like, and the association of living beings who have this sense makes a family and a state.[111]

And yet, though men are by nature social animals, equipped with an innate sense of good and bad, just and unjust, they do not easily form themselves into good societies. Certainly, men do not form good societies unthinkingly or without effort. It is the aim of political science, or politics, to show man how to organize society so as to ensure human happiness for its citizens. With this knowledge,

[105] *Politics* I.2, 1253a26.
[106] *Nicomachean Ethics* I.7, 1097b7–22; cf. v.6, 1134a27.
[107] *Nicomachean Ethics* I.7, 1097b15.
[108] *Nicomachean Ethics* I.8, 1099b3–6.
[109] *Politics* I.2, 1253a27–9.
[110] *Politics* I.2, 1253a29–30.
[111] *Politics* I.2, 1253a14–18.

men are more likely to attain the happiness which they all seek.[112]

The problem is that the knowledge of political science, though needed to ensure human happiness, provides a pessimistic vision of its possibility. The *Ethics* has already prepared us to accept the inability of mere theoretical understanding of the good life to secure the good life. Philosophy on its own is not enough. But by the end of the *Ethics* Aristotle seems to confess that even good training from youth and a good education are not enough:

> It is difficult to get from youth up a right training for virtue if one has not been brought up under right laws; for to live temperately and hardily is not pleasant to most people, especially when they are young. For this reason their nurture and occupations should be fixed by law; for they will not be painful when they have become customary. *But it is surely not enough that when they are young they should get the right nurture and attention; since they must, even when they are grown up, practise and be habituated to them, we shall need laws for this as well, and generally speaking to cover the whole of life; for most people obey necessity rather than argument, and punishments rather than the sense of what is noble.*[113]

The reason the *Politics* follows almost inevitably from the *Ethics* is that man is not an animal for whom the good life comes easily. For the mass of mankind it is not enough to be taught what the good life is; nor is it enough to be well trained. Laws are needed, for most people obey necessity rather than argument and punishments rather than a sense of what is noble. But if that is so, most people must stand in an odd relation to their own natures. For the ethical life is grounded in human nature: it is a good life precisely because it allows man to lead a rich, full, distinctively human life. So if the mass of mankind cannot live an ethical life without laws compelling them, this suggests that they must continually be forced to live according to their own natures. It would seem that most men do not really want to be men.

This odd vision seems to be confirmed by the study of politics.

---

[112] *Nicomachean Ethics* I.2; cf. *Politics* IV.11; VII.1–2, 13–15.
[113] *Nicomachean Ethics* X.9, 1179b31–1180a5 (my emphasis).

Aristotle engages in the study 'in order to complete to the best of our ability the philosophy of human nature,'[114] but what one learns about human nature is that men lack the ability to form themselves into healthy states. That is, although men may in an attenuated sense have the ability to form themselves into a healthy state, if one looks at the states which they actually have formed, one must conclude that they do not tend to exercise that ability. Why not? Here there seems to be a pronounced tension between Aristotle's role as descriptive biologist and his role as teleological biologist. The teleologist should see nature as producing its creations more or less for the best. The state is itself a creation of nature, yet Aristotle the descriptive biologist, committed to studying the human animal in the habitats he actually forms, cannot help but notice that man tends to form flawed societies. It is in the case of the creation of political states that Aristotle seems forced to admit that the real is not rational and the rational is not real.

Aristotle classifies constitutions according to the number of citizens in the state and for whose benefit they ruled. A citizen, for Aristotle, is one who is able to participate in the political life of the state: to hold political office, help administer justice, and legislate.[115] So citizens must be actual or potential rulers of the state. Of states which serve the common interest, the rule of one is a monarchy, the rule of the few is an aristocracy, and the rule of many is called by the generic name, a constitution. All of these forms of government have corresponding perversions in which one, few, or many rule in their own interests. These perversions are tyranny, oligarchy, and democracy.[116]

Why is democracy a perversion? For Aristotle, democracy is the rule of the poor seeking their own interests. The choice between oligarchy and democracy, in Aristotle's eyes, is the choice between the rich or the poor looking after themselves.[117] Aristotle thinks that democracies tend to arise through a natural cycle of decay.[118] The first governments, Aristotle says, were monarchical, but when the stability of a monarchical society produced many people of

114 *Nicomachean Ethics* x.9, 1181b14–15.
115 *Politics* III.1, 1275a22–3, b18–20.
116 *Politics* III.7, 1279a32–b10.
117 *Politics* III.8, 1280a1–6. Aristotle actually describes four forms of democracy: see *Politics* IV.4–6; VI.4.
118 *Politics* III.15, 1286b8–22.

equal merit, they wanted to establish a constitutional government. Under this pressure the ruling classes deteriorated and confined themselves to the pursuit of their own interests. Thus the monarchy naturally decayed into an oligarchy:

> ... riches became the path to honor, and so oligarchies naturally grew up. These passed into tyrannies and tyrannies into democracies; for love of gain in the ruling classes was always tending to diminish their number, and so to strengthen the masses, who in the end set upon their masters and established democracies. *Since cities have increased in size, no other form of government appears to be any longer even easy to establish.*[119]

Democracy, then, naturally emerges out of an even worse form of oppression, tyranny, but it remains a form of domination: domination by the masses. But why do human societies tend to go through this cycle of perversions? If states are creations of nature, why is there no natural process of growth tending toward the best state? We who live in an age which at least aspires to democracy might put the question this way: even if we grant Aristotle that democracy is government by and for the poor, why does he not take more seriously the possibility of constitutional government, government by the many for the benefit of all? Aristotle's answer is that the many will, by their nature, not be governing for the benefit of all. It takes a virtuous person to be a good citizen of a good state, and there are not that many virtuous people.

In a good state the best men rule.[120] No society can contain more than relatively few virtuous men, so one cannot hope for a wider citizen body than is found in an aristocracy. That is, one cannot hope for a wider citizen body if one wishes to construct an ideal or perfect state. The tension between Aristotle's role as descriptive biologist and his role as teleological biologist is especially manifest in his discussion of the ideal state. On the one hand, if he is to talk about how men should govern and be governed, he is forced to talk about an *ideal* state. He must, therefore, implicitly acknowledge that man is not an animal who naturally tends to form good governments. A good government may be beneficial to man and an

---

[119] *Politics* III.15, 1286b15–22 (my emphasis).
[120] *Politics* III.18, 1288a33–4.

expression of his nature, but then man in his actual behavior does not tend to realize his nature. On the other hand, he insists that the conditions of an ideal state must be conditions which can actually be realized.[121] Aristotle has no interest in a utopia: he wants to describe a state in which men, as he knows them, can actually live. An ideal state, though as yet unrealized, should be realistic.

To know the best form of state, Aristotle says, one must know the best life for man.[122] For a good state, simply, is one which enables man to live the best life. Since the best life for man is a life of happiness and a happy life is a life lived according to virtue or excellence, the best state will be one that encourages its citizens to live a virtuous life.[123] Thus Aristotle can say that political society exists for the sake of noble actions.[124] Producing noble actions is not the obvious goal of political society: the goal is to secure the good life for its citizens. It is because the good life consists in a life of noble actions that political society can have noble actions as a goal.

The good state, then, can be thought of as an environment in which man is encouraged to realize his nature. And, since the good state is defined as one which secures the good life for its citizens, it is only in the good state that a good citizen can be a good man.[125] The idea of a good citizen is a relative notion: a good citizen is one who is actively helping to pursue the ends of the state. So if the ends of the state are themselves not good, a good citizen of that state will be pursuing bad ends. Insofar as he is a good citizen of a bad state, he cannot be leading a virtuous or happy life. The good state, by contrast, is directly aimed at encouraging a virtuous life for its citizens. Since encouraging the virtuous life helps to constitute the virtuous life, and since the aim of the good state is virtuous actions, the good citizen of the good state will be leading a good life. In the best state, good citizens are good absolutely:

> ... the virtue of the good man is necessarily the same as the virtue of the citizen of the perfect state.[126]

[121] *Politics* VII.4, 1325b35–9; IV.11, 1295a25–31.
[122] *Politics* VII.1, 1323a14–21; VII.2, 1324a23–25; VII.13, 1332a4–10. Cf. *Nicomachean Ethics* I,2.
[123] *Politics* VII.1, 1323b21–1324a4; VII.13, 1332a28–38; IV.11, 1295a35–b1.
[124] *Politics* III.9, 1281a2–4.
[125] *Politics* III.4, 18; IV.7; VII.9, 13–15.
[126] *Politics* III.18, 1288a38–9.

In the perfect state the good man is absolutely the same
as the good citizen; whereas in other states the good citizen is only good relatively to his own form of government.[127]

It is because in a good state the good citizen must be a good man
that Aristotle restricts the citizenry. A good man, as the song goes,
is hard to find.[128] In any society there will be relatively few virtuous
men – for, after all, virtuous men are men who display human
excellence – and the citizenry of a good state must be restricted to
them. Aristotle did think that an absolute monarchy could be a
good state: for a good king will govern in the interest of his subjects.[129] But if we are concerned with a good state that is governed
by laws rather than by the judgements of an absolute ruler, and if
we wish to enlarge the citizen body as much as possible, we cannot
get beyond the rule of the few: 'one man or a few may excel in
virtue; but as the number increases it becomes more difficult for
them to attain perfection in every kind of virtue.'[130] The rule of the
few best, in the common interest, is an aristocracy, the only form
of government in which political office is distributed according to
merit.[131]

That citizenship in a good state is restricted to the virtuous men
has dramatic consequences. Almost all of society is excluded from
participation in political life. It is not merely slaves and the poor
who are excluded; tradesmen, craftsmen, mechanics, and laborers
– those who perform functions necessary for the state's existence
and well-being – are denied a role in civic life.[132] Citizens, for their
part, are barred from performing many of the tasks required for a
healthy society:

Since we are here speaking of the best form of government, i.e. that under which the state will be most happy
(and happiness, as has already been said, cannot exist
without virtue)[133] it clearly follows that in the state

[127] *Politics* IV.7, 1293b5–7.
[128] Cf., e.g., *Politics* III.7, 1279a39–b2.
[129] *Politics* III.7, 1279a32–3.
[130] *Politics* III.7, 1279a40–b2.
[131] *Politics* III.8.
[132] *Politics* III.5; VII.9.
[133] *Politics* VII.1, 1323a21–1324a4; VII.8, 1328a37ff.

which is best governed and possesses men who are just absolutely, and not merely relatively to the principle of the constitution, the citizens must not lead the life of artisans or tradesmen, for such a life is ignoble and inimical to virtue. Neither must they be husbandmen, since leisure is necessary both for the development of virtue and the performance of political duties.[134]

Citizens of the ideal state do not work. They run the state – deliberating, legislating, and adjudicating the law; perhaps, too, some will lead armies, and they will run their own households. In youth they may have served in armies, but even that experience in being ruled was part of their preparation for ruling.[135] Above all, the state will offer them ample opportunity to exercise their virtues. For the point of the state is to promote the happiness of its citizens, and happiness is the exercise of the virtues. The citizens will be the only members of society truly capable of virtuous action.

From the perspective of an age committed to democratic ideals, Aristotle's conception of the ideal state is unattractive. But is there anything more substantive to say than that Aristotle lived in his time, not ours? One cannot expect an act of critical reflection to catapult Aristotle out of his age and give him a timeless, absolute perspective on it. The question is whether there is anything internal to Aristotle's own critical reflection which might have made him uncomfortable with it. At first one might think that the answer is no: Aristotle simple did not think that human excellence was democratically distributed. But if one considers Aristotle's general theory of nature, there does seem to be reason even for Aristotle to be concerned. Aristotle did not think that the reproduction of a good member of each species was a rare occurrence. Why, then, did he think the production of a good human being occurred so infrequently? Perhaps the answer is historical: in the mid-fourth century BC, Aristotle was witnessing the breakdown of the democratic *polis*.[136] His political philosophy reflects his lack of faith in democratic Athens's ability to shore itself up and survive. However, even if Aristotle's political philosophy is informed by the political reality he witnessed, it is supposedly grounded in his theory

[134] *Politics* VII.9, 1328b33–1329a2.
[135] *Politics* VII.14.
[136] See Cynthia Farrar, *The Origins of Democratic Thinking*, chapter 7.

of nature. And his theory of nature might at least have suggested that good men should be occurring in nature more often than his political theory allows.

Moreover, the very fact that he had to conceive of an *ideal* state ought to have been puzzling to Aristotle. One does not have to engage in speculation to determine the ideal conditions of, say, frog life. One has only to inspect ponds and marshes in which frogs actually live to find out how it is best for them to live. But one cannot simply look to the societies in which men actually live to find out how they ought to live. Humans tend to live in flawed societies. And so, the human species is the only species in nature which tends to live in an unhealthy environment. Of course, humans are the unique species which creates its own environment. But if nature is sufficiently kind to endow man with the ability to form political societies, one would have thought that Aristotle's nature would have been more liberal in its distribution of the ability to create a good state.

Why are there not more good states? This ought to have been an urgent and troubling question for Aristotle. It is by pursuing this question that Aristotle, without transcending his time, could have subjected his own political philosophy to further critical scrutiny.

6

Understanding the broad structure of reality

Man is not only a political animal. He also has within his breast the desire to understand. And there is a serious question as to how man can both fulfill his nature as a political animal and fully satisfy his innate desire to understand. The conflict is one which takes time to develop. For to a certain extent the desire to understand helps man to live the life of an active citizen. For man comes to understand that the ethical life within society is a way to achieve genuine human happiness; and when man comes to understand what happiness is, he is more likely to achieve it. However, if man pursues his desire to understand to the full he will find himself drawn outside the ethical life. It seems that it is man's nature to transcend his nature. Man is by nature a political animal, but he is also an animal who by nature desires to understand the world. And in coming to understand the world, he will leave the ethical life behind. His nature will take him beyond (or outside) his natural life as a political animal.

How are we to understand such a paradoxical conception? One way is to investigate the structure of theoretical understanding. For if we grasp what the desire to understand is a desire for, we may be able to see how satisfying the desire – achieving theoretical understanding – takes one outside the ethical life in society.

6.1 Aristotle's logic[1]

One of Aristotle's greatest intellectual achievements, and one for which he is rightly famous, is the discovery of formal logic. Indeed, Aristotle himself was uncharacteristically proud of his achieve-

---

[1] Appropriate reading: *Prior Analytics* 1.1–7, 23; *Posterior Analytics* 1.1–4; 11.19.

ment. At the conclusion of his logical treatises, he writes:

> That our programme, then, has been adequately com-
> pleted is clear. But we must not omit to notice what has
> happened in regard to this inquiry. For in the case of all
> discoveries the results of previous labors that have been
> handed down from others have been advanced bit by bit
> by those who have taken them on, whereas the original
> discoveries generally make an advance that is small at
> first though much more useful than the development
> which later springs out of them... This is in fact what
> has happened in regard to rhetorical speeches˙ and to
> practically all the other arts: for those who discovered
> the beginnings of them advanced them in all only a little
> way, whereas the celebrities of today are the heirs (so to
> speak) of a long succession of men who have advanced
> them bit by bit, and so have developed them to their
> present form... Of the present inquiry, on the other
> hand, it was not the case that part of the work had been
> thoroughly done before while part had not. Nothing
> existed at all... Moreover, on the subject of rhetoric
> there exists much that has been said long ago, whereas
> on the subject of syllogism we had nothing else of an
> earlier date to speak of at all, but were kept at work for a
> long time in experimental researches. If, then, it seems to
> you after inspection that, such being the situation as it
> existed at the start, without the other inquiries that have
> been developed by tradition, there must remain for all of
> you, or for our students, the task of extending us your
> pardon for the shortcomings of the inquiry, and for the
> discoveries thereof your warm thanks.[2]

What is the syllogism, and why was Aristotle so proud of it?

For as long as there has been anything recognizable as philosophizing there has been rigorous argument. Philosophers do not
just look to the world to understand it; they think about what must

---

[2] *Sophistical Refutations* XXXIV, 183b15–184b8. (I have used the term 'syllogism'
in the translation rather than the Oxford translation, 'deduction.' The reasons for
so doing are, first, that if a syllogism turns out to be a deduction that should be the
outcome of our inquiry into what a syllogism is; second, at least some syllogisms
are not easily conceived of as deductions.)

be true given what they already know about the world. That is, they use argument as a form of extending their knowledge. They also use argument to persuade others of the truth of their beliefs. If an argument begins with premisses that everyone believes to be true and proceeds with sufficient rigor and clarity, then anyone who believes the premisses *ought* to come to believe the conclusion. Of course, someone may nevertheless fail to follow the argument or be too stubborn to admit that he ought to accept the conclusion. But if the argument is a good argument one can at least rest assured that any rational person will be persuaded by it. In fact, it is a sign of his rationality that he accepts the argument as a good argument. And, since rationality lies at the heart of man's essence, in constructing, following, and accepting rigorous arguments, man manifests what he most truly is.

The rigorous arguments with which Aristotle is primarily concerned are about the nature of the world. The premisses express basic truths about the world that can be known through themselves: that is, without appeal to any other premisses.[3] The rigorous arguments are meant to reveal other necessary truths about the world which cannot be known through themselves, but only by deducing them from basic premisses. Thus the rigorous arguments not only manifest man's rationality; they reveal the rationality of the world. The world, for Aristotle, is a good place. And the world's goodness is partially manifested in its intelligibility. But the world would not be intelligible if there were no systematic way of relating that which is immediately intelligible to that which is not. There must be a systematic relation between those truths about the world which can only be known on the basis of other more basic truths and these basic, immediately intelligible truths. Otherwise the world would not be intelligible – and thus not a fundamentally good place. So there is a crucial lacuna in the demonstration of the world as being a good place which exists so long as we do not understand the systematic relation which exists between immediately intelligible truths and truths whose intelligibility depends upon them.

Now there are two senses in which one might say that a truth is 'immediately intelligible.' Aristotle captured these senses with his

---

[3] See *Posterior Analytics*, especially I.1–4, II.19.

distinction between what is immediately intelligible *to us* and what is immediately intelligible *without qualification*. By the time we are in a position to investigate the broad structure of reality, we are no longer primarily concerned with the things that seemed immediately obvious to us when we first began our exploration of the world. We are concerned with ontologically basic truths: with definitions which state essences. A definition which states, for example, what it is to be a man is immediately intelligible in the sense that its truth does not depend upon the truth of anything else. Such an 'immediately intelligible' truth will only be immediately intelligible *to us* after we are far along into our inquiry into man's nature. It is only then that we will understand that man's essence is true of man not in virtue of anything else, but solely in virtue of what man most basically is.

It is at this point that we stand in greatest need of a logical system. Owing to the promptings of our innate desire to understand and the responses of an intelligible world, we have *already* moved from what is immediately obvious to us along a path which has led us to basic truths about the world. As Aristotle puts it, we have already made what is immediately intelligible without qualification immediately intelligible to us. The question now is: how do we work our way back? How do we systematically relate the basic truths of the world, which have by now become immediately intelligible to us, to the less basic truths which depend upon them? Until we answer this question, we cannot lay bare, and thus make intelligible, the broad structure of reality.

In order to explain Aristotle's logic, it is necessary to introduce a few concepts. Let us say that an inference from premisses to conclusion is *valid* if when all the premisses are true the conclusion *must* be true. For example, consider the inference

$$\frac{\text{x is a square}}{\text{Therefore} \quad \text{x is a rectangle}}$$

This inference is valid because the square is just a special type of rectangle; a rectangle whose sides are all the same length. Notice, first, that even if x is not a square, the inference is still valid. To be a valid inference the premisses need not be true. All that is required is that *if* the premisses are true, the conclusion *must* be true. Second, even if an inference is valid, that need not make it a good argument. Suppose one simply stated the axioms of Euclidean geometry and then stated an arbitrary theorem. Even if that inference is valid – if the axioms are true the theorem must be true – it is not a good argument because the proof of the theorem is missing. A good argument is more than a valid inference, it is a valid inference or set of valid inferences in which one can *see* that the inferences are valid. The conclusion of a valid inference is said to be a *logical consequence* of the premisses. In a good argument the conclusion is a logical consequence of the premisses and one can see how it is that the conclusion follows logically from the premisses.

Any inference that is not valid is invalid. In particular, the premisses and conclusion of the inference may both be true. For example

The sky is blue
Therefore   You are reading this book

is invalid. Both the premiss and the conclusion are true, but it is not true that if the premiss is true the conclusion *must* be true. The sky would be blue even if you were doing something else.

Now there are some inferences which we can see to be valid in virtue of their form alone. Consider, for example:

All bachelors are unmarried men
All unmarried men are mortal
Therefore   All bachelors are mortal

Or

All swans are birds
All birds are bipeds
Therefore   All swans are bipeds.

These inferences are both of the form

All a's are b's
All b's are c's

Therefore   All a's are c's

And it is in virtue of having this form that the inferences are valid. Such inferences are said to be *formally valid*. By contrast, the inference

x is a square

Therefore   x is a rectangle

is informally valid. For the form of the inference is

x is a P

Therefore   x is a Q

and this form is not valid. The inference

x is a triangle

Therefore   x is a rectangle

is of the very same form, but it is not valid. So if an inference of this form is valid, it is not valid in virtue of its form. To know that

x is a square

Therefore   x is a rectangle

is valid, we cannot look to its form. Rather we must know what a square is, what a rectangle is and know that a square is a special type of rectangle. By contrast, we can know that

All quarks are glarks
All glarks are narks

Therefore   All quarks are narks

is valid even if we don't know what the terms mean, just so long as we know that the terms are genuine.

Aristotle was not the first to recognize that an inference can be valid in virtue of its form alone, but he was the first to devise a complex and sophisticated system of formal inferences. But before introducing Aristotle's system, it is worth understanding why *formally* valid inferences are of such importance. For Aristotle, the concept of valid inference and proof was bound up with the axiomatic method. The paradigm of an *informal* axiomatic theory is

Euclid's *Elements*. In an axiomatized geometry certain basic statements called axioms are posited: these should be of such a simple or obvious nature that one can simply see that they are true, just by understanding them. From these axioms one can then deduce further statements: these are the theorems of geometry. While Euclid (*c.* 300 BC) would have been a contemporary of Aristotle's grandson, it is generally thought that he helped to codify and wrote down an axiomatic system that existed well before his time. The realization that disparate geometrical results could be organized around a few basic geometrical ideas – the kernel of the idea of axiomatization – goes back at least to Pythagoras (born *c.* 582 BC). The Pythagoreans encouraged the axiomatized organization of geometry, rather than the pursuit of disparate geometrical results, for they thought that the organization revealed a basic harmony in nature. It has been said by later commentators that Pythagoras sacrificed oxen to the gods on the discovery of the axiomatic method. Actually Pythagoras did not believe in such sacrifices; but one can see that the discovery that so many disparate geometrical results can be so simply organized is cause for awe.

If one wants to achieve the highest degree of rigor, one should assume no truths except those explicitly stated in the axioms. The only inferences allowed would be valid inferences: those in which the conclusion is a logical consequence of the stated premisses. A purely axiomatized geometry would then consist only of those statements which can be deduced from the axioms by purely logical means. It is possible that this was Euclid's objective. There is evidence that he wished to make all assumptions explicit as axioms and definitions and to deduce the theorems by logic alone.

If this was Euclid's goal, he failed to achieve it.[4] For, while there is little doubt that he tried to put all his extra-logical assumptions in the axioms, in various places Euclid unconsciously assumes geometrical propositions which are neither included in his axioms nor proved to follow from these. Take, for example, the very first proof in Euclid.[5] This proof, which is very easy, is supposed to show that we can construct an equilateral triangle on any finite straight line. In brief, we are, first, given a line AB and asked to draw a circle with center A and radius AB.

[4] Here I am indebted to Charles Parsons's lucid discussion of the axiomatic method in 'Mathematics, Foundations of,' *Encyclopedia of Philosophy*, vol. 5, pp. 190–2.
[5] See table 1 (pp. 217–18 below).

Understanding the broad structure of reality

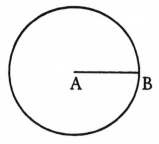

Next, we construct a circle with center B and radius AB.

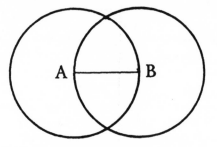

Both of these steps are authorized by the axioms (see table 1). Next we are asked to draw a line from A to the point C where the two circles intersect, and to draw a line from B to C.

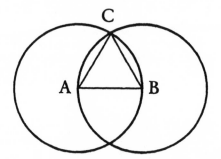

The axioms allow us to draw lines between any two points. Since all the sides of the newly constructed triangle are also radii of equal length, the triangle must be an equilateral triangle. QED.

Table 1. *Euclidean geometry*

Postulates:
Let the following be postulated:
1 To draw a straight line from any point to any point.
2 To produce a finite straight line continuously in a straight line.
3 To describe a circle with any center and any distance.
4 That all right angles are equal to one another.
5 That, if a straight line falling on two straight lines make the interior angles on the same side less than two right angles, the two straight lines, if produced indefinitely, meet on that side on which the angles have less than the two right angles.

Common notions:
1 Things which are equal to the same thing are also equal to one another.
2 If equals be added to equals, the wholes are equal.
3 If equals be subtracted from equals, the remainders are equal.
4 Things which coincide with one another are equal to one another.
5 The whole is greater than the part.

Definitions:
15 A *circle* is a plane figure contained by one line such that all straight lines falling upon it from one point among those lying within the figure are equal to one another;
16 And that point is called the *center* of the circle.
20 Of trilateral figures, an *equilateral triangle* is that which has its three sides equal, an *isosceles triangle* that which has two of its sides alone equal, and a *scalene triangle* that which has its three sides unequal.

Book I, Proposition 1:
On a given finite straight line to construct an equilateral triangle.

Let AB be the given finite straight line.
Thus it is required to construct an equilateral triangle on the straight line AB.
    With center A and distance AB, let the circle BCD be described (post. 3) again with center B and distance BA, let the circle ACE be described; (post. 3) and from the point C, in which the circles cut one another, to the points A, B let the straight lines CA, CB be joined. (post. 1).

    Now, since the point A is the center of CDB, AC is equal to AB. (def. 15).
    Again, since the point B is the center of the circle CAE, BC is equal to BA. (def. 15)
    But CA was also proved equal to AB; and therefore each of the straight lines CA, CB is equal to AB.
    And things which are equal to the same thing are also equal to one another (C.N. 1). Therefore CA is also equal to CB.
    Therefore the three straight lines CA, AB, BC, are equal to one another. Therefore the triangle ABC is equilateral; and it has been constructed on the given finite straight line AB.

What could be more rigorous than that? Well, there is nothing in Euclid's postulates which allows us to assume the existence of a point C where the two circles intersect. Euclid failed to notice that he must postulate the existence of two points of intersection where the circles intersect. His postulates allow the existence (or construction) of lines and circles, but nothing in his postulates allows that when the circles are drawn as described there is a point C which can form one of the vertexes of the triangle. It may seem obvious that there is such a point C just by looking at the diagrams, but the use of diagrams is supposed to be purely heuristic. The use of a diagram may help us to concentrate our attention, it may help us heuristically to follow or discover a proof; but if we accept propositions merely because they seem evident to us when we are looking at a diagram, we are in effect adding to our axioms without due notice.

This raises a general problem: how can one prevent such a failure of proof? How can one tell that one's proof does not depend on important assumptions that have not been stated? One way is to abstract so much from the meanings of the terms used in the proof that the validity of the proof does not depend on the validity of the terms used, but only on the form. For example, we can recognize that the inference

> All bachelors are unmarried men
> All unmarried men are mortal
> ---
> Therefore   All bachelors are mortal

is valid without knowing what 'bachelors,' 'unmarried men' or 'mortal' mean. Euclid's proof, by contrast, depends on one's knowing what a circle, straight line, triangle and point are. (The danger, then, is that one has not explicitly stated what one understands, or that one thinks one understands something that one does not.)

Aristotle's project was to devise a system of formal inferences in which any valid inference could be expressed. The idea was that any informally valid inference, like a proof in Euclid, could be translated into a series of *formally* valid inferences. If this could be done it would provide us with a test for the validity of informal inferences. If they could be translated into formally valid inferences, one could know that an inference is valid without relying on any knowledge of the subject-matter. One would be able to see that the inference is valid in virtue of its form alone. This is important if one's overall project is to lay bare the broad structure of reality. For the different sciences which constitute our knowledge of the world are about different subject-matters. Geometry, for example, is about triangles, spheres, and their spatial relations; biology is about living organisms. Yet if both sciences are rigorously organized, the *forms* of argument ought to be common to them both. At the beginning should be basic axioms stating definitions: for example, what it is to be a triangle or what it is to be a man. Though of course these statements are different, they are both conceived by Aristotle as being of the same form: 'All a's are b.' And since the premisses have a common form, the conclusions which can be formally derived from them will also be alike in form. Thus by formalizing the different sciences we are in a position to appreciate a higher unity which links them: a common formal structure.

Had Aristotle accomplished his goal, the axiomatic method, one of the high-water marks of abstract thinking, would have reached its flowering – and two generations before Euclid even wrote down the *Elements*! Aristotle did not succeed in his project. His system of formally valid inferences, known as the *syllogistic*, is not, as it turns out, sufficiently sophisticated to express a single proof in Euclid. But Aristotle did think he had succeeded, and he had an argument to back him up. Alas, the argument is faulty. But the failure of Aristotle's project should not blind us to the brilliance of the attempt – the first attempt to put the axiomatic method on a firm foundation. Nor should it blind us to the birth of formal logic.

The first sentence of the *Prior Analytics* states that the subject of inquiry is proof.[6] However, Aristotle first presents his theory of the syllogism because, he says, it is more general: every proof is a syllogism, but not every syllogism is a proof.[7] Aristotle defines a *syllogism* as 'discourse (a *logos*) in which certain things being stated,

---

[6] *Prior Analytics* I.1, 24a10–11.
[7] *Prior Analytics* I.4, 25b28–31.

something other than what is posited follows of necessity from their being so.'[8] This sounds like our earlier definition of valid inference or logical consequence. There is nothing in the definition of a syllogism which mentions form, and there is no mention of any of the well-known Aristotelian syllogisms, for example,

> All a's are b's
> All b's are c's
>
> Therefore   All a's are c's

A syllogism is *any* argument in which certain things are laid down (as premisses) and other things follow from them.[9] Aristotle does set out a complex system of formal inferences, which we more commonly think of as syllogisms. But the point of the system of formal syllogisms is to show that every syllogism in the broad sense of the definition – for example, every deduction in Euclid – can be represented as a series of formal syllogisms.

A syllogism is said to be *perfect* if it needs nothing other than what is stated to make evident what necessarily follows.[10] An example of an informal perfect syllogism is

> x is a square
>
> Therefore   x is a rectangle

One need only know what a square and a rectangle are to see that the inference is valid. An example of a formal perfect syllogism is the by now familiar

> All a's are b's
> All b's are c's
>
> Therefore   All a's are c's

---

[8] *Prior Analytics* I.1, 24b18–20. (I use 'posited' rather than the Oxford translation's 'stated,' for the Greek suggests a stronger notion than just stating: it suggests the idea of asserting, positing, or laying down hypotheses.)

[9] That is why one cannot comfortably identify syllogisms with deductions. If one states the axioms of a theory and then any arbitrary theorem, one has a syllogism, but it would be a strain to call this a deduction. Indeed, it would seem that in such a case the deduction of the theorem from the axioms is precisely what is missing.

[10] *Prior Analytics* I.1, 24b22–5.

A syllogism is *imperfect* if, although the conclusion does follow from the premisses, it needs one or more statements to be added which are indeed necessary consequences of the premisses to make it clear that the conclusion really does follow. If, for example, one simply stated the axioms of Euclidean geometry and then said 'therefore, a triangle has interior angles equal to two right angles,' one would have an imperfect informal syllogism. The conclusion might follow from the premisses, but one would lack the proof which makes it evident that it follows.

Aristotle says that in a syllogism the conclusion follows of necessity from the premisses. What is it to follow of necessity? Aristotle never explains, *but he does not have to* in order to set up his system of formal logic.[11] Since there are perfect formal syllogisms, he can begin simply by pointing to paradigm examples of inferences in which the conclusion follows of necessity from the premisses. The perfect inferences which Aristotle uses are:

All a's are b	All a's are b	Some a's are b	Some a's are b
All b's are c	No b's are c	All b's are c	No b's are c
All a's are c	No a is a c	Some a's are c	Not all a's are c

Because the inferences are perfect, we can simply see that the conclusion follows. Aristotle does not offer a definition of 'following of necessity' and then show that the syllogisms are true to it. Rather, he begins by presenting a few obviously valid inferences and invites one to agree that these are cases in which the conclusion follows of necessity from the premisses.[12]

Aristotle is introducing a logic of predication. It is a study of what predicational relations follow from others. This logic was important for Aristotle because he was interested not so much in axiomatizing geometry as in axiomatizing reality as a whole. The basic axioms would state essences – for example, 'man is a rational

---

[11] I discuss the significance of this in more detail in *Aristotle and Logical Theory*, chapter 1.
[12] *Prior Analytics* 1.4, 25b37–26a2, 26a23–7.

animal' – and the syllogisms would deduce consequences of these essences.

The perfect syllogisms are said to be in the *first figure*, for the relation of the predicates is in each case the same:

$$————a's\ are\ b$$
$$————b's\ are\ c$$

Therefore ————a's are c

But then, just by shifting the order of the predicates, we can formulate other syllogisms. Syllogisms of the second figure are formulated by applying the operators 'All,' 'No,' 'Some,' 'Not all' to

$$————a's\ are\ b$$
$$————c's\ are\ b$$

Therefore ————a's are c

The 'third figure' is made up of syllogisms of the form

$$————b's\ are\ a$$
$$————b's\ are\ c$$

Therefore ————a's are c

Aristotle tries to construct syllogisms by applying the operators in all combinations to the three figures. In the three figures Aristotle considers the various pairs of premisses that can be formed by attaching the operators 'All,' 'Some,' 'Not all,' and 'No.' Aside from the perfect first-figure syllogisms, he is able to eliminate by counter-example all but ten other premiss-pairs as being invalid. Here is how Aristotle shows that a pair of premisses has no syllogistic consequence. Consider, for example, the premiss-pair

No a's are b
All b's are c

Aristotle shows that these premisses have no valid consequence of the form

————a's are c

as follows.[13] He first finds terms that will make both the premisses true and make a conclusion of the form 'All a's are c' also true:

| No horse is a man | | No a's are b |
All men are animals	is of the form	All b's are c
All horses are animals		All a's are c

Since all these sentences are true, no syllogism with these premisses could have a negative conclusion – 'Not...' or 'Not all...'. For we have just seen an example where the premisses are both true and so is a universal affirmative conclusion, 'All horses are animals.' Since it is possible for two premisses of this form to be true and a universal affirmative conclusion also to be true, the premisses clearly do not *necessitate* a negative conclusion. But they must necessitate a conclusion, if there is to be a syllogism.

Similarly, if one can find terms that make the premisses true and also make true a conclusion that is of the form

No a's are c

then the possibility of the premisses of this form having an affirmative conclusion – 'All...' or 'Some...' – is eliminated. Since

No stone is a man
All men are animals
and No stone is an animal

are all true, and since these sentences are of the form

No a's are b
All b's are c
and No a's are c,

it follows that the premisses do not necessitate an affirmative conclusion. The elimination of these two possibilities ensures that premisses of the form

---

[13] *Prior Analytics* I.4, 26a2–9.

No a's are b
and All b's are c

have no syllogistic consequence.

Aristotle is left with ten syllogisms which are not in the perfect first figure and which he cannot eliminate as invalid (see table 2). To give just two examples from the second figure:

	All a's are b	No a's are b
	No c's are b	All c's are b
Therefore	No a's are c	No a's are c

These two syllogisms Aristotle thinks are *imperfect* – they are valid, but not obviously valid. How, then, can one establish their validity? Aristotle thinks that all imperfect inferences can be perfected. That is, for every inference that is valid, but not obviously valid, one can derive another set of inferences from the same premisses to the same conclusion in such a way that every inference is obviously valid. To this end Aristotle introduces three rules of conversion:[14]

From	No b's are a	infer	No a's are b
From	All b's are a	infer	Some a's are b
From	Some b's are a	infer	Some a's are b

Although Aristotle gives examples – 'if every pleasure is good, some good must be pleasure' – he again invites the reader to see that these rules are obviously valid. Here is an example of the perfection of an imperfect syllogism

	All a's are b
	No c's are b
Therefore	No a's are c

---

[14] *Prior Analytics* 1.4, 25a5–26.

The second premiss,

> No c's are b,

can be converted to

> No b's are c,

and thus we can form the perfect first-figure syllogism

> All a's are b
> No b's are c
> ―――――――――
> No a's are c

Aristotle's strategy is thus to isolate a handful of obviously valid inferences and justify the remaining valid inferences by showing that one can move from premises to conclusion using only obviously valid inferences. In the opening chapters of the *Prior Analytics* Aristotle sets out a comprehensive set of predicational relations, and he shows that each inference is either invalid (and thus can be dismissed) or valid and either perfect or perfectible.[15] Within his formal system of inferences, all unobvious valid inferences can be reduced to obviously valid inferences. This is important, for two reasons. First, Aristotle guarantees that man can come to see the rationality of every formally valid inference. Since every formally valid inference is either perfect or perfectible, formal validity cannot lie beyond man's ability to comprehend. Not only can man appreciate the rationality of every formally valid inference; he can appreciate that he is a being who is capable of doing this. Second, Aristotle provides a neat strategy for justifying all the formally valid inferences. He takes a handful of inferences which are obviously valid and does not try to justify these at all. He simply points to them and appeals to the reader to recognize that they are obviously valid. For unobvious inferences, he shows that they are valid, not by producing any abstract argument, but by showing that one could move from premises to conclusion without them. They are, strictly speaking, redundant – though one might use them to make a quicker leap from premises to conclusion.

[15] See *Prior Analytics* I.1–7, 13, 23. I shall not go through all the details here. Those who are interested, see my *Aristotle and Logical Theory*, chapter 1, and J. N. Keynes, *Studies and Exercises in Formal Logic*.

Table 2. *Aristotle's syllogistic*

	Barbara	Celarent	Darii	Ferio
1st figure	Abc Aab	Ebc Aab	Abc Iab	Ebc Iab
	Aac	Eac	Iac	Oac
	Cesare	Camestres	Festino	Baroco
2nd figure	Ecb Aab	Acb Eab	Ecb Iab	Acb Oab
	Eac	Eac	Oac	Oac
	Darapti	Felapton	Disamis	Datisi
3rd figure	Abc Aba	Ebc Aba	Ibc Aba	Abc Iba
	Iac	Oac	Iac	Iac
	Bocardo	Ferison		
	Obc Aba	Ebc Iba		
	Oac	Oac		

Rules of conversion:
From Eba infer Eab
From Aba infer Iab
From Iba infer Iab

The symbolization is as follows.* 'Abc' is read either as 'All b's are c' or as 'c belongs to all b.' 'Ebc' is read either as 'No b's are c' or as 'c belongs to no b.' 'Ibc' is read either as 'Some b's are c' or as 'c belongs to some b.' 'Obc' is read as 'Not all b's are c' or as 'c does not belong to some b.' The names of the syllogisms, given by later commentators, encode relevant information. The three vowels of each name give the type of premisses and conclusion in the syllogism. For example, *Barbara* is of the form A . . . A . . . /A . . . The first consonant in each name shows which of the first-figure syllogisms are used in the perfection of the second- and third-figure syllogism. For example, Cesare and Camestres are both perfected by Celarent.†

* This natural deduction formalization is due to T. J. Smiley, 'What is a Syllogism?', and to J. Corcoran, 'Aristotle's Natural Deduction System.'
† There is yet more information encoded. For those who are interested, see J. N. Keynes, *Studies and Exercises in Formal Logic*.

It is important to realize that Aristotle is here demonstrating a truth *about* his logical system. He is not here using his logical system to formulate proofs; rather, the logical system is itself being made an object of study, and truths are being proved about it. The study of logical systems is called *metalogic*. It is clear that Aristotle must be the first metalogician: for no one before him had a rigorous system of formal inferences that could be subjected to serious study. Thus Aristotle opened a whole new realm of thought and discourse: he was able to inquire into the nature of proof and consequence in a way that was not available to any of his predecessors.[16] What is so fascinating is that as soon as metalogic was possible, it was made use of: the birth of logic was simultaneously the birth of metalogic. The reason for this, I suspect, was that Aristotle needed metalogic to demonstrate the intelligibility of the broad structure of reality. By partitioning all valid inferences into those that were obvious and those that were not and showing that all non-obvious inferences could be perfected – that is, transformed into a chain of obvious inferences – Aristotle demonstrated that the broad structure of reality could be known. Metalogic was of a piece with Aristotle's metaphysical aspirations.

It is precisely because Aristotle's study of logic is part of a larger project that he does not rest content with proving theorems about his formal logic. Aristotle has proved that the imperfect syllogisms of the second and third figures can be perfected by means of the obviously valid first-figure syllogisms and the rules of conversion.[17] But in the beginning of *Prior Analytics* I.4, Aristotle says that he can state how *all* syllogisms come to be.[18] In *Prior Analytics* I.23 he argues that *all syllogisms without qualification* come about through the three figures.[19] Aristotle's claim is that *any deductive argument*, even if it is an informal proof, can be expressed as a series of formal syllogistic inferences.[20] Aristotle is declaring that any non-formal deduction, such as the proof that a triangle has interior angles equal to two right angles, can be recast as a formal deduction. If Aristotle's argument were successful it would systematically relate all of our rigorous reasoning to his system of formal syllogisms.

Aristotle does not try to formalize particular deductions, but rather presents an abstract argument for his thesis. He assumes that the conclusion of every non-formal deductive argument –

---

[16] The significance of Aristotle's role as a metalogician is one of the central themes of my earlier book, *Aristotle and Logical Theory*.

[17] On occasion he has to use slightly more complex means: see my *Aristotle and Logical Theory*, pp. 5ff.

[18] *Prior Analytics* I.4, 25b27.

[19] *Prior Analytics* I.23.

[20] Aristotle excepts so-called hypothetical syllogisms. For a discussion of this, see my *Aristotle and Logical Theory*, chapter 3.

every syllogism in the broad sense – is essentially of the form of a syllogistic formula. For example, he assumes that the conclusion that

all triangles have interior angles equal to two right angles

is essentially of the form

All a's are c.

He then argues that the only way such a conclusion can be directly derived is through premisses which link the terms much as a formal syllogism does.[21] That is, the proof begins with an axiom stating that all triangles have a certain property,

All a's are b,

and then shows that such b things have the property of having interior angles equal to two right angles:

All b's are c.

Of course, we may need a chain of inferences to get to the conclusion:

	All a's are b
	All b's are d
Therefore	All a's are d
But	All d's are e
So	All a's are e
But	All e's are c
So	All a's are c

The 'middle terms' b, d, e function more or less like the proof which links triangles with the property of having interior angles equal in sum to two right angles. The ways in which the terms of the conclusion can be related by the 'middle terms' correspond, as Aristotle sees it, to the three figures of the formal syllogism.[22]

Aristotle's argument is overly optimistic. It is so schematic that he is not in a position to realize that informal geometrical proofs require a formal system so complex that only thousands of years later was anyone able to devise it. Aristotle's logic reigned as the

---

[21] *Prior Analytics* I.23, 40b30–41a20.
[22] *Prior Analytics* I.23, 41a4ff.

unquestioned paradigm of logic until the end of the nineteenth century. But it is not sufficiently sophisticated to realize his dream. If Aristotle is to present a unified and coherent logical theory without giving an analysis of the concept of following of necessity, it is essential that all deductions, non-formal and formal, be systematically related to the perfect syllogistic inferences. Aristotle has provided, first, an analysis of the three syllogistic figures which reduces imperfect inferences to perfect ones; and, second, an argument that the three syllogistic figures are adequate for the expression of all non-formal deductions. If that argument were valid, it would follow that any deductive consequence of any set of premises could be reached by a series of obviously valid inferences. For any deduction could, in theory, be expressed as a chain of syllogistic inferences, and those formal inferences could be perfected. In actual deductive practice one moves quickly, making large inferential steps, with, perhaps, a passing reference to theorems already proved. On Aristotle's account, this practice is licenced, not by an analysis of consequence, but by the guarantee that, in doubtful cases, any non-formal deduction can be formalized, and any formalized deduction can be perfected – transformed into an argument in which every step follows obviously.

It is a magnificent vision, and Aristotle actually thought he had attained it. It enabled him to envision the possibility of laying bare the broad structure of reality. At the apex were essences and the predications which expressed them. Flowing from these essences were consequences which could be derived by rigorous reasoning. Were one able to set out reality's structure along these lines, the order of reality and the order of one's knowledge of reality would be one and the same. Indeed, it is precisely *by* understanding the broad structure of reality that what is most knowable *to us* finally comes to coincide with what is most knowable.

It is important to remember that the point of Aristotle's syllogism is not to provide a logical theory *per se*, but to provide a theory of proof. As we have already seen, the first sentence of the *Prior Analytics* states that the subject of inquiry is proof.[23] The theory of the syllogism is presented first because it is more general: every proof is a syllogism, but not every syllogism is a proof.[24] It is

[23] *Prior Analytics* I.1, 24a10–11.
[24] *Prior Analytics* I.4, 25b26–31.

the task of the *Posterior Analytics* to show what is required to turn a syllogism into a proof. The point of a proof, Aristotle says, is to give us understanding without qualification. And we understand something without qualification when we grasp its explanation or cause and understand that this is the explanation.[25] But if a proof is to be genuinely explanatory it cannot rely on premisses that themselves require explanation. The ultimate premisses of a proof must, as we have seen, be knowable in themselves – mind simply grasps them – and they must be ontologically basic.[26] Otherwise they would not form the basis of a genuine explanation. The premisses of a proof are most knowable in that they accurately express what is fundamental about reality. In knowing them, we know the basis of reality. So in learning a proof our knowledge takes on the structure of reality.

This is a vision which guided and inspired Aristotle in his most abstract inquiries into the nature of reality. If, as we come to investigate the broad structure of reality, the order of our knowledge comes to reproduce the order of reality, then there is an important sense in which subject and object of inquiry come to coincide. Until now the object of our inquiry has been held at an intellectual arm's length. The inquiry into nature revealed the world as meant to be known; the inquiry into man's soul revealed him as a being who is meant to be a knower. Man and world are, as it were, made for each other. But now, as man comes to understand the broad structure of reality, there is no longer any firm distinction to be made between 'subjective' mind inquiring into the world and 'objective' world yielding up its truth. For now the order of our knowledge and the order of reality coincide: there is no longer any gap between what is most knowable *to us* and what is most knowable. The world is constituted of essences and so is our thinking: indeed, it is the very same essences that constitute world and mind. Moreover, our inquiry into the world has become an inquiry into ourselves. For the essences we discover there are the essences we become. This is where the desire to understand leads us. The opposition between the essential structure of reality and what is essentially human begins to disappear. Our inquiry can thus simultaneously be about man and about the world, because at this level

[25] *Posterior Analytics* I.2, 71b10–19.
[26] *Posterior Analytics* I.2; II.19.

of inquiry there is an internal coincidence between what is essential to man and what is essential about the world: in coming to understand the world, man realizes his essence.

6.2 Aristotle's philosophy of mathematics[27]

It was impossible for Aristotle to investigate the broad structure of reality without confronting the role of mathematics in that inquiry. For Plato, his teacher and predecessor, thought that the mathematical realm provided a key to a deep understanding of reality. But what is the mathematical realm? Mathematics seems to be a form of understanding which, paradoxically, is about a realm of unchanging objects, and yet which also seems to be applicable to the physical world. The spheres, triangles, and cubes of geometry, the numbers of arithmetic, seem to be unchanging, pure entities quite unlike anything found in nature, and yet geometry and arithmetic are used to build buildings, measure land, exchange in trade. It is for the mathematician to engage in mathematical activity, but it is for the philosopher to ask: how is this activity possible? Plato's answer, in brief, was that there was a separate realm of ideal mathematical objects – pure numbers and shapes – and mathematics was a study of those objects. Two questions immediately arise about Plato's answer. First, how do we have mental access to this mathematical realm? It cannot be by any of our senses, which only gives us access to the physical world. Second, how is it that mathematics is applicable to the physical world? If mathematics must be about a separate realm of pure, unchanging objects, how can it be used in the changing world of nature? If one were a committed Platonist, one might try to answer these questions by, say, endowing the mind with a special quasi-visual faculty which could perceive this realm, but Aristotle decided on a completely different strategy.

Mathematics, Aristotle argues, is directly about the changing objects of the natural world. There is no separate realm of numbers and geometrical objects. We shall see how he thought this was possible, but we ought to see immediately what an ingenious strat-

---

[27] Appropriate reading: *Physics* II.2; *Metaphysics* XIII.2–3. There are many difficult issues in the interpretation of these texts which I here ignore. For those who are interested, I discuss them in 'Aristotle's Philosophy of Mathematics.'

egy it is: for it allows Aristotle simply to bypass the two problems which plagued Plato. There is no need for special mental access to the mathematical realm, for there is no special mathematical realm. There is just the realm of nature. Nor is there a special problem about how mathematics is applicable to the physical world: it is only if mathematics is about a removed realm that special problems of applicability arise. If mathematics is directly about the physical world, then of course it is applicable.

The mathematician does differ from the physicist, Aristotle says, not in virtue of the objects he studies, but in virtue of the way he studies them.

> The next point to consider is how the mathematician differs from the student of nature; for natural bodies contain surfaces, volumes, lines and points, and these are the subject-matter of mathematics ... Now the mathematician, though he too treats of these things does not treat them *as* the limits of a natural body; nor does he consider the attributes indicated *as* the attributes of such bodies. That is why he separates them, for in thought they are separable from change and it makes no difference nor does any falsity result if they are separated. The holders of the theory of the forms do the same, though they are not aware of it ...[28]

Several fundamental features of Aristotle's philosophy of mathematics emerge quite clearly from this passage. First, physical bodies do actually contain the surfaces, lengths, and points that are the subject-matter of geometry. Second, the mathematician does study the surfaces, volumes, lengths and points of physical bodies, but he does not consider them *as* the surfaces, etc., *of* physical bodies. Geometry does investigate physical lengths, but not *as* physical. Third, the mathematician is able to study the surfaces, volumes, lengths, and points in isolation from their physical instantiations, because (in some way which needs to be explained) he is able to separate them *in thought*. The Platonist confusion, according to Aristotle, is to mistake this mental activity of abstraction for the perception of a separate realm of objects. In fact, the Platonists are doing no more than engaging in this process of

---

[28] *Physics* II.2, 193b23–36 (my emphasis). (I translate *kinesis* as 'change' rather than as 'motion'.)

separation in thought. Fourth, having been separated in thought, mathematical objects are free from the changes which physical objects undergo. Finally (for some reason which needs to be explained), no falsity results from this separation.

It is clear that Aristotle allows that there is some legitimate type of separation (which differs from Plato's separation of a realm of ideal objects), such that, if we understand how this separation occurs and why it is legitimate, we will understand how mathematics is possible. But what does Aristotle mean when he says that the mathematician studies physical bodies but not *as* physical? Aristotle says a bit more about this in *Metaphysics* XIII.3:

> ... it is possible for there to be formulae and proofs about sensible magnitudes, but not *as* sensible but *as* possessed of certain definite qualities. For as there are many formulae about things merely *as* changing, apart from the essence of each such thing and from their accidents, and as it is not therefore necessary that there should be either something changing separate from sensibles, or a separate substance in the sensibles, so too in the case of changing things there will be formulae and sciences which treat them not *as* changing but only as bodies, or again only as planes, or only as lines, or as divisibles, or as indivisibles having position, or only as indivisibles ...
>
> Many properties attach to things in virtue of their own nature as possessed of some such property; e.g. there are attributes peculiar to the animal as female or as male, yet there is no female nor male separate from animals. And so there are attributes which belong to things merely *as* lengths or *as* planes ...
>
> Thus if we suppose things separated from their attributes and make any inquiry concerning them as such, we shall not for this reason be in error, any more than when one draws a line on the ground and calls it a foot long when it is not; for the error is not included in the propositions.
>
> Each question will be best investigated in this way – by supposing separate what is not separate, as the arithmetician and the geometer do. For a man *as* man is one

indivisible thing; and the arithmetician supposes one indivisible thing, and then considers whether any attribute belongs to man *as* indivisible. But the geometer treats him neither *as* man nor *as* indivisible but *as* a solid. For evidently the attributes which would have belonged to him even if he had not been indivisible, can belong to him apart from these attributes. Thus, then, geometers speak correctly – they talk about existing things, and their subjects do exist ...[29]

The point of the argument is to show that, *contra* Plato, one can allow that the mathematical sciences are true without having to admit the existence of ideal objects. Aristotle points to our ability to abstract certain features of a physical body and consider them in isolation from the other features of that body. For example, one can treat physical objects solely *as* changing bodies, in isolation from all their other particular properties. There is nothing special about Zeno's arrow's being *an arrow* that features in Aristotle's account of how it can move from one spatial position to another. He would have considered its being an arrow in detail if, say, he had been in an archery workshop trying to design a better arrow. But, as it was, Aristotle was only trying to account for the possibility of a physical object's changing position. The arrow was considered not *as* an arrow, but *as* a physical body.

Reality, Aristotle seems to be saying, can be considered under various aspects. Given a physical object, like a man, horse, table, or planet, we are able to consider certain features of this object in isolation. Suppose that for a paperweight you have a bronze equilateral triangle on your desk. It is possible to consider this paperweight solely *as* a triangle. One abstracts from the fact that it is made of bronze, one even abstracts from the fact that all its sides are of the same length, and one considers only what is true of this object insofar as it is a triangle. Although it is true that

this triangle is bronze,

it is not true that

---

[29] *Metaphysics* XIII.3, 1077b21–1078a31 (my emphasis). (I use 'as' rather than the Latin *qua* of the Oxford translation. I also use the more familiar 'proof,' rather than 'demonstration,' for *apodeixis*.)

this triangle *considered as a triangle* is bronze.

For, although the triangle is bronze, its being bronze does not follow from the fact that it is a triangle. Nor is it even true that

this triangle *considered as a triangle* is equilateral.

Although the triangle is equilateral, it is not insofar as it is a triangle that it is equilateral; for it could equally well have been a triangle that is scalene or isosceles. Yet it is true that

this triangle *considered as a triangle* has interior angles equal to two right angles.

For the fact that this object has interior angles equal to two right angles follows directly from the fact that it is a triangle. The proof in Euclid that all triangles have interior angles equal to two right angles depends solely on the fact that the triangle is a triangle.[30]

Generalizing, one might say that Aristotle is introducing an *as*-operator which works as follows. Let b be a physical object and let b-as-F signify that b is being considered as an F. Then a property P is true of b-as-F if and only if b is an F and its having property P follows of necessity from its being an F.[31] Thus to use the *as*-operator is to place ourselves behind a veil of ignorance: we allow ourselves to know only that b is an F and then determine on the basis of that knowledge alone what other properties must hold of it.[32] For example, Aristotle thought that the heavenly bodies must be composed of a special stuff different from and more divine than earth, air, fire, or water; he also thought that the heavenly bodies must be indestructible.[33] However, if one considers a heavenly body like

[30] See Euclid, *Elements* 1.32.

[31] To symbolize this, let us use

P(b-as-F)

to mean that property P holds of b-as-F. And let us use '≡' to mean 'if and only if,' and '⊢' to mean 'follows of necessity.' Then

P(b-as-F) ≡ P(b) & ((F(x) ⊢ P(x)).

[32] If we are considering b as being a P, then every predicate that is not essential to its being P is considered incidental, even though it may be essential to b's being the substance that it is. That is why in the definition of *P(b-as-F)* one should have '(F(x) ⊢ P(x))' on the right hand side of the equivalence rather than 'F(b) ⊢ P(b).' For one might have F(b) ⊢ P(b) in virtue of what b is instead of in virtue of what F and P are.

[33] *On the Heavens* 1.2, 10.

the sun solely *as a sphere*, all the properties that do not follow from its being a sphere (its being composed of special stuff, its indestructibility, etc.) are *from this perspective* incidental. By applying a predicate filter to an object instantiating the relevant geometrical property, we will filter out all predicates which concern the material composition of the object. Thus the geometer is able to study perceptible material objects – this, indeed, is all that he studies – but he does not study them *as* perceptible or *as* material.

So far Aristotle has argued that in studying geometry one need study only physical objects, not Platonic objects, though considered independently of their particular physical instantiation. The second major step in his argument begins when he says that if someone should postulate and investigate objects that are separated from incidental properties, he would not because of this be led to speak falsely.[34] Why is this? Suppose, for example, we assume that there is an object c such that

> For all properties P, P is true of c if and only if
> P is true of *c-as-a-triangle*.

That is, we are assuming the existence of an object whose only properties are those that are logical consequences of its being a triangle. This is the assumption of a geometrical object, a triangle, separated from any material instantiation. Now, suppose that we should prove that c has interior angles equal to two right angles – which I shall symbolize as '2R(c).' Since, by hypothesis, we are guaranteed that the only properties of c are logical consequences of its being a triangle, we can argue from

$$2R(c)$$

to

> For all objects x, if x is a triangle, then 2R(x).

We can then infer

$$2R(b)$$

for any triangle b.

The reason one will not be led to speak falsely as a result of the

[34] The argument begins at *Metaphysics* XIII.3, 1078a17, quoted above.

fiction that there are separated objects, according to Aristotle is that 'the falsity is not in the premisses.'[35] The analogy offered is with the case in which one draws a line (on a blackboard or in sand) and says 'Let the line AB be one foot long.' Aristotle correctly sees that the line is drawn for heuristic purposes and is not part of the proof. How is this analogous?

In the above proof one has assumed that there is a separated geometrical object c, but in fact from the point of view of the proof there is no difference between c and any actual triangular object b considered as a triangle. For the properties one can prove to hold of c are precisely those that one can prove to hold of *c-as-a-triangle*. And it is easy to show from the definition of the *as*-operator that these are the same as the properties one can prove to hold of *b-as-a-triangle*, regardless of the choice of b, provided only that it is a triangle. For heuristic purposes we may indulge in the fiction that c is a separated triangle, not merely some b considered as a triangle. This is a harmless fiction because the proof is indifferent as to whether c is really a separated triangle or just b considered as one. It is in this sense that the falsity does not enter the premisses.

That the postulation of separated objects is of heuristic value Aristotle is certain. He thinks that the more predicates we can filter out, the more precise and simple our knowledge will be.[36] Our knowledge is simpler because we have been able to filter out extraneous information. For if we have proved

(1) 2R(c)

then we know we can infer that any particular triangle whatever has interior angles equal to two right angles. If, by contrast, we had proved only that

(2) b-as-bronze-equilateral triangle implies 2R(b)

then, given a wax, scalene triangle d, we could not infer on the basis of (2) that

(3) 2R(d).

For it is not clear on what properties the proof of (2) depends.

[35] *Metaphysics* XIII.3, 1078a20–1.
[36] *Metaphysics* XIII.3, 1078a9–13.

However (3) is an obvious consequence of (1) and of the fact that d is a triangle.

The postulation of separated geometrical objects enables us to attain knowledge that is more general. And it is through this general knowledge that one can discover the explanation of why something is the case. For by abstracting one can see that the full explanation of a triangle's having the 2R property is that it is a triangle and not, say, that it is bronze or equilateral.[37] In a limited sense, though, the abstract proof is unnecessary. For of any particular physical triangle d we can prove that it has interior angles equal to two right angles without first proving this for c: we can prove that d has the property directly. The proof that a physical object possesses a geometrical property via proof that a pure geometrical object has the property is a useful but unnecessary detour. However, if we want to know why the object possesses the property, the abstract proof is of crucial importance.

Thus it is that the best way of studying geometry is to separate these geometrical properties of objects and to posit objects that satisfy these properties alone. Though this is a fiction, it is a helpful fiction rather than a harmful one: for, at bottom, geometers are talking about existing things and properties they really have.[38]

This interpretation of Aristotle's philosophy of geometry rests on the assumption that Aristotle thought that physical objects really do instantiate geometrical properties. This might at first seem odd, for it is commonly assumed that it is obvious that objects in the natural world do not perfectly instantiate mathematical properties: a physical sphere is not truly spherical, a straight edge is not truly straight. But this is not at all obvious. And there is strong evidence that Aristotle did believe that physical objects perfectly instantiate mathematical properties. The passages from *Physics* II.2 and *Metaphysics* XIII.3 which we have already considered repeatedly emphasize that the geometer studies physical objects, but not *as* physical objects. There is no mention that the physical objects do not possess geometrical properties, yet one would certainly expect Aristotle to mention this if he believed it. Further, throughout the Aristotelian corpus there are scattered references to bronze spheres and bronze isosceles triangles: there is

---

[37] Cf. *Posterior Analytics* I.5.
[38] *Metaphysics* XIII.3, 1078a21–2, 28–9.

no suggestion that these objects are not really spherical or really triangular.[39]

To be sure, there is a passage or two in which Aristotle looks as though he is denying that physical objects instantiate geometrical properties. But looks can deceive. Consider, for example, the following passage from *Metaphysics* III.2:

> And astronomy also cannot be dealing with perceptible magnitudes nor with this heaven above us. *For neither are perceptible lines such lines as the geometer speaks of (for no perceptible thing is straight or curved in this way; for a hoop touches a straight edge not at a point, but as Protagoras said it did in his refutation of the geometers)*, nor are the movements and complex orbits in the heavens like those which astronomy treats, nor have geometrical points the same nature as the actual stars.[40]

Reading Aristotle can be a tricky business. Sometimes a particular passage will look as though Aristotle is clearly asserting something, but when one looks to the larger context in which the passage occurs one can see that he is not asserting anything of the kind. This is one of those times. *Metaphysics* III.2 is a catalogue of philosophical difficulties (*aporiai*) presented from various points of view. None of it should be thought of as a presentation of Aristotle's considered view on the subject. It is rather a list of difficulties in response to which he will form his philosophical position. Immediately before the quoted passage Aristotle puts forward a problem for the Platonists: the belief in Form-like mathematical objects involves many difficulties.[41] The quoted passage can thus be read as an imagined Platonist's response: 'Yes, the belief in special mathematical objects is problematic, but giving them up involves difficulties too.' Here it is an imagined Platonist speaking, and not Aristotle. So Aristotle is not endorsing Protagoras' view; he is presenting it as one horn of a dilemma that must be resolved. We have already seen Aristotle's proposed resolution: and it is one

[39] See *Metaphysics* VII.8, 1033a28–b10; VII.10, 1035a25–b3; VII.11, 1036a31–b2; *On the Soul* 403a10–16.

[40] *Metaphysics* III.2, 997b34–998a6 (my emphasis).

[41] *Metaphysics* III.2, 997b12–34.

that involves asserting that some physical objects perfectly possess geometrical properties.[42]

One might ask: 'Does this mean that Aristotle is committed to saying that the hoop-as-a-circle touches the straight edge at a point?' The straightforward answer to this is, 'Yes, it does,' but this is not as odd as it may initially appear. Protagoras' objection looks plausible because the hoops we tend to see are not perfectly circular, and so they obviously would not touch a straight edge – let alone the surfaces on which they actually rest, which are not perfectly straight – at a point. But Aristotle is not committed to saying that there are any perfectly circular hoops existing in the world. All Aristotle must say is: (i) insofar as a hoop is a circle it will touch a straight edge at a point; (ii) there are some physical objects that are circular. (Such circular objects need not be hoops.) Claim (i) is true: inasmuch as a hoop fails to touch a straight edge at a point, thus much does it fail to be a circle. And there is certainly evidence that Aristotle believed claim (ii). Aristotle thought that the stars were spheres and that they moved in circular orbits.[43] But there is also evidence that he thought that even in the sublunary world physical objects could perfectly instantiate geometrical objects. In his many references to, say, the craftsman's ability to make a bronze sphere, there is never a mention that the sphere is not truly spherical.

There does, however, remain room for skepticism. Even if one grants that there are, for example, perfect spheres in the physical world, must there be perfect physical instantiations of every figure the geometer constructs? Surely, the skeptic may object, Aristotle should not commit himself to there being, for example, perfectly triangular bronze figures. And, the skeptic may continue, even if there were perfectly triangular physical objects, there are no physical instantiations of the more complex figures which a geometer constructs when he is proving a theorem. I think it is clear how Aristotle would respond. At the end of *Metaphysics* IX.9 he says:

> It is by actualization also that geometrical constructions
> are discovered; it is by dividing the given figures that

---

[42] The other passage in which Aristotle appears to deny that physical objects instantiate geometrical properties (*Metaphysics* XI.1, 1059b10–12) can be handled in the same way. See my 'Aristotle's Philosophy of Mathematics,' pp. 178–9.

[43] *On the Heavens* II.11, 8.

people discover them. If they had been already divided, the relations would have been obvious; but as it is the divisions are present only potentially. Why are the angles of the triangle equal to two right angles? Because the angles about one point are equal to two right angles. If, then, the line parallel to the side had been already drawn, the theorem would have been evident to anyone as soon as he saw the figure... Obviously, therefore, the potentially existing relations are discovered by being brought to actuality (the reason being that thinking is an actuality).[44]

The geometer, Aristotle says, is able to carry out geometrical constructions in thought: the activity of thinking makes the actual constructions which existed only potentially before the thinking occurred.

Has, then, Aristotle severed the tie between pure mathematics and the physical world? Does the geometer contemplate pure mathematical objects that are not in any way abstractions from the physical world? I do not think so. For to retain the link between geometry and the physical world Aristotle need only maintain that the elements of a geometrical construction are abstractions from the physical world. Not every possible geometrical construction need be physically instantiated. In Euclidean geometry, constructions are made from straight lines, circles, and spheres. We have already seen the evidence that Aristotle thought that there were perfectly circular physical objects. Evidence that he thought there were also physical objects with perfectly straight edges is in *On the Soul*:

> If there is any way of acting or being acted upon proper to soul, soul will be capable of separate existence; if there is none, its separate existence is impossible. In the latter case, it will be like what is straight, which has many properties arising from the straightness in it, e.g. that of *touching a bronze sphere at a point*, though straightness divorced from the other constituents of the straight thing cannot touch in this way; it cannot be so divorced at all, since it is always found in a body.[45]

[44] *Metaphysics* IX.9, 1051a21–31.
[45] *On the Soul* I.1, 403a10–16.

What Aristotle takes to be touching a bronze sphere at a point is a physical straight edge, for when the straight line has been abstracted it cannot touch a physical object at all.[46] Since a geometrical triangle can be constructed in thought from straight lines, Aristotle does not have to say that a particular bronze figure is perfectly triangular. If it is – and given that he thought there could be a physical straight edge, there is no reason for him to deny that there could be a physical triangle – then one can apply the *as*-operator to it and proceed to prove theorems about it *as a triangle*. If it is not, then the properties that have been proved to hold of triangles will hold of it more or less, depending on how closely it approximates being a perfect triangle. We could then relax our claim that this object *as a triangle* has interior angles equal to two right angles, and say only that insofar as it is a triangle it has such angles.

The important point is that direct links between geometrical practice and the physical world are maintained. Even in the case where the geometer constructs a figure in thought, one which perhaps has never been physically instantiated, that figure is constructed from elements which are direct abstractions from the physical world. Otherwise it will remain a mystery how, for Aristotle, geometry is supposed to be applicable to the physical world. Now Aristotle does make the cryptic remark that mathematical objects have 'intelligible matter' – and one might suspect that this is a special stuff which makes up a separate realm of pure mathematical objects.[47] That suspicion is, I suspect, misplaced. Aristotle is only trying to do justice to the nature of mathematical thinking: that is, when one carries out a geometrical proof it seems as though one has a particular object in mind. To prove a general theorem about triangles, it seems as though one chooses an arbitrary *particular* triangle on which one performs a construction.[48] It does not

---

[46] *On the Soul* III.7, 431b15–17; III.8, 432a3–6. Note also Sextus Empiricus' report: 'Aristotle, however, declared that the length without breadth of the geometers is not inconceivable: 'For in fact we apprehend the length of a wall without having a perception of the wall's breadth ...' (*Adversus Mathematicos* IV, 412).

[47] For his references to intelligible matter, see *Metaphysics* VII.11, 1036a2–12; 1036b32–1037a5; VIII.6, 1045a33–5. See also XI.1, 1059b14–16; XI.3, 1061a26–30.

[48] Cf. Euclid, *Elements* I.32 and the interpolation after III.3. See also *Posterior Analytics* II.11, 94a24–35; *Metaphysics* IX.9, 1051a26; T. L. Heath, *Mathematics in Aristotle*, pp. 31–9, 71–4, 216–17.

seem that one merely has the form of, for example, triangularity in mind: intelligible matter is invoked to account for the fact that we are thinking about a particular object.

But Aristotle has not postulated a separate realm of pure mathematical objects. For he does not have to postulate the existence of an object that does not exist in the physical world to be the object of thought. He merely has to explain how we think about objects that do exist in the world. It is true that we can both perceive a sphere and think about it. In fact, we can think about it in abstraction from the fact that it is composed, for example, of bronze. We can even perform mental constructions and form a figure that we have perhaps never perceived. But even in this case we are doing no more than constructing a figure in thought from elements that are direct abstractions from the physical world. One might wonder whether, on this interpretation, it follows that ordinary perceptible objects have intelligible matter. The answer is that they have intelligible matter insofar as they can be objects of thought rather than perception: that is, it is the object one is thinking about that has intelligible matter. The evidence for this is Aristotle's claim that intelligible matter is the matter 'which is present in sensible things not *as* sensible, i.e. in the objects of mathematics.'[49]

Aristotle's philosophy of arithmetic differs significantly from his philosophy of geometry, though Aristotle is not especially sensitive to this difference. The predominant mathematics of ancient Greece was geometry, and thus it is not surprising that his philosophy of mathematics should be predominantly a philosophy of geometry.

The main obstacle preventing Aristotle from giving a successful account of arithmetic is that number is not a property of an object.[50] Something may be at the same time *one* book, *two* stories, *thirty* pages, a *billion* molecules. To assign a number, we must first bring the object under a concept. Thus one cannot legitimately think of a number as one of the various properties of an object that can be separated from it in thought. One can, however, see Aristotle grappling with the problem:

Each question will be best investigated in this way – by

---

[49] *Metaphysics* VII.10, 1036a11–12.
[50] See G. Frege, *The Foundations of Arithmetic*.

> supposing separate what is not separate, as the arith-
> metician and the geometer do. For a man *as* man is one
> indivisible thing; and the arithmetician supposes one
> indivisible thing, and then considers whether any attri-
> bute belongs to man *as* indivisible. But the geometer
> treats him neither *as* man nor *as* indivisible but *as* a solid.
> For evidently the attributes which would have belonged
> to him even if he had not been indivisible, can belong to
> him apart from these attributes.[51]

Aristotle's position is, I believe, that members of natural kinds
carry a concept with them as their most natural form of desig-
nation. A man is first and foremost a man. Thus when one considers a man as a man, one is not abstracting one of the many
properties a man may possess from the others; one is rather selecting a unit of enumeration.[52] Elsewhere Aristotle allows that the
number of sheep, of men, and of dogs may be the same even though
men, sheep, and dogs differ from each other.[53] The reason is that
we are given the individual man (or sheep or dog) as a unit, and the
enumeration of each group yields the same result. The arithmetician posits a man as an indivisible because he posits him as a unit,
and as a unit he is treated as the least number of men.[54]

Aristotle thus uses the as-locution for two distinct purposes. In
geometry it is used to specify which property of a physical object is
to be abstracted from others and from the matter. In arithmetic it is
used to specify the unit of enumeration. It is easy to see how these
two uses could be run together. Both uses could be loosely
expressed as 'considering an x in respect of its being a P.' In one
case we can consider a bronze sphere in respect of its being a
sphere; in the other we can consider Socrates in respect of his being
a man. Indeed, in both cases one can be said to be 'abstracting': in
the former one abstracts from the fact that the sphere is bronze; in
the latter one abstracts from the fact that one man is many-limbed,
snub-nosed, etc. But to run these two uses together may be misleading. For in the former case we are picking out one of the
object's many properties and separating it in thought; in the latter

---

[51] *Metaphysics* XIII.3, 1078a22–8.
[52] In Fregean terms one is bringing objects under a first-level concept.
[53] Cf., e.g., *Physics* IV.12, 220b8–12, 223b1–12, 224a2–15.
[54] Cf. *Physics* IV.12, 220a27–32; *Metaphysics* XIV.5, 1092b19.

case we are picking out the object itself, under its most natural description, and specifying it as a unit for counting. If one thinks that, strictly speaking, abstraction is the separation of a property of the object, then in the case of arithmetic there is no abstraction at all. Aristotle would have had a more difficult time conflating these uses if he had not instinctively switched to natural-kind terms when discussing arithmetic. For suppose Aristotle had asked us to consider a *sphere as a sphere*: there would be no way of knowing on the basis of the locution whether we were to treat the sphere as a unit in counting spheres or to consider the spherical aspect of a sphere in abstraction from its other properties.

Of course, Aristotle's philosophy of mathematics does have its limitations, but what is remarkable is that, even from a contemporary perspective, it retains certain strong virtues. The limitations are obvious. In arithmetic we are given only a means of selecting a unit of enumeration; and since Aristotle's time there have developed whole realms of abstract mathematical thinking to which he did not address himself.

But one virtue of Aristotle's account is that he takes great pains to provide an account of mathematical truth that is harmonious with our understanding of how we come to know mathematical truths.[55] One reason for positing a separate realm of mathematical objects, as Plato did, is that it gives us something for our mathematical statements to be about. We can think of our mathematical statements as true because they truly describe these objects. The question then arises: how can we come to know about these mysterious objects? That question never gets a satisfying answer. Aristotle, by contrast, tries to show how geometry and arithmetic can be thought of as true *even though* the existence of separated mathematical objects, triangles and numbers, is a fiction.[56] Aris-

---

[55] Plato, *Meno* 73e–87c; *Republic* 5073–527d. Cf. Paul Benacerraf, 'Mathematical Truth.'

[56] Let us use the word 'Platonist' to describe the position in the philosophy of mathematics held by Plato and his followers in the Academy. Let us use 'platonist' to describe anyone who believes that mathematical statements are true in virtue of the existence of abstract objects which exist outside space and time. Finally, let us say that a 'mathematical realist' is someone who believes that mathematical statements are determinately true or false independently of our knowledge of them. Then one can say that Aristotle defends a form of mathematical realism while denying both Platonism and platonism.

totle considered geometry to be true in virtue of there being clear paths which lead one from the physical world to the (fictitious) world of geometrical objects (and back again). There may be no purely geometrical objects, but they are a *useful* fiction, because they are an *abstraction* from features of the physical world. If, as we have seen, one wants to prove of a particular bronze equilateral triangle b that it has interior angles equal to two right angles, one may 'cross' to the realm of pure geometrical objects and prove the theorem of a triangle c. The 2R property has been proved to hold of c in such a way that it is evident that it will hold of any triangle, so one can then 'return' to the physical world and conclude that b has the 2R property. The crossing was not, however, strictly speaking necessary: one could have proved directly of the bronze equilateral triangle b that it had interior angles equal to two right angles. The reason why the 'crossing' is valuable, though, is that one thereby proves a general theorem applicable to all triangles rather than simply proving that a certain property holds of a particular triangle.

Aristotle's suggestion, then, seems to be that what is needed for mathematics to be both true and knowable is for there to be a bridge between the physical world and the (fictitious) world of mathematical objects. Aristotle uses the *as*-operator to provide a bridge between bronze triangles and geometrical triangles. This, for Aristotle, ensures the applicability of mathematics: for mathematics to be applicable to the world it must reproduce structural features that are found (at least to some approximate degree) in the physical world. Moreover, there must be a bridge by which we can cross from the structural features of the world to the mathematical analogues and then return to the physical world.[57] The bridge

---

[57] An example of a bridge, suggested by Hartrey Field, is Hilbert's representation theorem for Euclidean geometry (see Hartrey Field, *Science Without Numbers*, chapter 3; and David Hilbert, *Foundations of Geometry*). The proof of the representation theorem shows that, given any model of Hilbert's geometrical axioms, there will be functions from points in space into the real numbers which satisfy conditions for a distance structure. Given that, one can show that the standard Euclidean theorems are equivalent to theorems about relations between real numbers. So if one thinks of models of space as being abstract, there is a two-stage process of moving from the physical world to the mathematical. The first stage is Aristotle's, where one moves from the physical world to a Euclidean model of space; the second is where one moves from the Euclidean model to a model of Euclidean space in the real numbers. The homomorphic functions would then provide the second span of the bridge and Aristotelian abstraction

enables us to conceive of mathematics as true without there being a special realm of mathematical objects which mathematics is allegedly about.

The other great virtue of Aristotle's account concerns not mathematics *per se*, but the study of the broad structure of reality. Aristotle's philosophy of mathematics reveals that there is a way of considering *this world* in abstraction. The beauty of our abstract thinking about triangles does not force us to consider it to be about an otherworldly realm of triangles. As Aristotle says, mathematics studies the physical world, but not *as* physical. But this opens the conceptual possibility of there being other forms of abstract thinking about the world. Certainly, the very fact that a form of abstract thinking has a certain purity and beauty need not imply that it is about another world: the thinking may gain its purity not because it is about a pure world, but because it is about this world considered in abstraction from its impurities. Once Aristotle realized how abstract thinking can be about this world, the question must have arisen for him: just how abstractly can man think about the world? Metaphysics was his answer.

6.3 Metaphysics: the inquiry into being *as* being[58]

Man is an inquirer who is able to abstract from certain features of reality in order to consider other features in depth. As we have just seen, when the mathematician considers a triangle *as* a triangle, he abstracts from the fact that it is made of bronze and considers only the properties it has in virtue of its being a triangle. Aristotle saw that this process of abstraction could be continued: ultimately it would yield a very abstract inquiry into reality. 'There is a science,' he says, 'which investigates *being as being*.'[59] The expression '*being as being*' may seem odd, but Aristotle's idea is that man is able to conduct an inquiry into the broad structure of reality. Rather than focussing solely on particular aspects of reality – say,

---

would provide the first. Or one could just take physical space as the model for the axioms (assuming that the axioms are true of physical space), and then one needs only the homomorphic functions as a bridge.

[58] Appropriate reading: *Metaphysics* IV.1–3.

[59] *Metaphysics* IV.1, 1003a21.

the heavens or living organisms, as the sciences of astronomy and biology do – man can also abstract from all the particular properties which make things the things they are and consider them merely as existing things. That is, man can inquire into reality as such. The desire to understand propels a man on from the first explorations of his immediate environment, to a search for explanations of why the world is the way it is, to, finally, the realization that man can transcend the explanation of this or that phenomenon and begin to inquire into the broad structure of reality. Aristotle discovered that there could be an inquiry into reality as such: as he put it, there is a single science which studies being as being.

Reality, in Aristotle's eyes, has a certain organized structure. Although there are many senses in which a thing is said to be, all refer to one starting-point: substance.[60] Now it may at first seem odd to a modern reader to see Aristotle call substance a 'starting-point' or 'principle.'[61] Is it not certain premises or thoughts that are starting-points, not bits of reality? But by this stage of our inquiry there is no longer a significant distinction to be made between the order of our thoughts and the order of reality. Thus a certain portion of reality itself, substance, can be thought of as a starting-point. Some things are substances, other things are properties of substance, processes toward substance, etc. All reality either is substance or is somehow dependent on or related to substance. Thus the inquiry into reality as such is an inquiry into substance. This inquiry Aristotle calls first philosophy.[62] Later commentators named this inquiry 'metaphysics,' signifying that it is an inquiry which comes after (*meta*) the study of nature (physics).[63]

There is, I think, a philosophically important sense in which metaphysics comes after physics. Until now the object of our inquiry has been held at an arm's length. The inquiry into nature revealed the world as meant to be known; the inquiry into man's

[60] *Metaphysics* IV.2, 1003b5–19. See also *Metaphysics* VII.1.
[61] Both words are acceptable translations of the Greek word '*archē*.'
[62] *Metaphysics* IV.2, 1004a2–4.
[63] There is also a story that the *Metaphysics* is so called simply because some librarian catalogued it and placed it on the shelf after the *Physics*. The 'things that come after the *Physics*' is so named simply because it comes after the *Physics*. I don't believe this story: or, at least, if a librarian did place the *Metaphysics* after the *Physics*, he did so because he was a very smart librarian and had a deep reason for doing so.

soul revealed him as a being who is meant to be a knower. Man and world are, as it were, made for each other. But now, as man comes to understand the broad structure of reality, there is no longer any firm distinction to be made between 'subjective' mind inquiring into the world and 'objective' world yielding up its truth. For now the order of our knowledge and the order of reality coincide: there is, for the metaphysical inquirer, no longer any gap between what is most knowable *to us* and what is most knowable. The world is constituted of essences and, when we are doing metaphysics, so is our thinking: indeed, it is the very same essences that constitute world and mind. We are now at a point where it becomes possible to understand that understanding itself is not just a part of reality, but plays a constitutive role in the overall structure of reality. At the same time, we can see that our inquiry into the world is at the same time an inquiry into ourselves. For the essences we discover there are the essences we become. This is where the desire to understand leads us. The opposition between the essential structure of reality and what is essentially human begins to disappear. Metaphysical inquiry can thus simultaneously be about man and world, because at this level of inquiry there is an internal coincidence between what is essential to man and what is essential about the world. Moreover, we come to see how man, in pursuit of understanding, becomes something more than mere man. This transcendence is more sweeping than that which he undergoes in becoming a political animal. In the ethical life, the individual transcends the (lack of) organization of desires that are given to him by nature: his desires become organized in such a way as to promote a flourishing human life within society. But with the inquiry into the broad structure of reality, man surpasses the 'human' perspective altogether.

6.4 The most certain principle of being[64]

It is the philosopher's task to know the basic principles of reality:

> ...he whose subject is being must be able to state the

---

[64] Appropriate reading: *Metaphysics* IV.3–7. Some of the argument in this section is adapted from chapter 6 of *Aristotle and Logical Theory*. However, my current views about the argument have changed significantly from those expressed in that chapter.

most certain principles of all things. This is the philosopher, and the most certain principle of all is that regarding which it is impossible to be mistaken; for such a principle must be both the best known (for all men may be mistaken about things they do not know) and non-hypothetical. For a principle which everyone must have who knows anything about being, is not a hypothesis; and that which everyone must know who knows anything, he must already have when he comes to a special study. Evidently then such a principle is the most certain of all; which principle this is, let us proceed to say. It is, *that the same attribute cannot at the same time belong and not belong to the same subject in the same respect*; we must presuppose, in face of dialectical objections, any further qualifications which might be added. This then is the most certain of all principles, since it answers to the definition given above. For it is impossible for anyone to believe the same thing to be and not to be, as some think Heraclitus says; for what a man says he does not necessarily believe. If it is impossible that contrary attributes should belong at the same time to the same subject (the usual qualifications must be presupposed in this proposition too), and if an opinion which contradicts another is contrary to it, obviously it is impossible for the same man at the same time to believe the same thing to be and not to be; for if a man were mistaken in this point he would have contrary opinions at the same time. It is for this reason that all who are carrying out a proof refer it to this as an ultimate belief; for this is naturally the starting point even for all the other axioms.[65]

The most certain principle is that a property cannot both belong and not belong to a subject at the same time and in the same respect. This principle is commonly known as the *principle of non-contradiction*. Although Aristotle says that this principle is the most certain, he does not mean that we have what we would call Cartesian certainty: that by merely entertaining it in thought we will recognize its truth. Heraclitus, for example, may sincerely assert that the principle of non-contradiction is false. There are

[65] *Metaphysics* IV.3, 1005b8–34 (I use 'as' rather than the Latin *qua* and 'proof' rather than 'demonstration.')

two conditions which a principle must satisfy if it is to be the most certain of all. First, it must not be possible to be mistaken about it.[66] Second, anyone who understands anything understands the principle.[67] It may at first appear that these conditions do demand Cartesian certainty, but this appearance is misleading. Aristotle believes that the principle of non-contradiction satisfies these conditions, but if Heraclitus can sincerely assert that the principle of non-contradiction is false, his assertion cannot be a mistake about the principle. Nor can it reveal that he does not understand the principle. For Heraclitus clearly understands many things, so he must understand the most certain of principles. Therefore, what it is to make a mistake about the principle or to fail to understand it must be something other than sincerely to assert a falsehood about it. But how can Aristotle say that Heraclitus believes the principle of non-contradiction, that he understands it, that he cannot make a mistake about it, when he sincerely asserts that it is false?

Aristotle seems to be focussing on a deeper sense of belief than what an agent thinks he believes. Heraclitus *thinks* he believes the principle of non-contradiction is false, but Aristotle's point is that he is wrong about his own beliefs. By denying the principle of non-contradiction, Heraclitus reveals that he does not know the contents of his own mind. This idea should no longer be strange to us. The incontinent thinks that he knows that it is best for him, say, to refrain from temptation, but his action reveals that he does not have the knowledge he thinks he has. Heraclitus, by contrast, does have the knowledge he thinks he does not have. He does know that the principle of non-contradiction is true, even though he thinks he believes it false. But what notion of belief and knowledge is such that one can believe what one sincerely asserts to be false? The way to uncover this notion of belief is to study Aristotle's argument that everyone must believe the principle of non-contradiction. For his strategy is not to try to persuade someone who does not believe the principle of non-contradiction to change his mind: there is no such person to whom the argument should be addressed. The argument is designed to show us that we all – even

[66] *Metaphysics* IV.3, 1005b12.
[67] *Metaphysics* IV.3, 1005b16.

those who deny it – really do believe the principle of non-contra-diction.

It might initially appear that Aristotle's argument begs the question. For Aristotle assumes that *the belief that a certain property holds of a subject* is itself a property which is true of the person who has the belief. Beliefs are properties of believers. And, he says, the contradictory belief – that is, *the belief that the property does not hold of the subject* – is itself the contrary property of the believer. So for Heraclitus actually to believe that the same property both applied and did not apply to a given subject, contrary properties would have to be true *of him*. And, since contrary properties cannot hold of a given subject simultaneously, he cannot actually believe the principle of non-contradiction is false. Or so Aristotle thinks. But suppose Heraclitus were right: suppose the same property could both apply and fail to apply to a subject at the same time. Then there would be no reason to think that contrary properties could not be true *of him* at the same time: no reason, that is, to suppose that he could not believe that the principle of non-contradiction is false. So it seems that Aristotle's argument that everyone must believe the principle of non-contradiction depends upon the truth of the principle of non-contradiction itself.

The charge of begging the question is typically difficult to adjudicate. One usually charges an opponent with begging the question when one thinks he has assumed in his argument the very thing he should be arguing for. And yet, from the opponent's perspective the charge usually seems unfounded: directed against a basic and (to him) self-evident principle for which argument is impossible. One man's begging of the question is another man's self-evident truth.

In the case of Aristotle's argument, I think the situation is as follows. If the principle of non-contradiction is true, then Aristotle has not begged the question; if it is false, then he has. Remember, Aristotle is not trying to prove the principle of non-contradiction; he is trying to show that it is the most certain of principles. He does this by showing that everyone must believe it, no matter what they think they believe. The argument may use the principle of non-contradiction, but, far from begging the question, this is the heart of Aristotle's strategy. For he is not only inquiring into the basic structure of reality, but also trying to show that we are capable of making such an inquiry. Aristotle's argument establishes a basic harmony between thought and reality. Although the principle of non-contradiction is a basic principle constraining the structure of reality, it also harmoniously constrains the way we can think about the structure of reality. But what is the nature of this harmony? One might ask: is it because the principle of non-contradiction is a basic principle of *reality* that it constrains the way we must think if we are to think about reality? Or is it a principle of *intelligibility*, governing all thinking, to which the world must conform if it is to be understood? By now it should be clear that this is a false dichotomy. One of the key insights which emerged from the investigation of logic was the possibility of a structure which was at once the order of reality and the order of thought. Indeed, as we shall see, thinking constitutes reality at its highest level.[68]

But if the principle of non-contradiction so permeates thought and reality, it would seem to be inevitable that one must rely on it in any argument on its behalf. Aristotle certainly recognizes that he uses it in his argument: 'We have now posited that it is impossible for anything at the same time to be and not be, and by this means have shown that this is the most indisputable of all principles.'[69] However, if the principle of non-contradiction is false, then a case can be made that Aristotle has begged the question. For the claim that a person cannot simultaneously believe that a property does and does not apply to a subject depends on the principle of non-contradiction holding with respect to that person. If the principle of non-contradiction is not generally true, it may not be true of that believer: so he may well believe that contradictory properties hold of a subject. It seems odd to suppose that whether or not an argument begs the question depends not on the structure of the argument itself, but on the truth of the claims made in the argument. We tend to think that question-begging is a failure of argument, not of truth. But that is why the charge of begging the question is difficult to adjudicate and why it is often unfair to charge one's opponent with begging the question. It may be that one has simply not yet understood what he recognizes to be a basic truth. Aristotle is confident that the principle of non-contradiction is a basic prin-

[68] See section 6.7 below.
[69] *Metaphysics* IV.4, 1006a23–4.

ciple of reality, and therefore that his argument that everyone must believe it does not beg the question.

Still, there is a problem of persuasiveness. The reason an opponent might be tempted to charge Aristotle with begging the question is that he would not find Aristotle's argument, at least as presented so far, at all persuasive. Even if Aristotle is right that his opponent only *thinks* he believes the principle of non-contradiction is false, from the opponent's (mistaken) perspective it will look as though Aristotle is simply helping himself to the truth of the principle. But should not a good argument be persuasive? Ought it not to convince people who are not already convinced? An opponent might admit that if the principle is true, then it is the most certain of principles and he must be incapable of disbelieving it. Yet he might deny that the principle is true, and he might take his own alleged belief in its falsity as evidence that the principle of non-contradiction could not be the most certain of principles. So, even if Aristotle has not begged the question, there is a serious issue about how he will be able to persuade someone of the certainty of the principle of non-contradiction.

The claim that a good argument ought to be persuasive needs to be handled with care. A good argument ought to be persuasive, but it does not follow that it ought to convince those who are not already convinced. Consider, for example, Aristotle's argument that the ethical life is the good life for man. This argument was addressed only to those who were already living an ethical life, and Aristotle assumed that, in an important sense, the argument would not be available to a bad man. That is not a fault in the argument; it is a fact about the restricted availability of the truth. Now the realm of rationality is wider than the ethical: it encompasses us all. Yet though all rational beings are subject to the principle of non-contradiction, it does not follow that all rational beings must come to appreciate this. And yet, being rational beings, we ought to be capable of appreciating the rationality of our thought. Thus the aim of Aristotle's argument is not only to make the truth of the principle of non-contradiction self-evident to us; it is to place us in a position in which we can recognize that the argument for it is itself a good argument.

Aristotle is aware that a certain dialectical finesse is required. He admits that a direct proof is the wrong strategy:

Some indeed demand that even this [the principle of non-contradiction] shall be proved, but this they do through want of education, for not to know of what things one may demand proof, and of what one may not, argues simply want of education. For it is impossible that there should be proof of absolutely everything: there would be an infinite regress, so that there would still be no proof. But if there are things of which one should not demand proof these persons cannot say what principle they regard as more indemonstrable than the present one.

We can, however, prove negatively even that this view is impossible, if our opponent will only say something; and if he says nothing, it is absurd to attempt to reason with one who will not reason about anything, in so far as he refuses to reason. For such a man, as such, is seen already to be no better than a mere plant. Now negative proof I distinguish from proof proper, because in a proof one might be thought to be assuming what is at issue, but if another person is responsible for the assumption we shall have negative proof, not proof. The starting-point for all such argument is not the demand that our opponent shall say that something either is or is not (for this one might perhaps take to be assuming what is at issue), but that he shall say something which is significant both for himself and for another; for this is necessary, if he really is to say anything.[70]

Proof has its limitations. By its very nature, a proof enables one to gain knowledge of the conclusion based upon a knowledge of the premisses. But the problem is not to prove the principle of non-contradiction from more basic principles — for there are no more basic principles — but to respond to someone who seems to be denying it. Negative proof, or proof by refutation, is Aristotle's indirect strategy for establishing the certainty of the principle of non-contradiction. Negative proof is designed to show that the possibility of saying anything, even that the principle of non-contradiction is false, depends on belief in the principle of non-contradiction. If a person is to deny the principle of non-contradiction, he must do just that: assert that the principle is

[70] *Metaphysics* IV.4, 1006a5–22.

false. There is no point, Aristotle says, in trying to argue with someone who says nothing: for insofar as he says nothing he is no better than a plant.[71] But Aristotle is not arguing with a plant. He is arguing with someone who can present an understandable, if fallacious, argument for the falsity of the principle of non-contradiction. The opponent of the principle, while disowning reason, listens to reason.[72] He is able to argue in a reasoned way against the principle of non-contradiction, and the possibility of such argumentation depends on adherence to the principle of non-contradiction.

Therefore, a person reveals his belief in the principle of non-contradiction not so much by *what* he says as by the fact that he *says* anything. His belief in the principle is revealed by the fact that he both speaks and acts in understandable ways. That is why everyone must believe the principle of non-contradiction. For, since this belief is manifested in all speech and action, if a 'person' did not believe the principle of non-contradiction, 'he' would not be able to speak or to act. But a being who has the capacity neither to speak nor to act has no claim to being a person; and so 'he' would rightly be considered as no better than a plant. The principle of non-contradiction is most certain, then, in the sense that it is absolutely unshakeable: the very possibility of speech, thought, and action depends on adherence to its truth.

If a man is to *say anything* – even that the principle of non-contradiction is false – he must say something significant both to himself and to others.[73] What is it to say something significant? In a statement, according to Aristotle, a person either affirms or denies something of a subject.[74] Thus the speaker must be able *to pick out or refer to* the subject about which the affirmation or denial is being made. For an affirmation can affirm something of something only if the subject-term picks out the subject of which something is being affirmed. In general, I believe that what an expression signifies corresponds *both* to what, if anything, the expression refers to *and* to its meaning.[75] An important part of what

[71] *Metaphysics* IV.4, 1006a15.
[72] *Metaphysics* IV.4, 1006a26.
[73] *Metaphysics* IV.4, 1006a21–2.
[74] Cf. *On Interpretation* 17a25ff; and see 16b26, 16b33, 17a8.
[75] Of course, one must avoid attributing to Aristotle the sophisticated semantic distinctions which have been made only recently. His notion of signifying some-

it is for someone to say something significant is for him to pick out or refer to the subject about which he is going to make an affirmation or denial.[76] Since all statements are affirmations and denials of a subject, it is clearly necessary for the speaker to pick out or refer to a subject if he is going to say anything.

Now the subject of a paradigmatic Aristotelian statement will be a substance. However, to *signify a substance* is not merely to refer to it, but to refer to what it is: namely, its essence.[77] As we shall see later, Aristotle ultimately argues that primary substance is identical with its essence.[78] So simply to refer to substance is to refer to essence. But the way to think about it for the moment is that a substance-term does not just *happen* to pick out a substance – as 'featherless biped' might happen to pick out man; a substance-term picks out a substance in virtue of what that substance is. 'Man,' for example, picks out man just in virtue of what he is: 'If *man* signifies one thing, let that be biped animal. What I mean by *signifying one thing* is this: if *this is a man, then if anything is a man that thing will be what being a man is.*'[79] If a subject-term signifies one thing, it will refer to something that is both substance and essence. Let us suppose that 'biped animal' states the essence of man, and consider the assertion

Man is [a] biped animal.

(I have put the indefinite article in brackets because Greek has no indefinite article.) On Aristotle's theory, if 'man' signifies one

---

thing will cause heartache to the modern philosopher who tries completely to assimilate it to that of either sense or reference, at least as these notions are commonly understood. The lack of precision does not, however, impugn the suggestion that part of what it is for a subject-term to signify is to refer.

[76] As Aristotle says at *Categories* v.3b10–13, 'Every substance seems to signify a certain "this something." As regards primary substances it is indisputably true that each of them signifies a certain "this something"; for the thing revealed is atomic and numerically one.'

[77] See *Posterior Analytics* I.22, 83a24–35.

[78] See *Metaphysics* VII.6, and section 6.6 below.

[79] *Metaphysics* IV.4, 1006a28–34 (The Oxford translation here uses the expression 'means' where I use 'signify' (for *sēmainō*). The advantage of the Oxford translation is that it makes for easier reading. The disadvantage is that, for Aristotle, 'to signify' is a term of art being put to technical use. There is no reason why the meaning of an expression should pick out the essence. And to say that an expression has one meaning seems to suggest nothing more than it is unambiguous. Moreover, as we shall see, the Oxford translation will find itself unable to stick with this translation. So it seems better to use the slightly artificial 'signify' to indicate that Aristotle has a special meaning for it.)

thing, it refers both to the man's substance and to what man is – the essence of man. But if 'man' signifies *one* thing, the man's substance and the essence of man cannot be two distinct things to which the expression refers. The man's substance and the essence of man must be identical. The above assertion is true, then, because it is a statement of identity. *Biped animal* is not a property that is true *of* man, it is what man *is*.[80]

Aristotle distinguishes *signifying one thing* from *being predicable of one subject*:

> It is not impossible, then, that being a man should signify precisely not being a man, if 'man' is not only predicable of one subject but also signifies one thing (for we do not identify 'signifying one thing' with 'being predicable of one subject,' since on that assumption even 'musical' and 'white' and 'man' would have signified one thing, so that all things would have been one; for they would all have been synonymous). And it will not be possible for the same thing to be and not to be, except in virtue of an ambiguity, just as one whom we call 'man' others might call 'not-man'; but the point in question is not this, whether the same thing can at the same time be and not be a man in name, but whether it can in fact.[81]

Even if 'man,' 'pale,' and 'musical' could all be predicated of a single subject, these terms would not signify one thing. Only a substance-term like 'man' can signify one thing: for it picks out something that is both substance and essence.

Aristotle says that if 'man' and 'musical' and 'white' signified one thing 'all would be one because synonymous.'[82] For Aristotle it is *things*, not words, that are synonymous. Two things are synonymous if they share not only a name in common, but also the '*logos* of substance' that corresponds to the name.[83] Again the *logos* of substance need not be thought of as merely verbal:[84] the *logos* may be the order or arrangement which is the essence. To state that

---

[80] See Alan Code, 'Aristotle: Essence and Accident.' He distinguishes predications of properties a thing *has* from predications which express what a thing *is*.

[81] *Metaphysics* IV.4, 1006b13–22.

[82] *Metaphysics* IV.4, 1006b17–18.

[83] *Categories* 1a7.

[84] See J. L. Ackrill, *Aristotle's Categories and De Interpretatione*, pp. 71–91.

biped animal is the *logos* of man is not to say that the linguistic expression 'man' means *biped animal*: it is to say that to be a biped animal is what it is to be a man. Similarly, if *biped animal* is what 'man' signifies, it is not that 'biped animal' gives the verbal definition of what 'man' means.[85] If 'man,' 'white,' and 'musical' signified one thing, then 'man,' 'white,' and 'musical' would share a *logos*. Aristotle says that all would be one because synonymous: this means that if things shared not merely a name but a *logos*, they would be essentially the same:

> Therefore, if it is true to say of anything that it is (a) man, it must be a two-footed animal; for this was what 'man' meant; and if this is necessary, it is impossible that the same thing should not be (a) two-footed animal; for this is what 'being necessary' means – that it is impossible for the thing not to be. It is, then, impossible that it should be at the same time true to say the same thing is (a) man and is not (a) man.[86]

Because Greek lacks an indefinite article, this argument can be carried out at two levels. First, we can suppress the indefinite article and take the argument to be about the substance man. Since man signifies biped animal, it is necessary that anything which can be said to be man be biped animal. For 'man' signifies its essence: and the essence is just what man is. Man cannot cease to have its essence and remain man. Second, we can insert the indefinite article and understand the argument to be about an individual man, Socrates. If it is true to say of Socrates that he is a man, then it is necessary that he be a biped animal. For since 'man' signifies biped animal, what it is for Socrates to be is to be a biped animal: so it is not possible that he should not be a biped animal. For if he is anything he is that. But if we cannot say that he is not a biped animal, we cannot say that he is not a man.

Aristotle's argument is persuasive only if one accepts his views of substance and essence. Aristotle seems to be aware of this, for he

[85] For a different interpretation, see R. M. Dancy, *Sense and Contradiction: A Study in Aristotle*, especially p. 46. Dancy takes what a word signifies to be its sense and is thus led to make criticisms that I do not think are justified.

[86] *Metaphysics* IV.4, 1006b28–34. (I have placed the indefinite article in parentheses.)

accuses those who deny the principle of non-contradiction of destroying substance:

> In general those who use this argument do away with substance and essence. For they must say that all attributes are accidents, and that there is no such thing as being essentially man or animal. For if there is to be any such thing as being essentially man this will not be being not-man or not being man (yet these are negations of it); for there was some one thing which it signified, and this was the substance of something. And signifying the substance of a thing means that the essence of the thing is nothing else.[87]

If 'not-man' could be said of the very same thing of which 'man' is said, there could not be substance, for there would be nothing which was just what it is to be a man. In Aristotle's view this is tantamount to destroying the possibility of discourse, for there is no longer a subject about which to make any affirmation or denial:

> But if all statements are accidental, there will be nothing primary about which they are made, if the accidental always implies predication about a subject.[88]

But accidental properties are properties of a subject. The white thing may be musical and the musical thing may be white, but that is because they are both properties *of* a man.[89] If accidental properties are always properties of a subject, then an enduring subject is needed for any predication whatsoever. Any account, then, that destroys substance must, in Aristotle's view, be incorrect.

> There must, then, even in this case be something which signifies substance. And it has been shown that, if this is so, contradictories cannot be predicated at the same time.[90]

[87] *Metaphysics* IV.4, 1007a20–7. (Here the Oxford translation gives '*denoting* the substance of a thing' where I continue to use 'to signify.' The translator is forced here to acknowledge the referring aspect of 'to signify,' and thus he has had to use two English expressions, 'to mean' and 'to denote,' to translate one Greek verb *sēmainō*.)

[88] *Metaphysics* IV.4, 1007a33–b1.

[89] *Metaphysics* IV.4, 1007b2–17.

[90] *Metaphysics* IV.4, 1007b16–18. (Again, I use 'to signify' where the Oxford translation uses 'to denote.')

A true opponent of the principle of non-contradiction is robbed of the possibility of saying anything. For to say something, on Aristotle's account of language, is to affirm or deny something of a subject. And if we attempt to say of a subject both that it is man and that it is not-man we have not succeeded in making two statements; we have failed to make one:

> It follows that all would then be right and all would be in error, and our opponent himself confesses himself to be in error – And at the same time our discussion with him is evidently about nothing at all; for he says nothing. For he says neither 'yes' nor 'no', but both 'yes' and 'no'; and again he denies both of these and says 'neither yes nor no.'[91]

This is the ultimate reason why the opponent of the principle of non-contradiction cannot say anything. The opponent (if he is consistent) must admit not only that what he says is true, but also that what he says is in error. This seems to be the paradigm of proof by refutation: the opponent is forced to say that what he says is false.

Why, however, should this opponent be worried? That everything he says is false does not for him rule out the possibility that everything he says is also true, which he also firmly believes. In fact he should cheerfully admit that everything he says is false – of course it is false – and he should chide us for not seeing that it is false (and true) as well. Similarly with Aristotle's argument that it is not possible for the same thing to be a man and not be a man.[92] Why cannot the opponent agree that it is not possible, but also conclude that it is? Why should the opponent object to any inference we make? Should he not accept all the inferences we accept, and complain only that we have not recognized all the valid inferences? (Of course, he should also say that we have!) Indeed, why can this opponent not accept Aristotle's entire argument, and complain only that he has not recognized the other side of the story? He may even charge Aristotle with begging the question, for Aristotle's argument only appears to be an objection to his position if one already accepts the principle of non-contradiction.

However, Aristotle's proof by refutation has a purpose more

---

[91] *Metaphysics* IV.4, 1008a28–33.
[92] *Metaphysics* IV.4, 1006b28; see above.

profound than the mere attempt to extract a confession of error from such a slippery opponent. His argument is not primarily intended for the 'opponent' of the principle of non-contradiction, whoever he is; it is addressed to the reader. The proof by means of refutation is constructed so as to reveal *to us* that Aristotle's opponent is in a contradictory position. At first it might appear that the revelation that one is in a contradictory position would hardly be felt as damaging to the opponent of the principle of non-contradiction. But Aristotle is not trying to persuade him: the argument is for our sake, not for his. Aristotle thinks that there is no one who does not believe the principle of non-contradiction. So the strategy to adopt is one designed to get us to see the incoherent position Aristotle's opponent is in.

This cannot be achieved merely by having him admit that he is in error. Although he admits to this, we do not yet recognize the incoherence of his position. Proof by means of refutation is designed to show us that if the opponent is capable of saying anything – even if what he is capable of saying is that he is opposed to the principle of non-contradiction – then his assertive and inferential practices, his general behavior, must be in accord with the principle of non-contradiction. And when a man is sufficiently confused to assert that he does not believe the principle, his general behavior is a far better guide to his beliefs than his assertions. That he will walk to Megara rather than stay where he is when he considers that he should walk there, that he will do one thing rather than another, reveals decisively that he is not the opponent of the principle that he thinks he is.[93] Were he a true opponent he would not think Aristotle's arguments damaging, but neither would he think anything else – he would be a vegetable. Even in such a case we could not justly call him a 'true opponent' of the principle of non-contradiction, for we would not be able to ascribe to him any beliefs at all. The opponent of the principle of non-contradiction tries to argue rationally that one should not accept it. Aristotle's point is that there is no conceptual space in which such a rational discussion can occur. Argument is useless to persuade him to 'accept the principle of non-contradiction,' whatever that might mean, but his very ability to argue reveals that the alleged opponent is not genuine, even though we may have thought he was. The opponent

[93] *Metaphysics* IV.4, 1008b12–27.

may cheerfully admit that everything he says is false, and, momentarily, we may find that amusing and challenging, but after the proof by refutation we should not find it deeply interesting.

A more serious objection to Aristotle's proof by refutation is that it depends on his theory of substance and essence. Is that not a major weakness in his argument? For it is overwhelmingly likely that the opponent who claims to disbelieve the principle of non-contradiction would also disbelieve Aristotle's theory of substance and essence. The opponent might also dispute Aristotle's philosophy of language. Aristotle argues that an opponent of the principle of non-contradiction must eliminate substance, so that there can be nothing that his statements are about. But that an opponent cannot *say anything* follows only if one assumes that the correct account of language-use is the one Aristotle gives: that to say anything is to affirm or deny something of a subject. Indeed, the very way in which Aristotle defines a contradiction and poses an objection to the principle of non-contradiction assumes an ontology of things about which our language speaks. In a contradiction 'the negation must deny the same thing as the affirmation affirmed and of the same thing ...'[94] Similarly, the opponent of the principle of non-contradiction as Aristotle thinks of him is not someone who completely gives up an ontology of substances and properties, but rather someone who asserts the opposite of the principle: that it is possible for the same thing to belong and not to belong to a subject simultaneously and in the same respect.[95] But why could not a more sophisticated opponent completely reject this world-view and theory of language? Could he not hold that, since the principle of non-contradiction is false, Aristotle's argument only shows that we must give up the picture of the world as composed of substances and properties? The truth of sentences would then have to be accounted for in ways that did not invoke the existence of substance.

In the grip of this objection, one might wonder why Aristotle did not formulate a more abstract argument, one which is independent of his particular theory of substance. Certainly, he had an argument immediately to hand. For within the details of his proof by refutation a valid point is being made which transcends both his

[94] *On Interpretation* VII, 17b38.
[95] *Metaphysics* IV.3, 1005b23.

theory of substance and his philosophy of language. An assertion divides up the world: to assert that anything is the case one must exclude other possibilities. This exclusion is just what fails to occur in the absence of the principle of non-contradiction, even when it is construed in its most general form:

for any statement S, it is not the case that both S and not-S.

One cannot assert S and then directly proceed to assert not-S: one does not succeed in making a second assertion, but only in canceling the first assertion. This argument does not depend on any theory of substance or on any theory of the internal structure or semantics of statements. It is a completely general point about the affirmation and denial of statements. Why, then, did Aristotle not focus on such a general argument if he wanted to make his proof as strong as possible?

If this objection looks strong, it is because one has lost sight of Aristotle's project. Aristotle's goal is neither to prove the principle of non-contradiction nor to convince an opponent of the principle to change his mind: in Aristotle's view, there is no such opponent. What Aristotle is trying to do is to show how the structure of reality constrains the structure of our thought. The very fact that the world is constituted of substances and properties forces us to think, speak, and act in certain ways. In a world made up of substances, any thinker must be someone who believes the principle of non-contradiction. It is because the structure of our thought is responsive to – indeed, expressive of – the structure of reality that we thinkers are capable of conducting a very general inquiry into reality. Since substance is the basis of reality, we thinkers are capable of conducting a general inquiry into substance. That is, we are capable of being philosophers engaged in metaphysical inquiry.

The next step in Aristotle's progress is to show that substance is identical with essence. For if substance is identical with essence, inquiry into substance cannot be a study of a subject-matter which is distinct from the inquiry itself. For, as we have seen, when mind inquires into essence it becomes the very essence it is contemplating. It is only when Aristotle has shown that substance is essence that he finally establishes metaphysics as an inquiry in which subject and object of study are identical. This is one of the central tasks of the central books of Aristotle's *Metaphysics*.

6.5 What is substance?[96]

We are beings capable of conducting an inquiry into the broad structure of reality, and it is the desire to understand that urges us on. We have not carried out that inquiry, we have not satisfied our desire, though, until we know what substance is. For substance is that which is basic, that upon which the reality of other things depends. But one can know *that* substance is basic without knowing *what* it is. One can know that substance is the most real sort of thing there is, and still inquire into what that real thing is. That was Aristotle's position. He never questioned that reality had an organized structure: that everything that existed was either substance or somehow dependent on substance for its existence. But over his life his thinking about what deserved to be considered substance developed. The idea that Aristotle changed his mind is very recent. Until the twentieth century, scholars assumed that Aristotle's philosophy formed a consistent whole; thus apparent inconsistencies had to be explained away. The problem is that certain things Aristotle says about substance do seem to contradict others. Of course, one possibility is that Aristotle simply made a mistake and contradicted himself. But a fascinating suggestion, made only recently, is that the apparent discrepancies in Aristotle's statements can be seen as the developing thought of someone who is changing his mind as his inquiry deepens and matures. The suggestion, then, is that we abandon the assumption that Aristotle's writings on substance are thoroughly consistent. And yet, instead of merely accepting inconsistency and contradiction, the idea is that we can find a greater coherence by finding in these inconsistencies the developing thought of a maturing thinker.

The question then becomes: how are we to trace the development of Aristotle's thought? The most famous attempt to answer this question uses the following organizing thesis: that Aristotle as a young man was heavily under Plato's influence and that as he grew older he saw more and more problems with Plato's meta-

---

[96] Appropriate reading: the *Categories*, and *On Interpretation* VII.

physics and developed his own distinctively Aristotelian outlook.[97] On this suggestion, the Aristotelian texts which are more Platonic in outlook are dated as earlier than those which are less Platonic. One problem with this suggestion is that what it is to be 'Platonic' is itself a matter of debate; so it is not at all clear when Aristotle is being more or less Platonic. Another problem is that the situation might be precisely the reverse: that Aristotle started out as a young man concerned to distance and distinguish himself from Plato as much as possible and, as he matured, came to realize the deeper truths in Plato's metaphysics. In that case, under some interpretation of what it is to be 'Platonic,' a work which is less Platonic should be dated earlier than one which is more Platonic. I have some sympathy with this suggestion, and I shall present an interpretation of Aristotle's investigation into substance which is in harmony with it. However, the reader should bear in mind that this is only one interpretation of Aristotle's developing thought; there are others.[98] This is only to be expected since the very idea that Aristotle's thought changed over time is so recent. It is so easy to think of the study of Aristotle as an almost timeless activity which has been carried out in more or less the same way since antiquity. It is exciting therefore to realize that the very idea that Aristotle changed his mind is extremely recent. As a result, Aristotle's mature view of substance is currently an issue of intense debate among scholars. The reader should also keep in mind that, although, as I interpret him, Aristotle becomes more Platonic in a certain respect, there are other respects in which he remains a staunch anti-Platonist all his life. But there is a serious issue about how we are to conceptualize Aristotle's debate with Plato. Is he to be seen as offering a fundamental critique of Platonism, as offering a polar opposite world-view? Or is he rather to be seen as working within Plato's general research project, offering criticisms and improvements, but preserving the overall approach and strategy? I tend to think that Aristotle did preserve Plato's overall approach:

[97] The classic text is Werner Jaeger, *Aristotle*. For a brilliant critique of this thesis, see G. E. L. Owen, 'The Platonism of Aristotle.'

[98] The interpretation I present has been deeply influenced by two pioneering articles of Alan Code: 'On the Origins of some Aristotelian Theses about Predication,' and 'Aristotle: Essence and Accident.' See also John A. Driscoll, '*EIΛH* in Aristotle's Earlier and Later Theories of Substance.' For alternative interpretations, see, e.g., Michael Frede, 'Individuen bei Aristoteles'; Rogers Albritton, 'Forms of Particular Substances in Aristotle's Metaphysics.'

he, like Plato, believed that the world was a fundamentally good place, that it was teleologically organized, and that it was accessible to man's philosophical inquiry. Their arguments occurred within this framework: over the precise structure of the teleological world-view.

In his study of predication, Aristotle focussed on a special type: those predications in which an essence is predicated of a substance. Let us suppose that the essence of man is *rational animal*. Then a predication like

Man is [a] rational animal

does not just predicate a property of a subject, it tells us what it is to be a man. One might call this an *essential predication*: a predication which gives the essence of the subject. This is one type of predication which Aristotle said is true *in virtue of itself (kath' hauto)*.[99] The predication is not one in which a property is predicated of an independently existing subject; rather, the predication helps to express what the subject itself is. In a non-essential predication, an ordinary property is predicated of a subject. For example, the sentence

Socrates is pale

is true just in case Socrates happens to have pale skin. But although Socrates may have pale skin, having pale skin is in no way part of Socrates' essence. Pale skin does not help to constitute what Socrates is. Aristotle called this an *incidental predication (kata sumbebēkos)*.

Not only are there two different types of predication, there are two different *levels* at which predication can occur: at the level of reality and at the level of thought or language. The reason that a linguistic predication, like

Man is [a] rational animal

is true is that a certain predication exists in reality. The word 'man' names the species *man*, the expression 'rational animal' names the essence of man, and that essence, *rational animal*, is essentially predicated of man. In general, the definition of a substance both states

[99] For other types of *kath' hauto* predication, see *Posterior Analytics* 1.4, 73a34–b4; 1.6, 74b6–10.

its essence *and signifies it*. But we have already seen that a substance-term like 'man' also signifies what it is to be a man, that is, the essence of man. It follows that the expression 'man' and the expression 'rational animal' signify the very same thing.[100] We might say, then, that *man* is a *thoroughly definable* entity. For the definition of man states the essence, but that is precisely what the term 'man' signifies. In the predication 'Man is [a] rational animal,' what the subject-term 'man' signifies is identical to what the predicate 'rational animal' signifies.

Now this is to be distinguished from an essential predication like

Socrates is [a] rational animal.

For the name 'Socrates' signifies the individual Socrates, and if 'rational animal' is the definition of man, it signifies the essence of man, *rational animal*. This sentence is true not because its subject and predicate signify the same thing, but because it expresses an essential predication which exists in reality. The essence of man, *rational animal*, is essentially predicated of the individual Socrates: being a rational animal is just what Socrates is.[101] Socrates is not identical with his essence, but his essence is what he most truly is. Thus we can say that Socrates' essence, *rational animal*, is what Socrates most truly is, but it is not *all* that he is. As we have just seen, in addition to essential predications, we can also make incidental predications of Socrates: for example, 'Socrates is pale.' This linguistic predication is true because a certain predicational relation exists in reality. The universal *pallor*, which is predicated of many distinct things – of Alcibiades, of Kallias, etc. – is also predicated of Socrates.[102] This predication is true of Socrates but is no part of his essence. Yet definition states the essence. So there are more things true of Socrates than are stated in a definition

---

[100] Although what 'man' signifies is identical to what 'rational animal' signifies, this does not imply that 'Man is a rational animal' has the form of an identity statement, 'Man = rational animal.' It can be a regular predication in which subject and predicate are identical.

[101] Indeed, Aristotle uses an expression which means just that: *hoper to ... estin.* See *Categories* 3b6; *Metaphysics* VII.4, 1030a3; cf. *Posterior Analytics* 73b8–9, 83b9, 89a35, 83a28–30.

[102] *On Interpretation* VII. (I am, for simplicity, suppressing the *Categories* distinction between something being predicable of and something being present in a subject. Those who are interested, see *Categories* II.)

expressing his essence. Socrates, unlike the species man, is not a thoroughly definable entity.[103]

Aristotle differs from Plato in his belief that certain items in the natural world embody essences. Plato believed that no item in the natural world could be the bearer of an essential predication.[104] It may be true that Socrates is a man, but Socrates, like all other individual men, falls short of being what it is to be (a) man.[105] Plato posited a separate realm of Forms and restricted essential predications to them. For Plato, only an ontologically separate Form, the Man Itself, can be said to be a man in virtue of itself. One may say that an individual like Socrates is a man, but, Plato thought, that is only because he stands in some relation (participation, imitation) to the Man Itself. For Plato, only thoroughly definable entities are bearers of essential predications. Aristotle disagrees. For Aristotle, items in the natural world have essences, and thus one can make essential predications of them. Socrates is a man, not because he stands in some relation to a separate Platonic Form, but because he himself has an essence. If being a rational animal is the essence of man, then it must be true not merely to say that 'Man is a rational animal,' but also to say 'Socrates is a rational animal.' This predication states what Socrates essentially is. Aristotle's disagreement with Plato about embodied essences and essential predication is one which he maintains throughout his career, and the disagreement has a profound effect on his view of the route human understanding should take. For if essences are *in* the natural world, it is by penetrating deeper into that world that we get beyond it.

In the *Categories*, which I take to be an early work, the primary substances are individual men, animals, plants, etc. By 'primary substance' or 'substance in the primary sense,' Aristotle meant to designate the paradigm of substance. Various sorts of things may be called 'substance' when speaking loosely, but when one is en-

---

[103] That is why when I gave an example of an incidental predication I had to resort to a particular, Socrates, rather than continue using the subject man. Since man is thoroughly definable, all the predications which are true of it are essential predications.

[104] At least, Plato as Aristotle understood him: see *Phaedo* 74.

[105] Here I am using Aristotelian terminology to make a Platonic point. I take this liberty because we are here primarily concerned with an understanding of Aristotle and of how he differed from Plato. Again, I put the indefinite article in parentheses not simply because Greek lacks an indefinite article, but because if one reads the claim without it, the Platonic position gains a certain plausibility.

gaged in a philosophical inquiry into what substance in the primary sense is, one is engaged in trying to answer the questions: what is most real?, what is ontologically basic?, what is that upon which the reality of other things depends? The salient reason for this early choice of primary substance is that a particular man, animal, or plant is a subject of properties which are predicable of it, but it is not predicable of anything further.[106] One might think of (non-essential) predication as expressing a relation of dependence. The universal *pallor* may exist, but it can only exist as something that is predicable *of* an underlying subject. Thus a universal cannot be ontologically basic. *Pallor* must exist as the color of an individual like Socrates, but since Socrates is not predicable of anything else, he is not dependent on anything else for his existence. Thus a particular like Socrates counts as ontologically basic.

Because an individual like Socrates is a particular thing with an essence, he is something definite: Aristotle calls him a 'this something' (*tode ti*). Some translators even translate *tode ti* as 'a particular' or 'an individual' rather than use the artificial 'this something,' but I think this translation misses Aristotle's point. Aristotle uses the expression 'this something' as a placeholder for a definite, ontologically basic item. Thus he can insist that primary substance must be a 'this something' before he even knows what primary substance is. It is important, therefore, not to presuppose Aristotle's answer to the question 'What is substance?' in advance of his inquiry into substance. Translating *tode ti* as 'a particular' makes this very presupposition. So instead of translating *tode ti* as 'a particular,' one should see the *Categories* as *trying to answer* the question 'What is ontologically basic?' by offering particulars as primary substances. His reasoning, in brief outline, is, first, that primary substance is a subject for predicables, but is not itself predicable of anything further; second, that a particular is something which is not by its nature predicable of anything else.[107] Since particulars are themselves subjects of predication, it follows that to be a primary substance is simply to be a particular.

However, when Aristotle wrote the *Categories* he had not yet developed the concepts that would enable him to conceive of a particular like Socrates as a composite of form and matter. He knew that Socrates had an essence, but he had not yet come up with the

---

[106] *Categories* V, 2a11–14.
[107] *On Interpretation* VII.

idea that the essence was the formal aspect of Socrates, his body being the matter. Nowhere in the *Categories* is any primary substance subjected to an analysis in terms of form and matter. Indeed, Aristotle had not yet developed his technical concept of matter, a concept which he developed only when he came to explain how change was possible.[108] Once he had the concept of matter, though, it became possible to reformulate his concept of form. The early idea of form was, so to speak, relatively unformulated: it was the idea of the shape or structure of something. However, once he developed the concept of matter, it was possible to conceive of form as the complement of matter. He was then able to regard particular animals and plants as composites of a potentially living body (the matter) and a soul (the form or first actuality of a potentially living body). Look at how the concept of form changed: it was no longer just the shape of something, but had become a principle of life. But this must have re-opened the question of what counts as primary substance. For if a particular like Socrates is a composite of form and matter, the following question becomes unavoidable: is not Socrates dependent on his form or his matter for being what he is? If the answer to this question is 'yes,' then Socrates cannot any longer be regarded as primary substance.

Moreover, it looks uncomfortably as though Aristotle's developed concept of matter turns out to be primary substance as defined in the *Categories*. For matter is a subject of properties and is not itself predicable of anything further. And yet matter cannot be substance, for it is not something definite, nor is it intelligible, nor is it ontologically independent. As Aristotle puts it, matter is not a 'this something.' His point is not that matter is not a particular, but that matter is not an ontologically definite, independent

[108] The concept is introduced to help explain the persistence of something or other through a change. Of course, substantial changes provide the most difficult case, for there is no persisting subject of change. (See *Physics* I.7 and *On Generation and Corruption*.) But in fact all physical change seems to require matter. If, for example, a craftsman shapes a hunk of gold into a sphere, one wants to say that it is *the very same yellow* that was in the hunk that is now in the sphere. (That is, we want to say not merely that the very same shade of yellow is in the hunk and the sphere, but the very same property token.) But since yellow is a property, for that property to persist through the change, it seems that there must be a something that is also persisting through the change that it is the property of. That something is matter. (See Brian O'Shaughnessy, *The Will*, vol. 2, pp. 172–4.)

entity. Therefore, once Aristotle developed the complementary concepts of form and matter, the whole issue of what primary substance is had to be re-thought.

It is the task of *Metaphysics* VII to do the re-thinking. *Metaphysics* VII represents Aristotle's mature thoughts on substance, yet understanding what he says there is extraordinarily difficult. As usual, this is not a finished work, but unpolished notes; yet these notes are unusually cramped and impenetrable. There are several reasons for this. First, when *Metaphysics* VII begins, Aristotle is already well into the inquiry into substance, a sophisticated inquiry which has occupied him on and off for most of his adult life. He simply takes the inquiry thus far for granted. If he were lecturing from these notes, he would assume that his audience already knew in detail the intricacies of Plato's and his own previous inquiries into substance. Perhaps the most impenetrable passages are ones in which Aristotle is clearly in the throes of a heated debate with a Platonist opponent, though it is not clear exactly what Platonic doctrine Aristotle is attacking. Of course, anyone listening to Aristotle's lectures would most likely have been familiar with the fine points of the current debates about substance, and so it would have been unnecessary to set the stage. But those once current debates are by now so unfamiliar that, even as you read this, some of the best Aristotle scholars of the present generation are trying to figure out what those debates were. Second, the inquiry is carried out in such abstract terms that it is often not clear at what level of generality Aristotle is speaking. For example, it is on occasion very difficult to recover either from the Greek vocabulary or from the content of the argument whether Aristotle is talking about a particular man, the species man, or the form of the species man. Since there is a serious question whether any of these is primary substance, it is of the utmost importance to determine which Aristotle is talking about. Finally (for those who are reading *Metaphysics* VII in translation), there is the troubling fact that the most available translations have not taken seriously the idea that Aristotle changed his mind about what counts as primary substance.[109] Since individual animals and plants are clearly the primary substances of the *Categories*, translations sometimes force a

---

[109] An exception is Montgomery Furth, *Aristotle, Metaphysics Books Zeta, Eta, Theta, Iota*. (His interpretation nevertheless differs from the one given here.)

reading of the *Metaphysics* in which these things remain primary substance.

Because *Metaphysics* VII is so difficult, there are very different views as to what Aristotle's argument is. A definitive interpretation will, I am sure, be the size of a small encyclopedia. That being said, I do not intend to present any of the alternative interpretations; nor do I even intend to present an interpretation of all the difficult passages. I am writing for someone who is reading *Metaphysics* VII for the first or the second or the third time. The reader should not expect to understand everything that is said there. The aim of the next section is to orient the reader: to give some idea of the central issues, arguments, and conclusions of Aristotle's mature inquiry into substance.

6.6 A tourist's guide to *Metaphysics* VII[110]

There are two thoughts about the world which permeate Aristotle's thinking. The first is that the world is ultimately intelligible. The second is that reality forms a hierarchy: at the base is substance, which is ontologically independent, and upon which the reality of everything else depends. Aristotle's task in *Metaphysics* VII is to find a candidate for substance which will satisfy both these beliefs. As Aristotle puts it, substance must be both a 'this something' and a 'what-it-is.'[111] The idea of something's being a 'what-it-is' is that of its being a thoroughly definable, and thus an intelligible, entity. The idea of something's being a 'this something' is the idea of its being an ontologically basic, definite item. Only if something can be both a 'what-it-is' and a 'this something' is the intelligibility and the ontological basicness of substance secured. If Aristotle

---

[110] Appropriate reading: *Metaphysics* VII. Please do not feel that you have to make a visit. This is a very technical book of the *Metaphysics* and, though I shall try to present the central ideas as clearly and simply as possible, the discussion cannot fail to be a bit technical without also failing to be about *Metaphysics* VII. For those who do not wish to work through the arguments, read the first and last paragraphs of this section and then skip to the next section, which presents Aristotle's account of God.

[111] *Metaphysics* VII.1, 1028a11–18. The centrality of these two demands to the arguments of *Metaphysics* VII was pointed out by G. E. L. Owen in 'Particular and General.' Unfortunately, Owen assumed that a 'this something' must be a particular; and thus, I believe, he could not appreciate the actual structure of Aristotle's argument.

cannot show that what is ontologically basic is also intelligible, the ultimate intelligibility of the world is threatened.

Now before Aristotle begins his inquiry in *Metaphysics* VII, it does seem as though the intelligibility of the world is under threat. For in *Metaphysics* III, where Aristotle catalogues the difficulties which confront the philosophical inquirer, he asks whether substance is a particular or a universal.[112] It looks as though the answer must be 'neither.' For if substance is a particular, it will not be knowable. A particular like Socrates is, as we have seen, not a thoroughly definable entity; and to the extent that he is not definable, he is not intelligible.[113] But it is unacceptable that substance be unknowable. If, on the other hand, substance is a universal, it will be knowable, yet it will not be capable of independent existence. For a universal is something which is predicated of many particulars, and thus it seems to be dependent on the particulars for its existence.[114] But substance was supposed to be ontologically independent. It looks, then, as though substance can be either knowable or ontologically basic, but not both. This is untenable.

Aristotle solves this dilemma, but he does so without opting either for the particular or for the universal as primary substance. What he realizes in *Metaphysics* VII is that the choice between particular and universal is not exhaustive. There is, he discovers, a way of being a 'this something' which is neither a particular nor a universal.[115] That is why it is crucial not to assume that a 'this something' is a particular. The form or essence of each species is, Aristotle discovers, a 'this something,' yet it is neither a particular nor a universal.[116] Why it is neither we shall soon see. First, we ought to see what the form of a species is. Once Aristotle discovered that an individual like Socrates could be conceived as a composite of form and matter, it was a short step to realizing that the species *man* could be conceived as a universal which itself has a formal and material aspect. The species *man* could be conceived as

---

[112] *Metaphysics* III.6, 1003a5–17. And cf. *Metaphysics* XIII.9–10. See Alan Code, 'The Aporematic Approach to Primary Being in Metaphysics Z.' I discuss this issue in more detail in 'Active *Epistēmē*.'

[113] Cf. *Posterior Analytics* I.8, 31, 33.

[114] See *On Interpretation* VII.

[115] See Joseph Owens, *The Doctrine of Being in the Aristotelian Metaphysics*, chapter 13.

[116] The idea that species-form emerges as primary substance is due to Alan Code, 'Aristotle: Essence and Accident,' though he does not agree with the further claim that species-form is neither particular nor universal.

human soul embodied in such and such a type of flesh and bones. *Human soul* is thus the form of the species *man*.[117]

There is one such form per species. You and I differ in matter, but we are the same in form: each of us is human soul embodied in this or that matter.[118] This is a very different idea of soul from what we, influenced by two thousand years of Christianity, are used to. Strictly speaking, there is only *one soul* animating numerically distinct human bodies. Now Aristotle can, if he wishes, talk about your soul or my soul: he can, for example, insist that it is my soul, not yours, that is the principle of life for me.[119] But this is just an elliptical way of saying that it is human soul embodied in *these* flesh and bones which is a principle of life for me.

Now if there is a way that the form of a species can be a 'this something,' then this form can count as ontologically basic. *Human soul*, for example, is the form of the species *man* and so it can count as one of the basic things there is. Each species-form is eternal, and Aristotle thinks that each individual organism, by realizing its form, participates to the best of its ability in something that is ontologically basic and divine.[120] And yet the form or essence of each species is also definable, and so it is thoroughly intelligible. Species-form satisfies both of the constraints on primary substance – basicness and intelligibility – and thus the hierarchy and intelligibility of reality can be secured.

How does Aristotle arrive at this outlook? He lays down a set of positive and negative constraints which any successful candidate for primary substance must satisfy. As it turns out, only form will

---

[117] Note that Aristotle uses the same word (*eidos*) for 'species' and for 'form.' So passages in which it might at first look as though he is talking about the species *man* may, upon further inspection, turn out to be about the *form* of the species *man*.

[118] *Metaphysics* VII.8, 1034a5–8. (I should like to mention an alternative interpretation in which each individual has his own form which is peculiar to him. For an exposition of it, see Michael Frede and Gunther Patzig, *Aristoteles, Metaphysik Z*.)

[119] One might at first think that *Metaphysics* XII.5, where he says that individuals rather than universals are causes, might pose a problem for me. However, species-form is not a universal; so the contrast that is made in this passage does not affect the point I am making either way. I think one should understand this passage in terms of the old *Categories* ontology of particular vs. universal, with primacy being given to the particular. It simply does not apply to the new ontological framework which Aristotle is developing in *Metaphysics* VII.

[120] See *On the Soul* II.4, 415a26–b7, quoted in section 4.1 above. We have yet to discover the divine aspect of this activity.

satisfy all the constraints. It is often said that *Metaphysics* VII is aporematic: whether or not this is true depends on what one means by 'aporematic.' Often what is meant is that Aristotle makes contradictory demands on substance which nothing could possibly satisfy and thus that *Metaphysics* VII is unfinished, unresolved, and inconsistent. I do not think that this is true. The constraints on substance might at first look inconsistent, but that is not because they actually are inconsistent, but because they are drawn so tight that only one candidate for primary substance can emerge: substantial form. The work is, though, aporematic in Aristotle's sense. He lays down a set of problems (*aporiai*) and demands concerning substance, he begins with his own and other respectable beliefs, and he tries to work his way through the problems.[121] *Metaphysics* VII is simply a working through of those problems.

One respectable belief with which Aristotle begins is that substance is that which underlies the various properties (*to hupokeimenon*).[122] Of course, this is an idea which once attracted Aristotle. When he wrote the *Categories*, a particular like Socrates was treated as a primary substance because he was a subject of properties but was not himself predicated of anything else. But now that Aristotle has the concept of matter, the old *Categories* criterion of primary substance becomes unclear: in particular, it is unclear whether or not matter is primary substance. For if primary substance is that which underlies and supports the various properties of a thing, then if in thought we 'strip away' the various properties of a thing, what we are left with is the matter.[123] This is the old idea of substance as the ultimate supporter of properties, revamped for a world which includes matter. Matter is the ultimate supporter of properties.

The problem with matter so conceived is that it seems to be something that is in itself an indeterminate, unknowable stuff: 'By matter I mean that which *in itself* is neither a particular thing, nor of a certain quantity nor assigned to any other of the categories by which being is determined.'[124] This does not imply that matter has no properties; it only implies that matter *in itself* has no properties.

[121] See, e.g., *Metaphysics* VII.3, 1029a33–b12; and see Alan Code, 'The Aporematic Approach to Primary Being in *Metaphysics* Z.'
[122] *Metaphysics* VII.3; see especially 1028b36–1029a1.
[123] *Metaphysics* VII.3, 1029a10–26.
[124] *Metaphysics* VII.3, 1029a20–1 (my emphasis).

There are no properties matter has in virtue of its being what it is. It is not in its own right a definite thing: it is a mere supporter of properties. This is the conception of underlying thing which Aristotle is now concerned to dismiss as a possible candidate for primary substance. He does so by introducing two constraints on substance.[125]

(1) Substance must be a 'this something' (*tode ti*), a definite thing.

(2) Substance must be separate (*chōriston*), ontologically independent.

Matter is neither capable of existing on its own nor a definite thing, so it cannot be substance.

Aristotle then seems to rush headlong to his conclusion. For he says that of the three candidates for substance – form, matter, and the composite of form and matter – both the matter and the composite may be dismissed.[126] Matter has already been dealt with. As for composites, a composite is ontologically posterior to its form and matter. But Aristotle has already insisted at the beginning of *Metaphysics* VII that

(3) Substance is prior in every sense: in *logos*, in knowledge, in time.[127]

A composite like Socrates is dependent on his form to be what he is, so the paradigm primary substance of the *Categories* must be dismissed.

It looks, therefore, as though Aristotle has already concluded

---

[125] *Metaphysics* VII.3, 1029a27–8; cf. VII.1, 1028a33–4. (The numbering is to some degree arbitrary. One can, if one wishes, consider (1) and (2) as forming a single constraint, with (2) providing an explication of what is involved in claiming (1).)

[126] *Metaphysics* VII.3, 1029a29–32.

[127] *Metaphysics* VII.1, 1028a31–b2. A substance is prior in *logos* in the sense (1) that in the *order* of reality other things are dependent for their existence on substance, but substance is not dependent on anything else; so (2) when one gives an *account* or *definition* of other things one will ultimately have to mention their dependence on substance, and thus include the *logos* of substance. Substance is prior in knowledge in the sense that if our knowledge reflects the order of reality – if what is most knowable to us is what is most knowable – then substance will be known to be that which is prior in reality. Cf. *Posterior Analytics* I.2; *Metaphysics* IV.11; *Categories* XII.

that form must be the new primary substance. Yet we are only at the beginning of *Metaphysics* VII. Indeed, in the very first few lines of the chapter Aristotle says: 'That which is primarily is the "what it is" which signifies the substance of the thing.'[128] The 'what-it-is' gives us the form or essence of a thing. What, then, does Aristotle do in the rest of *Metaphysics* VII? He shows us how form can be primary substance. That is, he works through the other constraints which form must meet if it is to be worthy of the title of primary substance. He shows how other candidates for substance, like the genus (rather than the species) or Platonic Forms, are inadequate. And he shows how form can be both ontologically basic and intelligible. He solves the problem about whether substance is particular or universal, by developing a conception of a basic intelligible substance that is neither particular nor universal. In effect what he is doing is narrating for us, his students, the conceptual search for substance: it is a search we must work our own way through if we wish to discover for ourselves why the form or essence of species emerges as primary substance.

It is clear to Aristotle that substance bears some relation to essence, and it is the task of *Metaphysics* VII.4–6 to hammer out what that relationship is. In *Metaphysics* VII.4–5 Aristotle restricts both definition and essence to substance.[129] His reason is that only substance can be said to be something in virtue of itself. Other things can be said to be what they are only in virtue of their relation to substance: for other things depend on substance for their existence. But the essence of something is what that thing is in virtue of itself.[130] Since only substance is what it is in virtue of itself, essence must be restricted to substance. Now a definition is an account which states an essence: an essence is the ontological correlate of a definition.[131] Thus Aristotle can lay it down that, strictly speaking,

(4) Only substance is definable.[132]

---

[128] *to ti esti*: *Metaphysics* VII.1, 1028a13–15.
[129] *Metaphysics* VII.4, 1030a28–31, b4–6; VII.1031a1–2, a11–14. Indeed, even at this early stage Aristotle says that it is only the species of a genus that will have an essence: for only they are primary and do not involve the predication of one thing of another (*Metaphysics* VII.4, 1030a10–14). The argument for this claim, though, is yet to come.
[130] *Metaphysics* VII.4, 1029b14.
[131] *Metaphysics* VII.4, 1030a6–7; VII.5, 1031a11–12. See also *Topics* I.5.
[132] *Metaphysics* VII.5, 1031a1–2.

And yet, although Aristotle can conclude that 'definition and essence in the primary and simple sense belong to substances,'[133] it is not yet clear what the relationship is between substance and essence. Is it that primary substances alone *have* essences, or that primary substances alone *are* essences?

In *Metaphysics* VII.6 Aristotle argues that

(5) Each primary substance is identical with its essence.

It is worth realizing that this is a condition on substance which, by now, we should have expected. For Aristotle has already argued that substance is definable (condition (4)): this is a condition that has been imposed to secure the ultimate intelligibility of substance. For the definition of a thing states the essence, and it is essence that mind comprehends. Now a particular like Socrates has an essence, but he is not definable: as we have already seen, there are properties true of him that are no part of his essence. And he is a composite of form and matter, but his matter is no part of his form or essence. It would seem, then, that to be a definable entity, something must be identical to what its definition signifies. Since a definition signifies the essence of a thing, it would seem that if primary substance is definable it must be identical with its essence.

Aristotle's own argument takes the shape of a complex and interwoven series of arguments directed against Platonic Forms.[134] For simplicity, I shall extract only one central idea which is sufficient for our purposes. Let us suppose, for the purposes of a *reductio*, that a primary substance X is distinct from its own essence. Then it follows that X itself is unknowable: for mind grasps essences. Mind may comprehend the essence of X, but since that essence is distinct from X, mind will not in that act comprehend X. But then X fails one of the fundamental constraints on substance: namely, that it be intelligible. So if X is a primary substance, it must *be* its essence. As Aristotle concludes, 'each thing that is primary and said to be what it is in virtue of itself is one and the same as its essence.'[135]

This forces a dramatic revision in Aristotle's conception of substance. For although Socrates *has* an essence, he is not *identical*

133 *Metaphysics* VII.4, 1030b4–6.
134 *Metaphysics* VII.6, 1031a28–b22.
135 *Metaphysics* VII.6, 1032a4–6; cf. VII.6, 1031b18–20.

279

with his essence: he is a certain essence embodied in certain matter. A concrete individual like Socrates, the paradigm primary substance of the *Categories*, can no longer be treated as primary substance. In general, Aristotle believes that

(6) No material particular is a primary substance.[136]

This is a complete reversal of the position he held when he wrote the *Categories*. With the development of the concept of matter and the corresponding concept of form, a material particular like Socrates can no longer without qualification be considered a basic underlying subject of properties. Socrates is himself a composite of form and matter, and thus he seems to be ontologically posterior to his form and matter. Moreover, the very idea of an underlying subject being the criterion of primary substance is called into question by the idea of matter. For there is some sense in which matter is an underlying subject of properties, and yet, as we have seen, it lacks ontological independence and definiteness. Finally, the idea that a material particular like Socrates can be conceived as a certain form embodied in certain matter raises to a new level the possibility that the world is fundamentally intelligible. For forms or essences are intelligible, so if it turns out that form is primary substance, a new meaning is given to the idea that the world can be understood. What is most basic ontologically and what is most knowable will coincide.

Metaphysics VII.7–9 is devoted to the items that come to be in the natural world, both natural organisms and products of art. Each item comes to be by a certain form's being realized in certain matter. The form itself is neither created nor destroyed. In natural generation, the male parent passes on his form to his offspring. So each member of the species has the same form or essence.[137]

> And when we have the whole, such and such a form in
> this flesh and in these bones, this is Callias or Socrates;
> and they are different in virtue of their matter (for that is
> different), but the same in form ...[138]

Artefacts too depend on antecedently existing form and matter.

---

136 Cf. *Metaphysics* VII.11, 1037b3–7.
137 *Metaphysics* VII.7, 1032a24–5.
138 *Metaphysics* VII.8, 1034a5–8.

The artist has the form in his soul, and this is the active principle and starting-point of his creation.[139] This form is a completely matter-less substance:

> ... from art proceed the things of which the form is in the soul. (*By form I mean the essence of each thing and its primary substance.*) ... There it follows that in a sense health comes from health and house from house, *that with matter from that without matter*: for the medical art and the building art are the form of health and of the house, and *I call the essence substance without matter*.[140]

Creation consists in the realization of a form in matter.[141] The craftsman has the form *house* in his soul and is thus able to impose that form on the appropriate matter. Both the form and matter exist antecedently to the creation. Of course, there is some sense in which it is possible to create matter. For example, a builder may make bricks from straw and mud and later use them to build a house. Aristotle's point is that even the creation of the bricks is to be conceived as the imposition of a certain form on antecedently existing matter (mud and straw). The created bricks can now serve as the antecedently existing matter for another creation. Creation thus depends on some antecedently existing matter or other. The form, however, is never created.[142]

The term 'house,' then, is ambiguous. It may refer to the totally matter-less form in the builder's soul or it may refer to the composite of form and matter in which one lives. The form in the builder's soul, Aristotle insists, is not itself a *particular*. There is no need for a Platonic Form – the House Itself – to explain how all the material houses that exist in the world come into being.[143] The form in the builder's soul Aristotle calls a 'such.'[144] Since it is not realized in any matter, the form in the builder's soul has no particularity at all. It represents the builder's ability to impose that form on the appropriate matter. When the builder has imposed such a

139 *Metaphysics* VII.7, 1032a32–b1, b21–3.
140 *Metaphysics* VII.7, 1032a33–b14 (my emphasis).
141 See *Metaphysics* VII.8.
142 *Metaphysics* VII.8, 1033b5–7, b16–17; VII.9, 1034b10–19.
143 *Metaphysics* VII.8, 1033b19–29.
144 *toionde: Metaphysics* VII.8, 1033b22.

form on certain bricks and wood, the resultant particular house Aristotle calls a 'this such.'[145] It is from the form *house* that the composite of form and matter gets its name.[146] So when one says 'This is a house' one may be predicating the form: that is, one may be saying that this particular house has the form of a house. Or one may be predicating a *universal composite* of form and matter: that is, one may be predicating a universal which is true of a subject in virtue of that subject's being a composite. One may be saying that *this* house is an instance of the form house realized in a certain type of matter.

Some terms, however, refer unambiguously to form realized in certain matter. 'Man,' for example, signifies a composite of human form realized in flesh and bones.[147] According to the *Categories*, *man* is a secondary substance, the species to which a primary substance like Socrates belongs. However, once Aristotle realized that Socrates was a composite of form and matter the predication took on a different look. The species itself could now be conceived as having a formal and a material aspect: human soul embodied in flesh and bones. In saying 'Socrates is a man,' one is now predicating a universal of Socrates that signified both his form and his matter. Aristotle now says that *man* is a 'universal composite.' *Man* is a *universal* in the sense that it is said of individual men: of Socrates, of Plato, etc. *Man* is a *composite* in the sense that it signifies both the form and the matter of men: it signifies *human soul* embodied in flesh and bones. But if *man* is now a universal composite, the essence of man can no longer be thought of as identical to *man*. Here again Aristotle is forced to change his mind. The essence of *man* is *human soul*, the formal aspect of the universal composite man.

This, however, raises a question as to whether a definition of *man* should include an account of the flesh and bones in which human soul is embodied. On the one hand, it is hard to imagine that we can give an account of man which does not mention his peculiar matter; on the other hand, definition is supposed to state the essence or form, and matter is not part of the form. It is the task of *Metaphysics* VII.10–11 to work through this dilemma. One can

---

[145] *tode toionde*: Metaphysics VII.8, 1033b23–4.
[146] *Metaphysics* VII.8, 1033b17–18.
[147] *Metaphysics* VII.10, 1035b27–30.

give an account of man which includes both his form and his matter, but Aristotle insists that a strict definition will be not of man, but of human soul, the form of man. The definition will make no mention of his matter. Of course, it is hard to imagine human soul other than as instantiated in a certain type of matter, flesh and bones, but Aristotle does not think that the mere fact that we cannot imagine something is philosophically significant:

> *Definition is of the universal and of the form.*[148] If then it is not evident which of the parts are of the nature of matter and which are not, neither will the *logos* of the thing be evident. In the case of things which are found to occur in specifically different materials, as a circle may exist in bronze or stone or wood, it seems plain that these, the bronze or the stone, are no part of the essence of the circle since it is found apart from them. Of things which are *not* seen to exist apart, there is no reason why the same may not be true, e.g. even if all circles that had ever been seen were of bronze (for none the less the bronze would be no part of the form); but it is hard to effect this severance in thought. E.g. the form of man is always found in flesh and bones and parts of this kind. Are these then also part of the form or the *logos*? No, they are matter; but because man is not found also in other matters we are unable to effect the severance.[149]

Because a circle can be realized in various types of matter, it is easy to realize that no part of the definition of a circle will mention the matter. In fact, one can use the term 'circle' to refer to the matterless form *circle* which is identical with its essence:

> Only the parts of the form are parts of the *logos* and *the logos is of the universal*: for *being a circle* is the same as *the circle* and *being a soul* the same as *the soul*. But when we come to the concrete thing, e.g. *this* circle, i.e. one of

---

[148] *Metaphysics* VII.10, 1035b34–1036a1.

[149] *Metaphysics* VII.11, 1036a28–b3 (my emphasis). (I leave *logos* untranslated; the Oxford translation gives 'formula.') It seems odd to me that Aristotle does not here take advantage of his idea that matter is a relative item: that flesh and bones are themselves composites of form and matter. Aristotle could then allow that the definition of human soul does include the *formal* aspect of flesh and bone. See section 2.4 above.

the individual circles ... of these there is no definition.[150]

So the situation is as follows.[151] One can define *the human soul, the
circle*, or *the house*, for these are all matter-less forms. The definition
will state the essence which is identical to the form. *Human soul* is
identical to *what it is to be human soul*; the circle is identical to what it
is to be a circle. One cannot define *man*, the universal composite of
form and matter, nor can one define an individual man, except insofar
as one can define its primary substance, human soul. Primary substance is immaterial and identical to its essence. So only primary substance is definable: it alone *is* what the definition states.

However, if definition is only of the form it is not easy to see how
Aristotle avoids contradicting himself. For in *Metaphysics* VII.13 Aristotle argues that

(7) No substance is a universal.

A universal is that which is said of many things.[152] Aristotle has
already insisted that definition is of the form and of the universal,[153]
but *only* substance is definable.[154] How can it be that (1) no substance
is a universal, but (2) only substance is definable, and (3) definition is
of the universal?[155] If no substance is a universal, how could form
emerge as primary substance? To answer this question, one must look
to the context in which Aristotle makes the claim that no substance is
a universal. If we probe the context, I wish to argue, the appearance of
contradiction vanishes.

One of Aristotle's major discoveries in *Metaphysics* VII is that the
form of a species can be considered to be a 'this something' (*tode ti*).[156]
Once he has made this discovery, he can go on to say that substance is
not a universal, for by universal he means something which is importantly different from a 'this something.' So as his conception of a 'this
something' develops one might expect a corresponding change in his
conception of a universal. Now if one simply assumes that a 'this
something' is a particular, one will not be able to follow the pro-
gression of Aristotle's thought. Aristotle never defines the notion, so

[150] *Metaphysics* VII.10, 1035b34–1036a5 (my emphasis). (I leave *logos* untranslated; the Oxford translation gives 'formula.')
[151] See *Metaphysics* VII.11, 1037a21–b7.
[152] Cf. *Metaphysics* VII.13, 1038b11–12; and *On Interpretation* 17a38–40.
[153] *Metaphysics* VII.11, 1036a28; 10, 1035b34–1036a1.
[154] See constraint (4) above, and cf. *Metaphysics* VII.5, 1031a1–2.
[155] See J. H. Lesher, 'Aristotle on Form, Substance and Universals: A Dilemma.'
[156] For Aristotle's references to form as a 'this something,' see *Metaphysics* V.8,
1017b21–26, VIII.1, 1042a28–31; cf. VII.12, 1037b27.

we have no clear statement of what it is to be a 'this something.' However, his examples of what counts as a 'this something' change as his
thought develops. In the *Categories*, a particular like Socrates is a
paradigm 'this something.' This, as we have seen, has caused the widespread belief that a 'this something' must be a particular. But there is
no linguistic evidence that 'this something' means 'particular.'[157] The
'this' does function to pick out a 'something'; but whether it picks out
a particular or not will depend on what 'something' stands for. Take
for example the expression 'this animal': it could be used at the zoo to
pick out a particular lion; or it could be used by Platonists to refer to a
Form, the Man Itself; or it could be used to ₌efer to the species man; or
it could be used to refer to the (Aristotelian) form of the species man.
The phrase itself gives no guidance as to how it is being used. What it
picks out will depend on the context of its use.

Although Aristotle never defines the concept, being a 'this something' is regularly associated with two other metaphysical notions:
that of being ontologically independent (*chōristos*) and that of being
definite (*horismenos*).[158] At the heart of Aristotle's metaphysics lies
the belief that substance must be both independent and definite. But
what is it to be independent and definite? Suppose Aristotle adopted
the following research strategy. The inquiry into substance is to be
pursued at an extremely high level of abstraction. Aristotle believes
that substance must be independent and definite in some way or other,
but even the notions of independence and definiteness are subjects of
inquiry. One may discover what it is to be independent at the same
time as one discovers what turns out to be primary substance. Aristotle would then need an abstract expression which will express the
ontological independence and definiteness of substance, but which
will leave undetermined what this independence and definiteness consist in. A bare 'this something' (whatever it is) performs that function
perfectly. This, I suspect, was Aristotle's strategy; but if one assumes
that a 'this something' is a particular, one cannot see this strategy as
even a possible one for Aristotle to adopt.

---

[157] Indeed, in *Metaphysics* IX.7, Aristotle says that a form or 'this something' is predicated of matter (1049a34–b1). So this 'this something' could not possibly be a
particular.

[158] See *Metaphysics* VII.1, 1028a12, 25–28; 3, 1029a28–30, 13, 1039a1, 14,
1039a30–32; VIII.1, 1042a29, b3; IX.7, 1049a35; XII.3, 1070a35; XIII.10,
1087a15–18; V.8, 1017b23–26. Cf. VII.4, 1030a5–6; XI.2, 1060b1; *Categories*
v.3b10; *Posterior Analytics* I.4, 73b7. (*Chōristos* is often literally translated as
'separate' or 'separable.' The problem is that it is unclear what is meant by
'separate.' I think that 'ontologically independent' both makes sense to us and
captures the central idea involved in the claim that substance is *chōristos*.)

Nor can one appreciate Aristotle's solution to what he considered to be the great problem posed in the *Metaphysics*.[159] As we have already seen, Aristotle posed a dilemma which seemed to suggest that substance could be neither particular nor universal. If substances are particulars, they will not be knowable, for knowledge is of what is universal. This is unacceptable, for substances must be knowable. If, however, substance is universal (and thus knowable) it will not be capable of independent existence. This too is unacceptable, for substance must be capable of independent existence. Now if one takes a 'this something' to be a particular, it is hard to see how Aristotle could successfully resolve this puzzle. One will naturally see him as pulled between the legitimate demands of the particular and the legitimate demands of the universal to be substance.[160]

One will thereby miss the genius of Aristotle's solution. Aristotle does not remain trapped by this dilemma. Nor does he solve it by granting the title of primary substance either to the particular (thus ignoring what is legitimate in the claim of the non-particular to be substance) or to the universal (thus ignoring what is legitimate in the claim of the non-universal to be substance). Rather, he discovers that there is a way of being a 'this something' which is neither particular nor universal. Aristotle discovers a gap in what previously had looked like an exhaustive dilemma.

To see why the species-form emerges as a 'this something,' one must look to the argument of *Metaphysics* VII.12. There Aristotle returns to a puzzle that has bothered him before: if one can give a definition of substance, why should substance be a unity? For example, if the definition of (the form of) man is 'biped animal,' why is man one and not a plurality, namely *biped* and *animal*?[161] The problem is that definition is discursive, but 'substance is a certain unity and *signifies a "this something"*.'[162] Aristotle's answer, in outline, is that one must not think of the substantial form as composed of two prior elements, *biped* and *animal*. The genus *animal* does not exist independently of the species-form; and it should be thought of along the lines of the matter to which the species-form provides the form.[163] Although a

---

[159] See *Metaphysics* XIII.10, 1087a13, and the family of problems set out in *Metaphysics* III.

[160] This is G. E. L. Owen's analysis in 'Particular and General.'

[161] *Metaphysics* VII.12, 1037b8–14.

[162] *Metaphysics* VII.12, 1037b27.

[163] *Metaphysics* VII.12, 1038a5–9.

definition is discursive, it does not state elements which mysteriously make up a certain unity. So a definition which is formulated by starting with the genus and working one's way down through the differentiae in the appropriate order should not be conceived as a move from the more real to the more dependent: it is in fact the reverse. The final differentia will be the form of the species and the substance.[164] It will imply all the higher-level differentiae and the genus in the sense that they will all be universals predicable of the form, but they are not elements that make up the form. Aristotle has thus given content to the idea that species-form is an atomic form: on the one hand it is not composed of prior elements, on the other it is itself the last differentia, so it cannot be further divided into differentiae.[165]

One might think of Aristotle as employing the same *sort* of argument as he did in the *Categories*, only one octave up. Socrates can no longer be treated as a primary substance, for he is dependent on his form, human soul. But if we move the argument one octave higher and treat human soul as basic, the Aristotelian argument can be re-employed. The genus animal may exist, but it depends for its existence on the various species-forms of which it is the genus.

But then species-form passes all the tests of a 'this something.' First, it is a genuine unity, and so can be referred to as a 'this.' Second, it is ontologically independent in the following sense: if one moves either in the direction of the more general or in the direction of the particular one moves toward items that are dependent on it. The particular composite of form and matter is dependent on form for its reality.[166] And as one moves up the scale of differentiae one moves toward ever more general universals which do not have independent existence, but which are dependent on and predicable of species-form. Finally, species-form is definite. In the physical world it is the most definite thing there is. Again, as one moves toward the particular or toward the general one moves toward matter or what is *like* matter in the sense that it is less definite. Thus species-form is a 'this something.'

Yet, though species-form is a 'this something,' there is no particularity about it. Any two humans have the same form. The crucial feature of a particular is its particularity. It is the very particularity of a

---

[164] *Metaphysics* VII.12, 1038a19–20, a25–26, a28–30.
[165] Note that *Metaphysics* VII.8, 1034a5–8 supports the view that the same atomic form can be the form of distinct individuals. Callias and Socrates have the same atomic form but differ in matter.
[166] E.g., *Metaphysics* VII.3, 1029a27–32; VII.11, 1037a27–30; cf. VII.17, 1041b6–9.

particular that, Aristotle argues in *Metaphysics* VII.15, a definition could not possibly capture. The most difficult case for Aristotle is posed by unique, eternal, imperishable objects.[167] Aristotle says that with a unique, eternal object, like the sun or moon, it is very difficult to realize that it is not definable. The idea is presumably this: with a unique, eternal object one can in principle specify a set of conditions which it uniquely satisfies. Since the object is unchanging in the relevant respects, it will never fail to satisfy these conditions. Why, then, is this not a definition?

Aristotle answers this question with an ingenious thought experiment. Suppose that 'going around the earth' is the candidate definition for the sun. Aristotle asks us to consider two counterfactual conditionals:

> Even if the sun were to stop in its tracks, it would still be the sun.

> If some other body were to start going around the earth, it would nevertheless not be the sun.

Aristotle argues that both these statements are true. The reason the first conditional is true is that 'the sun' signifies a certain substance, and the substance in question is a particular.[168] Signifying at least partially consists in referring; and Aristotle is arguing that a substance-name like 'the sun' is not an abbreviated or disguised description. It refers directly to the particular substance, the sun, independently of any descriptive conditions the sun might satisfy. Therefore the description 'going around the earth' cannot be the definition of the sun, for it cannot specify what it is to be the sun. It cannot explain why if the sun failed to meet that very condition it would still be the sun. The second conditional is also true, because if some other object were to start going around the earth, it would not thereby become the sun. The sun is a particular, and the particularity of the particular cannot be captured by a *logos* which other objects could conceivably satisfy.

Note that the antecedents of both conditionals specify situations which are not only counterfactual, but which, on Aristotle's view, are impossible. For Aristotle, as we shall see, the movement of the heavens is itself an expression of the world's relation to God.[169] It is, for him, impossible that it should ever cease. This is a pure thought exper-

---

[167] *Metaphysics* VII.15, 1040a8–b2.
[168] *Metaphysics* VII.15, 1040a32–33, b1.
[169] See *Physics* VII; *Metaphysics* XII.7–9; *On the Heavens* I.10. I discuss this further in section 6.7 below.

iment: the antecedents could not possibly obtain, though they can be envisaged. And in envisaging them we realize that, even if we can specify a condition which a particular object will satisfy for all eternity, even if it is impossible for the particular object to fail to satisfy it, nevertheless the condition cannot be the definition of a particular.

Species-form, by contrast, is definable. It lacks the particularity of a particular, yet it is a 'this something.' But if there is a way of being a 'this something' which is not a particular, then one should expect a change in what counts as a paradigm universal. A universal, Aristotle says, is that which naturally belongs to many things.[170] Thus the concept of a universal is as vague or ambiguous as are the 'things' to which a universal belongs.[171] For example, in the *Categories* the universal *animal* is predicable both of the species *man* and of individual men.[172] So the 'things' of which *animal* is predicable would include the species *man, horse, shark* as well as individual men, horses, and sharks. The vagueness of the definition of a universal is an advantage, for Aristotle is able to capture with it the full range of predicational relations.

Yet there is no doubt but that there is a paradigm predicational relation: that in which the universal is predicated of a 'this something.' In this case above all others, a universal is predicated of a genuine subject. Within the framework of the *Categories*, the individual man or horse has been identified as primary substance and a 'this something.'[173] Thus the paradigm universal within the *Categories,* ontology is that which is predicated of many particulars. However, in his mature metaphysics Aristotle sees that the form of a species can also be considered a 'this something.'[174] The paradigm predicational re-

---

[170] *Metaphysics* VII.13, 1038b11–12. Cf. *On Interpretation* VII, 17a38–40.

[171] This fact is masked by the *On Interpretation* definition, which, I think misleadingly defines a particular in terms of a universal. In that definition Aristotle gives a negative characterization of a particular. A universal is that which is naturally said of many things; a particular is that which is not (17a39–40). Here the dichotomy between particular and universal is genuine; but the problem with any negative characterization is that it purchases exhaustiveness at the cost of negativity. If one has any positive conception of a particular, there is a danger that the positive conception will not be coextensive with the negative characterization. Some non-universal may not share the positive characteristics of a particular.

[172] *Categories* III.1b10–15.

[173] *Categories* v.3b10–18.

[174] He does not thereby abandon the view that a particular like Socrates can be considered a 'this something' (see *Metaphysics* VIII,1, 1042a25–31; and cf. *On the Soul* II.1, 412a8–9); but his primary concern now is with form as a 'this something.'

lationship is that in which a universal is predicated of a 'this some-thing.' But since species-form emerges as a 'this something' in the later books of *Metaphysics* VII, one ought to expect the universal discussed there to be a genus. As the 'this something' moves one octave up, so too does the universal.

If one lifts *Metaphysics* VII.13 out of context, it will read as though Aristotle is arguing that particulars must be substances. For he argues that no universal can be substance. And, since he elsewhere argues that particulars are not definable, but substance is, one will be forced to conclude that *Metaphysics* VII is inconclusive. But *Metaphysics* VII.13 follows Aristotle's demonstration in VII.12 that form is a 'this something' and the universal is explicitly contrasted with a 'this some-thing,' not with a particular.[175] Aristotle also contrasts essence with the universal: within the context of VII.13, essence is not a univer-sal.[176]

Moreover, the doctrine that the universal is substance is not merely an abstract doctrine that is investigated for its own sake; it is a doc-trine with adherents.[177] One ought thus to be able to recover in more detail what this doctrine is. Aristotle's target is a type of Platonist who believes that as one ascends the scale of generality one moves toward what is ever more real.[178] For him the genus is more real than the species, and the Form *man* should be thought of as composed of the genus *animal* plus a differentia *biped*.[179] Indeed, *Metaphysics* VII.13 investigates the inverse position to that which emerged in VII.12. There Aristotle argued that if one carries out a proper division from the genus down through the differentiae, it is at the *bottom* of the division that one finds substance. *Metaphysics* VII.13 investigates the claim that one must move up the scale to find substance. Now if Aristotle's opponent is such a Platonist, then *nothing* Aristotle says in *Metaphysics* impugns the claim of species-form to be primary sub-stance. For he has already shown species-form to be a 'this something' in VII.12. Indeed, in the opening lines of VII.13 the universal to be in-vestigated is distinguished from essence. In VII.13 Aristotle only attacks the claim that the (paradigm) universal – that which is

[175] *Metaphysics* VII.13, 1039a1–2.
[176] *Metaphysics* VII.13, 1038b3.
[177] *Metaphysics* VII.13, 1038b7–8.
[178] This is Aristotle's major antagonist in *Metaphysics* VII.13–17. But he also plays a significant role in the problems in *Metaphysics* III: see III.1, 995b27–31, 996a4–11; 3, 998a21–25, b3–8; 4, 999a24–b4, b24–1000a1; cf.VIII.1, 1042a13–16.
[179] *Metaphysics* VII.13, 1038b16–18, b33–1039a19; 14, 1039a24–b15; 15, 1040a16–25; 17, 1041b11–17, b25–33; VIII.6, 1045a14–22.

predicated of a 'this something' – is substance. Substantial form is not a universal – it is not a genus – it is a 'this something.'[180]

So when Aristotle claims that

(7) No substance is a universal,

what he really means is that

(7*) No substance is a genus.

Aristotle can correspondingly relax his earlier demand that definition be of the universal. What is important about this demand is that definition must be non-particular: as we have seen, definition cannot capture the non-particularity of a particular. But now that Aristotle has discovered that there is a way of being a 'this something' which is thoroughly non-particular, he can allow that definition may be of a 'this something.' The appearance of contradiction ultimately dissolves.[181]

[180] The argumentative structure of *Metaphysics* VII.13 is extremely difficult. Those who would like to probe it, see M. F. Burnyeat, ed. *Notes on Zeta*; M. J. Woods, 'Problems in Metaphysics Z, Chapter 13'; John A. Driscoll, '*EIΔH* in Aristotle's Earlier and Later Theories of Substance.' I must confine myself to two quick hints. First, the Oxford translation of 1038b10–11 is misleading. It says: 'For primary substance is that kind of substance which is peculiar to *an individual*, which does not belong to anything else; but the universal is common.' A literal translation of the Greek is: the 'substance *of each* is that which is peculiar *to each*, which does not belong to another, but the universal is common.' Now if one, first, ignores the context of the argument and, second, assumes that by 'each' Aristotle must mean a particular individual, it will appear that he is saying that each individual must have its own form. But Aristotle's use of 'each' is systematically ambiguous and depends on the context of use. He regularly uses it to refer to items that are not individuals: indeed, there are cases where he is clearly referring to species (cf. *Posterior Analytics* B13, 97b28–31; *Parts of Animals* 1.4, 644a28–33, b6–7. I am indebted to John Cooper, *Reason and Human Good in Aristotle*, p. 29, for these references). The most specific item that has emerged in VII.12 is species-form; and it is certainly true that species-form is peculiar to the species of which it is the substance and does not belong to another. The universal genus-form *animal*, by contrast, is common (1038b11): it is said of *man*, of *lion*, etc. Second, do not assume that Aristotle is speaking in his own voice throughout the chapter: from 1038b16–30, Aristotle is voicing a Platonist objection to which he must respond. This is discussed in detail in the works cited above, and I discuss it further in 'Active *Epistēmē*.'

[181] There is a further reason, independent of the argument of *Metaphysics* VII.13, for denying that species-form is a universal. The idea of a universal is of something that is predicable of a plurality of thing (*On Interpretation* VII). But there is no plurality of things existing antecedently to the predication of form. It is only in virtue of *already having* a form that Socrates, Callias, etc., constitute a plurality of things. Species-form is predicable not of a plurality of things, but of the matter which, once form is predicated, constitutes the plurality of things (see Alan Code, 'Aristotle: Essence and Accident,' and *Metaphysics* VII.16, 1040b5–9; VII.11, 1037a6–10).

Metaphysics VII concludes that form is substance. Aristotle argues in VII.17 that, when we inquire why something is the way it is, we are actually inquiring into its essence or form,[182] But that which explains why something is the way it is is its substance, the primary cause of its being.[183] Moreover, if we look back through the arguments of *Metaphysics* VII, we can see that form can meet all the constraints that have been laid down.

The only constraint that raises any problem is

(2) Substance must be separate: ontologically independent.

How, one might ask, can form be capable of independent existence? Aristotle certainly does not give up on this constraint, for at the end of *Metaphysics* VII he says that his inquiry should give a clear view 'of that substance which exists apart from all sensible substances.'[184] Is there any way that form can exist apart from the matter of which it is the form? The only way we have seen is for form to be contemplated by a mind. For mind is immaterial, and when it is contemplating form it *is* the form it is contemplating. However, form cannot purchase this independence from matter at the cost of becoming dependent on *our* choosing to contemplate it. For substance to be capable of independent existence, it must not depend on a mind to contemplate it; it must *be* a mind that is actively contemplating.

What this mind thinks must be form at its highest level of actuality, primary substance that is identical with its essence. But that is not enough to secure the independence of primary substance. This mind itself must be identical with its essence; it must itself *be* form at the highest level of actuality.[185] There is, then, an internal demand, within Aristotle's world, for there to be a mind that *is* form at the highest level of actuality. Such a mind must exist if Aristotle's theory of substance is ultimately to be consistent. And this mind cannot be a (subjective) ability to learn and think about the (objective) world. If substance is to be mind actively contemplating, it cannot have the *potentiality* to think anything: its essence must consist entirely in the ac-

---

[182] *Metaphysics* VII.17, 1041a20–2, b3–11.
[183] *Metaphysics* VII.17, 1041b27–8.
[184] *Metaphysics* VII.17, 1041a8–9. Aristotle here uses the perfect participle, *kechorismenē*, so it is clear that he is not talking here merely about substance which is *separable*, but about substance which is separate.
[185] Thus it would also satisfy the constraint of *Metaphysics* IX.8 that actuality is always prior to potentiality.

tivity of thinking. Active understanding cannot be just a part of reality; it must play a constitutive role in the overall structure of reality. Here 'subjective' (a mind whose essence is active thinking) coincides with 'objective' (the forms which, as they are thought, constitute the very thinking that thinks them). Thinking and the thought, knowledge and the knowable must coincide. How can this coincidence occur? For substance genuinely to be ontologically independent it would seem that it would have to be mind actively contemplating substance. But how can such a mind exist?

6.7 Mind's place outside of nature[186]

Aristotle's world needs a mind that is actively thinking primary substance. Such a mind would be the primary substance that it is thinking. And it would be primary substance in its highest state of actuality. If that mind existed eternally, it would thereby establish the eternal existence of primary substance. If everything in the physical world somehow depended on this mind, that would establish the primacy and ontological independence of primary substance.

Aristotle has already argued that motion or change must be eternal.[187] Since, he believed, every change requires a distinct cause, he argued that there must be an eternal cause of change that is itself unchanging. An infinite succession of perishable causes was unsatisfactory, for Aristotle thought it was possible that they all should perish and then there would be no further change.[188] That, in Aristotle's eyes, would be absurd. In fact, Aristotle thought he could *see* in the heavens the eternal motion which he had proved must exist: precisely because the world is intelligible, one can expect sensory experience to corroborate the dictates of reason, and one can expect reason to explain what one encounters in experience.

> There is, then, something which is always moved with an unceasing motion, which is motion in a circle; and *this is plain not in theory only but in fact*. Therefore the first heavens must be eternal. There is therefore also something which moves them. And since that which is moved and moves is intermediate, there is a mover which moves

---

[186] Appropriate reading: *Metaphysics* XII.6–10.
[187] *Physics* VIII.1–2; cf. *Metaphysics* XII.6.
[188] *Metaphysics* XII.6, 1071b5–6. See sections 3.3–4 above, on the media of change.

without being moved, being eternal, substance and actuality. *And the object of desire and the object of thought move in this way: they move without being moved. The primary objects of desire and of thought are the same.* For the apparent good is the object of appetite, and the real good is the primary object of wish ...[189]

Desire provides the means whereby something can cause motion without moving itself. An object of desire need not itself move in order to cause motion in those who desire it. But how can the world's relation to God be one of desiring?

One popular answer is that God only moves the 'first heaven,' thereby causing the rotation of sun, stars, and planets around the earth. These heavenly bodies are thought of as living beings, so presumably they are capable of feeling love and desire for God.[190] The motion of the heavens then imparts motion to the rest of the natural world. The standard answer may be true as far as it goes, but it seems too impoverished to be the whole truth. First, we are not given any explanation of what it is about God that makes him peculiarly lovable to the stars. Second, God's relation to the world as a whole is incredibly remote. It is as though God bears a special relation only to the stars, and the stars bear a more or less mechanical relation to the rest of the world. This seems unlikely, for Aristotle thinks that God is cause of the world *as a whole* being well ordered:

> We must consider also in which of two ways the nature of the universe contains the good or the highest good, whether as something separate and by itself, or as the order of the parts. Probably in both ways, as an army does. For the good is found both in the order and in the leader, and more in the latter; for he does not depend on the order but it depends on him. And all things are ordered together somehow, but not all alike – both fishes and fowls and plants; and the world is not such that one thing has nothing to do with another, but they are connected. For all are ordered together to one end ... all share for the good of the whole.[191]

[189] *Metaphysics* XII.7, 1072a21–8 (my emphasis).
[190] *On the Heavens* 285a29, 292a20, b1.
[191] *Metaphysics* XII.10, 1075a11–25.

The world is a good place: that can be seen in its order, its harmony, its accessibility to reason. And God is somehow responsible for the fact that the world forms a well-ordered whole. It is incredible to suppose that this responsibility is exhausted by his getting the stars to move. Now Aristotle's God is not a directing general: he does not directly intervene in the world, or in any sense create it. He does not create matter or form, nor does he intervene in any way so as to be considered responsible for the bringing together of form and matter. Nor is he a divine engineer. He has no purposes or intentions: so the teleological organization to be found in the world cannot be the expression of divine purpose. Nevertheless, the world manifests a rational order for which God is responsible, even though he did not plan the world, even though the world is not working out God's purposes. God is the final cause: the order depends on him. The order of this well-ordered world must bear some relation to God if he is to be responsible for it.

What is needed is a conception of the order of the world as a *response* to God. God does not intervene in the world, but the world can be conceived as an expression of desire for God. And this expression of desire must be conceived within the general framework of Aristotle's world. I should like to offer a conjecture. Suppose that God is actively thinking the primary substances to be found in the world. Suppose, further, that his thinking forms a well-ordered whole. Then we can see the world as a whole as dependent on God: for the realization of form in the natural world depends upon the antecedent existence of form at its highest level of actuality. But form or primary substance at its highest-level actuality simply is God. And the desire which God inspires is *none other than the desire of each organism to realize its form*. Each natural organism has within it a desire to do those things necessary to realizing and maintaining its form. This desire is part of the organism's form or nature itself: form is a force in the organism for the realization and maintenance of form. It is the desire in each individual organism to sustain its life and reproduce that is responsible for the eternality of the species. By reproducing, the individual organism can partake in (divine) immortality of the only sort available to it – the immortality of the species.[192] From

---

[192] *On the Soul* II.4, 415a26–b7.

the perspective of a physicist or a biologist, all that a developing natural organism is trying to do is to realize its form. However, from a metaphysical perspective, one can see that in trying to realize its form, the organism is doing all that it can do to become intelligible. It is also doing the best job it can do to imitate God's thought – and thus to imitate God himself. God's thought does not reproduce the structure of the world: the order of the world as a whole is an attempted physical realization of God's thought.

This is a conjecture. And yet this conjecture does have the quality of the missing piece in a jigsaw puzzle. For using nothing other than the basic principles of Aristotle's world – form, mind, higher-level actualities, substance – we can make sense of God's relation to the world. And, aside from the fact that the world as a whole depends upon God, there is another piece of evidence which supports the conjecture. God's thinking is to some extent like ours:

> On such a principle, then, depend the heavens and the world of nature. And *its life is such as the best which we enjoy, and enjoy but for a short time. For it is ever in this state, (which we cannot be)*, since its actuality is also pleasure. (And therefore waking, perception, and thinking are most pleasant, and hopes and memories are so because of their reference to these.) And thinking in itself deals with that which is best in itself, and that which is thinking in the fullest sense with that which is best in the fullest sense. And mind thinks itself because it shares the nature of the object of thought; for it becomes an object of thought in coming into contact with and thinking its objects, so that mind and object of thought are the same. For that which is *capable* of receiving the object of thought, i.e. substance, is mind. And mind is *active* when it *possesses* this object. Therefore the latter rather than the form is the divine element which mind seems to contain, and the act of contemplation is what is most pleasant and best. If, then, God is always in that good state in which we sometimes are, this compels our wonder; and if in a better this compels it yet more. And God is in a better state. And life also belongs to God; for the activity of mind is life, and God is that activity; and God's essential actuality is life most good and eternal.

> We say therefore that God is a living being, eternal, most
> good, so that life and duration continuous and eternal
> belong to God, for this *is* God.[193]

God is a principle of heaven and nature: Aristotle calls him *a way
of life*.[194] And it is a way of life that is 'such as the best which we
enjoy,' though because of our natures we can only live it for short
periods of time. This way of life to which we have intermittent
access is clearly the life of contemplation which Aristotle describes
at the end of the *Nicomachean Ethics*:[195] a life in which man contemplates essences or primary substance. This ought to give us
insight into the principle of heaven and nature. For our understanding of the divine is not confined to that which can be revealed
by rigorous argument: 'from the outside' as it were. Some of our
life, that part which we spend contemplating, is divine: our appreciation of the divine ought thus to be enhanced by our recognizing in ourselves a way of life that we at times live. Now when we
are actively contemplating, our minds become identical with the
objects of thought.[196] What we are contemplating are essences
which we have encountered embodied in natural organisms, so our
minds become identical with the essences we are contemplating. So
mind contemplating an essence is itself that very essence. It is that
essence at the highest level of activity.

It is *this* activity that Aristotle says is pleasure or is most
pleasant. We have all experienced the pleasure which attends
philosophical activity.[197] For Aristotle, this pleasure is not an
adventitious charm which accompanies the thinking like a charm-
ing escort; the pleasure is internal to the thinking itself. This activity of thinking-cum-pleasure is essence at the highest level of
actuality. Aristotle says that that which is most desirable and that

---

[193] *Metaphysics* VII.7, 1072b13–30 (my emphasis). (The Oxford translation uses
'thought' as a translation both for *noēsis* (which I translate as 'thinking' to
stress the activity implied) and for *noûs* (which I translate as 'mind': see section
4.3 above). Also, I translate *energeia* as 'activity,' to stress the active nature of
thinking and of God's being, but the Oxford translation of 'actuality' is also
correct. The one word *energeia* suggests both that God is an activity and that he
is an actuality.)

[194] *diagōgē: Metaphysics* XII.7, 1072b14.

[195] *Nicomachean Ethics* x.7.

[196] See section 4.3 above.

[197] I say that with confidence because you have gotten this far in the book!

which is most intelligible are the same.[198] For all natural organisms, the strong desire to survive, to sustain life, flourish, and reproduce is, from another perspective, a striving to become intelligible. However, no organism other than man is capable of appreciating this other perspective. A frog may participate in and thus express the intelligibility of frog life, but it can never understand what it is to be a frog. So the pleasure that attends a frog flourishing and thus manifesting the intelligibility of frog life is the pleasure the frog achieves in satisfying its desire to live and reproduce. Man too derives pleasure from living and reproducing, but, unlike all other animals, he is not a being who merely strives to become intelligible; he can come to understand the intelligible order that is being manifested in the world. Man is not only intelligible, he is intelligent. So the pleasure man derives from the intelligible is not only the pleasure that attends living and reproducing (and thus manifesting intelligibility); it is the pleasure that attends satisfying the desire to understand. This is the pleasure of active thinking, an altogether higher-order pleasure than that of reproducing. And this is to be expected, since mind contemplating form is form at a higher level of actuality than as it exists in an embodied animal. Both thinking and reproducing are expressions of form, though at different levels of actuality. Now it is part of man's nature to satisfy the desire to understand. In coming to understand the world, man realizes his own essence. And in fulfilling his nature, man comes to imitate God in an altogether deeper sense than is available to other animals. For man is able to engage in the very same activity, contemplating, that is God. In coming to understand the world we become like God, we become God-like.

God's activity is thinking, an activity in which we can engage. His way of life seems to be one in which he thinks primary substance. Of course, in thinking primary substance, he *is* primary substance. Since his life is like the best life is for us, it would seem that he is thinking the primary substances we think. These are the essences or forms found embodied in the natural world. So it would seem that God stands to the essences or forms embodied in the world as a higher-level activity of form – active contemplating – stands to its lower-level embodied counterpart.

Now there are a few obstacles which seem at first to stand in the

[198] *Metaphysics* XII.7, 26–7.

way of this conjecture. Aristotle characterizes God's activity as a 'thinking of thinking.' Aristotle also insists that God is Mind that thinks itself. But if God is thinking the substances which (at a lower level of activity) are found in the physical world, how could his thinking be a thinking *of thinking*? Why is he not characterized as thinking the world rather than himself? To answer these questions, we should look to the context in which they are made. Aristotle is posing certain problems confronting any characterization of the divine. He poses a dilemma.[199] What does the Divine Mind think? If, on the one hand, God thinks nothing, he is no better than a sleeping person. If, on the other hand, he is actively thinking something, it would seem that Mind is dependent on the object of thought. For, as we have seen, it is only by its activity, thinking, that God has stature. But what about the object of thought? If it is worse than God, then is not God diminished by thinking about it? But if it is better than God ... The question Aristotle is posing is whether it is the *act* or the *object* of thinking that is best. At first, it seems as if the answer must be 'neither.' It cannot be the mere activity of thinking that is best, because thinking can have a bad object. Neither can something which is merely an object of thought, no matter how good, be the best. For then thought would be a mere potentiality for understanding this good object and, as a potentiality, could not be fully divine.

But Aristotle answers the question by saying that both the act and the object of thinking are the best. As is his wont, he answers the dilemma by finding a passage through it:

> Therefore it must be itself that Mind thinks (since it is the most excellent of things) and its thinking is a thinking of thinking. But evidently knowledge and perception and opinion and understanding have always something else as their object, and themselves only by the way. Further if thinking and being thought are different, in respect of which does goodness belong to Mind? For being an act of thinking and being an act of thought are not the same. We answer that in some cases the knowledge is the object. In the productive sciences (if we abstract from the matter) the substance in the sense of essence, and in the theoretical sciences the *logos*, or the act

[199] *Metaphysics* XII.9, 1074b15–35.

thinking, *is* the object. As, then, mind and the object of thought are not different in the case of things that have not matter, they will be the same, i.e. the thinking will be one with the object of thought.[200]

Aristotle's solution escapes the dilemma, but is that all it does? What does God's thinking himself consist in? Is this a totally empty conception, a mere solution to a puzzle? If so, how could Aristotle have believed that God was an unmoved mover of the world? Or is that too an empty conception: did Aristotle merely need an unmoved mover to halt the regress of moved movers? Did he use one empty conception to 'solve' two distinct problems. The answer must be 'no': it is incredible that Aristotle should allow the bare solution to a dialectical puzzle to serve as one of the foundations of his entire metaphysical outlook. We do have before us a rich conception of God's relation to the world. The task then is to show how God's thinking himself can be woven into this conception.

When Aristotle describes God's activity, it is remarkably reminiscent of his account of how mind is thinkable.[201] Mind is thinkable just as any object of thought is thinkable, for thinking consists in mind's becoming the object of thought. This is all that mind, in thinking, is. Thus in all thinking mind is thinkable – indeed, mind is thought. For understanding and the object of understanding are the same. One might suppose that this at least begins to provide an analysis of what it is for God to think himself: in active thinking, the Divine Mind and its object are one and the same. Yet this can not provide a complete analysis of what it is for God to think himself. For one problem that bothers Aristotle is that God's stature might be increased or diminished by what he thinks. This problem cannot be lightly dismissed by saying that whatever thinking he does (no matter how awful) he is only thinking himself. So to understand what it is for God to think himself, we must also con-

---

[200] *Metaphysics* XII.9, 1074b33–1075a5. (When Aristotle says that being an act of thinking and being an object of thought are not the same, what he means is that the *accounts* one would give of the two differ. For, as we see, Aristotle does believe that, when fully understood, an activity of thinking and the object of thought are the same. Again, I use 'Mind' as a translation for *noûs*, rather than 'thought'; I capitalize it because here Aristotle is clearly considering the Mind that is God.)

[201] *Metaphysics* XII.9, 1074b33–35; 7, 1072b19; cf. *On the Soul* III.4, 429b22–430a7. See section 4.3 above.

sider the respects in which God's thinking differs from ours.

There are at least two important differences. First, God's activity is eternal, unmoved, and unaffected by that which is intelligible in the world (though it does bear some relation to it), while our thinking is sporadic and affected. Our minds are receptive to the forms found embodied in the world.[202] God, by contrast, is unmoved by the intelligible essences found in the world. In this sense, God's activity transcends the world and is unaffected by it. But it does not follow that his activity stands in no relation to the world. God's activity is unmoved, unaffected, and separated from perceptible things: nevertheless, his eternal activity is a higher-level actuality whose corresponding lower level may yet be found in enmattered essences. So while our thinking the intelligible essences and God's thinking these essences stand in a similar relation to the embodied essences – both thinkings stand as a higher-level actuality of form to a lower-level embodied actuality – the explanation of the relation differs in each case. Unlike God, we must journey through the world and interact with the essences found there if we are ever to be able to contemplate them. Our ability to contemplate essences develops from our experience.[203] It is to this fact that Aristotle is drawing our attention when he says that our mind is *receptive* of the intelligible forms and uses the metaphor of a tablet on which nothing has yet been drawn.[204] Aristotle's point is that humans, by contrast to God, can only become active thinkers *in response to the world*.

This asymmetry allows us to fill out the picture of God thinking himself. Our active thinking is a single actualization of two distinct potentialities: our capacity to think and an embodied essence. God, by contrast, requires no interaction with anything external to be in his active state. Since in his case as well subject and object of thought are identical, there is no objection to saying that he thinks himself. Further, we can characterize his activity as a thinking of thinking, rather than as a thinking of essences in the world. Since our thinking, though of the same general kind as God's, depends on interaction with the world, it would be misleading to charac-

---

[202] *On the Soul* III.4, 429a15, a29–b9, b23; cf. *Metaphysics* XII.7, 1072a30.

[203] See *Posterior Analytics* I.8, II.19; *On the Soul* III.7, 432a7ff.

[204] *On the Soul* III.4, 429a15–16, b31–430a2; cf. III.7, 431a28–9; *Metaphysics* XII.7, 1072b22.

terize it as a thinking of thinking. We are thinking about the embodied essences or primary substances found in the world. However, what makes our thinking *about* something is not anything in the *quality* of the thought, but a feature of how that thought arises. Though God's thinking may be the highest-level actuality of primary substance found (at a lower-level actuality) embodied in the world, it is not *about* the enmattered substance. God's activity is thinking. Since subject and object of thought are identical, the object of God's thought is thinking. Thus God's activity can justly be characterized as a thinking of thinking.

Although God's thinking does differ from ours in this way, his thinking is nevertheless 'a way of life such as the best which we enjoy.' And there is an attenuated sense in which when we come to understand and contemplate the world we are thinking ourselves. For we are by nature systematic understanders of the world, rational animals. But we cannot know what it is to be a systematic understander until we know what the full exercise of the ability to understand consists in. So it is by the very activity of understanding the world that we come to understand ourselves. We could never understand ourselves simply by turning our intellectual gaze inward. It is only in understanding and contemplating the essences found in the world that we can come to understand who we are.

So it would seem that the desire to understand leads us toward an activity of thinking that is at once an understanding of the world, an understanding of ourselves, and an understanding of God. In coming to understand the world, our minds become the essences found embodied in the world. In that activity we also realize our essence as understanders and come to understand our essence. Understanding the world brings self-understanding in its wake. Of course, we have not fully understood the world until we understand that it is, in an important sense, a response to God. If we are ignorant of the world's relation to God, we do not know why the world is the way it is. But if we must understand the world in order fully to appreciate what is involved in being a systematic understander of it, it would seem that we must understand God and his relation to the world before we can fully understand ourselves. And in coming to understand God, and thus the world, and thus ourselves, we both fulfill our own essence and imitate God. Our understanding is a re-enactment of the very activity we are understanding. That is why we must, paradoxically, transcend our own nature in order to realize it. For until we re-enact God's thinking and thus become God-like in our own activity, we cannot understand God or the world. The re-enactment is required for us to fulfill our role as systematic understanders: to become fully human we must become God-like.

But if it is in the very activity of understanding the world and God's relation to it that man comes to understand himself, then the idea of man thinking himself is as rich as the world that he understands. Now God has no need of interacting with essences found in the world; his thinking need never have been mediated by interaction with a distinct object; but if his thinking is *something* like ours, then in thinking the essences that are embodied in the world, he would be thinking himself. The conception of God thinking himself need not be empty.

The second important difference between God's thinking and ours lies in the unity and indivisibility of God's thought.[205] Everything that does not have matter is indivisible (*adiairetos*). Each second-level essence is indivisible in the sense that it is thought as a unity.[206] God himself is a substance without matter, so it follows that both he and his thought are indivisible. Does this threaten to sever the conjectured relation between God's thinking and the essences found in the world? For if each higher-level activity of contemplating essence is indivisible, it would seem that, were God to be thinking the essences whose lower-level counterparts are found embodied in the world, he would have to think many distinct indivisible thoughts. It seems, however, that it is precisely because he thinks himself that his thought is not composite and does not change, as it would if he were to think the distinct parts of a whole. It might appear that we are forced back to a bare conception of God thinking himself. But appearances can be misleading, for the indivisibility of a thought ought not to be considered as due solely to the indivisibility of the object of thought. Since mind actively thinking and its object are identical, the indivisibility is as much due to the thinking as to its object.

The word 'indivisible,' says Aristotle, is ambiguous. It can refer both to what is potentially indivisible and to what is actually indi-

205 *Metaphysics* XII.9, 1075a5–11.
206 See *Metaphysics* IX.10, 1051b26ff.; *On the Soul* III.6.

visible.[207] Now what it is for something to be *actively indivisible* is for mind to think it as a whole. For instance, mind can actually consider a length as a whole, and it is in virtue of this active thinking that the length is 'actually indivisible.' The time of this active thinking is also indivisible: for time is a measure of change, a measure carried out by the soul marking successive distinctions. Here, however, mind is engaged in a single thinking – its thinking is without change or succession – so the time is reciprocally indivisible. Of course, if we had chosen we could have first considered one bit of the length, then another bit. We would then have divided the length in thought, and the time too would have been divided by the thought.

This account of actual indivisibility has greatly disturbed commentators, for they have not seen how a length could under any circumstances be called actually indivisible. A length, after all, is Aristotle's paradigm of something that is divisible. Indeed, it has been suggested that one translate the Greek expression as 'actually undivided' rather than as 'actually indivisible.'[208] When we consider the length as a whole it is actually undivided, though it is div*isible*. Though this suggestion tames Aristotle's account, it ought to be rejected, for it does not do justice to the fact that Aristotle is discussing active thinking.[209] Of course, when we consider the length as a whole it has not been divided, so in that obvious sense it is 'actually undivided.' But Aristotle meant more than this. During the act of thinking there is an actuality which does not exist before or after the thinking. It is this actuality, the length being thought as a unity (not the length lying on the ground) that Aristotle calls 'actually indivisible.' This active thinking is actually indivisible, not just undivided: what would possibly divide it? It is the length lying on the ground that is both potentially indivisible and potentially divisible.[210]

---

[207] *On the Soul* III.6, 430b6–20.

[208] D. W. Hamlyn, *Aristotle's De Anima, Books II, III*, p. 143. Though 'undivided' is an acceptable translation for the Greek term, it does not accord with Aristotle's general use of that term. Cf., e.g., *Physics* III.5, 204a9–13, a24–8; *On the Soul* III.2, 426b23–427a16; cf. *Metaphysics* XIII.9, 1075a7.

[209] *Metaphysics* IX.9, 1051a29–30.

[210] Both ancient and modern commentators have suggested that the phrase 'the indivisible is ... potentially and actually' should be interpreted as 'the not potentially divisible' and 'the not actually divisible,' with 'potentially' and 'actually' modifying 'divisible' rather than 'indivisible' (430b6–7). (See Themi-

Reality, for Aristotle, can be considered under different aspects. One can, as in this example, consider a length as a single length or as two lengths. However, in the active consideration of each, two distinct second-level actualities come into existence, one of them being actually indivisible – an active unity – the other being actually divided. The length can be considered both as one and as many; but in the active consideration of it as one, a single, indivisible, second-level actuality exists, whereas in the consideration of it as many, there is a multiplicity of second-level actualities, each of them actually indivisible.

God, as we have seen, is a substance without matter. Everything without matter is indivisible, and, since God is an eternal actuality, he is actually indivisible. Since he thinks himself, the object of his thought is actually indivisible. It does not follow that his thinking bears no relation to the world or that his self-contemplation is barren. For the possibility lies open that God thinks the (essences embodied in the) world as a whole. This thinking would differ from the essences found in the world as a higher-level actuality differs from its lower-level counterpart. The lower-level essences, one might say, are both potentially divisible and potentially indivisible. It is possible for us to think this essence, then think that essence: the essences found in the world would then be actually divided. God's thinking, by contrast, is actually indivisible. He does not first think this essence, then that: he thinks the essences found in the world as a whole. So God, who is identical to his thinking, is not to be found in the world. Further, his thinking differs from the second-level activity which constitutes our contemplating this or that aspect of the world. And so it is at least possible for our con-

stius 110, 5H., 202,22 Sp; Simplicius 251, 14; Ross, *Aristotle, De Anima*, p. 301; but cf. Philoponus 549, 5–7. And cf. R. D. Hicks, pp. 516–17; though cf. also his own translation on p. 137. The one sentence of Aristotle which Hicks cites as allegedly supporting this type of interpretation, *Metaphysics* xii.8, 1073a23, does not do so.) Given that the length lying on the ground is *potentially* indivisible, it might seem odd that Aristotle says we can call it 'indivisible' (430b6–7). The oddness stems, I think, from the fact that for a wide range of cases that which is potentially F is not F. The oddness disappears when we realize that there are some cases where that which is potentially F may be called F. As we have already seen, 'sound,' 'color,' and 'smell' may all be used to refer both to the potentiality and to the actuality. In general this phenomenon seems to occur when the actuality is an active mental apprehension of something that, unapprehended, is a potentiality.

templation to be of composites and to occur in some time and yet for it still to be true that both we and God are contemplating the same essences – in the one case as divided, in the other case as indivisible. Aristotle's conception of God thinking himself would then be as rich as the conception of contemplating the world as a whole.

Aristotle, I believe, seizes on this possibility in explaining God's relation to the world. He points out a problem for human mind or any mind which thinks of composites in a certain period of time: '[mind] does not have the good in this bit or in that bit, but *the best is in a certain whole*, being something different.'[211] But if the best is in a certain whole, then God's thinking must form a certain whole. It is upon this thinking, as we have already seen, that the order of the whole of nature depends: 'For the good is found both in the order and in the leader, and more in the leader; for he does not depend on the order, the order depends on him.'[212] The world has an order and thus can be thought of as a whole. God's thinking is a thinking this whole, but in a strange sense he is not thinking about the world at all. His thinking is independent of the world; yet it is because of his thinking that the world comes to have the order it has. Therein lies the explanation of the world's goodness.

If this account of God's relation to the world correctly represents Aristotle's beliefs, then a common conception of the history of philosophy has to be revised. It is widely believed that before Kant philosophers tended to conceive the mind as a mirror of nature.[213] But Aristotle does not seem to have held a 'mirror theory' of the mind. The belief that he did so derives from considering a particular aspect of mind's relation to the world in isolation: that of man's development from ignorance to wisdom. Man is born in ignorance, but he is a creature capable of gaining experience through his interactions with the world. Through repeated experience and instruction, his mind takes on the forms that he has encountered in the world. Yet this is the perspective of man's development, not of mind's relation to the world.

The perspective is corrected when we consider the physics of contemplating. The essence of a physical object expresses what

---

[211] *Metaphysics* XII.9, 1075a7–9 (my translation; my emphasis).
[212] *Metaphysics* XII.10, 1075a14–15.
[213] See, e.g., Richard Rorty, *Philosophy and the Mirror of Nature*.

that object most truly is: it is the substance and actuality of that object. But from the point of view of mind, that which the object most truly is is a potentiality to be comprehended. And the actualization of this potentiality occurs in mind: indeed, it is mind. Every potentiality in Aristotle's world depends on a prior actuality.[214] This cannot merely be the essence as embodied in a previously existing natural object, for the essence as such remains a potentiality to be comprehended. The prior actuality must be God or Active Mind: the essence at the highest level of actuality. Thus it is truer to say that, for Aristotle, nature does its best to imitate mind than that mind does its best to mirror nature.

Kant describes his 'Copernican Revolution' in philosophy as the shift from the supposition 'that all our knowledge must conform to objects' to the supposition 'that objects must conform to our knowledge.'[215] The problem with this description is that it permits the reader to suppose that Kant's distinctive contribution lies in the suggested direction of the conforming relation rather than in the characterization of the mind to which objects are conforming. Both Aristotle and Kant believe that objects must conform to knowledge rather than vice versa. But for Kant this implies that the conforming objects of knowledge must be 'appearances': empirical knowledge is possible only if it is partially but significantly constituted by a contribution of the human mind. Thus it is very much *our* knowledge to which objects must conform. This 'subjective' contribution does not, according to Kant, rob us of the claim to objective, empirical knowledge: it provides the conditions for the possibility of such knowledge. Kant, one might say, humanizes knowledge: having knowledge is manifestly not a matter of seeing the world as God does.[216] The 'distortions' of the human mind, Kant thinks, do not rob us of the possibility of knowledge, they provided its conditions. His originality lies not in the hypothesis that objects must conform to mind, but in his portrayal of the mind to which objects are conforming.

For Aristotle, by contrast, objects must conform to our knowledge not because they must conform to the human mind, but

---

[214] *Metaphysics* IX.8, especially 1050a30–b8.
[215] Kant, *Critique of Pure Reason*, Bxvi.
[216] See H. E. Allison, 'Kant's Transcendental Humanism,' and *Kant's Transcendental Idealism*.

because they must conform to God or Active Mind. Aristotle is thus, one might say, an *objective idealist*. He is an idealist in the sense that the order of the physical world is ultimately dependent on mind. Yet there is not a trace of subjectivity in his idealism. Objects must conform to knowledge, but that does not in the least reveal them to be constituted by any contribution from us. Aristotle and Kant differ not over whether objects must conform to mind, but over the location of the mind to which they are conforming. Since, for Aristotle, there is nothing distinctively human about the mind to which objects are conforming, there is no basis for saying that the essences we contemplate are mere appearances.

There are in broad outline two ways one can view philosophy's history: as marked by discontinuities or by continuities. The most familiar way is in terms of discontinuities. For example, Descartes's focus on the individual ego and what it can know, and his radical investigation of skepticism, led to the invention of subjective idealism. After Descartes, the philosophical quest for knowledge had to begin with the ego and its experience and work its way out from there. Given this map, we see emerging in the seventeenth century a set of problems to which previous philosophers simply did not address themselves.[217] It then becomes questionable whether a previous philosopher's solutions to dead problems can valuably be applied to a new problematic. There is, however, another map: one can view philosophy as concerned throughout its history with the question of how mind relates to reality or (perhaps equivalently) of how and where to draw the boundary between subjects and objects. These are certainly fundamental issues for both Plato and Aristotle, and they are arguably the central problems of Kant's first *Critique*. Indeed, one of the central ideas of Kant's transcendental idealism is to re-draw the boundary between subjective and objective so that what, from an empirical perspective, are the objective conditions of empirical knowledge are, from a transcendental perspective, the subjective conditions of mind to which appearances must conform. In fact, even the problem of how concepts apply to objects, a manifestation of the problem of how mind relates to reality which fascinated Plato and Aristotle, spans the divide between ancient and

[217] See M. F. Burnyeat, 'Idealism in Greek Philosophy: What Descartes Saw and Berkeley Missed.'

modern philosophy. Metaphysics had degenerated, according to Kant, because it had confined itself to a 'groping among mere concepts.' Metaphysics could only advance, Kant thought, if it broke away from the barren study of the relations of concepts and began again to inquire how concepts relate to objects.[218] By now it should be clear that the relation of subjective mind to objective world is one of the central issues in Aristotle's philosophy. And so it would seem that the concern with mind's relation to the world spans the supposed gap between ancient and modern philosophy. On this reading of philosophy's history, Cartesian and Humean skepticism remain issues for Kant, but they are secondary to the traditional problems of metaphysics: the relation of mind to reality, the boundary between subjective and objective, the relation of concepts to objects. And the problem of radical skepticism does not form a self-contained problematic. It occurs as a relatively recent perturbation within a larger conceptual framework which spans Western philosophy.

In this regard, it is perhaps worth noting that one of the central responses to Kant's philosophy has been an attempt to relocate the mind to which objects are conforming. Hegel tried to locate the mind in the Idea or the Absolute; the later Wittgenstein tried to locate it in the activities and customs of a community – what he called a form of life. Both argued that there is no legitimate vantage-point from which knowledge can be judged a mere appearance, the product of systematic, human distortions. Though they shared with Kant the belief that objects must conform to our concepts, they both thought that the individual human mind was an inadequate candidate for the Mind to which objects conform. What I am suggesting, of course, is that the location of the mind to which objects are conforming remains a serious philosophical problem. And it is a problem to which, in a different guise to be sure, Aristotle was sensitive.

6.8 Man's place outside of nature[219]

This book began with a highly paradoxical conception of man: as driven by his nature to transcend his nature. Let us return for a moment to a plausible train of thought which, when first sketched

[218] *Critique of Pure Reason*, Bxv.
[219] Appropriate reading: *Nicomachean Ethics* x.7–9.

out, seemed so bizarre.[220] At the beginning of the *Metaphysics*, Aristotle says that the understanding of first principles and causes is divine.[221] He is not speaking metaphorically. God himself is a first principle and cause, so in coming to understand first principles we come to understand God. It is our natural desire to understand that drives us on until we reach this understanding. This understanding would, for God, be self-understanding. Indeed, as we are now in a position to see, this self-understanding *is* God. We are also in a position to see that this understanding is, in an attenuated sense, self-understanding for us as well. For we come to understand ourselves as understanders of the world through our activity of learning and understanding. We come to realize and to recognize something of God's mode of activity in our own activity of understanding the world and the principles and causes which govern its intelligible shape. That is why this understanding, even as *our* understanding of the world, is in some measure divine.

In chapter 1, I mentioned two remarkable consequences of the claim that the understanding of first principles and causes is divine. First, since God is a principle of all things and is constituted by self-understanding, it follows that this understanding is itself a cause or principle of all things. Thus the understanding of first principles – philosophy – is not an understanding of something which exists independently of that understanding. The understanding is itself a principle or force in the world. We can now see how this can be so. Philosophical understanding of the world is an understanding of primary substance: an understanding of what the world most basically is. But this understanding *is* primary substance at the highest level of actuality. It is here that philosophical understanding, divine understanding, and primary substance coincide. Form or essence is a basic driving force in the world, and when mind understands the world it becomes this driving force. Philosophic activity, then, is one of the basic forces in the universe. This, of course, is a misleading way of putting a deep truth about Aristotle's world. 'Philosophical activity' is a name we give to substantial form only belatedly: form was operating as a basic force long before humans ever organized themselves into societies with a leisure class – a class whose members were in a position to indulge their desire to understand.

[220] See chapter 1 above.
[221] *Metaphysics* 1.2, 982b28–983a11.

Second, when man fully satisfies his desire to understand, when he comes to understand the principles and causes of the world, he is not acquiring understanding of a distinct object which, as it turns out, is divine. The understanding is itself divine. Since 'human mind contemplating form,' 'substantial form,' 'primary substance,' and 'God thinking himself' may be various ways of describing the same thing – form at the highest level of actuality – man's understanding is not merely *of* the divine, it *is* divine. It is here that we come face to face with the paradoxical conceptions of man driven by his nature to leave his nature behind. In satisfying his desire to understand, man must transcend his own nature precisely at the point he finally realizes it. But if Aristotle's account suggests that man must go beyond what it is to be a man precisely in order fully to become a man, does that mean that man must ultimately leave himself behind?

If we are to understand this paradox, I think we must grasp another: that, for the mature Aristotle, man is to a significant degree alienated from his own nature. At first sight, this claim must look absurd. Man's nature or form is what he most essentially is. There can be no sense in saying that he is alienated from his own nature: that is tantamount to saying that he is alienated from himself. Or so one might think. But let us consider the path of inquiry along which Aristotle's desire to understand led him. In the course of his inquiries, Aristotle discovered the possibility of a basic metaphysical inquiry into primary substance. This inquiry led to a discovery about man: namely, that he may conceive of himself in two ways. He may conceive of himself as a composite of form and matter: human soul realized in flesh and bones. Or he may conceive of himself in terms of his substance, what he most truly is: human soul. 'Man' is a term Aristotle reserves for the composite. In this sense 'man' is like 'snub,' which refers to form as it is realized in certain matter. It is unlike 'concave,' which refers to a form on its own – a form which can be realized in various types of matter.

Man, the composite of form and matter, is a creature of the physical world. He is by nature a political animal; and the good life for him is the life of ethical virtue. The political life is the active flourishing life within society, man's natural habitat. Let us call the outlook of man engaged in active life within political society 'the merely human perspective.' Once Aristotle discovered that man's form is what he most truly is, it was only a short step to discovering that there is more available to man than the merely human perspective: when man has achieved his deepest self-understanding he will realize that he is in a very important sense unmanly. He is human soul; and human soul at its highest level of activity, active mind, has no material instantiation at all. But once man can conceive of himself as importantly unmanly, the possibility opens of a radically different form of life:

> If happiness is activity in accordance with virtue, it is reasonable that it should be in accordance with the highest virtue; and this will be that of *the best thing in us*. Whether it be mind or something else that is this element which is thought to be our natural ruler and guide and to take thought of things noble and divine, whether it be itself also divine or only the most divine element in us, the activity of this in accordance with its proper virtue will be perfect happiness. That this activity is contemplative we have already said.[222]

Man is a creature who bridges the gap between the divine and the natural world. As an animal, he is a creature of the natural world; as mind, he is a totally immaterial capacity to engage in divine activity. Now one might think that, for Aristotle, there is no single way of life which harmoniously blends both sides of man's character. Man must inevitably be pulled in contrary directions: toward a political life within society and toward an anti-social life of contemplation. This is not quite right. The life of ethical virtue, described in the bulk of the *Nicomachean Ethics* is intended to be a harmonious one: after all, it is not a life for flesh and bones alone, but for human soul embodied in flesh and bones. The problem for Aristotle's man is not the impossibility of a harmonious life, but the possibility of a certain type of disharmonious life so valuable that it is worth leaving considerations of harmony behind.[223]

So, although Aristotle's man is not denied the possibility of a harmonious life, fit for man, he nevertheless faces a fundamental

---

[222] *Nicomachean Ethics* x.7, 1177a12–18. (I translate *aretē* by 'virtue,' rather than 'excellence,' *noûs* by 'mind' rather than 'intellect'.)

[223] That the contemplative life is an alternative to the ethical life is also mentioned in *Politics* vii.2.

choice. Of course, the mass of mankind never has to confront this choice: either by material necessity or by lack of innate ability, most men are excluded from the life of contemplation. It is the rare person who has both the material means and the intellectual ability to pursue the contemplative life, who will be forced to choose. For his innate desire to understand will lead him on until he faces a conflict between fundamentally different ways to live a life. Aristotle does offer us this solace: it is not a tragic choice. If we are genuinely in a position to choose, there is no question but that we should choose the contemplative life. There will be no basis for regret or remorse at having left the ethical life behind.

Aristotle commends the contemplative life above all others. When reading his praise, it is hard not to think that the life he is commending is rather unlovely. First, the contemplative life is the most self-sufficient of lives. At the beginning of the *Nicomochean Ethics*, self-sufficiency is described as a political virtue.[224] As a political virtue, self-sufficiency is expressed in one's relations with one's family, friends, and fellow-citizens. The self-sufficient man is one who has both the material resources and the resources of character to be able to live temperately, liberally, and justly with his fellow-citizens. On this conception, the self-sufficient life could only be lived within political society: indeed, Aristotle contrasts it with the solitary life, in which, he thought, man cannot flourish.[225] However, when he comes to commend the contemplative life, there is a form of self-sufficiency which transcends ethical life. The temperate man, the just man, and the brave man depend upon a social environment in which to carry out their virtuous acts, 'but the philosopher can contemplate *even when by himself.*'[226] By the end of the *Ethics*, self-sufficiency is no longer a political virtue, it is a *metaphysical* virtue. It is God's activity that shows us, ultimately, what self-sufficiency consists in, and man has the opportunity to partake in what might be called metaphysical flourishing. Divine self-sufficiency – the absolute identity of thought and object in the highest actualization of form – is the paradigm of metaphysical flourishing. It is because man is by nature a thinking being, because by nature he desires to understand, that he desires, ultimately, to

---

[224] *Nicomachean Ethics* I.7, 1097b7–22.
[225] *Nicomachean Ethics* I.8, 1099b3–6. See section 5.6 above.
[226] *Nicomachean Ethics* X.7, 1177a32–3.

leave the merely human perspective behind. Of course, there is a serious question as to how successful any man can be in this project. For, no matter how lofty his thoughts, man remains a composite being who can never fully transcend the distinction between subjective mind capable of understanding and objective world capable of being understood. Nevertheless, man does stand to gain a type of self-understanding which is *like* God's. For in his contemplation, thinking mind and object of thought are identical. Man, man the active understander, has no need of anything outside himself. He is metaphysically flourishing.

The second way in which Aristotle commends the contemplative life is by saying that contemplation is productive of nothing and has no value beyond itself.[227] Acting bravely may help to constitute a good life and thus be good in itself, but it is also for a further end: for example, defending the Athenian state. Contemplating is not for the sake of anything beyond itself. In this sense, it imitates God's life, which is productive of nothing.

Aristotle's third commendation is that the life of contemplation is one of leisure.[228] The ethically virtuous man will often be taken up with the demands of his social existence. The statesman and the general will take pleasure in the demands of political life and may achieve nobility and greatness, but their lives will be to some extent harried and demanding. The birth of philosophy, Aristotle thought, was an historical event. It occurred only after society was so organized as to secure the necessities of life and free a master class for the pursuit of leisure activities.[229] The life of contemplation is only a choice for members of a leisured master class. Although a contemplater will shed his obligations to society, he will nevertheless depend on society to confer upon him the material benefits which make an anti-social contemplative life possible. To be blunt: the contemplative life is socially parasitic. In mitigation, it can be said that the contemplative life does make a human contribution. For if mind is the best thing in us, then contemplative man, in living the life of mind, contributes to humanity an example of human form in its highest realization, an example of the rule of the best thing in us.

[227] *Nicomachean Ethics* x.7, 1177b1–26.
[228] See again *Nicomachean Ethics* x.7, 1177b4–26.
[229] *Metaphysics* I.1, 981b13–25; 2, 982b20–4. See chapter 1 above.

Nevertheless, leaving all concerns for one's fellow-man may not appear to be the most attractive life for man to lead. Yet if the contemplative life does look unlovely, there is a more important lesson to be learned than that Aristotle's values differ markedly from our own. The contemplative life looks unlovely because we are looking at it from an ethical and merely human point of view. The contemplative life is by its nature unethical. Aristotle's point is that certain men may have overwhelming reason to lead an unethical life. The reason is that man is one part divine: and if he is in a position to live a divine life, there is no question but that he should:

> [The contemplative] life would be too high for man; for it is not in so far as he is man that he will live so, but in so far as something divine is present in him; and by so much as this is superior to our composite nature is this activity superior to that which is the exercise of the other kind of virtue. If mind is divine, then, in comparison with man, the life according to it is divine in comparison with human life. But we must not follow those who advise us, being men, to think of human things and, being mortal, of mortal things, but must, so far as we can, make ourselves immortal, and strain every nerve to live in accordance with the best thing in us; for even if it be small in bulk, much more does it in power and worth surpass everything. This would seem too to be each man himself, since it is the authoritative and better part of him. It would be strange then if he were to choose not the life of his self but that of something else. And what we said before will apply now; that which is proper to each thing is by nature best and most pleasant for each thing; for man, therefore, the life according to mind is best and pleasantest, since mind more than anything else *is* man. This life therefore is also the happiest.[230]

Perhaps we moderns do not feel the same pull toward the contemplative life as Aristotle did. But we certainly do recognize with Aristotle that the disparate strands of man's nature may not all fall comfortably within the ethical. The creative demands of a great

---

[230] *Nicomachean Ethics* x.7, 1177b26–1178a8. (Again, I translate *noûs* as 'mind' rather than 'intellect.')

artist, we moderns tend to believe, may lead him to ignore his responsibility to family, friends, or society.[231] One can imagine a latter-day Aristotle arguing that the divine element in man is his creativity. The artist, like God, is a creator, so if one is able to choose between the artistic and the ethical life, one should choose the artistic.

Aristotle identifies man with his mind. Man is first identified with his substance or form and then with the highest or ruling element in his substance. This is an immaterial capacity to contemplate immaterial forms. What man most truly is, in Aristotle's eyes, is not anything personal or particular. When he contemplates essences, lives the life of a philosopher, he leaves the nooks and crannies of his personality behind. His contemplation will be perfectly general and impersonal. Of course, he has to have a particular history in order to get to the stage where he can contemplate essences. He traces a particular path through the world, encountering essences embodied in natural objects and artefacts. It is through his experience and study that his mind takes on the forms embodied in the world. Thus the philosopher's mind comes to reproduce the (forms found in the) world. Aristotle's man is most himself when he is least himself – when he has become the world (at least in form). By the very same activity he also imitates God. For God is actively thinking/being the forms. Man is most truly divine, mental activity.

Thus, although contemplative man leaves his social commitments to his fellow-man behind, there is nothing selfish about his choice, for the contemplative man leaves behind any self to be selfish about. In one sense, of course, the contemplative man chooses the best life for himself. But the unselfishness of the choice is revealed by asking what sort of *self*-understanding the contemplative man achieves. It is certainly not an understanding of the individual personality. If anything, it is an understanding of the best thing in him, mind, which the contemplative man has identified himself with and allowed to become his life. But mind, as we have seen, can only be understood through its activity. It is only through investigating the world and coming to understand it that one comes to understand what mind is. Such investigation and understanding,

---

[231] See Bernard Williams, 'Persons, Character and Morality,' and 'Moral Luck,' in *Moral Luck*; and *Ethics and the Limits of Philosophy*, chapter 3.

the complete satisfaction of the desire to understand, ultimately constitute the highest form of self-understanding. That is, once we have penetrated deeply into the world's intelligible structure, we come to understand God – or, equivalently, God's understanding. But divine understanding simply *is* the intelligible ground of the world. And so we discover that what we have been thinking (in our investigation of the world) simply *is* Mind. At this point, our thinking is imitating and re-enacting God's thinking. It is in this re-enactment that man comes to understand the world and to understand God, but he also comes to understand himself. For it is only with this re-enactment that man fulfills his highest nature, and thus only then can he come to appreciate the best thing in him: mind, which is divine. It is this form of 'self-understanding' that the desire to understand is, ultimately, a desire for. Man comes to comprehend fully what is involved in being meant to be a systematic understander of a world that is itself meant to be understood.

The idea of a re-enactment of God's thinking may seem abstract and difficult to grasp. Perhaps an analogy will be of help. Throughout this book, Aristotle's world has been the object of our study. Indeed, we have taken a stance toward Aristotle's world – his system of beliefs and outlook – similar to the one Aristotle took toward the world as a whole. Now, if this book has been successful, we have not remained at an intellectual arm's length from Aristotle's world: we have come to understand his world by working through the very problems and thoughts which Aristotle did. Thus our understanding of Aristotle is to some extent a re-enactment of his thinking. There is, then, no firm distinction to be drawn between the subject/mind which sets out to understand (Aristotle) and the object (Aristotle) which is meant to be understood. In understanding Aristotle, subject and object of inquiry coincide. Aristotle thought that the very relation which holds between our study and Aristotle's own thinking holds generally between thinking and the object of thought. When we are thinking about the world, our thinking is a re-enactment of the forms that are found embodied in the world. When we are thinking about God, our thinking is a (perhaps partial) re-enactment of God's thinking. For Aristotle world and God are both meant to be understood, just as for us Aristotle is meant to be understood. In both cases the understanding comes through a re-enactment. But if self-understanding comes through re-enactment in thought of the forms found in the world, one should expect that 'self'-understanding would be a deeply impersonal affair.

Now, man is able to express his personality and character in the ethical life. And he is able to live a flourishing, happy life within the arena of the ethical. But, by contrast to the life of contemplation, the ethical life is second best.[232] From the perspective of the ethical, the contemplative life looks unethical; from the perspective of the contemplative, the ethical life looks human, all too human: 'The ethical virtues must belong to our composite nature; and the virtues of our composite nature are human; so, therefore, are the life and the happiness which correspond to these. The virtue of mind is a thing apart.'[233] The ethical virtues focus on the fact that man is an enmattered being, living with his fellow-men in the natural world. This may be the human condition, and yet there is another sense in which the contemplative life is the most 'human' life there is. But, then, what is 'all too *human*' about the ethical life, such that, in transcending it, the contemplative life brings us to the highest realization of the human? The answer is that there are virtues which belong to our composite nature, and that from 'the merely human perspective' the life of these virtues appears the best life for man to lead. But the philosopher comes to see that 'the merely human perspective' is *merely* human. He comes to see the existence of *metaphysical* virtues: excellences, so to speak, from the point of view of the universe. And he comes to see that man is the only creature on earth whose life offers him the opportunity for metaphysical flourishing. By studying the world man finds his highest place by occupying mind's place. By realizing what is best in him man transcends his own nature: he no longer lives the life that it is best *for man* to live; he simply lives the life that is best.

It is important to recognize that the contemplative life does not leave the world completely behind. Insofar as man does succeed in living the contemplative life, he does not thereby cease to be an enmattered being. Material needs are unimportant to the contemplative man, not because he no longer needs them, but because if he

---

[232] *Nicomachean Ethics* x.8, 1178a9–24.
[233] *Nicomachean Ethics* x.8, 1178a19–22. (I translate *ethikē aretē* as 'ethical virtue' rather than 'moral excellence,' and *noûs* as 'mind' rather than 'intellect.')

is lucky enough to be able to live a contemplative life, those needs will be taken care of for him. But there is a deeper sense in which the contemplative life is involved in its earthy being. For man's inquiry into nature itself helps to constitute the contemplative life. There is no substitute, then, for going out into the world – whether it be ponds where frogs live, or societies where men live – and studying it. For human beings, unlike God, must discover primary substances if they are to contemplate them. And such discovery can only be accomplished by active querying of the world. Contemplative man must use his arms and legs as well as his perceptual equipment and mind. Of course, what ultimately constitutes the contemplative life, the thinking of primary substances, is performed by that part of man which has no material instantiation. But being a thinking being is what man most truly is. We are now in a position to appreciate in what respect man can transcend the human and become divine and in what respect he must remain man and fail to achieve identity with God. Man's active contemplating is divine, yet man himself, even in leading the contemplative life, can only become *like* God. For all there is to God's way of life is *thinking*. The contemplative man can only approximate such a way of life, for even in his contemplating he remains an enmattered being. The contemplative life can only be *like* God's, not identical with it.

It is often said that Aristotle's philosophy is unfinished: that it remains torn between two ideals, the ethical and the contemplative lives. This is not so. What is so hard for a modern reader to take seriously is Aristotle's claim that man has a divine element in him. If we think of man as that earthy, embodied animal we know so well, it is hard not to think that the bulk of the *Nicomachean Ethics* provides one of the great descriptions of all times of the life appropriate to him. From this perspective, the end of the *Ethics* looks like an unworked-out appendage, perhaps (one hopes) tacked on by a witless editor. This is to ignore two aspects of Aristotle's thought from which modern readers tend to shy away: his metaphysics and his theology. The problem is not that Aristotle has not worked out how one should live; it is that his metaphysical analysis of man as a composite of form and matter enables him to conceive man as radically divided. Man is a composite, and yet he is *most truly* the highest element in his form.

It is man's natural desire to understand that propels him forward through a life of inquiry and experience until he is able to realize what he truly is. It is this natural desire that propels him to transcend his nature. And yet there is a trace of humanity which remains even in this divine life: it can only be lived for a short period. Death overtakes even the philosopher. But, while it lasts, the life of the mind is god-like. Aristotle, no doubt, thought that he had lived such a life.

Select bibliography

(*Note:* I have decided to keep this bibliography short. It is intended for those who have read this book and would like to pursue some line of thought a step further. Thus I have listed only works that have been footnoted and some others that are clearly relevant. Obviously, further references can be found in the works cited here. Also, there is an extended bibliography of articles and books on Aristotle to be found in *Articles on Aristotle*, volumes 1–4 (ed. J. Barnes, M. Schofield and R. Sorabji), cited below. For texts, I have relied primarily on the Oxford Classical Texts of Aristotle's and Plato's works. Exceptions are the Ross editions of *The Analytics*, *Physics*, and *Metaphysics*, and the Hicks edition of *De Anima*, cited below.

J. L. Ackrill, *Aristotle's Categories and De Interpretatione*. Clarendon
    Press, 1963
    'Aristotle's Definitions of *Psuchē*,' in *Articles on Aristotle*, vol. 4
    Aristotle the Philosopher. Oxford University Press, 1981
Rogers Albritton, 'Forms of Particular Substances in Aristotle's
    Metaphysics,' *Journal of Philosophy*, 1957
D. J. Allan, *The Philosophy of Aristotle*. Oxford University Press, 1970
Henry Allison, 'Kant's Transcendental Humanism,' *The Monist*, 1971
    Kant's Transcendental Idealism. Yale University Press, 1983
Julia Annas, *Aristotle's Metaphysics Books M and N*. Clarendon Press,
    1976
D. M. Balme, *Aristotle's Use of Teleological Explanations*. Athlone Press,
    1965
Renford Bambrough, ed., *New Essays on Plato and Aristotle*. Routledge
    & Kegan Paul, 1979
Sir Ernest Barker, *The Political Thought of Plato and Aristotle*. Dover,
    1959
Jonathan Barnes, *Aristotle's Posterior Analytics*. Clarendon Press, 1975
    The Presocratic Philosophers. Routledge & Kegan Paul, 1979
    Aristotle. Oxford University Press, 1982
    ed., *The Complete Works of Aristotle, The Revised Oxford
    Translation*. Princeton University Press, 1984
Jonathan Barnes, Malcolm Schofield, and Richard Sorabji, eds., *Articles
    on Aristotle*, volumes 1–4. Duckworth, 1975–9

Select bibliography

Paul Benacerraf, 'Tasks, Supertasks and the Modern Eleatics,' *Journal of Philosophy*, 1962
   'Mathematical Truth,' *Journal of Philosophy*, 1973
Jonathan Bennett, *Linguistic Behaviour*. Cambridge University Press, 1976
Franz Brentano, *The Psychology of Aristotle*. University of California Press, 1977
M. F. Burnyeat, 'Idealism in Greek Philosophy: What Descartes Saw and Berkeley Missed,' in *Idealism Past and Present*, ed. G. Vesey. Cambridge University Press, 1982
   'Aristotle on Understanding Knowledge,' in *Aristotle on Science: The Posterior Analytics*. Editrice Antenore, 1984
   'Is Aristotle's Philosophy of Mind Still Credible?' (unpublished)
   ed., *Notes on ZETA*. Oxford Sub-faculty of Philosophy, 1979
   ed., *Notes on ETA and THETA*. Oxford Sub-faculty of Philosophy, 1984
R. G. Bury, trans., *Sextus Empiricus*, vols. 1–4. Loeb Classical Library, Harvard University Press, 1933–49
S. H. Butcher, *Aristotle's Theory of Poetry and Fine Art*. Dover, 1951
Harold Cherniss, *Aristotle's Criticism of Plato and the Academy*. Russell & Russell, 1972
Alan Code, 'The Aporematic Approach to Primary Being in Metaphysics Z' (abstract), *Journal of Philosophy*, 1982
   'The Aporematic Approach to Primary Being in Metaphysics Z,' *Canadian Journal of Philosophy*, 1984
   'Aristotle: Essence and Accident,' in *Philosophical Grounds of Rationality: Intentions, Categories and Ends*, ed. R. Grandy and R. Warner. Clarendon Press, 1985
   'On the Origins of Some Aristotelian Theses About Predication,' in *How Things Are: Studies in Predication and the History of Science*, ed. J. Bogen and J. McGuire. D. Reidel, 1985
John Cooper, *Reason and Human Good in Aristotle*. Harvard University Press, 1975
   'Aristotle on Natural Teleology,' in *Language and Logos: Studies in Ancient Greek Philosophy Presented to G. E. L. Owen*, ed. M. Schofield and M. Nussbaum. Cambridge University Press, 1982
John Corcoran, 'Aristotle's Natural Deduction System,' in *Ancient Logic and Its Modern Interpretations*, ed. J. Corcoran. D. Reidel, 1974
R. M. Dancy, *Sense and Contradiction: A Study in Aristotle*. D. Reidel, 1975
Donald Davidson, 'How is Weakness of Will Possible?,' in *Essays on Action and Events*. Clarendon Press, 1980
   Inquiries into Truth and Interpretation. Clarendon Press, 1984
Richard Dawkins, *The Selfish Gene*. Granada, 1978

Hermann Diels, *Die Fragmente der Vorsokratiker*, 6. verbesserte Auflage hrsg. von W. Kranz, 3 vols. Weichmann, 1951–2.

John A. Driscoll, '*EIΔH* in Aristotle's Earlier and Later Theories of Substance,' in *Studies in Aristotle*, ed. D. J. O'Meara. Catholic University Press, 1981

Michael Dummett, *Truth and Other Enigmas*. Duckworth, 1978

Troels Engberg-Pederson, *Aristotle's Theory of Moral Insight*. Clarendon Press, 1983

Cynthia Farrar, *The Origins of Democratic Thinking: The Invention of Politics in Classical Athens*. Cambridge University Press, 1988

Hartrey Field, *Science Without Numbers*. Blackwell, 1980

Michael Frede, 'Individuen bei Aristoteles,' *Antike und Abendland*, 1978

Michael Frede and Gunther Patzig, *Aristoteles, Metaphysik Z*. Beck, 1987

Gottlob Frege, *The Foundations of Arithmetic*. Blackwell, 1968

David Furley, *Two Studies in the Greek Atomists*. Princeton University Press, 1967

Montgomery Furth, *Aristotle, Metaphysics Books Zeta, Eta, Theta, Iota*. Hackett Publishing Co., 1986

Marjorie Grene, *A Portrait of Aristotle*, University of Chicago Press, 1963

D. W. Hamlyn, *Aristotle's De Anima, Books II, III*. Clarendon Press, 1968

W. F. R. Hardie, *Aristotle's Ethical Theory*. Clarendon Press, 1980

Edwin Hartman, *Substance, Body, and Soul: Aristotelian Investigations*. Princeton University Press, 1977

T. L. Heath, *Mathematics in Aristotle*. Clarendon Press, 1970

G. W. F. Hegel, *Philosophy of Right*, trans. T. M. Knox. Clarendon Press, 1952

Lectures on the History of Philosophy. Humanities Press, 1974

Phenomenology of Mind, trans. A. V. Miller. Clarendon Press, 1977

Robert Heinaman, 'Knowledge of Substance in Aristotle,' *Journal of Hellenic Studies*, 1981

R. D. Hicks, *Aristotle, De Anima*. Cambridge University Press, 1907

David Hilbert, *Foundations of Geometry*. Open Court, 1971

Jaakko Hintikka, *Time & Necessity*. Clarendon Press, 1973

Werner Jaeger, *Aristotle: Fundamentals of the History of his Development*. Oxford University Press, 1934

B. Jowett, *The Politics of Aristotle*. Clarendon Press, 1885

Immanuel Kant, *Foundations of the Metaphysics of Morals*, trans. L. Beck. Bobbs–Merrill, 1959

Critique of Pure Reason, trans. N. K. Smith. St Martin's Press, 1965

Critique of Practical Reason, trans. L. W. Beck. Bobbs–Merrill, 1966

Critique of Judgement, trans. J. C. Meredith. Clarendon Press, 1978

Anthony Kenny, *Aristotle's Theory of the Will*. Yale University Press, 1979

Select bibliography

J. N. Keynes, *Studies and Exercises in Formal Logic*. Macmillan, 1928

Christopher Kirwan, *Aristotle's Metaphysics, Books Γ, Δ, E*. Clarendon Press, 1971

Melanie Klein, *Love, Guilt and Reparation*. Hogarth Press, 1981

L. A. Kosman, 'Aristotle's Definition of Motion,' *Phronesis*, 1969
'Understanding, Explanation and Insight in the Posterior Analytics,' in *Exegesis and Argument*, ed. E. N. Lee, A. P. D. Mourelato, and R. M. Rorty, *Phronēsis*, supplementary volume 1, 1973
'Perceiving that We Perceive,' *Philosophical Review*, 1975

Jonathan Lear, 'Aristotelian Infinity,' *Proceedings of the Aristotelian Society*, 1979–80
Aristotle and Logical Theory. Cambridge University Press, 1980
'A Note on Zeno's Arrow,' *Phronesis*, 1981
'Aristotle's Philosophy of Mathematics,' *Philosophical Review*, 1982
'Leaving the World Alone,' *Journal of Philosophy*, 1982
'The Disappearing "We",' *Proceedings of the Aristotelian Society*, supplementary volume, 1984
'Moral Objectivity,' in *Objectivity and Cultural Divergence*, ed. S. C. Brown. Cambridge University Press, 1984
'Transcendental Anthropology,' in *Subject, Thought and Context*, ed. P. Pettit and J. McDowell. Clarendon Press, 1986
'Active *Epistēmē*,' in *Mathematik und Metaphysik bei Aristoteles: X Symposium Aristotelicum*, ed. A. Grasser. Bern, 1987

J. H. Lesher, 'Aristotle on Form, Substance and Universals: A Dilemma,' *Phronesis*, 1971
'The Meaning of *Noûs* in the Posterior Analytics,' *Phronēsis*, 1973

G. E. R. Lloyd, *Aristotle: The Growth and Structure of His Thought*. Cambridge University Press, 1968

G. E. R. Lloyd and G. E. L. Owen, eds., *Aristotle on the Mind and the Senses*. Cambridge University Press, 1978

John McDowell, 'Are Moral Requirements Hypothetical Imperatives?,' *Proceedings of the Aristotelian Society*, 1978

Alasdair MacIntyre, *After Virtue*. Duckworth, 1981

A. Mansion, *Introduction à la physique aristotelicienne*. Louvain, 1945

S. Mansion, 'La Première Doctrine de la Substance,' *Revue Philosophique de Louvain*, 1946

R. G. Mulgan, *Aristotle's Political Theory*. Clarendon Press, 1977

Thomas Nagel, *The Possibility of Altruism*. Clarendon Press, 1970
'The Limits of Objectivity,' in *The Tanner Lectures on Human Values*, vol. 1, ed. S. McMurrin. University of Utah Press, 1980
The View From Nowhere. Oxford University Press, 1986

Martha Nussbaum, *Aristotle's De Motu Animalium*. Princeton University Press, 1978
The Fragility of Goodness. Cambridge University Press, 1986

Select bibliography

Brian O'Shaugnessy, *The Will*. Cambridge University Press, 1980
G. E. L. Owen, 'Zeno and the Mathematicians,' *Proceedings of the Aristotelian Society*, 1957–8
  'Logic and Metaphysics in Some Earlier Works of Aristotle,' in *Aristotle and Plato in the Mid-Fourth Century*, ed. I. During and G. E. L. Owen. Studia Graeca et Latina, 1960
  'Tithenai ta Phainomena,' in *Aristote et les problèmes de methode*, ed. S. Mansion. Louvain, 1961; reprinted in *Articles on Aristotle*, vol. 1
  'The Platonism of Aristotle,' *Proceedings of the British Academy*, 1965; reprinted in *Articles on Aristotle*, vol. 1
  'Inherence,' *Phronesis*, 1965
  'Particular and General,' *Proceedings of the Aristotelian Society*, 1978–9
Joseph Owens, *The Doctrine of Being in the Aristotelian Metaphysics*. Pontifical Institute of Mediaeval Studies, 1978
Charles Parsons, 'Mathematics, Foundations of,' in the *Encyclopedia of Philosophy*, vol. 5, ed. P. Edwards. Macmillan, 1967
T. Penner, 'Verbs and the Identity of Actions,' in *Ryle*, ed. G. Pitcher and O. P. Wood. Doubleday, 1970
Hilary Putnam, 'Philosophy and Our Mental Life,' in *Philosophical Papers, Volume 2: Mind, Language and Reality*. Cambridge University Press, 1975
W. V. Quine, 'Two Dogmas of Empiricism,' in *From a Logical Point of View*. Harper and Row, 1961
John Rawls, *A Theory of Justice*. Harvard University Press, 1971
Amelie Rorty, *Essays on Aristotle's Ethics*. University of California Press, 1980
Richard Rorty, *Philosophy and the Mirror of Nature*. Princeton University Press, 1979
W. D. Ross, *Aristotle's Physics*. Clarendon Press, 1936
  Aristotle, De Anima. Clarendon Press, 1961
  Aristotle's Prior and Posterior Analytics. Clarendon Press, 1965–1954
  Aristotle. Methuen, 1971
  Aristotle's Metaphysics. Clarendon Press, 1975
  ed., *The Works of Aristotle translated into English*. Clarendon Press, 1928–54
Bertrand Russell, *The Principles of Mathematics*. Allen and Unwin, 1972
David Sanford, 'Infinity and Vagueness,' *Philosophical Review*, 1975
Wilfred Sellars, 'Substance and Form in Aristotle,' *Journal of Philosophy*, 1957
  Science, Perception and Reality. Routledge & Kegan Paul, 1963
Richard Shute, *On the History of the Process by which the Aristotelian Writings arrived at their Present Form*. Clarendon Press, 1888
T. J. Smiley, 'What is a Syllogism?,' *Journal of Philosophical Logic*, 1972

Friedrich Solmsen, *Aristotle's System of the Physical World*. Cornell
　　University Press, 1960
Richard Sorabji, 'Body and Soul in Aristotle,' in *Articles on Aristotle*,
　　vol. 4
　Aristotle on Memory. Duckworth, 1972
　Necessity, Cause and Blame. Duckworth, 1980
Charles Taylor, *The Explanation of Behavior*. Routledge & Kegan Paul,
　　1964
　'The Explanation of Purposive Behavior.' in *Explanation in the
　　Behavioral Sciences*, ed. R. Borger and F. Cioffi. Cambridge
　　University Press, 1970
Gregory Vlastos, 'A Note on Zeno's Arrow,' in *Studies in Presocratic
　　Philosophy*, vol. 2, ed. R. E. Allen and D. Furley. Routledge & Kegan
　　Paul, 1975
Sarah Waterlow (Broadie), *Nature, Agency and Change in Aristotle's
　　Physics*. Clarendon Press, 1982
N. P. White, 'Origins of Aristotle's Essentialism,' *Review of Metaphysics*,
　　1972–3
Wolfgang Wieland, 'The Problem of Teleology,' in *Articles on Aristotle*,
　　vol. 1
　Die aristotelische Physik. Vandenhoeck & Ruprecht, 1970
Bernard Williams, *Morality: An Introduction*. Cambridge University
　　Press, 1972
　Moral Luck. Cambridge University Press, 1981
　Ethics and the Limits of Philosophy. Harvard University Press, 1985
Timothy D. Wilson, 'Strangers to Ourselves: The Origin and Accuracy of
　　Beliefs about one's own Mental States,' in *Attribution, Basic Issues
　　and Applications*, ed. J. H. Harvey and G. Weary. Academic Press,
　　1985
Ludwig Wittgenstein, *Philosophical Investigations*. Blackwell, 1978
M. J. Woods, 'Problems in Metaphysics Z, Chapter 13,' in *Aristotle: A
　　Collection of Critical Essays*, ed. J. M. E. Moravcsik. Doubleday,
　　1967
　Aristotle's Eudemian Ethics. Clarendon Press, 1982
Crispin Wright, 'Language Mastery and the Sorites Paradox,' in *Truth
　　and Meaning*, ed. G. Evans and J. McDowell. Clarendon Press, 1976

Index

Made in the USA
Middletown, DE
10 January 2018